THE AMERICAN EDUCATOR

Introductory Readings in the History of the Profession

Edited by
Charles M. Dye

UNIVERSITY
PRESS OF
AMERICA

Copyright © 1980 by
University Press of America, Inc.

P.O. Box 19101, Washington, D.C. 20036

All rights reserved
Printed in the United States of America
ISBN: 0-8191-1221-6 (Perfect)

Library of Congress Catalog Card Number: 80-5759

DEDICATION

This book is dedicated to Margaret Louise Dye Upchurch and Charles Marvin Upchurch.

But for them I would have languished, if not perished.

To her I owe my understanding of the sacrifices demanded and of the dedication required from those in the human services professions.

To him I owe my understanding of the values of duty, responsibility, and reliability.

To both of them I owe my appreciation of the strength of marital love, the bastion of family life, and the obligation to contribute in the service of humankind.

ACKNOWLEDGEMENTS

I wish to acknowledge my colleagues in the Department of Educational Foundations, College of Education, The University of Akron.

Their energies, support, encouragement, and unrelenting commitment to make sense of and to bring some order out of the chaos that surrounds us in our world has provided me with the opportunity to experience that excitement, challenge, and fulfillment that can only be found within relationships of positive professional colleagueship.

To strive to know, to comprehend, to understand, all this is legitimate labor.

To share and instruct is honest toil of useful purpose.

The university is the workbench of the scholar.

TABLE OF CONTENTS

Preface xi

Semester: Week One Schedule 1
   Ennis, Robert H. "The Believability of People" 3

Semester: Week Two Schedule 11
   Church Chapter 1 Study Guide 13
   Bronson, David B. "Thinking and Teaching" 15
   Karier, Clarence J. "American Educational History: A Perspective" .. 23
   Strain, John Paul. "Idealism: A Clarification of an Educational Philosophy" 33

Semester: Week Three Schedule 43
   Church Chapter 2 Study Guide 45
   Stanton, H. E. "Teacher Education and the 'Good Teacher'" 47
   Crockenberg, Vincent. "Poor Teachers Are Made Not Born" 53

Semester: Week Four Schedule 63
   Church Chapter 3 Study Guide 65
   College of Education, The University of Akron. "Objectives" 67
   College of Education, The University of Akron. "Teaching Competencies: A Working Model" 69
   Florida Council on Teacher Education. "Essential Teaching Competencies" .. 77

Bowers, C. C. "The Messianic Tradition in American Education" 81

Semester: Week Five Schedule 89
   Church Chapter 4 Study Guide 91
   Swineford, Edwin J. "Critical Teaching Strategies" 93

Semester: Week Six Schedule 101
   Church Chapter 5 Study Guide 103
   Black, Hugh C. "Educational Philosophy and Theory in the United States - A Commentary" 105

Semester: Week Seven Schedule 115
   Church Chapter 6 Study Guide 117
   Cuban, Larry. "Urban Superintendents: Vulnerable Experts" 119
   Riley, Glenda. "Origins of the Argument for Improved Female Education" 125

Semester: Week Eight Schedule 141
   Church Chapter 7 Study Guide 143
   Gersman, Elinor Mondale. "Progressive Reform of the St. Louis School Board, 1897" 145
   Johnson, Ronald M. "Politics and Pedagogy: The 1892 Cleveland School Reform. 165

Semester: Week Nine Schedule 177
   Church Chapter 8 Study Guide 179
   Arnstine, Donald. "The Use of Coercion in Changing the Schools" 181
   Snook, I. A. "Neutrality and the Schools" 193

Semester: Week Ten Schedule 201
    Church Chapter 9 Study Guide 203
    Bagenstos, Naida Tushnet. "The Teacher as an Inquirer" 205
    Spring, Joel. "Education and Progressivism" 213
    Wirth, Arthur G. "The Deweyan Tradition Revisited" 233

Semester: Week Eleven Schedule 239
    Church Chapter 10 Study Guide 241
    Hunt, Thomas C. "The American High School in Crisis: A Historical Perspective" 243
    Wirth, Arthur G. "Charles A. Prosser and the Smith-Hughes Act" 255
    Wirth, Arthur G. "John Dewey's Philosophical Opposition to Smith-Hughes Type Vocational Education" 263

Semester: Week Twelve Schedule 273
    Church Chapter 11 Study Guide 275
    McFarland, Mary A. "A Consideration of Educational Decision-Making" 277
    O'Connor, James J. "Teaching: A Questionable Career" 283

Semester: Week Thirteen Schedule 289
    Church Chapter 12 Study Guide 291
    Goodenow, Ronald K. "The Progressive Educator, Race and Ethnicity in the Depression Years: An Overview" 293
    Violas, Paul. "Fear and the Constraints on Academic Freedom of Public School Teachers, 1930-1960" 323

American Federation of Teachers.
"Bill of Rights of the American Federation of Teachers" 335

National Education Association.
"Bill of Teacher Rights" 339

Semester: Week Fourteen Schedule 343

Church Chapter 13 Study Guide 345

Goetz, William W. "The Schools and Their Critics: An Angry Comment From Within the System" 347

Gowin, D. Bob. "The Structure of Knowledge" 351

National Education Association. "Code of Ethics of the Education Profession". 361

Semester: Week Fifteen Schedule 365

Church Chapter 14 Study Guide 367

Covert, James R. "Second Thoughts About the Professionalization of Teachers" 369

Taggart, Robert J. "Accountability and the American Dream" 375

Carper, James C. "In The Way He Should Go: An Overview of the Christian Day School Movement" 385

Sponsorship of the Periodicals in this Text 399

Bibliography of Professional Periodicals. 401

x

PREFACE

Course Information

Title   Introduction to Professional
             Education
Number   150
Sections   001, 002, 003, 004, 080
Department   Educational Foundations
College   Education
Prerequisites Admission, The University of Akron

Course Description

Nature and purposes of education in the United States. Emphases on the social, historical, and philosophical foundations of public education and on the roles of the professional educator.

Course Rationale

Introduction to Professional Education is the introductory course of all undergraduate programs offered by the College of Education of The University of Akron. It is the first professional course in the pre-service teacher education curriculum. I.P.E. provides a broad introduction to the study of American education by an examination of the historical and social-philosophical foundations of American Schooling, with special emphases on the origins and the development of the contemporary public education scene.

Long a tradition in teacher preparation, such an introductory course provides the undergraduate student commencing pre-service preparation, or the undergraduate student contemplating a career in professional education, with a substantive basis for understanding the values and traditions that have been and that are now operable in our society's educational institutions, particularly as they relate to American educational organization, curricular theory, and pedagogical practice. Special attention in the course is placed upon the roles expected of professional educators in this society, so as to provide the undergraduate student with added perspective in considering the career opportunities available in the education profession.

Committed to cognitive achievement and to affective success, I.P.E. provides an opportunity for the undergraduate student to select or to design an Independent Learning Project that will permit him to participate in an active, contemporary educational setting. This early experience in a supporting role in an ongoing educational program provides the pre-service student with further insights and an initial awareness of the potential contributions that he might make to the profession.

As I.P.E. is the first professional course in the teacher preparation program, it is appropriate that it serve to model different instructional and evaluational techniques, while organized in a team-teaching format. To that end, therefore, only those with a history of successful teaching and/or administrative experience will be permitted to serve as Graduate Assistants and members of the Instructional Team. It is preferred that those Graduate Assistants be engaged in advanced study and in original research in a masters or doctoral program of the College of Education of The University of Akron.

Course Objectives

Knowledge

The student will demonstrate his knowledge and comprehension of the historical and social-philosophical foundations of American education by correctly responding to a minimum of seventy per cent of the items on each objective examination, which will include multiple choice, matching, and true-false items. There will be three objective examinations administered at regular intervals throughout the course calendar.

Demonstrated knowledge and comprehension of the foundations of American education will relect topics such as:

- a. contemporary opinions,
- b. teaching traditions,
- c. school organization models,
- d. traditions of curricular philosophies,
- e. leadership case studies,
- f. teacher organizations,
- g. school finance,
- h. educational legal concerns,
- i. traditions of reform,
- j. professional role expectations,
- k. minority education,
- l. traditions of teacher education,
- m. elementary education,
- n. junior high school/middle school education,
- o. secondary education,
- p. vocational education,
- q. higher education,
- r. federal legislation in education, and
- s. professional terminology.

Skills

1. The student will synthesize and assess his Initial Field Experience(Independent Learning Project) by writing an essay so as to describe and evaluate his semester's experiences. This must be typed.

2. The student will interpret and evaluate one outside reading that pertains to a contemporary foundational topic in American education by writing a book critique using a prescribed model. This must be typed.

3. The student will engage in rational discourse with student colleagues and with members of the Instructional Team during the weekly meetings of the semester calendar.

4. The student will obtain specific aid from members of the Instructional Team pertaining to those areas perceived as needing improvement during the semester calendar.

5. The student will participate in simulated instructional settings in The University of Akron Micro-Teaching Laboratory for a specified number of clock hours and through a prescribed schedule.

Attitudes and Values

1. The student will complete his commitment for service in an Initial Field Experience of his choosing or design for a specified number of clock hours and will fulfill minimal expectations for participation at that I.F.E. site.

2. The student will complete his commitment for participation in simulated instruction in The University of Akron Micro-Teaching Laboratory for a specified number of clock hours through a prescribed schedule.

3. The student will regularly attend two large group meetings throughout the semester calendar on a weekly basis.

4. The student will regularly attend one small group meeting throughout the semester calendar on a weekly basis.

5. The student will demonstrate his awareness and understanding of the Teaching Competencies required by the College of Education of The University of Akron by employing and

demonstrating those competencies within the parameters of I.P.E. course activities.

6. The student will complete an evaluation instrument pertaining to I.P.E. as provided by members of the Instructional Team.

Final Grade Scheme

A Final Grade in I.P.E. is achieved by earning grade points assigned to the various lactivities in the course. The grade points that have been earned are added at the end of the semester calendar, points for absences are deducted, and a Final Grade is then assigned to each student in accordance with the following scheme:

Grade Point Range	Final Grade
1,000-931	A
930-900	A-
899-871	B+
870-831	B
830-800	B-
799-771	C+
770-731	C
730-700	C-
699-671	D+
670-631	D
630-600	D-
599-000	F

Attendance

Each student is expected to attend all classes for which he is registered.

Textbook Availability (Required and Optional)

The University of Akron Bookstore
Gardner Student Center

Required Textbooks

Church, Robert L. and Michael W. Sedlak.
<u>Education in the United States:
An Interpretative History.</u>
New York: The Free Press, A Division of Macmillan Company, Inc., 1976.
(hardback)

Dye, Charles M. (ed.)
<u>The American Educator:
Introductory Readings in the Traditions
of the Profession.</u>
Washington, D.C: University Press of America, 1980.
(paperback)

Office Hours: Instructional Team

Extensive office hours have been scheduled by your Major Instructor and by your Graduate Assistants, so as to make themselves readily available to you during your out-of-class time. Appointments may be made for specific conferences, however, they are not necessary. Feel free to drop by during the scheduled office hours.

The members of the Instructional Team are available to you for assistance in your achieving the highest possible level of success in this course. Use them!

Optional Textbooks

See handout distributed at the first large group meeting.

Course Activities

Activity	Maximum Points
Three examinations	600
Initial Field Experience (field experience)	100
Micro-Teaching Laboratory (clinical experience)	50
Book critique	100
Independent Learning Project Essay	50
Small group evaluation	100
	1,000 points*

*Each absence from the weekly small group meetings will result in the loss of five grade points which will be deducted from the total points earned at the end of the course calendar.

200 **Examination One:** An objective examination that evaluates learning from the required readings, lectures, and glossary items, Week One through Week Five.

200 **Examination Two:** An objectives examination that evaluates learning from the required readings, lectures, and glossary items, Week Six through Week Ten.

200 **Final Examination:** An objective examination that evaluates learning from the required readings, lectures, and glossary items, Week Eleven through Week Fifteen.

100 **Initial Field Experience:** Completion of the I.F.E. by accumulation of a minimum number of specified clock hours of service.

  50   **Initial Field Experience Essay:** An essay that describes and assesses the **I.F.E.** (see model elsewhere in the course syllabus).

  50   **Micro-Teaching Laboratory:** Completion by accumulation of a minimum number of specified clock hours of participation in simulated instruction.

100   **Book Critique:** A description and evaluation of an approved outside reading using the prescribed model(see model elsewhere in the course syllabus).

100   **Small Group Evaluation:** Learning activities supervised by the Graduate Teaching Assistants and related to communications skills and demonstration of values and attitudes objectives.

────────

1,000 maximum earnable points

Initial Field Experience

    Each **I.P.E.** student will select an approved site for their Initial Field Experience. By the end of the semester calendar, each student will have accumulated a specified number of clock hours of service at that site. A regular, weekly commitment throughout the semester will be the most efficient and effective method of completing this course requirement.

    The most appropriate service expectation for an Initial Field Experience in an introductory course is service as an _assistant_ to an instructor at a site. In this role of assistant, the site instructor has the responsibility of directing you in assisting with instructional and non-instructional activities perceived by the instructor as having the highest priority during your time at the site. The role of assistant is not meant to unduly restrict you in your creativity and imagination, but to clearly indicate that it is the site instructor who is in charge of that educational environment and that only they have the responsibility for determining those needs that you can assist in fulfilling.

You would minimally be expected to <u>assist</u> the site instructor in such instructional and non-instructional activities as follows:

    a. distribution and collection of instructional materials,

    b. development and maintenance of instructional materials,

    c. administration and scoring of evaluative instruments,

    d. recording student grades,

    e. provision of group instruction,

    f. provision of individual assistance to students,

    g. direction of student movement at the site,

    h. maintenance of student records,

    i. operation of instruction-related equipment, and

    j. supervision of student activities.

This list indicates minimal expectations of your service involvement on-site and is not meant to be all inclusive of the possibilities that might exist at a particular site. We expect that you will assist the site instructor in at least these ways.

Appropriate personnel from the Office of Educational Field Experiences must approve each student's selection of their Initial Field Experience.

Book Critique Model

The Book Critique will be composed of your responses to the following questions about the book that you selected:

1. What is the author's purpose in writing this book?
   Is the author presenting a position to you? i.e., is the author taking a stand?
   If so, are the arguments presented persuasive?

2. What are the different major points the author makes?
   What new terms or new ideas, if any, is the author introducing in this book?

3. What is the basis of the author's evidence in this book?
   He is sharing what he knows with you.
   Do you know <u>how</u> he knows?

4. With what do you agree in this work?
   With what do you disagree in this work?
   What is the basis for your agreement and/or disagreement?

5. How could this book be a more effective piece of scholarship?
   Could the author have employed other strategies in the writing? If so, what?
   Does the structure of the book make sense to you?
   Is the book readable?
   Could this book be improved? If so, how?

6. What contribution to your introduction to professional education has this book made?
   What added insights into American education have you gained from this reading?
   What new things do you now know as a result of having read this work?
   Do you see professional education differently

xx

as a result of having completed this book? How so?

7. In terms of your own personal growth, where does this book lead you?
Now that you've encountered this work, what other areas of professional concern do you feel that you should explore?
Because of this reading, what else do you feel the need to know?

8. Did this book touch you emotionally?
Do you have now a sense of "mission", some sense of philosophic purpose, as a result of reading this book?
What do you wish to do now as a result of reading this work in your own professional career?

There is no minimum or maximum number of pages expected in the Book Critique. We expect that you will do the most complete work possible and that you will treat each question as fully as possible.

This Book Critique is to be typed on 8½ X 11 white paper and all typing is to be double-spaced. On a cover sheet there will be your name, your Graduate Assistant's name, your section number, and the name and author of the book.

Initial Field Experience Essay

Please regard this writing task as an opportunity to share with us descriptions of your I.F.E. and what you feel that you have learned as a result of this experience. We expect that you will include in your essay topics such as the following:

1. In what ways did you provide assistance during your service on-site?

2. What different things did you learn from providing these different kinds of assistance?

3. Assess your relationship(s) with the site instructor.

4. Assess your relationship(s) with the site students.

5. Assess the specific and the general learning environment of the site.

6. What goals do you feel that you have accomplished as a result of the completion of your I.F.E?

7. What further goals have you now established for yourself as a result of this I.F.E. this semester?

There is no minimum or maximum number of pages expected in the Initial Field Experience Essay. We expect that you will do the most complete work possible and that you will treat each topic as fully as possible.

This Initial Field Experience Essay is to be typed on 8½ X 11 white paper and all typing is to be double-spaced. On a cover sheet there will be your name, your Graduate Assistant's name, your section number, and the name of the site and of the on-site supervisor.

Withdrawals(Drops)

Students have complete freedom to withdraw (drop) from this course at any time during the first half of the semester calendar without the permission of the Major Instructor.

If students wish to withdraw from this course during the second half of the semester calendar, signed permission from the Major Instructor is required by University regulations. While each request for withdrawal is decided on its own merits, only rarely has such permission been granted in the past.

If University regulations are now followed, the result will be the appearance of the student's name on the Final Grade Report form at the end of the semester. In such cases, the Major Instructor is required by University regulations to automatically award a permanent Final Grade of "F".

Incompletes

In the event that a student fails to complete the course requirements by the end of the semester, the Major Instructor may not automatically award the temporary grade of "Incomplete".

Students must request the temporary grade of Incomplete from the Major Instructor according to University regulations. Each request is decided on its own merits. Approval or rejection of the request will be made by the Major Instructor at the time of the request.

If the request for an Incomplete is approved by the Major Instructor, he will at that time specify for the student those tasks to be completed by the student that are necessary for the elimination of the temporary grade of Incomplete.

The temporary grade of Incomplete must be eliminated by the end of the next regular academic semester not including summer sessions) according to University regulations. Failure of the student to complete those specified tasks so as to eliminate the Incomplete will result in the award of a permanent grade of "F" by the Major Instructor as required by University regulations.

SEMESTER: WEEK ONE

REQUIRED READINGS

Dye

Preface (19 pp.)

Ennis, Robert H. "The Believability of People" *The Educational Forum*, V.38, No.3, March, 1974. (08 pp.)

Handouts

Glossary of Educational Terms

Optional Books List

Micro-Teaching Laboratory Information

Office of Educational Field Experiences Information

I.P.E. Contract forms

MEETINGS

Monday

Lecture: Course Introduction

Tuesday

Lecture: Course Introduction

Wednesday

Lecture: Field and Clinical Experiences

Thursday and Friday

Small Groups: Course Introduction continued
Distribution of Materials

SEMESTER: WEEK ONE

REQUIRED READINGS

Dye

Preface (19 pp.)

Ennis, Robert H. "The Believability of People," The Educational Forum, V.38, No.3, March, 1974. (08 pp.)

Handouts

Glossary of Educational Terms
Optional Books List
Micro-Teaching Laboratory Information
Office of Educational Field Experiences Information
I.P.E. Contract forms

MEETINGS

Monday

Lecture: Course Introduction

Tuesday

Lecture: Course Introduction

Wednesday

Lecture: Field and Clinical Experiences

Thursday and Friday

Small Groups: Course Introduction continues
Distribution of Materials

The Believability of People

ROBERT H. ENNIS

ALTHOUGH students continually need to judge whether a writer or speaker is believable, they are generally offered very little guidance in making the decision. The approach of The Institute for Propaganda Analysis in the Thirties and Forties is typical of one kind of advice: "Don't believe anything you hear or read." This approach is impractical, since we are unavoidably dependent on others for much that we know. At the opposite pole we find people who are ready to believe anything they hear or read, and this kind of credulity is equally unsatisfactory. Taking a reasonable path between these extremes is difficult, partly because general guidelines are not widely available, and partly because each situation is unique, requiring intelligent critical judgment.

In what follows I shall present a set of general criteria for judging the statements of people who speak or write with an air of authority, and shall apply these criteria to a particular case, a printed discussion of tooth care.[1] My goals are to illustrate the application of the criteria, to show that they have exceptions, and thus to show the need for flexibility and judgment in their application.

The phrase "people who speak or write with an air of authority" applies to teachers, authors of textbooks, television advertisers, news reporters who claim to tell us what happened in Washington, soothsayers who claim to tell us what will happen, people who offer pronouncements about what is right or good, the odd person on the street who informs us that the price of large eggs is now eighty cents at the grocery store in the next block, and an acquaintance who asserts that everyone running through Sather Gate in

---

Robert H. Ennis is a professor of philosophy of education at the University of Illinois.

Reprinted from The Educational Forum, Kappa Delta Pi, Volume 38, Number 3, March, 1974.

the last half hour was arrested. What these people have in common is that they speak as if they are telling us something that they are in a position to know. The believability of such people is the topic—not their right to be obeyed.

NINE CRITERIA FOR JUDGING BELIEVABILITY

The following set of criteria is a revision of an earlier uninterpreted list.[2] Though the list carries a range of applicative problems it reminds one of questions people often forget to ask. The criteria are useful, but can only serve as rough guides.

A person's statement is *believable roughly to the extent* that—

1. The statement is in his *area of experience*.
2. He *studied* the matter.
3. He was in *full possession of his faculties* when he made the statement.
4. He has a *reputation* for being honest and correct about the sort of thing considered.
6. His *reputation could be affected* by his statement, and he was aware of this fact when he made his statement.
7. He followed the *established procedures* in coming to his conclusion.
8. He is in *agreement with the others* who satisfy the above criteria.
9. The statement is *not in conflict* with what we otherwise have *good reason* to believe.

The phrase "roughly to the extent that" is intended to indicate that although no item in the list is an absolutely necessary condition, all of the items should be considered for their *combined* impact on a judgment about believability. No numerical weighting of each factor can be provided. Intelligent human judgment is needed to balance the impact of the various factors in the particular situation and produce a total critical judgment.

There is no implication here that a person's believability should be consciously questioned *every* time one is faced with a statement made by someone else. That policy would be paralyzing. However, it is generally reasonable to wonder about each new source with which one is faced, and one should always be ready to raise the question of believability and to invoke the criteria.

THE TOOTHPASTE CASE

Consider the application of these criteria to a particular case. A pamphlet entitled "Four Factors that Affect Your Child's Teeth" was distributed in a school I know. It is actually a folded sheet of 8½-by-11-inch paper with three-color printing and pictures. The four factors referred to in the title are the dentist, the toothbrush, the toothpaste, and food. There is a discussion of each of these factors followed by a five-item quiz. The author of the pamphlet (who is unnamed) speaks with an air of authority.

In this pamphlet one finds the following statement about the selection of a toothpaste:

> Your best guide is to check the label on the box to see whether the brand you are considering has received the official statement relating to effectiveness issued by the Council on Dental Therapeutics of the American Dental Association. The Council's Seal of Acceptance looks like this:

It is to this statement in that pamphlet that I shall apply the criteria. The question is: Can we take the author's word that the best guide in choosing a toothpaste is, in effect, the presence of the council's seal of acceptance? I am not asking about whether the presence of that seal is the best guide. Rather I am asking whether we can take the word of the pamphlet's author on the matter. It could be that the presence of the seal is the best guide even though we should attach no weight to the fact that the pamphlet says so.

1. *Area of Experience.* The first criterion asks that the statement be within its author's area of experience. So an obvious first question must be: Who said it?

A careful search reveals the source in small print:

© 1966, Professional Services Division of the Proctor & Gamble Company, Cincinnati, Ohio

Let us presume this company to be the author.

Proctor & Gamble satisfies this first criterion. The statement about choosing a toothpaste is in the company's area of experience, since it makes toothpaste.

An area of experience is not limited to scholarly or professional interests. The price of eggs is within the area of experience of the average person on the street. Hence the average person qualifies on this criterion. But the price of eggs is not a matter within my five-year-old son's area of experience, so I am automatically suspicious of any statements he makes about the price of eggs.

If, however, my son reports the price of eggs to me after consulting his mother, then I would find his report believable, even though the matter is not in his area of experience. He has a good memory and is an accurate listener. Hence such a statement by him would constitute an exception to this criterion. A person's statement might well be believable on the ground that he got it from an authority, even though the content of the statement is not within the area of experience of the statement maker.

2. *Study.* There can be no doubt that some people at Proctor & Gamble have studied the question of how to choose a good toothpaste. Hence, the statement comes out favorably on this criterion. We generally would not want to give weight to the words of someone who had not studied the matter under consideration, even though it was within his field of experience.

An exception to the study criterion is the case of the witness who noticed something that one could not help noticing, although he did not study the matter. In an army court martial case, for example, a witness noticed that a fellow soldier was in the lonely barracks after supper, as claimed, although the witness did not study the matter. If the other criteria are satisfied, lack of study should not disqualify this witness.

3. *Possession of Faculties.* It is desirable for our statement maker to have been in full possession of his faculties when he made the statement. This is a vague requirement, but understandably so. If we tried to specify in advance the sorts of things we want to guard against, then we would miss some. Had we made up the list in 1960, we would have omitted being under the influence of LSD. Better to leave it vague.

Again, there are exceptions to this criterion, if it is treated as a requirement. I have on occasion talked to learned men under the influence of alcohol. They were not in full possesion of their faculties.

Yet they knew their subjects well enough so that they were quite able to give me true information. Furthermore, on some occasions the alcohol loosened up their tongues sufficiently, and increased camaraderie to the point that I got more honest authoritative information from them than I would have if they had been cold sober.

The application of this criterion to the pamphlet statement under consideration yields a presumed plus for it. It certainly appears from the quality of the work that the author had full possession of his faculties.

4. *Disinterest.* By disinterest I do not mean lack of interest. Lack of interest is undesirable because it results in sloppiness and carelessness. But *dis*interest *is* desirable because it means a lack of conflict of interest. People being what they are, I feel much better about believing someone's statement if I know that he does not stand to profit from my believing it. Consider the used-car salesman who gives assurance of the accuracy of the odometer on a car he is trying to sell. Very often these men speak the truth. But, as a result of conflict of interest, the truth is violated enough times for us to have a right to be suspicious.

The notion of profit here is not limited to financial gain. Profit includes the promotion of a case that is dear to someone's heart, and it includes a variety of rewards that vary from person to person, including power, prestige, respect, notoriety, and all sorts of ego-gratification.

I very much regret that I have so many times seen people in important positions, people who are experts in the relevant area, make statements which are obviously twisted or slanted as a result of a conflict of interest. Hence I am justifiably suspicious of any statement made by someone who stands to profit from the acceptance of his statement. Application to cases is not always easy, however.

In my survey of the toothpaste boxes in the local pharmacy at the time of distribution of the pamphlet I found only one kind of toothpaste with the council's seal of acceptance printed on the box. It happened to be a toothpaste made by Proctor & Gamble. Hence, acceptance of this statement about the supposed best guide would be to the interest of Proctor & Gamble. This particular statement fails on the distinterest criterion. Proctor & Gamble is not disinterested on this matter.

The difficult question is whether a failure on the distinterest criterion should always disqualify the statement maker as an authority on the statement in question. Note that I am not raising the question of whether the statement is true. A statement might well be true even though it is made by a completely undependable person. Speaking the truth might well be to his interest.

But should we always ignore the statements made by interested parties—parties who stand to profit by our acceptance of their statements? The answer is negative. I do not want to disqualify all parties with an interest—even though I will always want to maintain a healthy skepticism. Consider the case of my hasty search for a book on study skills: I am looking for something to recommend to some undergraduates who managed to get through high school and into college without ever learning how to read effectively on the level that is required for survival. I ask a colleague for advice. He tells me the names of several books and approaches, including his own, but I reply that I am too busy to read these books now—and furthermore am not in a very good position to evaluate them. I ask him which one is most likely to be of help.

He is somewhat embarrassed, but names his own book as the one which is most likely to be of help. He asks me to be sure to mention the other books to the students, so that if they find his unhelpful they will have another place to go. I take his advice, and pass it on to my students, because, having known this man for a long time, I can judge him to have satisfied the other criteria, and because I have a special insight into his reputation: I know him to have been impeccably honest and straightforward in all my previous dealing with him. Under these conditions I am justified in giving some weight to his words, even though he fails on the criterion of disinterest.

The situation I have described is not a unique one. We are sometimes justified in overriding the criterion of disinterest, even though we should maintain a healthy suspicion. After all, people do have lapses in their integrity, and they do sometimes lose their objectivity in evaluating their own work.

I hope that any teacher who uses this toothpaste pamphlet is aware of its lack of satisfaction of the disinterest criterion. When students are asked to read it, I hope that somehow they, too, become aware of the problem. A teacher interested in promoting critical thinking should bring students to be duly suspicious of statements they read which are made by someone who stands to profit from the acceptance of the statement. This should not be an eyes-closed rejection, but a healthy suspicion.

5. *Reputation.* So far as I know, Proctor & Gamble has as good a reputation for being correct as any cleaning product company; but since sellers of products are often given to making rather exaggerated claims about their products, all of their reputations for credibility are suspect. Since the name of the company appears only once on the pamphlet, and then in smaller type than the text, Proctor & Gamble presumably did not want its reputation to play a large role in people's judgments about whether to believe the contents of this pamphlet. It was not intended to *look* like a sales pitch.

It is to the company's credit that *its* name, rather than no name, or the name of some unknown front organization, does appear on the pamphlet. Disguised authorship or lack of known authorship is generally more suspect than open sponsorship, even by a person of dubious reputation for credibility. But there are exceptions. For instance, in a censorship situation, where punishment is a possible consequnce of speaking the truth, we must be wary about condemning the disguised or anonymous source.

Furthermore a source need not always have a good reputation in order to be believable. A person with a poor reputation for being honest, but whom we know to be very religious, might swear (with this hand on the Bible, saying "so help me God") that a certain thing occurred. This sort of testimony might well be believable, providing that the other criteria are satisfied.

In any case, though, reputation is surely a factor to be considered. Other things being equal, the statement of a person with a good reputation for credibility deserves our belief more than that of a person with a poor reputation. In this situation Proctor & Gamble competes with others of equal reputation.

6. *Affectable Reputation.* Experts are well aware that they must guard their reputations in order that they can continue to play the role of experts. That a person's reputation can be affected by what he says, thus gives him a motive to speak the truth and to exercise due caution. Hence, it is desirable that a purveyor of

information believe that his reputation could be affected by what he says.

In the toothpaste pamphlet Proctor & Gamble does not stand to have its reputation suffer very much, should we discover that a check for the seal of acceptance is *not* the *best* guide—because we customarily find exaggerated claims made by companies selling products. They already tend to have weak reputations. Proctor & Gamble is taking some risk, however. If the seal of acceptance should somehow or other turn out to be an indication of a poor toothpaste, then Proctor & Gamble's reputation could be hurt slightly.

That its name appeared so unobtrusively in small print counts against Proctor & Gamble on this criterion. A reputation is less likely to be affected, if people find it difficult to know the source of a statement.

It is desirable that an authoritative-sounding statement somehow be checkable, since an uncheckable statement cannot hurt someone's reputation for veracity. However, it is difficult to check whether the use of the seal of acceptance is actually a good guide to choosing a toothpaste. Since statements made by a competing company about the ability of its toothpaste to produce sex appeal seem more easily checkable, these sex appeal statements score higher on this criterion for authority than does the statement about the use of the seal of acceptance. The more easily checkable the statement, the better it fares on this criterion.

Affectability of reputation is not a necessary condition for taking someone's word. Some statements are, for practical reasons, not checkable, but are acceptable. Suppose that an ornithologist reports that he saw a pileated woodpecker while on a solitary walk through the woods on Connecticut Hill near Ithaca, New York. Pileated woodpeckers, though rare, do exist in the area. I might well accept his statement, though I know no way to check it. Since his reputation can not be affected by his report, this situation shows that affectability of reputation need not necessarily be satisfied.

7. *Established Procedures.* Ordinarily we expect the preliminary work leading up to the making of a statement to be in accord with established procedures for doing this sort of preliminary work. A person making a blood count is supposed to follow certain established steps. A person whose duty it is to report the weather at the Ithaca airport is expected to follow certain procedures every hour—like spinning a wet bulb thermometer to determine the dew point. A person checking the effectiveness of a certain insecticide is expected to set up a control group. These are but a few examples.

But there are exceptions, and we should make clear to our students that there can be dangers in following the established procedures. In making the weather checks, one of the established procedures at Ithaca is to do it on the hour. Sometimes there is a radical change in the weather fifteen minutes later that goes unreported because nobody is looking out the window. If it is an unreported change for the worse, then a pilot might be caught unaware by this unfavorable change, even though he followed his established procedure of determining the reported destination weather.

The established procedures criterion, because of its conservative bent, must be used with caution. We all know of cases like that of the weather reporting procedures at Ithaca airport, in which the established procedures are inadequate. The established procedures criterion must be discarded when new and better procedures are offered in replacement of existing ones.

Now what are the established procedures for determining whether the *best guide* is the presence of the seal of approval? Established procedures for making that statement are not specified anywhere. I would investigate the results of research on other toothpastes and find out whether these results have been given due notice by the council; would look at the composition of the membership of the Council on Dental Therapeutics; and would examine the minutes of the council in an attempt to find out why no other seal-of-approval toothpaste appeared on my pharmacist's shelf. Furthermore inquiry about its reasons might well be addressed directly to the council, and since we know how committees work, one might inquire about the degree of unanimity found in the council's decisions. An absence of unanimity would suggest interviews with the minority members.

Basically, the point that I am trying to make is that the maker of the statement in question should have tried to find out *why* the council seal appeared on only one of my pharmacist's toothpastes. Did Proctor & Gamble do that? Probably so, because it is very much to Proctor & Gamble's interest to know *what* is going on in that council, to know *where* its seal appears, and to know *why*. Whether the statement represents an honest evaluation of the results of that investigation is another question. I do not know how to tell without doing a great deal of investigating myself.

If the procedures I outlined can be regarded as established procedures, then Proctor & Gamble presumably satisfies this criterion. If there are no established procedures, then the criterion does not apply.

   8. *Agreement with Others.* If we are to believe someone, generally it is desirable for people who are talking about the same thing to agree with that person. Proctor & Gamble, like all makers of toothpaste, does not do well on this criterion, for they are all in disagreement about what is the best guide in choosing a toothpaste.

Disagreement with others, however, should not automatically disqualify someone. The minority of one is often-enough correct for us to avoid making this criterion a necessary condition. But when people who fully satisfy the other criteria are in disagreement with each other, there is some reason not to accept the word of any—even though some of them might speak the truth. Once we have used the criteria together with good judgment and find inconsistency among those who otherwise get our approval, then we just have to be careful about basing our decision on someone else's word. To the extent that we can apply other critical thinking criteria to the statement under consideration, we should do so. For example, we might be able to apply the criterion of explanatory power to a statement; or we might apply the criterion of consistency with the evidence that we have or can get ourselves.

But sometimes we are not in a position to evaluate the statement (like a statement about the likelihood of deleterious radiation emission from a proposed nuclear power plant). If people who otherwise satisfy the criteria disagree on such a statement, then the reasonable person must admit that he just is not in a position to make a judgment about the statement in question. I am not suggesting that he give up—but merely that he suspend judgment until the situation improves.

   9. *Lack of Conflict With What We Otherwise Have Good Reason to Believe.*

Even if someone satisfies all the other criteria, conflict of what he says with what we otherwise have good reason to believe is often quite damaging to his statement. There are no precise criteria for resolving this conflict. Each person is in his own existential dilemma when it occurs. He must weigh and judge as best he can, given the circumstances.

An exception to this criterion is the statement in the summer of 1972 by a contemporary economist, Walter Heller, to the effect that the economy was becoming vigorous. This was in conflict with the conclusion that I drew on the basis of what I saw around me. It was to Heller's interest, especially prior to the re-election of Richard Nixon, to say otherwise. His satisfying the distinterest criterion counted heavily in his favor. I yielded to him.

The toothpaste statement is not in conflict with what I otherwise have good reason to believe. That is, I do not have good reason to believe that there is a better guide to choosing a toothpaste. Hence the toothpaste statement comes out favorably on this criterion.

The Decision

Ultimately some decision must be made: a positive decision, a negative decision, or suspension of judgment. After weighing the mentioned criteria in this particular situation my judgment on the quoted toothpaste claim is that Proctor & Gamble's word should not be taken on this matter, primarily because of conflict of interest and because of the general reputation of companies selling cleaning products. This is not to express doubt about the truth of what is said; I am only saying that I believe that we should not take the pamphlet as an authority on the matter.

I can see no way to make this sort of decision mechanically. Each person must weigh the evidence in a particular situation and decide for himself, taking the accompanying existential risks.

Summary and Comment

In examining the listed criteria for believability of people who speak as if they know, I have noted the looseness of the structure of the list of criteria, the need for intelligent human judgment in application, and the existence of outright exceptions when the criteria are treated as requirements. Although the application of these criteria is not easy, the list can be a useful tool, because it suggests questions that too often go unasked—in the schools and out.

Perhaps I have not sufficiently emphasized the magnitude of the task that accompanies the asking of the questions. Many students must overcome a set of social conditions that discourage one's asking such questions. These inhibiting conditions are common in all walks of life and in conjunction with all shades of political persuasion. Furthermore the tools, techniques, and resources for securing answers to the questions are often not at a student's disposal. The task admittedly is immense.

The alternatives, however, are unacceptable.

Do you believe that?

Notes

1. I am indebted to Terry Denny, Helen Ennis, David Nyberg, Hugh Petrie, Fred Rogers, Barak Rosenshine, and Decker Walker for helpful comments.

2. Robert H. Ennis, "A Concept of Critical Thinking," *Harvard Educational Review* 32 (1962): 106-107. Also "A Definition of Critical Thinking," *The Reading Teacher* 17 (1964): 611.

SEMESTER: WEEK TWO

REQUIRED READINGS

Church

Part I: Education in the New Nation, 1776-1830, Chapter 1: The District School (20 pp.)

Dye

Bronson, David B. "Thinking and Teaching" The Educational Forum. V.39, No.3, March, 1975. (07 pp.)

Karier, Clarence J. "American Educational History: A Perspective" The Educational Forum. V.37, No.3, March, 1973. (10 pp.)

Strain, John Paul. "Idealism: A Clarification of an Educational Philosophy" Educational Theory. V.25, No.3, Summer, 1975. (09 pp.)

MEETINGS

Monday

Lecture: Contemporary Opinions of Education

Tuesday

Lecture: The American Teacher

Wednesday

Lecture: The Liberal Arts Tradition in American Education

Thursday and Friday

Small Groups

SEMESTER: WEEK TWO

REQUIRED READINGS

Church

Part I: Education in the New Nation, 1776-1830. Chapter 1: The District School (20 pp.)

Dye

Bronson, David B. "Thinking and Teaching," The Educational Forum. V.39, No.3, March, 1975. (07 pp.)

Karier, Clarence J. "American Educational History: A Perspective," The Educational Forum. V.37, No.3, March, 1973. (10 pp.)

Strain, John Paul. "Idealism: A Clarification of an Educational Philosophy," Educational Theory. V.25, No.3, Summer, 1975. (09 pp.)

MEETINGS

Monday

Lecture: Contemporary Opinions of Education

Tuesday

Lecture: The American Teacher

Wednesday

Lecture: The Liberal Arts Tradition in American Education

Thursday and Friday

Small Groups

CHURCH TEXTBOOK STUDY GUIDE: CHAPTER 1

THE DISTRICT SCHOOL

1. Thomas Jefferson
2. <u>A Bill for the More General Diffusion of Knowledge</u>
3. meritocracy
4. national university
5. district school

6. moving school
7. decentralized school district
8. community control
9. professional prreparation of schoolmasters
10. terminal education

11. recitation method
12. child-centered pedagogy
13. Johann Heinrich Pestalozzi
14. spelling bee
15. spelldown

16. Noah Webster
17. blue-backed speller
18. orthography
19. socialization

CHURCH TEXTBOOK STUDY GUIDE: CHAPTER 1

THE DISTRICT SCHOOL

1. Thomas Jefferson
2. A Bill for the More General Diffusion of Knowledge
3. meritocracy
4. national university
5. district school
6. moving school
7. decentralized school district
8. community control
9. professional preparation of schoolmasters
10. terminal education
11. recitation method
12. child-centered pedagogy
13. Johann Heinrich Pestalozzi
14. spelling bee
15. spelldown
16. Noah Webster
17. blue-backed speller
18. orthography
19. socialization

13

Reprinted from *The Educational Forum*, Kappa Delta Pi, Volume 39, Number 3, March, 1975.

Thinking and Teaching

David B. Bronson

FOR teaching purposes *thinking* may be defined as *making connections,* and then teaching can be defined as showing people connections and helping them see and make their own connections.

This is no more than a practical kind of definition, but it is good enough to be useful in a discussion of teaching. It is useful, in the first place, because it is based on the understanding of the human mind as a pattern-making and pattern-finding mechanism or system, which is a crude representation of current cognitive psychology. It is useful, in the second place, because it helps to distinguish teaching and learning, which are often confused in such discussions. And it is useful, in the third place, because it points to something we are familiar with: the difference between connected and unconnected thinking, in and out of the classroom.

To start with the third and familiar point, the symptoms of unconnected thinking may be described in two ways. One is to say that some people act as if clusters of data were floating about in their minds without making any contact with each other. These clusters are like soap bubbles, delicate, airy, colorful, and there is a simple pleasure in playing with them, but it is not thinking. Thinking, in the sense of making connections, implies grasping, holding, considering, pushing and pulling the data, combining data to see how data and sets of data fit together, and eventually setting them in an appropriate place as part of a structure to be used as a working hypothesis, with the emphasis on the *working*. Only that which is located in a structure has "meaning."

David B. Bronson is an English teacher at Lincoln-Sudbury Regional High School in Sudbury, Massachusetts.

Another way of putting it is to compare this unconnected thinking with dreaming. At the dawn of philosophy Heraclitus said, "The waking have one world in common; sleepers have each a world of his own." The point is that *where there are no connections there can be no communication.* Connections make meaning, and connections make communication. The content of dreams is a series of sets, bits of verbal and visual images, which are recognizable and intelligible in themselves because they can usually be traced to experience. But what is characteristic of dreams is that the connections between these images and recollections are arbitrary, novel, incomplete, mysterious, sometimes frightening. The way they are combined literally makes no sense, though often we can read a weird sort of sense into them. Dreams make no sense except to the dreamer; they are not communication.

Much of what passes for thinking can be described, then, with reference to the image of the drifting soap bubbles or to the vivid but unconnected patterns of dreams. How often do we ourselves find that we have not been paying attention to what we are doing or to what someone is saying, and we exclaim protesting, "But I wasn't thinking!" How easy it is to see when the other person has failed to notice the implications—the connections—of what he is saying. How clear it is when someone is arguing hotly, for example, about the wrong aspect of a problem or getting excited about a side-issue and missing the point. How difficult it is to keep a conversation or a meeting on the subject.

This is all familiar and not a matter of urgent concern, but what *is* very serious is that unconnected thinking (or really nonthinking) characterizes too many of our traditional classrooms. We have all been raised and trained in such classrooms, and so we may not have noticed this. We see such classes busy and on one level evidently satisfying to young and old. In them one sees or has a genuine, if minute, sense of accomplishment, the kind of gentle accomplishment, perhaps, that is supplied by solitaire, by crossword or jigsaw puzzles, and possibly by television. There may be some slight cooperation or superficial communication, but it is essentially an individual experience. It is not wholly passive, for a pleasurable sense of activity fills the players. It is *entertaining*, which means that it *engages the attention without requiring decision*. The old chestnut is all too true that education consists of material passing from the notes of the teacher to the notes of the student without passing through the mind of either.

But there are no connections made between the activities in the traditional classroom and the lives of the people involved, or between one course and another. The traditional class is occupied with a course, which is part of a curriculum, or with a unit, which is part of a part of a curriculum. This set of data has been assembled by the teacher or by some other authority. It is then "covered," which means that various small tasks are performed and eventually assembled somehow, and the course is "done." The student can then say, "I did that last year," or, "I've had that already." If he has to "take" it again for some administrative or institutional reason, there is no great harm —there is no gain either—since mere repetition can neither add significantly to nor subtract from prepackaged material.

And right there is the trouble: it is prepackaged by someone other than the student. What he has to "learn," then, is someone else's arrangement, and it is the *arrangement* that he "learns," rather than to arrange the material himself, to connect it with his experience and with other sets of material from life and from books. That is why evaluation (grading) is so frustrating, because all we can measure is how much the student has remembered, and many a conscientious teacher worries because there seems to be a great gap between what the student has remembered in order to satisfy the teacher (the requirements of the course) and what we know to be the connections between this material and other material, between the course and "real life," between "what I taught them" and "what they learned."

It has been thought that this difficulty could be minimized, if not wholly avoided, if the students were to elect the course that interests them. This is done in college, but also increasingly in high schools and even in junior high schools. But the student can make his choice only on some basis other than the merits of the material itself, because he will not know what they are until he has completed the course. In practice he assembles a number of elements: the reputation of the course and of the teacher, how it appears to fit in with his personal or career interests (or the ambitions of his parents), departmental or curricular requirements, the limitations of the schedule, the presence of friends in the class, and, particularly in the case of younger students, the more or less valid advice of counselors.

It is difficult to imagine any system other than the one we have been raised and trained in, in which the teacher or authority determines the boundaries of the course. Our whole administrative structure is based on the validity of curricula and the departments which are responsible for them. As we try to imagine another way of organizing things, however, it will help to remember how much the departmental and administrative structure has to do with finances and politics and how little it has to do with the teacher's priorities, teaching, and learning. If we can make progress in solving the teaching-and-learning question (along the lines of connection-making), we may be able to relax our rigid grasp of the old structure.

Since the students have not been allowed to make their own connections, and since they have not generally been supplied with sets of connections made by other people, what they have to learn to deal with in their school years is *disconnectedness*. Many cannot handle this. The brightest tend to turn off, and the dullest tend to drop out. The lower middle range of students dutifully and in quiet desperation move the "soap bubbles" about, and the upper middle range of students, those best adapted to school, believe they have accomplished something, though they are hard put to say what it is.

The educational system is largely run by this latter group. These are the students who are best satisfied, and so the result is a perfect failure. It is perfect because it cannot be questioned by those in it. It is a closed system, an interlocked set of activities that cannot be broken. It is a failure because it encourages more of the same, more people not concerned with connections; more people who are not concerned with communication; more people who are irresponsible. Considered as a formal institution, the educational system does not significantly nourish the society which supports it. It leaves too many people careless of or callous to the interconnectedness of things and to the interrelatedness of people. Once one has "graduated" and become locked into a job and a growing family and all the attendant obligations, it is almost impossible to keep the "big picture" in view or to proceed in the guiding context of a set of pictures of increasing size and comprehensiveness. It is notoriously difficult to feel there is "meaning" in one's life, but nothing could be more important for a responsible citizen and parent. At the very least one should have the opportunity to see and work with the connections while he is still young and comparatively free to experiment.

There are some encouraging developments these days in educational practice that make it easier for the students to see and make connections: the integrated day, open classrooms, elective curricula, independent study, heterogeneous class groupings. These are as yet more common at the early stages of the system than at the latter, but it is safe to say that throughout the system there is some serious experimentation. The most common justification for these novel practices is the innate curiosity of the student and his expression in the act of discovery. There can be no doubt of the essential curiosity of human beings (and other primates), and this curiosity persists for a long time. But there are too many pressures for academic and social conformity from early school days, and there is too little reward for discovery and experiment in the complex social, business, and professional world.

A better basis for the programs which have courageously broken the rigid traditional pattern of passive students, memorized knowledge, and quantified scores is that *these programs make it easier to see and learn to use patterns, connected structures of knowledge.* Discovery presupposes patterns of connection, and history tells many stories of people who discovered things and did not know what to do with them. Curiosity is real and strong and persistent. It can be encouraged and reinforced from very early days, and when the habit is established of looking for connections, it will be lifelong. But it works with patterns. The mind is usefully considered as a pattern-making and pattern-using mechanism or system.

A better way of describing the unconnected thinking or "nonthinking" that is so common in school, as in life, is to speak of patterns that are too small or untested. The patterns that are too small consist of bits that are not connected with other bits and pieces to make larger patterns. Those that are untested are not compared with the patterns actually in use in the world, in the lives and experiences of living people, or with other patterns as hypotheses. There is, after all, no reason for people to connect and test and compare if they have never seen it done, if they do not know enough to do it, if they do not know its value or how it can enlarge experience and enrich one's life to have a maturing network of connections and patterns to give meaning to the whole of experience. If people have missed out on this, they may well think that patterns or structures cannot be connected, compared, evaluated; that "nothing matters", in other words. Connection is the key to communications and responsibility.

A start has been made with the new educational practices, and this can be understood and extended by focusing on the connections. A connection-making or pattern-using curriculum will deal with three kinds of connections: those between people, those between people and material, and those between different sets of material. The nature and usefulness of this kind of curriculum will be clearer when we consider each of these.

First, the connection between people includes that between teacher and student and that between student and student. The function of the teacher is to help the student see connections and make his own connections. This means that the teacher must see and make connections himself and not merely reiterate the old sets or someone else's. The advantage the teacher has—and his usefulness to the student—is that he has more experience in the subject and in life. This must be stated precisely: *he sees and makes more connections*. There is no separation, then, between "teaching" and "learning," for the same thing is going on in the mind of teacher and student. It is not really necessary to add that the "teacher" will naturally "learn" from the "student," for what is going on is an exchange of patterns.

There is no way the teacher can do this *for* the student; if no connections occur in the student's mind, nothing has been learned. To illustrate, when you climb a mountain with a professional guide, he does not stand at the bottom and point out the way, and he doesn't carry you on his back. He goes with you, and you do it together. A teacher does not simply point to the connections, and he does not make them for the student. The teaching/learning event is an exchange of patterns or structures. Both minds are pattern-making and pattern-finding systems, and they will work together or not at all.

That other set of personal connections, between student and student, is more important to the student than that between student and teacher, and the teacher must build on this fact. Communication is a pattern, a pattern of patterns, and it is with his contemporaries that one best communicates. It is easy to communicate with older and more experienced people because they (who have seen and made more connections) can make allowances and fill in the gaps. To communicate with younger people makes great demands on one's structure-building skill—which is why teaching is such a joy—and this is usually beyond the ability particularly of younger students, who are less experienced pattern-makers and finders. But if you cannot communicate what you have learned to a contemporary in some form, you have not learned it. So here is the point at which "instant feedback" is readily available. As long as "communication" is solely between teacher and student, or even between student and student *via* the teacher, there is no true feedback, no communication, no social reality. Small wonder that students rarely find school as exciting as many teachers do!

The second set of connections that a connecting-using curriculum will deal with includes the connections between the material, the course content, and the lives of people. People can handle unconnected or disconnected material, if they are forced to, only by memorizing or by a kind of fantasizing, and that certainly describes the work of some students. It is also fair to say that courses or subjects do differ in "connectability," but this is really to say that the connections have to be made in different ways. Everything, though, can be connected through the minds that do the thinking. Subjects grouped under humanities show human life more directly perhaps than the sciences, but it is the sciences which show the patterned context of life, the environment, and also the integrity of patterns in themselves.

The connections between the material and life are made by *models*. A model is

19

a construction, an assembly of elements, that *directs attention* to a process, to something going on. A table-top model of a river system, for example, shows you where you might look for erosion or silting. A mathematical model of a storm shows you what will happen if the elements of the atmosphere in their relations with each other continue to interact in this or that way. A historical model can show you how people might react in a given set of circumstances, and this applies also to many kinds of models in the social and behavioral sciences. A literary or artistic model can clarify your feelings and personal experience, bringing self-awareness, if not always self-knowledge. By arranging material into models one can see where to look and something of what to look for. Because they are models, they are subject to adjustment. Of course, since they are patterns, they can be exchanged. This is quite different from memorizing enough to get a good grade. The material is studied because it is "relevant," i.e., "connected," not because to "do" it will be rewarded with an appropriate number of points. The *means* of teaching, the *form* of studying, and the *shape* of learning start with relevance, or else it is all memorizing and fantasy.

Teaching can thus be considered as the clarification of pattern-making or model-constructing, that is, the process of making and using and seeing connections, both simple and complex. The practice and examination of this process is critical thinking, and the result of the process is a kind of realistic social responsibility.

The third set of connections is the curriculum itself, the whole set of data that a school or a department or a discipline deals with. For some time now, there have been few connections between the activities in the various parts of the whole curriculum, and the students' time has been rigidly apportioned between classes, fifty minutes of this and then fifty minutes of that, ten weeks of this and twenty weeks of that, with all tests jammed into one period with no integration, no reflection, no thought. And institutional fragmentation is simply the image of the pedagogic fragmentation. The actual schedules of the students show no relation between courses, and the curricula of the teachers show no relation between subjects.

Discussing the second set of connections, that between the material and the people, it was suggested that subjects can be connected through the minds that do the thinking. This is not to refer to metaphysical categories, but, instead, is to suggest that "subjects" originated in ways that people had found it profitable to think about certain things. What we consider subjects (and hence courses and curricula) are really modes of thought, and by way of illustration we can describe the curriculum of a general high school as follows:

Literature is produced by living people in a specific historical situation, using forms recognizable to their contemporaries.

The writing of *history* is a form of literature.

The *social sciences* describe historical situations using models developed in modern times.

Mathematics is an exercise in the rules of pattern-making and pattern-finding, and it demonstrates the reality and power of patterns.

Language study is the means of discovering the nature of language, its relation to thinking, and the structure of one's own language.

Science is an orderly way of studying the world you are in and in contact with, and of understanding both its orderliness and its complexity.

Art is the selection of patterns and a kind of miniaturization by which you can see the whole of life and its relations in ways inexpressible in words or formulae.

The *media* are extensions of the body and include technical education, home economics, and physical education, as well as photography, film, radio, and television.

The point is not this or that description, but, instead, that these things are all done by *people;* they do not exist except in the minds of the people who think in these ways. The connections between material and people and between sets of material are made by models or structures or patterns. People interact with each other and with their environment by means of patterns, and the mission of the school is to clarify and reinforce and improve the process of interaction.

It is no longer sufficient—if it ever was—for the school to be merely a supplier of information. The environment in which the student lives and into which he will go as a graduate is incalculably more complicated than that in and for which the school system was designed. And there are many sources of information in addition to the school, so it is not misleading to speak of an information or knowledge "explosion." The world is smaller, and the interrelatedness of people is more pressing; the degree of orthodoxy of a sheik's adviser may determine whether or not we are warm this winter!

The school must train people to handle information, and information comes in patterns and can be dealt with only by patterns. And patterns are *for* thinking.

Science is an orderly way of studying the world you are in and in contact with, and of understanding both its orderliness and its complexity.

Art is the selection of patterns and a kind of miniaturization by which you can see the whole of life and its relations in ways inexpressible in words or formulae.

The media are extensions of the body and include technical education, home economics, and physical education, as well as photography, film, radio, and television.

The point is not this or that description, but, instead, that these things are all done by people; they do not exist except in the minds of the people who think in these ways. The connections between material and people and between sets of material are made by models or structures

or patterns. People interact with each other and with their environment by means of patterns, and the mission of the school is to clarify and reinforce and improve the process of interaction.

It is no longer sufficient—if it ever was—for the school to be merely a supplier of information. The environment in which the student lives and into which he will go as a graduate is inescapably more complicated than that in and for which the school system was designed. And there are many sources of information in addition to the school, so it is not misleading to speak of an information or knowledge "explosion". The world is smaller, and the interrelatedness of people is more pressing; the degree of orthodoxy of a sheik's advisor may determine whether or not we are warm this winter. The school must train people to handle information, and information comes in patterns and can be dealt with only by patterns. And patterns are for thinking.

21

American Educational History: A Perspective[1]

CLARENCE J. KARIER

FRIEDRICH NIETZSCHE once said that, "You can only explain the past by what is highest in the present. Only by straining the noblest qualities you have to their highest power will you find out what is greatest in the past, most worth knowing and preserving."[2] History is inevitably written from a particular perspective of the present. The historian can no sooner divest himself of that present than it is possible for him to live in the past. To accept these conditions is not, however, to assume a position of historicism.[3] Although history is an imaginative creation of the past, it is not a fictional creation. Its validity is derived from both the artifacts of the past and the meanings that it illuminates in the present. History, I believe, is an art. The historian as an artist is different however from the painter as an artist. While both are ultimately judged by the meaning achieved in the present, the evidence with which the historian works must itself be validated by reason, logic and empirical analysis.[4] Context, internal consistency, cross referencing, authenticity of documentation are all instrumental tools with which the historian shapes and colors his picture of the past.[5]

---

[1] In writing this paper I have profited from both the research and the dialogue of a number of people at the University of Illinois. I am particularly indebted to the shared insights of Russell Marks, Jim Anderson, Joe Hamilton, Peter Sola, Leo Kazaniwskyj, Marian Metzow, Walter Feinberg, and Paul Violas.

[2] Oscar Levy, *Complete Works*, Vol. 5 (New York: Russell and Russell, 1924), p. 55.

[3] For a particularly sharp critique of John Dewey and George Herbert Mead's use of the past see Arthur O. Lovejoy, "Present Standpoint and Past History," *The Journal of Philosophy*, Vol. XXXVI, No. 18 (August 31, 1939).

The revision of the standard accounts of the development of education in this country casts grave doubts on the benign motives of our educational leaders and reformers. This article is an example of such revision. The author is Professor of the History of Education at the University of Illinois, Champaign-Urbana Campus, and is the author of Man, Society, and Education recently published by Scott Foresman. This article is an adaptation of a paper presented at the Southeastern Regional Meeting of the History of Education Society, Atlanta, Georgia, November 12, 1971.

[4] For a unique analysis of the ways a historian utilizes evidence see R. W. Winks, *The Historian as Detective* (New York: Harper & Row Publishers, Inc., 1969).

[5] Extended arguments supporting the above position will be found in: Carl Becker, "What Are Historical Facts" in Hans Meyerhoff (ed.), *Philosophy of History in Our Time* (New York: Doubleday Anchor Books, 1959), pp. 120-137; R. G. Collingwood, *The Idea of History* (New York: Oxford University Press, 1956), Part V; William Dray, *Laws and Explanation in History* (Oxford: Oxford University Press, 1957), Chapters IV and V; W. B. Gallie, *Philosophy and the Historical Understanding* (London: Chatto and Lindus, 1964), especially Chapters 3, 4 and 5.

For opposing arguments see: Carl G. Hempel, "The Function of General Laws in History" in Patrick Gardner (ed.), *Theories of History* (New York: The Free Press, 1966), pp. 344-356; John Passmore, "The Objectivity of History" in William Dray (ed.), *Philosophical Analysis and History* (New York: Harper & Row Publishers, Inc., 1969), pp. 75-94; and Ernest Nagel, *The Structure of Science* (New York: Harcourt, Brace & Co., 1961), pp. 547-606.

In many ways the mind of man is timeless. While he lives in the present, he transcends the barriers of the future and the past through imagination. Yet here also the imagination which allows one to wander in the future is different from that which works in the past. The imagination which recreates the past must not only grapple with the artifacts of a past world, but also the values and structure of that past which are a part of a living present. The past is thus inescapably linked to the present and any truly human quest for meaning involves a particular creation of a past. Historical inquiry is therefore an exciting fundamental search for meaning which imaginatively adds space—time and dimension to one's existence.

While one might profitably concern himself with the question why one historian views the past differently from another and why some people regard one past superior to another, perhaps a more fundamental question might be to ask why the historian writes history. I submit that the historian cultivates the art of history to add meaning to his present existence and that people prefer one history over another because it is that history which most satisfies their quest for meaning.[6] The art of historical scholarship, like the art of painting or sculpture, necessarily reflects the *Weltanschauung* in which the artist lives.[7] We can then attempt to understand and see, as well as feel, the relationship between Renaissance painting and Renaissance culture just as we can understand, see and feel the relationship of liberal historians to liberal progressive culture in 20th century America.[8] The intellectual, cultural, and educational histories written by Merle Curti, Henry Steel Commager, Richard Hofstadter, and Lawrence Cremin fundamentally reflect certain common assumptions about the world in which they moved. These assumptions guided their perceptions which in turn framed the picture of reality they created. Although each painted pictures depicting different aspects of the conditions of modern man, all held fairly similar assumptions about the idea of progress, rationality, community, science, and technology.

Broadly speaking, these men reflected a neo-enlightenment world view which emerged out of the intellectual debates over Spencerian-Darwinism combined with a pragmatic progressive temper to produce a kind of liberal humanitarianism which came to dominate the vital

---

[6] A sensitive and convincing case for this function of history is developed by Hayden V. White, "The Burden of History," *History and Theory*, Vol. V, No. 2 (1966), pp. 111-134. A less extensive treatment is located in Isaiah Berlin, "The Concept of Scientific History" in William H. Dray (ed.), *Philosophical Analysis and History* (New York: Harper & Row Publishers, Inc., 1969), pp. 5-53, especially Sections T and U.

[7] Even the staunch positivist Karl R. Popper recognized this in his *Poverty of Historicism* (New York: Harper & Row Publishers, Inc., 1964), especially Section 31; while the impact of *Weltanschauung* on social science is forcefully examined in Leon Bramson, *The Political Context of Sociology* (Princeton: Princeton University Press, 1961), especially Chapter 7.

[8] For a persuasive discussion of such relationships see: Carl Becker, *The Heavenly City of the Eighteenth-Century Philosophers* (New Haven: Yale University Press, 1932), especially Chapter I; and J. Huizinga, "The Idea of History" in Fritz Stern (ed.), *The Varieties of History* (New York: Meridian Books, Inc., 1956), pp. 290-303.

center of American social, intellectual and political life for half a century. These liberal historians believed in the American dream of progress. Progress was not seen as inevitable, but it was seen as possible. Through a process of social melioration, institutions might be so adjusted as to usher in a more satisfactory future. All believed that it was through the intelligent use of science and technology that a better life for mankind might be achieved. They further believed in a meritocracy where the professional expert would play an ever increasing role in using both state and corporate power to meliorate man's condition. They were not, however, naively optimistic either with respect to the social condition or the use of power to meliorate those conditions. While in general they viewed the straits of the Blacks, Southern European immigrants, the Mexican American, the Indians—in short, the disinherited—with compassion, they saw the solution to the problems of the disinherited not in questioning the system which cut people out, but rather as one of allowing more of the disinherited entrance into a growing middle-class America. Although some might have wished at times to radically change the system, their own pragmatic realism, applied especially to power situations, inclined them to approach change gradually from within the established system.

The world in which these historians moved was a world of growing power in international and national affairs. That progressive alliance between Government and Corporate Wealth that was put together during World War I and further developed during the great depression and World War II came to full fruition in the post-War decades in the form of the military-industrial state. This indeed was a world of burgeoning bureaucracies effectively allied with corporate wealth fashioning a mass system of schooling to maintain corporate security at home and abroad. The world the liberal historian viewed was sometimes his own creation, sometimes "out of joint", and at other times "accidental." Most however agreed that as much as they might disagree with the current trends, this social system was the best that could be wrested from what were difficult circumstances. Just as other historians, these men could not escape their own value orientations. More than others, however, they could not escape the fact that many of their own personal values were embedded in that corporate liberal state which they helped make intelligible if not to justify. Given the assumption that the society in which they moved was basically sound, it was almost inevitable that their histories would track along progressive lines. Under these circumstances the bloody violence and acts of repression committed against minority groups were not part of the mainstream of American history. In a similar vein, expansion of schooling for the masses was usually viewed as a progressive step forward, one generated by humanitarian motives while the possibility that the school was in fact a vehicle of control and repression escaped analysis. Schooling in American history was viewed as a positive "good" largely because educational historians viewed schooling as a positive necessity. Once again it was the present world which accounted for a particular interpretation. Other examples might be cited. For example, it was the liberal world of Lawrence Cremin which allowed him to fashion *The Genius of American Education* amidst the literal collapse of urban education and the burning of the cities. We do in fact live in different worlds, and we do therefore see our past differently.

Every new present, however, creates a need to re-examine our past. Those who still believe in the American dream and the basic soundness of this social system will still find the liberal progressive picture of the past meaningful. However, if one views the present world more critically, liberal history will be found short on meaningful criticism and heavy on apology. If one believes this society is not structured to enhance the dignity of man but is rather propelled by a de-humanizing quest for status, power and wealth, then the liberal histories fail to explain how we got where we believe we are. Under these circumstances, liberal history does not connect with and add meaning to our present world. If one starts with the assumption that this society is in fact racist, fundamentally materialistic and institutionally structured to protect vested interests, the past takes on vastly different meanings. Given these assumptions, material long ago passed over as unimportant takes on significance as indeed standard explanations of past events require fresh interpretation. The following instances are but a few examples, where, I believe, the liberal historical interpretations have failed to help us understand given historical phenomena and where a more critical perspective might be helpful.

Liberal interpretation of the Black educational experience is an example of one such failure. The liberals' commitments inclined them to view schooling as essentially positive. They, therefore, further assumed that a little schooling was better than none. Under the circumstances such a view tended to obscure the possibility that the school might have been a vehicle of social control and repression. The liberal historian thus interpreted philanthropic support of Black education as humanitarian in intent even though the statements of some of the key participants explicitly contradict such an interpretation. If we accept the notion that the school can be used for social control as well as repression, then we can more easily understand why such a strong advocate of slavery as J. L. M. Curry could rise so quickly to become, as Merle Curti put it, the "most influential figure in Southern education."[9]

Such a view of schooling can also help us to understand why both northern and southern industrialists took such a "philanthropic" interest in Black education by contributing so handsomely to the Peabody and Slatter funds as well as the General Education Board.

---

[9] Merle Curti, *The Social Ideas of American Educators* (New Jersey: Littlefield, Adams & Co., 1961), p. 264. For many of these insights with respect to Black education, I am indebted to James Anderson, Indiana University, Bloomington, Indiana.

It was in the economic interest of William H. Baldwin, John D. Rockefeller, and Andrew Carnegie to use the school as a vehicle to control and manage Black labor in the South. Just one year after granting Tuskegee Institute six hundred thousand dollars, Andrew Carnegie asserted that:

It is certain we must grow more cotton to meet the demands of the world, or endanger our practical monopoly of that indispensable article. Either the efforts of Europe will be successful to grow in other parts, even at greater cost for a time, or the world will learn to substitute something else for it. We can not afford to lose the negro. We have urgent need of all and of more. Let us therefore turn our efforts to making the best of him.[10]

William H. Baldwin, southern railroad magnate and close advisor of Booker T. Washington, also seconded Carnegie's position. As Baldwin put it:

The potential economic value of the negro population properly educated is infinite and incalculable. In the negro is the opportunity of the South. Time has proven that he is best fitted to perform the heavy labor in the Southern states. 'The negro and the mule is the only combination so far to grow cotton.' The South needs him; but needs him educated to be a suitable citizen. Properly directed he is the best possible laborer to meet the climatic conditions of the South. He will willingly fill the more menial positions, and do the heavy work, at less wages, than the American white man or any foreign race which has yet come to our shores. This will permit the Southern white laborer to perform the more expert labor, and to leave the fields, mines, and simpler trades for the negro.[11]

The purpose of education at Tuskegee was clearly an elaboration of this thesis. The Blacks were to be educated for their "natural" environment: the fields and the mines.

In brief, the aim of Tuskegee is to teach the negro boy or girl to be moral and religious, and how to make a living; to educate them in those lines in which the opportunity to make a living is open. They are educated for their natural environment and not educated out of it.[12]

In view of the rather obvious role philanthropy has played in the control of Black education, it might be a good idea to begin to critically question the role of philanthropic foundations throughout the twentieth century. Many of the major philanthropic foundations involving education came into existence between 1900 and 1918. This was the period in which capital, labor and goverment learned to function within the framework of the corporate liberal state. Part of that framework included the development of foundations as an instrument through which private wealth significantly influenced public policy in national and international affairs throughout the twentieth century.[13] By World War I, it became apparent

[10] Andrew Carnegie, "Proceedings of a Meeting Held in New York City Feb. 12, 1904, under the Direction of the Armstrong Association," Carnegie, Box 252, Library of Congress.

[11] As quoted in unpublished paper by James Anderson, "William Baldwin, Jr., Chairman of the Tuskegee Machine: An Interlocking Directorate of American Elites." University of Illinois, Champaign, May, 1971.
[12] *Ibid.*, p. 21.
[13] See David W. Eakins, "The Development of Corporate Liberal Policies Research in the United States 1885-1965" (Unpublished Ph.D. dissertation, University of Wisconsin, 1966).

that progressive liberal reformers had succeeded in creating a workable arrangement whereby the basic distribution of wealth would remain unchanged, as the overall interests of capital and labor were protected against undue competition through both the regulatory agencies of government and the liberally enlightened guidance of philanthropic foundations. In this context, the educational state emerged as a vital generator and reservoir of trained manpower.

The role of the liberal within that corporate society was that of the knowledgeable expert dedicated to the survival of the system. The liberal educational reformer, just as the liberal political reformer, in this sense, is an effective, flexible conservative. The conservative roots of American liberalism can best be seen in times of crisis when the survival of the system is in question.[14] From this perspective, one can understand why John Dewey, a socialist, would conclude in his study of the "Poles in the United States" for the War Department, that:

> The great industrial importance of Polish labor in this country must be borne in mind and the fact that there will be a shortage of labor after the war and that there is already a movement under foot (which should be carefully looked into) to stimulate the return of Poles and others of foreign birth in Southeastern Europe to their native lands after the war. With the sharp commercial competition that will necessarily take place after the war, any tendencies which on the one hand de-Americanize and on the other hand strengthen the allegiance of those of foreign birth to the United States deserve careful attention.[15]

John Dewey was committed to the economic growth and progress of the nation, even though that progress might require manipulation of Polish workers. Dewey's concerns at this point were not those of a socialist doing battle with conservative businessmen, but rather that of a liberal reformer worrying about making this system work. From this perspective, one can also account for his intense dislike and distrust of Papal Catholics as opposed to Protestant Catholics, as well as his condescending attitude toward ethnic differences which appear throughout the report. Ethnic and religious differences were viewed as a threat to the survival of the nation and had to be overcome through assimilation. Dewey, as well as other liberal reformers, was committed to flexible, experimentally managed, orderly social change which included a high degree of manipulation. It was this side of Dewey that one sees in his reports on the Soviet schools. The experimentally managed educational state which he saw emerging in Russia (1928) excited his imagination while the manipulative aspects of that totalitarian regime appeared of little consequence. In contrast, Emma Goldman visited the same schools and reacted negatively. Our observers have different perceptual screens. In the case of Dewey, we have a screen which places

---

[14] See Gabriel Kolko, *The Triumph of Conservatism* (New York: The Macmillan Co., 1963).

[15] John Dewey, "Confidential Report, Conditions Among the Poles in the United States," (Government Printing Office, 1918), p. 73.

a high value on flexible, managed social change; whereas, in the case of Emma Goldman, we have a screen which places high value on freedom and independence.[16]

A more critical perspective of the liberal progressive educational reformers might include a re-analysis of the thought of Jane Addams. A critical review of her work leads one to question why she should be viewed as such a grand humanitarian when, in fact, she held the people among whom she worked in such contempt. Her call for social control, efficiency and manipulation of the masses through propaganda techniques and her paternalistic attitude toward the ignorant immigrant reflect a very distinctive, but often overlooked side of American liberal thought and practice in the twentieth century. As Jane Addams put it:

Ethics as well as political opinions may be discussed and disseminated among the sophisticated by lectures and printed pages, but to the common people, they can only come through example—through a personality which seizes the popular imagination. The advantage of an unsophisticated neighborhood is, that the inhabitants do not keep their ideas as treasures.[17]

For Jane Addams, as well as Herbert Croly, Edward A. Ross and others, the school should be a vehicle to manipulate the psycho-social symbols so as to emotionally weld the masses to the corporate state which was thus emerging. As Jane surmised:

We are only beginning to understand what might be done through the festival, the street procession, the band of marching musicians, orchestrated music in public squares or parks, with the magic power they all possess to formulate the sense of companionship and solidarity. The experiments which are being made in public schools to celebrate the national holidays, the changing seasons, the birthdays of heroes, the planting of trees, are slowly developing little ceremonials which may in time work out into pageants of genuine beauty and significance. No other nation has so unparalleled an opportunity to do this through its schools as we have, for no other nation has so widespreading a school system, while the enthusiasm of children and their natural ability to express their emotions through symbols, gives the securest possible foundation to this growing effort.[18]

The mass psychology of the corporate state advocated by Addams would find parallel in more than one country in the twentieth century. In a similar vein, others such as Edward Ross and Herbert Croly called for spiritual reconstruction of society which could overcome the isolated self and weld the individual to a new nationalistic order.[19] Given this position, it should not come as a surprise to find Croly and other liberals viewing corporate fascism as a grand experiment in social engineering and warning their critics to ". . . beware of outlawing a political experiment which aroused in a whole nation an increased moral energy

---

[16] Compare John Dewey, *Impressions of Soviet Russia* (New York: New Republic, Inc., 1929) with Emma Goldman, *My Disillusionment in Russia* (New York: Thomas Y. Crowell Co., 1970).
[17] Jane Addams, *Democracy and Social Ethics* (New York: The Macmillan Co., 1964), p. 228.
[18] Jane Addams, *The Spirit of Youth and the City Streets* (New York: The Macmillan Co., 1909), pp. 98-99.
[19] See Herbert Croly, "Reconstruction of Religion," *New Republic*, XXXI, June 21, 1922, pp. 100-102.

and dignified its activities by subordinating them to a deeply felt common purpose."[20] The rather warm reception which Italian fascism received among such well known American pragmatic liberals as Charles Beard, Horace Kallen, Herbert Croly and Lincoln Steffens (1926-1930) was prompted by more than a simple desire to have the "trains run on time." While Beard was impressed with the flexibility of the fascist state and its freedom from "consistent scheme," others were more impressed with the ability of that state to act decisively by subordinating outworn "principles to method" and law to order. For many, corporate fascism seemed to satisfy the need of the corporate society for unity, order, efficiency, collective meaning, social engineering and experimentation as well as freedom from the older rationalistic liberal philosophies which tended to value individual liberty over state authority. It was not until the early 1930's that many liberals began to see the consequences of these ideas in terms of political refugees. At that point, they reversed their opinion about fascism. Historically, we have tended to treat this sympathetic treatment of fascism by pragmatic liberals as an "accidental flirtation,"[21] or perhaps, an aberration in which normally rational men got carried away with the *Zeitgeist* of the time. If we had a critical analysis of pragmatic liberal thought and the corporate state, we might understand the fascist flirtation as a logical and reasonable development of certain characteristics of liberal thought. If we took seriously the liberal's need for social experiment and reconciliation of opposites, we might have understood why Charles A. Beard looked upon Benito Mussolini's fascist Italy as working out "new democratic direction," and why he might conclude that:

Beyond question an amazing experiment is being made here, an experiment in reconciling individualism and socialism, politics and technology. It would be a mistake to allow feelings aroused by contemplating the harsh deeds and extravagant assertions that have accompanied the fascist process (as all other immense historical changes) to obscure the potentialities and the lessons of the adventure—no, not adventure, but destiny riding without saddle and bridle across the historic peninsula that bridges the world of antiquity and our modern world.[22]

Once again, if we had fully appreciated the liberal's commitment to the survival of the system through evolutionary, orderly change, we might have understood why it was the "liberal" dominated Committee for Cultural Freedom (1939) which assumed McCarthy-like solutions to the problems of communist teachers in the schools fully a decade ahead of the McCarthy era.[23] Nor

---

[20] Herbert Croly, "An Apology for Fascism," *New Republic*, XLIX, January 12, 1929, pp. 207-209.

[21] For example, see John P. Diggins, "Flirtation with Fascism: American Pragmatic Liberals and Mussolini's Italy," *American Historical Review*, LXXI, No. 2 (January, 1966), pp. 487-506. Although Diggins does an excellent review of the literature of the period, he fails seriously to consider the possibilities that there may be significant characteristics of liberal thought which can lead one to support enthusiastically a fascist regime.

[22] Charles Beard, "Making the Fascist State," *The New Republic*, LVII, January 23, 1929, p. 278.

[23] See Paul Violas, "Fear and Constraints in Academic Freedom of Public School Teachers, 1930-1960," *Educational Theory*, Vol. 21, No. 1 (Winter, 1971), pp. 70-81.

would it seem unusual that Sidney Hook would be one of the founders of the American Committee for Cultural Freedom (1951), an offspring of the C.I.A.-supported Congress for Cultural Freedom.[24] Finally, if we had an accurate historical analysis of the role the liberal has played in the development and maintenance of the corporate state, we would not have been so repeatedly surprised along the road from Berkeley to Attica to find a liberal mind behind the hand on the policeman's club or trigger.

Our educational history does not connect with the present, not only because we have failed to make connections, but because our earlier analysis does not allow us to perceive the roots of our present problems, whether these problems involve race, freedom or alienation. One must search long and hard to find any evidence in texts on twentieth century American educational history that key "professional" educators were prejudiced against Blacks, Southern Europeans, Mexican Americans, Orientals and Jews. If, however, one reads the journals and personal letters of David Starr Jordan, Edward Cubberly, William R. Harper, G. Stanley Hall, H. H. Goddard, Lewis M. Terman, Edward L. Thorndike and many others, one can readily understand why American educational institutions are so profoundly racist. One, however, has considerable difficulty in explaining how we could miss such blatantly obvious evidence. If we missed this because our perceptual framework did not allow us to pick up the evidence, then, isn't it time that we question our perceptual framework?

The framework used in conceptualizing our history is not usually derived from either a critical analysis of the present or the past. There is rather a distinct tendency to write in-house histories which accept the rhetoric of the "professional" as reality. For example, in the case of *The Sane Positivist*,[25] Edward L. Thorndike, one might maintain a skeptical attitude toward his assertions about being an "objective" social scientist, especially when one finds him discussing an applicant for a teaching position in the following manner: "Bair seems to be a pretty good man and he happens to be of some experience in the schools. But I am not sure that he will be a good enough teacher and I suspect that he is a Jew."[26] One wonders if Thorndike's anti-Semitism as well as his distinctive dislike for the poor and unwashed in our society ever interfered with his "objective" science of education and psychology.

Perhaps the most disturbing thing about American educational history is its failure to deal with the centers of power and influence in American life. We have considered one such center in terms of philanthropic foundation. If we consider the influence the General Education Board has had on Black education; the many Carnegie Foundations have had

---

[24] See Christopher Lasch, "The Cultural Cold War: A Short History of the Congress for Cultural Freedom," an essay in Barton J. Bernstein, *Towards A New Past* (New York: Random House, Inc., 1968), pp. 322-359.

[25] Geraldine Joncich, *The Sane Positivist* (Middleton, Conn.: Wesleyan University Press, 1968).

[26] Cattell Papers. Letter from Thorndike to Cattell, January 22, 1902, Box 42, Library of Congress.

on general education from kindergarten through the doctorate; and the role the Ford Foundation has played in educational television, it seems strange that we still do not have a solid critical history of the influence of these foundations in twentieth century American education. The irony of this, perhaps, will be that when a history of the foundations is written, it probably will be written by a scholar financed by the foundations.

Educational historians in the twentieth century have been reluctant to analyze centers of power, and through their reluctance have contributed to the liberal myth propounded by Michael Harrington about this being an *Accidental Century*. While I believe we do not know enough about how and why critical decisions have been made in American education, I do not believe that in this age of "accountability" we should blame an unseen hand at work in some nebulous bureaucracy for the difficulties we experience. A naive perspective with respect to past educational decision-making seriously interferes with our development of a more realistic understanding of our present. Here again, much depends on one's view of the present.

If we are satisfied with our present world, firmly believe that we live in the best of what could have been developed and generally espouse the liberal view of progress, then the kinds of problems of historical analysis I have raised will seem to have little meaning or significance. If, on the other hand, one sees this society as not structured to enhance the dignity of man but rather propelled by a dehumanizing quest for status, power, and wealth, then the liberal histories seem not only disconnected from our present, but also appear more as an apology than an explanation for what has transpired. Perhaps Nietzsche was correct, after all, when he said, "You can only explain the past by what is highest in the present. Only by straining the noblest qualities you have to their highest power will you find out what is greatest in the past, most worth knowing and preserving."

Reprinted from The Educational Forum, Kappa Delta Pi, Volume 37, Number 3, March, 1973.

Idealism: A Clarification of an Educational Philosophy

By John Paul Strain

One must search the journals of some years back before finding an article on Idealism as a philosophy of education. Even books about it are quite old. J. Donald Butler's 1966 paperback on Idealism is a rewrite of the chapters in his 1951 *Four Philosophies: And Their Practice in Education and Religion*.[1] The conspicuous absence of this philosophy of education in the literature is most notable, and a historian of our age might suggest that Idealism no longer exists in the thought and minds of 1970 man. But in order to prevent such a mistaken assumption from taking root, an article needs to be written to suggest that Idealism still exists, and clarification of its true outlook is required in dealing with people who hold to such a viewpoint. The following sketch attempts to accomplish this task.

I.

When one refers to Idealism as a philosophy of education, one has to have in mind Hegelian Idealism. Hegelianism, the dominant Idealism of the 19th century, carried in that day the same intellectual influence as John Dewey's Experimentalism of more recent times. What exists today of Idealism is a living remnant of that philosophy. Objective Idealism, as it is called, was considered by its author to be the climax of all philosophy, and provided for an explanation of the total realm of human experience, education included. Within its folds, the leading ideas of past Idealists had been integrated, and in a similar way, all subsequent developments were to be incorporated into its comprehensiveness.

Many American Idealists endeavored to adjust the Objective Idealism of Hegel to the life style of American political philosophy and social science discoveries. More explicitly, they attempted to incorporate the concept of American Individualism, the theory of Darwinian evolution, and the data of modern psychology into Objective Idealism or a synthesis theory of Idealistic philosophy. Josiah Royce's philosophy is an example as witnessed by Harry T. Costello's *Josiah Royce's Seminar, 1913-1914*[2] and Mary Briody Mahowald's *An Idealistic Pragmatism: The Development of the Pragmatic Element in the Philosophy of Josiah Royce*.[3] An examination of Royce's books and classes leaves no doubt that he was attempting a philosophical synthesis, and attempts of a like nature were made by many other American so-called Idealists.

The fact that such an approach was prevalent among Americans is an important consideration for understanding those whom history has designated as Idealist philosophers of education because many of them imitated their philosopher counterparts. Herman Harrell Horne, for example, stated that the most influential philosopher on his thinking was Josiah Royce, and that it was

---

John Paul Strain is a Professor of Philosophy of Education at the University of Redlands, Redlands California.

---

1. J. Donald Butler, *Four Philosophies: And Their Practice in Education and Religion* (New York: Harper & Brothers Publishers, 1951).

2. Harry T. Costell, *Josiah Royce's Seminar, 1913-1914*, ed. Grover Smith (New Brunswick, New Jersey: Rutgers University Press, 1963).

3. Mary Briody Mahowald, *An Idealistic Pragmatism: The Development of the Pragmatic Element in the Philosophy of Josiah Royce* (The Hague, Netherlands: Martinus Nijhoff, 1972).

from him that he developed his notions of philosophy, methodology, and education. As a result, Horne followed the role set by Royce, incorporating the information from the social sciences into traditional Idealism.

Horne knew Objective Idealism, and recognized its educational components. He wrote in his own book *The Philosophy of Education* that the "masterpiece" of Idealistic philosophy of education had already been written,[4] and this masterpiece is Karl Rosenkranz's *Paedogogik als System*.[5] "Written in the spirit of Hegel," wrote Horne, "this book is the classic text in education. As far as theoretical justification of education is concerned, nothing can surpass it." Horne suggested that since the masterpiece had already been written, it is the responsibility of people like himself to open new vistas by relating the theoretical ground of Idealism to the new empirical research from the social sciences.

The point that is clear in Horne's work is that he was a synthesizer of educational data. He never intended that his system be *the* representative system of Idealism in education. He was merely trying to correlate the traditional Idealistic philosophy of education with the developments in biology, physiology, psychology, and sociology. To be sure, there are clear strains of the Idealistic philosophy of education in Horne's work, and he indicates that they stem from Rosenkranz. But he considered his own contributions to be that of adding scientific information to an existing scheme. It is a serious mistake therefore to suggest that Horne's explanations of education are those which most represent the Idealistic position.

There are also certain special commitments that highlight the writings of Professor Horne. These commitments must be understood because they are often taken to be tenets of Idealism. These commitments are religious, i.e., (1) to God, as the infinite Person, the true Trinity of Father, Son, and Holy Ghost; (2) and to immortality as the infinite continuance of man's imperfect temporal existence. Indeed, the Absolute Idea is a fundamental notion in the philosophy of Hegel. But the religious connotations given to it by any number of Christian thinkers exploit Hegel's notion for purposes of Christian apologetics. Religious commitments of this nature are not commitments to Idealism as a philosophy but to Christianity as a religion. In many instances Idealism has become an academic designation for something which is initially religious. For example, the facts of evolution and experimental psychology (both anti-providential) can be incorporated into an interpretation for the continued belief in God and life-after-death. Horne himself recognized this strong commitment to religion. In order to clarify the situation, he wanted his system to be called Theistic Idealism.

In summary, if we are endeavoring to understand what Idealism as a philosophy of education stands for, we must be careful whom we classify as truly Idealists in thought and application. Even some of our declared modern day so-called Idealists are suspect on such grounds. Donald Butler's attempt at synthesis and incorporation is such an example.

II.

It is a paradox of education today that, while it is virtually impossible to find a true Idealist philosopher of education (in the academic sense of the term) who is publishing and writing on the subject, there exists the thought pattern of

---

4. Herman Harrell Horne, *The Philosophy of Education* (New York: The Macmillan Company, 1904), pp. 11, 12.
5. J. K. F. Rosenkranz, "Pedagogy as a System," in John Paul Strain (ed.), *Modern Philosophies of Education* (New York: Random House, Inc., 1971), pp. 128-143.

Idealism in certain places and components in American education. This thought pattern is held by a number of individuals and these people are recognized by virtue of their call for a return to traditional education and "the good old days" of American Society.

Now what is a thought pattern that is possessed by individuals and works to the degree of being an influence in education? A thought pattern is a belief system, consisting of an internalized order that gives direction and consistency to practices and ideas. This order is inherent within a person's feeling-cognitive system, functioning as the spring for accepting or rejecting data, ideas, or behavior. A thought pattern is an important phenomenon for the study of education because it is the intellectual foundation for an individual's practices.

For more than a hundred years the thought pattern of Idealism has been influential in American education. Its earliest and greatest prominence occurred in the last half of the 19th century under the leadership of William T. Harris, United States Commissioner of Education and Superintendent of the St. Louis Schools. Harris was not only a philosopher and translator of Hegel, but introduced Karl Rosenkranz's *Pedagogy as a System* to American intellectuals by way of the *Journal of Speculative Philosophy*.

A second important phase occurred in the 1930's as certain university philosophers of education stated an educational position distinct from the Pragmatism of the day. These individuals called themselves "Essentialists," the term signifying strong traditional values, and that the purpose of the schools being to teach the basics of the 3 R's in elementary school and the essential subjects of English, math, history, science, geography, and foreign languages in the secondary school. Michael Demiashkevitch initiated the term "Essentialism" and persuaded William Bagley to use it. The term has continued as a philosophy of education designation ever since.

The third influential phase of the thought pattern of Idealism followed in the wake of post-World War II conservatism. Writers and a few college professors, Arthur Bestor being the most noted, criticized the pragmatic philosophy in the American schools and called for a return to the basic and traditional subjects prevalent in the days before the advent of progressive education. These individuals organized the Council for Basic Education, and the following is a statement of its position which is an almost perfect synopsis of Idealism as a philosophy of education:

> The CBE believes that the school has many subsidiary purposes, but that its primary purpose is fourfold: (1) to transmit the facts about the heritage and culture of the race; (2) to teach young people to read and write and figure; (3) in the process of (1) and (2) to train the intelligence and to stimulate the pleasures of thought; and (4) to provide that atmosphere of moral affirmation without which education is merely animal training.[6]

The fourth phase of the thought pattern was the more recent political movement of law and order, stressing obedience to parental and legal authority, the value of work and discipline, and patriotic respect for country and leadership. Critical of "Dr. Spock and the so-called permissiveness in childrearing practices in America," "indolent hippies," "leniency toward criminals," "the unpatriotic stand of contemporary youth unwilling to fight for their country in Viet Nam," this movement sought to rally its views around certain political figures, hoping that they would turn the course of American events back to the

---

6. C. B. E. Bulletin, No. 2 (September 1957).

ways and manners of late 19th-century American life style. Along with this stand went the call for a return to traditional education.

III.

Clarification of the thought pattern of Idealism is required for fuller understanding of what relation traditional education has to the philosophy of Idealism. The following points are the earmarks of the thought pattern and can be seen as integral parts of a belief system in education that still exists today.

Progress A fundamental tenet in the thought pattern of Idealism is progress. Progress means growth and evolution. This is not the evolution of biological improvement as defined by Darwin, but the development of cultures from primitive societies to successive stages of higher and advanced civilizations. The history of man is the progress of human life through great civilizations. The advance is both intellectual and moral.

Knowledge of absolute truth and the practice of absolute moral right are the ends to which man must strive. Absolute truth never changes, nor does the ideal of absolute moral right. The Hegelian antithesis of logic—that of nature—also does not change. Man is the only entity which changes. Man begins as an entity of nature at one end of the continuum, and with the potential for thinking and development, advances toward the other end of absolute truth through human history. Man is different from the animals because he is capable of change, he progresses. The ultimate achievement of man is to acquire the absolutes in behavior and thought. Man is progressing when he works for these ends. Ambition and the search after truth are what characterize progressive man. A savage is content to live only for the moment, satisfying immediate needs. Civilized man, on the other hand, seeks higher values and truth. The signs of civilized progress are: (1) the growth of knowledge and the usefulness of discoveries, i.e., geometry for building bridges, steam and combustion for powering engines, water for producing electricity; and (2) advanced moral development, i.e., cleanliness in body functions (bathing and excretion), politeness and courtesy in social behavior, and respect for moral laws of state and church. Progress is never effortless. It requires discipline and perseverance.

Institutionalism The study of history shows that civilizations not only rise, they also decline and fall. Decline is caused by the growing loss of moral values and disregard for absolute truth. People become indifferent to religion, skeptical and agnostic toward truth, and vulgar and lazy in moral behavior. To prevent the possibility of decline and fall, civilization preserves religion, truth, and moral behavior by institutionalizing them. Institutions are the visible and objective realities of the mind of man. Man creates institutions to preserve the intellectual and moral gains he has achieved. All subsequent acquirements must be incorporated into these institutions so they may be preserved for the next generation. Memories do not last, habits are temporary and not valid unless they serve some system or organizational need, and the human individual is only significant and of value when he conforms to the laws and regulations of the institutions of society. From the standpoint of education, the young must be taught to conform to society's institutions, and to show them allegiance and respect. The young must learn that true freedom can only occur when the individual is protected from assault and lawlessness, and it is society's institutions which preserve the general public from anarchy.

Man's protective institutions are: (1) the family, for the control of sexual conduct and the rearing of children; (2) the nation, for preserving the standards of law and order in social behavior; (3) the church, for preserving moral behavior and the comprehensive view of the truth; (4) the school, for preserving past knowledge, discipline and practical skills. It must be noted, that teaching respect for institutions literally means respecting the past. Children go to school to prepare themselves for the future by learning the things that have been accomplished in the past.

Self-Control   A greater burden of learning is placed on the young with each new moral and intellectual achievement. This fact becomes clear when one recognizes a fundamental presupposition of this thought pattern, that an infant is born into the world as an animal. Indeed, the infant has the potential to become human; but in the first stages of life, the child is literally an animal, interested only in the immediate present, seeking to satisfy pressing desires, and displaying current emotions. In the course of becoming an adult, the child learns to control his animal drives and to live beyond the present. In so doing, the person learns to be human. If he fails to gain this control, he continues as a little animal—spoiled, selfish, and indulgent. He may even grow up to be an adult beast with all the brutality, inconsiderateness, and vulgarity that goes with adult power. To be human, one must have attained self-discipline. When one achieves this control, he is free, i.e., free from the immediacy of the moment and the pressing urges of animal drives. Self-control is the basis of human freedom, and it is the mind which accomplishes this control. This particular mind-function is called "will" or "will power."

Self-Estrangement   The first goal of education is to teach children self-control, the art of becoming free. The process by which this occurs is self-estrangement, and literally means, the estranging of oneself from one's original animal nature in order to learn a second nature, which is human nature. Learning the second nature goes by the name of "habit." To be human means, having attained a level of habitual conduct that is in agreement with the routines and habits of civilization at that level of progress. Habitual conduct is the means society has of preserving the social standards of civilized behavior, and the function of self-estrangement is to force the child away from his animal nature in order to learn civilized behavior.

Discipline   As a general rule, a child cannot attain the necessary habits of conduct unless assisted by adults. There are incidents, however, where the loss of parents has placed untold hardship and responsibility on a young lad or girl, and through self-discipline and hard work such a person attains proper habits. These individuals are often revered as self-made men and women. Although such cases do occur because of the unusual circumstances of heavy work and labor placed upon them, in most instances, a child learns the habits of civilized conduct through parental discipline. Since the tendency of a child is to be lazy, indulgent, and selfish, parents have to force the child into proper civilized habits. Discipline and punishment are parceled out to children in proportion to the need for producing correct habits and avoiding animal ways. Society charges parents with the responsibility of performing this function. If a child does not change from his original nature, the fault lies with parents who have failed in meeting their social obligations.

School   Discipline that begins in the home, must be continued in the institution of the school. Discipline shall be rational. Every possible wrong act must be identified with explanations and ensuing punishments. The teacher in the school is to be totally rational and composed. Order rather than spontaneity highlights the structure of the day. The proper habits to be taught in school are: cleanliness and neatness, orderliness and punctuality, courtesy and obedience, quickness and accuracy.[7] In the words of faculty psychologist Ruric Roark. "The how of forming habits in school may be summed up in two words—drill and imitation."[8] The possession of good habits is but another name for strong character. "As we sow habits in muscle and nerve and brain," says Roark, "so shall we, and those who come after us, reap in aptitude, in skill, in character."[9]

But the institution of the school has not only the responsibility of continued training in moral deportment, it also has the responsibility of preserving the knowledge of civilization. This is accomplished by mastering the summaries of knowledge found in textbooks. Books serve to preserve knowledge and truth. What is written down cannot be lost. The young need to master the skills that enhance this preservation, meaning, the children must all learn to read, write, and do arithmetic. Hence, the 3 R's are the essential subjects of the elementary school. In secondary education, the students are to put these skills to work in mastering textbooks in science, history, geography, foreign languages, literature. The textbook, indicates William T. Harris, is the greatest educational tool that has yet been devised. It organizes knowledge in an objective way, it is something that the student possesses so that he can read the material over and over again, and it prevents the teacher from bringing in subjective opinions on what is objectively true.

Educational Methodology   The method of education reflects the aims and function of the school. It relates to two tasks which society has ordered schools to perform: (1) strengthening the mind of students, and (2) furnishing the mind with knowledge.

Since mind is the human component which makes man different from animals and is the primary factor in human progress, one of the major functions in school teaching is training or exercising the mind. As Dr. Edward Brooks, late 19th-century superintendent of Philadelphia's public schools writes:

> The mind is a spiritual activity and grows by its own inherent energies. Mental exercise is thus the law of mental development. As a muscle grows strong by use, so any faculty of the mind is developed by its proper use and exercise. An idle mind loses its tone and strength, like an unused muscle; the mental powers go to rust through idleness and inaction. To develop the faculties of the mind and secure their highest activity and efficiency there must be a constant and judicious exercise of these faculties.[10]

Faculty psychology and the philosophy of education of Idealism are at root inseparable. It was the Idealist philosophers who utilized the method of psychological introspection to classify the mind's faculties, and this understanding is clearly visible in the works of Rosenkranz and William T. Harris. Faculty psychology, it should be noted, was also the part that the American philosophers of education such as H. H. Horne were most uncomfortable with. Nevertheless, the attitude of training and exercising the mind is a significant aspect of the thought pattern of idealism and must be recognized as one of its most significant dimensions.

The faculties of the mind are classified into three divisions: the intellect, the sensibilities, and the will. The intellect possesses the faculties of perception,

---

7. Ruric N. Roark, "Psychology in Education," in Strain (ed.), *op. cit.*, p. 147.
8. *Ibid.*
9. *Ibid.*
10. Edward Brooks, *Mental Science and Methods of Mental Culture: Designed for the Use of Normal Schools, Academics, and Private Students Preparing to be Teachers* (Philadelphia: Normal Publishing Co., 1891), pp. 37, 38.

memory, imagination, and reason, and all must be strengthened independently through exercise. Certain school subjects are to be performed for the sake of exercising particular faculties. Mental arithmetic is good exercise for the faculty of memory, object lessons for perceptions, literature for imagination, and diagramming and parsing sentences for reason. The suspected faculties, on the other hand, are the sensibilities of emotions, affections, and desires. What highlights their training is the control which reason must have over them. As in the case of affections, for example, duty and not passion should be the guiding force in such circumstances. In addition to reason, sensibilities must have worthy objects. It is worthy to have the desire to be successful and to do well in school. It is unworthy to desire money, sex, popularity. And finally, there must be the exercise and training of the will, involving practice in making decisions and practice in carrying out those decisions. The control of the will once again lies within reason. The worthy objects of practice are telling the truth, resisting temptation, observing good habits of behavior.

The teacher not only develops the power of the mind, he also works to furnish it with knowledge. Furnishing the mind with knowledge goes by the name of instruction, derived from *in* (into) and *struo* (I build), which means, according to Brooks, *I build into*.

> To instruct the mind is thus to furnish it with knowledge, or to develop and build up knowledge in the mind. The instructor puts the knowledge that is in his own mind into the minds of his pupils, and also develops knowledge in their minds from their own original sources of knowing. He is thus a builder of knowledge in the mind as an architect erects a building of brick and marble.[11]

William M. Bryant in his book *Hegel's Educational Ideas* suggests that the mature adult initiates instruction and the student submits himself to it. "The general psychological process is the same in both minds," he says. "But in the mind of the teacher, the given exercise has been repeated many times. In the pupil, the process is taking place for the first time."[12]

Maturity on the part of the teacher and the repetitious nature of knowledge to teaching technique reflect the Idealists' concern for past knowledge and the permanence of truth. New discoveries merely add to what is already known. Knowledge is found in books. What teachers repeat year after year is the subject matter existing in textbooks.

Teaching methods reflect the emphasis on textbook learning. Study lessons have two parts: (1) seatwork or homework, and (2) recitation. Assignments are made in textbooks to be completed at desks or at home. The teacher either assigns textbook study questions or asks the students to outline (skeletonize) the chapter. Study questions are either fact questions, detailed and concrete, or thought questions which ask who said what and why. Recitation is the time the teacher checks seat and homework. Suggestions for good teaching are: making sure all vocabulary words in the assignment are understood, utilizing a random method of calling upon students in the recitation period, and requiring the students to be absolutely correct in answering the questions.

Good teaching is defined as securing the attention of all pupils in the class, and keeping all pupils up to practically the same level of achievement. For this reason, believers of this thought pattern are strong supporters of ability grouping

---

11. *Ibid.*, p. 11.
12. William M. Bryant, *Hegel's Educational Ideas* (New York: American Book Company, 1922), p. 34.

and promotion gradewise for those who have successfully accomplished the course work. Unsuccessful students must repeat the grade. To keep pupil's attention and at somewhat the same level of achievement: (1) there must be no more than one class to a room or distractions will abound, (2) there should be only one teacher to a class in order to prevent divided attention and divided authority, (3) all the members of the class must be doing the same task, and (4) the textbook must be followed closely to prevent wandering either by students or teachers.[13]

State Schools Progressive levels of achievement are maintained when institutionalized. Therefore, institutions are the major structures of a civilization. One important institution is the school. But the school can only function properly when it is part of a higher institution, that of the state or nation. The nation is the major institution that binds man to man and upholds the ethical ideal of truth and right. For this reason, all institutions fit within dimensions of the state. The church, for example, exists in and for the nation. Hegel was critical of both Separatist Protestantism and Roman Catholicism for the promotion of a false dichotomy between the secular and the religious. Separatists err because they cultivate the separation of church and state. Catholics err because they consider the church as a sanctuary from the secular and independent of the state. The nation is the major institution of man's progress. All other institutions must abide by its laws, regulations, and purpose.

It goes without saying that the institution of the school should fall under the regulations and goals of the nation. For this reason, nations have established schools and means for regulating those schools. Such schools are called national schools, people's schools, or public schools. The nation taxes its inhabitants for their financial support, appoints a minister of education to oversee them, requires the young to attend them, and makes laws regulating content, administration, and employment. Schools, thus, are state institutions for encompassing the purpose of preserving the nation and the achievements of civilization.

National Progress One major function of the schools is to identify those few gifted students who may someday contribute to national progress. No doubt such students will learn the essentials of knowledge faster than others. In order to challenge them intellectually, these students should be separated either in special schools or special tracks within schools. Materials will be covered more quickly, the work will be more difficult. These special students will go on to higher education, where they can perform research and learn truths not yet discovered. It is from these persons that intellectual and moral progress occur. They are the intellectual leaders of society. In the course of time, the truths and benefits which these individuals discover will be written down for posterity and made useful for the general population. By utilizing the discoveries of intellectuals, the nation climbs a step higher toward absolute truth.

National Leadership Hegel states that the best form of government is a constitutional monarchy. It is very clear in Hegel that he never expected the philosopher to be a political leader as is the case with Plato's philosopher kings. The philosopher's role in Objective Idealism is that of the ivory towered intellectual who sees the comprehensive view of history and works to achieve the whole truth of reality. Political leadership is an immediate and practical enterprise, and would bore a first rate speculative philosopher.

A government of constitutional monarchy means first of all that society will rest on the rational foundation of the past. More explicitly, it will rest on the

---

13. William Chandler Bagley, *Classroom Management* (New York: Macmillan Co., 1907), pp. 188-213.

nation's constitution, the objectified and rational documents of society's order. "It is absolutely essential," writes Hegel, "that the constitution should not be regarded as something made, even though it has come into being in time. It must be treated rather as something simply existent and by itself, as divine therefore, and constant."[14] Society is rooted in the past by giving its allegiance to the nation's constitution.

But immediate and pressing issues of government must be managed. Therefore, national security and order require some kind of living head or person to make decisions. Just as the animal organism requires a head to determine what direction the body will go, so too with the organism of the state. The one head determines the course for the corporate body. Hegel suggests that this head be a monarch on a basis of hereditary succession. A monarch, indicates Hegel, guarantees continuity with the past and prevents factions from bringing discontinuity into government. A nation without a monarch, however, does not prevent its inhabitants from accepting a strong and similar role from its head of state no matter whether appointed or elected. The thought pattern presses them to interpret the head as the sole office of leadership. Such an office holder is to be respected, trusted, and unchallenged as the true head of the nation.

IV.

The thought pattern of Idealism has been and continues to be an influential educational position in the world today. People who have this belief system can be found in almost every section of the United States and in many parts of the world, especially where there has been a strong European influence. It is a philosophy of education that continues to exist because of tradition and economic pressure. Its relation to nationalism and capitalism is quite conspicuous. Since it is so very prevalent and often powerful as a system of thought, it must be studied and examined closely by those working in education.

---

14. George Wilhelm Friedrich Hegel, *Philosophy of Right* (Oxford: At the Clarendon Press, 1942), p. 178.

Reprinted from *Educational Theory*, Volume 25, Number 3, Summer, 1975.

41

SEMESTER: WEEK THREE

REQUIRED READINGS

Church

Part I: Education in the New Nation, 1776-1830, Chapter 2: The Antebellum College and Academy (22 pp.)

Dye

Stanton, H. E. "Teacher Education and the 'Good Teacher'" The Educational Forum. V.38, No.1, November, 1973. (06 pp.)

Crockenberg, Vincent. "Poor Teachers Are Made Not Born" The Educational Forum. V.39, No.2, January, 1975. (10 pp.)

MEETINGS

Monday

Lecture: The American Student

Tuesday

Lecture: American Teacher Education

Wednesday

Lecture: The Progressive Tradition in American Education

Thursday and Friday

Small Groups: Initial Field Experience Contracts are due.

CHURCH TEXTBOOK STUDY GUIDE: CHAPTER 2

THE ANTEBELLUM COLLEGE AND ACADEMY

1. college
2. academy
3. in loco parentis
4. revival
5. coeducation
6. Oberlin College
7. Emma Willard
8. Troy Female Seminary
9. Mary Lyon
10. Mount Holyoke Seminary
11. Vassar College
12. Smith College
13. Wellesley College
14. boards of trustees
15. self-perpetuating trustees
16. Harvard College
17. William and Mary College
18. Yale College
19. state charter
20. laizze-faire theory of economy
21. Adam Smith
22. David Ricardo
23. Dartmouth College case
24. more practical subjects
25. modern subjects
26. John Milton
27. Puritan dissenting academies of England
28. Benjamin Franklin
29. Proposals Relating to the Education of Youth in Pennsylvania
30. The Yale Report

45

31. mental discipline
32. faculty psychology
33. transfer of training
34. technical academy
35. technical institute

36. normal school
37. teacher training academy
38. traditional classical curriculum
39. extracurriculum
40. tertiary education

41. Latin Grammar schools
42. overbuilding
43. perpetual scholarships
44. boosterism
45. religiously-oriented organizational influences

46. non-denominationalism
47. denominationalism
48. social status

Teacher Education and the "Good Teacher"

H. E. STANTON

AFTER several decades in attempts to analyze teaching effectiveness, Professor A. S. Barr is reported as saying that his main contribution had been to find so many things that did not work.[1] The evidence of our not knowing what good teaching it has accumulated over the years and is embodied in numerous reviews of the literature, such as those conducted in 1954 by Marsh and Wilder[2] and in 1961 by the American Association of School Administrators. This latter survey concluded with the rather depressing statement that: "The notion of the 'good teacher' so basic to the study of teacher effectiveness turns out to be almost as vague and diffuse as the range of human experience relative to teaching."[3] In short, it would appear from the dozens, or more probably, hundreds of studies reporting the results of their search for a reliable index of good teaching, that there does not exist an essential relationship between teaching effectiveness and any single overall pattern of teacher conduct. Wilhelms sums up this matter when he states that we must "work on the assumption that there is no set of competencies and practices which equals the difference between good and poor teaching."[4]

Yet this "competencies" approach is still a dominant characteristic of many courses in teacher education. As Combs explains it, the thinking is of this nature: "If we know what the expert teachers do, or are like, then we can teach the beginner to be like that."[5] The result of such thinking is the production of voluminous lists of desired competencies which student teachers should attain; yet research evidence is quite unequivocal that good teaching cannot be seen as a direct function of general traits and methods. As Combs points out, this "competencies" approach has many weaknesses, not the least of these being that the methods people use are highly personal and can, therefore, not

---

H. E. Stanton is senior lecturer in education at The Flinders University of South Australia.

be abstracted from the personality of which they are a part. That is, teaching is a highly personal matter, and the highly successful practitioner of the art attains his eminence rather by being the sort of person he is than by practicing a set of competencies abstracted from the performance of other "master teachers."

If good teaching is looked upon as the result of the practitioner's personality, a rather different approach to teacher education seems to be indicated. Such an approach is implied in Combs' redefinition of the effective teacher as a "unique human being who has learned to use his self effectively and efficiently for carrying out his own and society's purposes."[6] This "self as instrument concept" rejects the concept of the teacher as a technician applying, rather mechanically, the methods he has been taught in favor of one seeing him ". . . as an intelligent human being using himself, his knowledge and the resources at hand to solve the problems for which he is responsible. He is a person who has learned to use himself as an effective instrument."[7] Teacher education courses should, then, see as their main concern persons and not competencies. This would involve a change from teaching students what to do, to helping them see themselves and their world in a different light. Perceptual psychology stresses that the way a person behaves is a direct function of his perception, of how things appear to him at the moment of his behavior.[8] Behavior change, then, involves changing a person's perceptions, and this might well be the most important aspect of a teacher education program.

This emphasis upon the teacher's personality is not a new idea by any means. In what was probably the most exhaustive study of teacher behavior yet undertaken, David Ryans[9] began with a detailed study of teaching procedures, skills, and methodology, but finished by placing emphasis upon highly personal characteristics. From the mass of data he collected, Ryans was able to abstract only three major dimensions of teacher behavior:

Pattern X_0 Friendly, understanding, sympathetic versus aloof, egocentric, restricted teacher behavior.
Pattern Y_0 Responsible, systematic, businesslike versus unplanned, slipshod teacher behavior.
Pattern Z_0 Stimulating, imaginative, surgent versus dull, routine teacher behavior.

It is hard to interpret these dimensions in terms of competencies or specific teaching skills. Rather they are integral aspects of personality, characteristics of the way a person operates over a wide range of human experience, not just in a teaching situation. Perceptual organization rather than an emphasis on competencies is reflected in other behaviors reported by Ryans. For example, outstanding teachers tend to "manifest extreme generosity in appraisals of the behavior and motives of other persons."[10] This finding—that it is more what a person is, rather than what he does that is important to the full development of his pupils—is supported by other studies.[11]

In summary, then, the kind of propositions which emerge from a concentration on the personal rather than the competencies approach would be these.[12]

1. The behavior of a teacher is a function of his personality.
2. Teacher education must be con-

cerned with personality and with methods which change personality.

The orientation outlined so far in this article would probably appeal in theory to many educationalists, but the problem lies in its implementation. Personality is a rather vague and amorphous concept. How can one define which aspects of personality are to be changed insofar as this may lead to the development of a "good teacher?" Such tampering with the essence of a person invokes shades of *1984* and Skinnerian behavioral control, the idea of which has proved abhorrent to so many people. Actually there are at least three important questions requiring answers if one contemplates changing the emphasis of a teacher education program in order to foster students' personality development. Firstly, there is the ethical issue. Does one have any right to attempt to change personality? This would seem to be a philosophical question and one I do not intend to elaborate upon in the present article. Secondly, do we have any guidance as to what particular aspects of personality may be desirable in a "good teacher?" Obviously, before we can attempt to modify personality we need guidelines as to what direction such modification should take. Thirdly, assuming desirable personality characteristics of the "good teacher" can be identified, how can the process of personality development in these directions be instituted? It is to a consideration of these last two questions that the remainder of this article is devoted.

The characteristics outlined by Ryans —friendly, understanding, sympathetic, systematic, responsible, stimulating, imaginative, and surgent—would provide one set of guidelines. Another set has been provided by Rogers when he discusses the client-therapist relationship in a psychotherapy context.[13] He hypothesizes that constructive personality change in a client is dependent upon three essential attitudes in the therapist. These are held to be more important than the therapist's professional qualifications, his therapeutic orientation, or his interview techniques, and are:

1. *Congruence*. This involves the genuineness in the relationship, the lack of a "facade" or "front" put on by the therapist.

2. *Acceptance*. The client should be prized for what he is, and accepted unconditionally as a person.

3. *Emphatic Understanding*. Understanding of the client's world. The ability to sense his inner feelings and perceptions. Rogers quotes research confirming the value of these attitudes to the therapist; and he also points out that conventional training courses for psychotherapists make it more, rather than less, difficult for students to develop these attitudes. It does appear intuitively reasonable to generalize these attitudes toward the teaching situation and to see them as personality characteristics of the "successful teacher." Congruence means being oneself, revealing oneself to pupils as a human being rather than as a person playing the role of teacher. Acceptance involves regard for the child as a person with his individual attributes and abilities. We give lip service to this idea of each child's individuality, but it is all too rarely translated into practice. It is necessary to accept the child as he is, rather than as we think he ought to be, and to help him develop as a person, realizing his human potentialities. Empathy is also important for a teacher. Although we can never fully experience the world as seen through the eyes of our pupils, surely it is important for us to try to share part of this view, to see things from

the pupils' point of view sometimes instead of always from our own.

Too idealistic? The present writer used to think so, too. Great in theory perhaps, but too far removed from the way things are, the realities of teaching. Yet eight years of teaching and eight of teacher education have brought home the futility of so much of traditional teacher education courses with their exclusive concentration upon the teacher as a "knower" and a practicer of "competencies." This is not a claim that subject matter knowledge and teaching skills should be dropped from such courses. This would be unwarranted overreaction. No, rather the claim would be for a change of emphasis from existing priorities, so that personal development of students would rank at least equal in importance with knowing subject matter and teaching skills.

There are encouraging signs that such a change of emphasis is occurring. For example, the program for elementary teacher education at the University of Massachusetts specifies three broad conceptual areas relating to teaching.[14] These are content knowledge, behavioral skills, and human relations skills, this latter area embracing the approach suggested in the earlier part of the present article. This Massachusetts example is particularly interesting in its attempt to specify particular human relations skills so that progress towards a goal may be evaluated. This is, of course, the prime difficulty with personality characteristics. How can they be defined and how can programs designed to aid development of the characteristics be evaluated?

Performance criteria is the method adopted in the example given.[15] Instructional and program goals have been specified in terms of behaviors to be exhibited by the trainee when instruction has been completed. Performance criteria, as so defined, are essential behavioral objectives. They state the behavior expected of the teacher, under what conditions the behavior will be performed, and how the behavior will be evaluated. In addition, at least two instructional alternatives are provided for each performance criterion, recognizing that there are alternative paths to reaching many of the criteria. To illustrate this approach further, and to link it to the discussion of Rogers' desirable characteristics, we could consider one aspect of the Massachusetts Human Relations Skills area, namely empathy or being fully aware of another person's experience. If we can accept empathy as being a valuable personality characteristic of a teacher, we can consider the Massachusetts approach as being one way of incorporating the developing of such a characteristic in a program of teacher education.

Although specifying behavioral objectives and performance criteria in the area of human relations is seen by the Massachusetts course planners as rather like an attempt to define the undefinable, they analyzed the basic characteristic of empathy into several specific behaviors. The first of these was "attending behavior" which could be described as (1) maintaining eye contact with another person; (2) physical attentiveness in terms of an attending yet relaxed posture; and (3) verbal following behavior in which the individual simply stays on the other person's topic and does not offer any new information of his own. A second aspect of empathy is the "reflection of feeling" which is so much a part of Rogers' client-centered therapy. The student is expected to attend primarily to the feeling or emotional statements of the other person. Yet another aspect involves physical empathy, whereby the trainee teacher is to assume the physical posture of the person with whom he is attempting to empathize in an attempt to feel more closely what the other is feeling.

Course planners do not claim that the specific skills mentioned above are empathy. Rather, their claim is that such skills are often considered parts of the empathic person. Minimum empathy might be defined as simple attending behavior, whereas stronger empathy would involve reflection of feeling and physical imitation. For each of the three aspects of empathy described, two levels of performance criteria were developed. The first of these was directly *behavioral,* depending on observations of eye contact, number of verbal following statements, etc. The second level, when *one forgets self* and loses himself in the other person, can be measured only by self-reports which can be partially verified by others. For example, verification of the trainee's report that he "lost himself" in the attending session would require the other person involved to say whether he felt the trainee had really attended to and understood him. Also, external observers could express their feelings as to whether the intense involvement did or did not seem to occur.

The example quoted above does suggest that "operationalization" of human relations skills may be possible. Other institutions, such as the University of Georgia, are also aware of the importance of including a personality development component in their teacher education program, as evidenced by the following statement in the preamble to this course:

> The teacher education program should also attempt to develop a teacher with adequate personality characteristics. Consequently, humanistic learnings, attitudes, and values were incorporated into the program. It is acknowledged that evaluative criteria for measuring attainment in this are inadequate. Despite this problem, the indicators are that the personality development of the teacher is as important as is his intellectual development.[16]

Six generalizations were translated into objectives for the development of an adequate personality. These were:

1. To develop and accept an accurate perception of self.
2. To acknowledge and accept one's social, psychological, and physical needs.
3. To acknowledge, accept, and deal appropriately with one's feelings, emotions, and intuitions.
4. To develop and enlarge one's capacity for human understanding and compassion for others.
5. To identify more fully and achieve towards one's aspirations and goals.
6. To awaken to and develop an awareness of the process of becoming.

In the development of the Georgia program, sample personality characteristics for each of these objectives are expressed more specifically and in behavioral terms.

No one would pretend that it is an easy matter to specify the desirable personality characteristics which make for success in teaching. Neither is it easy to translate such characteristics into performance criteria capable of evaluation. However, it does seem important for educators to examine more critically traditional courses in teacher education which emphasize the "knowing of subject matter" and the "training of competencies" and tend to ignore the personality of the trainees. We hear much talk about educating the "whole child," his personality and his emotions as well as his intellect. Surely the same exhortation is equally applicable to the student teacher whose intellect alone is, at present, being educated. If "what the teacher is" is the important variable in teaching efficiency that the writers quoted in this article seem to believe, it would appear that traditional teacher education programs are in dire need of revision.

Notes

1. Fred T. Wilhelms, "Actualizing the Effective Professional Worker in Education," in Eli H. Bower and William C. Hollister, eds., *Behavioral Science Frontiers in Education* (New York: John Wiley and Sons, 1967), p. 59.
2. J. E. Marsh and E. W. Wilder, "Identifying the Effective Instructor: A Review of Quantitative Studies, 1900-1952," *Research Bulletin*, AFPTRC-TR-54-44 (San Antonio, Texas: USAF Personnel and Training Center, 1954).
3. American Association of School Administrators, *Who's a Good Teacher?* (Washington, D.C.: American Association of School Administrators, 1961), p. 2.
4. Wilhelms, "Actualizing Professional Worker," p. 360.
5. A. W. Combs, "The Personal Approach to Good Teaching," *Educational Leadership* 21 (1964):369-377.
6. Ibid., p. 373.
7. Ibid., p. 373.
8. A. W. Combs and D. Snygg, *Individual Behavior*, rev. ed. (New York: Harper and Row, 1959).
9. D. G. Ryans, "Research on Teacher Behavior in the Context of the Teacher Characteristics Study," in Bruce J. Biddle and William J. Ellena, eds., *Contemporary Research on Teacher Effectiveness* (New York: Holt, Rinehart and Winston, 1964), pp. 67-101.
10. Ibid., p. 76.
11. For instance, M. M. Hughes, "What is Teaching? One Viewpoint," *Educational Leadership* 19 (1962):251-259; and Wilhelms, "Actualizing Professional Worker."
12. Wilhelms, "Actualizing Professional Worker."
13. C. Rogers, "The Therapeutic Relationship: Recent Theory and Research," *Australian Journal of Psychology* 17 (1965): 95-108.
14. University of Massachusetts, *Summary of a Proposed New Program for Elementary Teacher Education* (Washington, D.C.: Department of Health, Education and Welfare, Proj. No. 9-9023, 1968).
15. H. E. Stanton, "Performance Criteria in the Service of Teacher Education," *Australian Journal of Education,* in press.
16. University of Georgia, *Summary of the Georgia Educational Model Specifications for the Preparation of Elementary Teachers* (Washington, D.C.: Department of Health, Education and Welfare, Proj. No. 8-9024, 1968), p. 2.

Reprinted from The Educational Forum, Kappa Delta Pi, Volume 38, Number 1, November, 1973.

Poor Teachers Are Made Not Born

VINCENT CROCKENBERG

THERE is a disturbing sameness to the indictments that informed observers of the public schools have continued to bring against American public school teachers. Broudy's statement, in 1972, that "The single outstanding fact about teachers—especially in American public schools—has been their docility,"[1] echoes Beale's charge, in 1936, that "... American teachers are dominated by cowardice and hypocrisy. There are admirable exceptions. Yet almost universally, teachers teach not what they would like, but only so much of it as they dare."[2] And Silberman's assertion, in 1970, that "... what is mostly wrong with the public schools is not due to venality or indifference or stupidity but to mindlessness"[3] reflects Dewey's criticism, expressed in 1904, of "... the lack of intellectual independence among teachers, their tendency to intellectual subserviency."[4]

What I shall argue in this article is that the mindlessness, intellectual docility, and subservience that have continued to characterize teachers are directly a function of the working conditions of teachers; more specifically, that teachers are denied the conditions necessary for the development of mind because of the way in which schools are organized and controlled. In the course of the argument, I also hope to show that the many current proposals for "improving" the schools—from community control to voucher programs to performance contracting; from cost-benefit analysis to

Vincent Crockenberg is a professor of education at the University of California, Davis.

Reprinted from The Educational Forum, Kappa Delta Pi, Volume 39, Number 2, January, 1975.

behavioral objectives to systems analysis to "teacher-proof" curricula—are wrong-headed because they fail to establish the conditions for mindfulness, and in some cases exacerbate existing conditions that already contribute to the failure of mind. Any proposal for reforming the schools that depends to any significant extent on teachers for its success can ignore these conditions only at the price of yet another failure.

Silberman's analysis of the problems of the schools nicely illustrates the difficulties erstwhile school reformers have of grappling with the underlying issue of control. "If mindlessness is the central problem," he argues,

> ... the solution must lie in infusing the various educating institutions with purpose, more important, with thought about purpose, and about the ways in which techniques, content, and organization fulfill or alter purpose. ... we must find ways of stimulating educators ... to think about what they are doing, and why they are doing it.[5]

Well and good so far, but what does this amount to in practice? For Silberman, it amounts to (1) a liberal dose of British informal education with its "deep and genuine concern for individual growth and fulfillment," and its "equally genuine concern for cognitive growth and intellectual discipline";[6] (2) a "thoroughgoing reform of teacher education, to make sure that teachers are equipped with a strong sense of direction [i.e., purpose] ... as well as the ability to transmit that ... sense of direction to their students";[7] and (3), a "liberalizing and humanizing education" for those who want to become teachers.[8] All to the end,

and with the faith, that "when schools become warm and humane, teachers grow as human beings as well as teachers";[9] that is, they become mindful.

Silberman's proposals suffer, however, from a variety of afflictions. The recommendation that teachers cultivate "a deep and genuine respect for individual growth and fulfillment" is open-ended and rhetorical and subject to a multitude of contested interpretations. There is little agreement, too, on what constitutes a "liberalizing and humanizing education"— one man's "humanizing education" is another man's "permissiveness." And while it is certainly important that teachers have aims and purposes, "it is well to remind ourselves," as John Dewey pointed out,

> ... that education as such has no aims. Only persons, parents, and teachers, etc., have aims, not an abstract idea like education. And consequently their purposes are infinitely varied, differing with different children, changing as children grow and with the growth of experience on the part of the one who teaches.[10]

With which of these "infinitely varied" purposes are we to infuse—perhaps "indoctrinate" is a more fitting word— teachers? How shall we justify equipping teachers with one set of aims and purposes rather than any other, except at the most abstract and general level?

There is a more serious objection to be raised, however, and that is that Silberman's specific recommendation that the objectives, methods, and techniques of British informal education be adopted by American teachers is inconsistent with the development of purpose he so highly prizes. For in making this recommendation, Silberman is, in effect, telling teachers what their purposes should be and how they should organize and run their classrooms to achieve these purposes. However well-intentioned he may be, he is making decisions for teachers that the teachers themselves should be making. He fails to see that the "mindlessness" of teachers that so disturbs him is directly a consequence of the lack of decision-making control that teachers exercise over the purposes and procedures of the institutions within which they work. There may be much to the methods of informal education. But if our concern is with the development of intellectually vigorous and independent teachers, there is nothing to recommend any reform that fails to recognize that the development of such teachers is possible only if teachers are able and encouraged to act on their own initiative and to make their own decisions about how to run their classrooms and their schools, without outside interference or direction.

More generally, proposals for community control of schools, performance contracting, "teacher-proof" curricula, and the like, are all similarly encumbered. The problems of public schooling in this country—the failure of innovative change, dull teaching, inflexibility, unresponsiveness, the whole litany of charges that are included in the general indictment that "the professionals have failed" —and the problems of teachers—mindlessness, docility, intellectual subservience —will not be solved by vesting more and more control in the community, or in private corporations, or in scholarly curriculum commissions. These problems are primarily attributable to the structure of public schooling, a structure that already denies to classroom teachers any measure of significant control over the determination of school policies and practices. And these problems will be resolved only when teachers, not others, are given or seize greater control over the schools.[11]

To establish the relationship between mindlessness and the lack of control—or, better, the lack of autonomy—consider by way of analogy John Stuart Mill's classic argument against benevolent despotism. For Mill, as for classical democratic theorists generally, one of the goals of political society was to secure the intellectual growth and development of the citizens of that society. Free speech, press, assembly, and more generally, the direct and unhampered participation by citizens in the give and take of public affairs were to serve these outcomes. And, at least for Mill, the contribution to the intellectual growth and development of the citizenry consequent upon these procedures for arriving at policy decisions in a democracy overrode any considerations about the ultimate desirability of a perfectly benevolent despot dictating social policy without the participation or consent of the people. For if we had a perfectly good despot, argued Mill, we would, as a natural consequence, have "a mentally passive people."

Their passivity is implied in the very idea of absolute power. The nation as a whole, and every individual composing it, are without any potential voice in their own destiny. They exercise no will in respect to their collective interests. All is decided for them by a will not their own, which it is legally a crime for them to disobey. What sort of human beings can be formed under such a regimen? What development can either their thinking or their active faculties attain under it? . . .

A person must have a very unusual taste for intellectual exercise in and for itself, who will put himself to the trouble of thought when it is to have no outward effect, or qualify himself for functions which he has no chance of being allowed to exercise. The only sufficient incitement to mental exertion, in any but a few minds in a generation, is the prospect of some practical use to be made of its results.[12]

While there is not yet an education czar, benevolent or otherwise, in this country, the school establishment is organized in such a way that teachers are treated in much the same fashion as the subjects of Mill's benevolent depotism. We can expect, and have in fact seen, the same consequences for the intellectual development of teachers as Mill saw for the subjects of despotism—passivity and mindlessness. To strengthen and ground the analogy, consider the position of teachers in the educational decision-making hierarchy.

Teachers are the least-ranking members of a far-flung educational establishment that diffuses educational decision-making powers so broadly that accountability and responsibility are difficult to locate precisely. The legislative, executive, and judicial branches of government, national testing organizations and accrediting associations, nationally organized curriculum reform groups dominated by university scholars, foundations, nationally organized citizens' advisory groups (the Council for Basic Education is perhaps the best known), textbook publishers, corporations and commercial organizations (broadly, the "knowledge industry"), state legislatures and departments of education, district superintendents and local school administrators—in some loosely connected way, this "professional establishment" controls educational policy and practice.[13] This diffuse establishment is the counterpart in education to Mill's benevolent despot. The teachers are their subjects, their hired hands.

If one wonders why teachers are not included in the listing of the professional establishment, consider the decisions that teachers, in all but a few cases, do not make. Teachers have no or very little say about how many or what kinds of students are in their classes or how long they have to bring their students to a level of achievement predetermined by others. They are apportioned their teaching schedule and their students like a dime store clerk is handed a shelf inventory. Nor do they have any control over hiring, firing, or tenure decisions. In most states, teachers cannot reach any binding written contracts or agreements with school systems. In California, for example, the State Court of Appeals recently ruled that in the absence of collective bargaining legislation it is illegal for school boards to give teachers any formal authority over matters of employment conditions or educational policy, including textbook selection, approval of the curriculum, or the setting of pupil discipline policies. Even if the school board should reach agreements with teachers and incorporate these in the form of school regulations, the court held that the board is free to reverse itself at any time, unilaterally.[14]

Classroom teachers have little or no control over teacher preparation and licensing, and hence have little control over what the qualifications are for entry into teaching and who will be licensed to teach in any particular state. Teachers have traditionally had limited representation on the boards that license teachers, and little or no power either to select or to veto the appointments of members of the licensing board. In 1970, only eight states required that all or a majority of the members of the state advisory council on teacher education and certification be practicing classroom teachers. This contrasts sharply with the composition of the licensing boards for physicians, dentists, and lawyers, and even for such occupational groups as barbers and beauticians.[15]

In addition, in twenty-three states, the state board of education currently adopts the textbooks that will be used uniformly throughout the public schools of those states.[16] In the rest of the states, district boards of education, by way of the ubiquitous Approved Textbook List, tell teachers what textbooks they will be allowed to use in their classrooms. All states typically disapprove certain books for classroom use; and in New York, to choose just one example, any teacher who permits the use of a state disapproved book in his class can be charged with a misdemeanor.

The curriculum reform groups that have recently made such a large impact are dominated, again not by teachers, but by university scholars and researchers (Physical Sciences Study Committee, Biological Sciences Curriculum Study, CHEMS, and others), large publishing houses, regional laboratories (Educational Development Center, Southwest Regional Laboratory, and so on), and private corporations (General Electric, Westinghouse, IBM). Of twenty-six curriculum projects recently reviewed by the National Council for the Social Studies,[17] twenty-two were headquartered at the universities, two at the Educational Development Center (which is the successor to the Physical Sciences Study Committee), and one at the Boston Children's Museum. The one other project was headquartered at and financed by a local school district. In none of the programs were public school teachers centrally involved in research and development.

The finished curriculum projects themselves are often constructed in such a way that teachers are given no encouragement to think for themselves about how best to use the materials in teaching a particular subject. These curriculums are usually preorganized for the teachers, and their role is then simply to do as the teacher's manuals prescribe. To cite just a few examples, in *Man—A Course of Study,* a widely used elementary social studies curriculum developed by the Educational Development Center, the accompanying teacher's manual, with its detailed lesson plans, discussions of preclass preparation, questions to be asked, activities, homework assignments, and possible variations on the lessons, relieves the teachers of any need to think for themselves about what and how they should teach. Essential Modern Mathematics (distributed by Ginn and Company) and the Distar Reading and Mathematics programs go even further in this regard. Not only does each of these programs require teachers to introduce and develop each lesson according to detailed instructions in the teacher's manuals, the developers of these curricula even go so far as to write out for every lesson exactly what the teachers are to say and how they are to say it. An example of a script from a Distar Arithmetic lesson:

Teacher: "Listen. You're going to count to six. What are you going to count to?"
(Wait for children's response.)
"Yes, what are you going to count to?" (Wait.)

"And you're going to count *from* three. Get it going."
(The children should count quickly: 4, 5, 6.)
"Good counting. You counted to six and you counted *from* three."

The Sullivan Reading and Mathematics programs and a variety of computer-based curricula carry this trend to its culmination—the teacher is removed altogether, replaced by programmed texts.

As these examples should make clear, teachers are not encouraged or not allowed to make decisions on a wide range of important educational policies and practices. At best, they might be permitted to suggest; at worst they are reduced to the status of ventriloquists' puppets. To return briefly to Mill's argument against benevolent despotism: "All is decided for them by a will not their own. . . . What sort of human beings can be formed under such a regimen?"

"To a very great degree," wrote John Holt in *How Children Fail*, "school is a place where children learn to be stupid."[18] Holt was referring partly to the boredom, routinization, and the "sit down, shut up, read chapter seven, and do the questions at the end" syndrome that characterizes much of school life for children. His more central reference, however, was to the conditions of fear that dominate classrooms, that cause children to develop habits of stupidity to protect themselves from punishment. It is ironic that while we are beginning to accept the general relationship between fear and stupidity when applied to children in schools, we have failed to see the relationship between fear and mindlessness in the case of teachers.

Howard Beale, in his classic study, *Are American Teachers Free?*,[19] has described in close detail the oppressive conditions within which American teachers worked in the 1920s and 30s. Peace views expressed by teachers in the schools were frequently suppressed by the American Legion, the Daughters of the American Revolution, fearful principals, and self-proclaimed defenders of the republic. During and after World War I, a variety of agencies, established by law, investigated the loyalty of teachers and prosecuted cases of alleged disloyalty. A proliferation of vaguely-worded loyalty oaths allowed suppression of teacher criticism generally. Although dismissals were few, the climate established by the threat of investigation—a climate that continued up through the 1950s and the McCarthy era—cowed many teachers and stilled critical thinking about governmental policy and practice in classrooms.

Not only were teachers dismissed or threatened with disciplinary measures for criticizing the government, Beale documents numerous instances where teachers were vulnerable to sanction if they commented favorably about the Soviet Union, expressed sympathy with labor, criticized specific evils in the American economic system, argued the merits of free trade or government regulation of business or public ownership of public utilities, or discussed dishonest advertising or unethical business practices.

In the area of curriculum, some thirty-seven bills were introduced in twenty different state legislatures in the period between 1921 and 1929 making it a crime to teach evolutionary theory in the public schools. These sentiments were backed up in many places by local regulations and organized community opinion that assumed, according to Beale, that the teacher was simply a hired hand, "bound to do the bidding of his taxpaying employer even if, in obeying, he violates his own integrity in teaching scientific, or economic, or social theories he believes to be erroneous."[20]

The out-of-school life of teachers was also vigorously circumscribed. Teachers were routinely discouraged or forbidden, often by contract, from doing any or all of the following: drinking, smoking, attending the theatre, playing cards, gambling, swearing, marrying, divorcing, falling in love, being immoral, keeping late hours, using cosmetics, dressing in gay colors, bobbing their hair, wearing short skirts or low cut dresses or sheer stockings, belong to the American Civil Liberties Union or to the American Federation of Teachers, and generally from engaging in any behavior that might reflect unfavorably upon the school's or the teacher's reputation.[21]

It is only comparatively recently that teachers have been given any protection against arbitrary disciplinary procedures and dismissals. In several recent cases, for example, the courts have held that teachers can be dismissed from their jobs only if it can be shown that their conduct in or outside of class interferes seriously with the work of the school or compromises necessary working relationships between a teacher and his administrative superiors.[22] But while the days of indentured teacher servitude may be waning, the legacy of docility and submissiveness is not so easily overcome. The effects on teachers of the suspicion, distrust, and oppression that Beale and others have documented are continuing effects. Young people entering teaching have been in some 10,000 hours of close contact with *their* teachers during the course of their public schooling. They have had, consequently, a lengthy prior socialization into the habits of submissiveness. As Lortie points out: "Few occupations have entrants with more precise knowledge of the work activities of practitioners than does public school teaching. Persons whose aspirations do not match the teacher's work round are not likely to enter the occupation willingly."[23] And in a time of alleged oversupply of teachers, the difficulties of getting a job and gaining tenure reinforce the attitude that one should simply do as one is told and, without fuss, open one's teacher's manual and memorize the "teaching" script on page thirty-eight.

Many people, including students in teacher education programs, react adversely to the suggestion that teachers should be given greater decision-making responsibility. Their reaction is typically that the teachers they had in school were either too incompetent, too insensitive, or too dumb to be entrusted with such responsibility. What they fail to recognize is that teachers are not naturally inept adults, but that the context within which they work encourages, among other things, mental dullness. Just as fear turns otherwise normal, intelligent children into members of the dumb class of students, so too conditions of oppression and domination turn otherwise normal, intelligent adults into members of the dumb class of teachers. "Yet released from the dumb class to their private lives," observes James Herndon,

> ... teachers are marvelous gardeners, they work on ocean liners as engineers, they act in plays, win bets, go to art movies, build their own houses, they are opera fans, expert fishermen, champion skeet shooters, grand golfers, organ players, oratorio singers, hunters, mechanics ... all just as if they were smart people. Of

course it is more difficult to build a house or sing Bach than it is to teach kids to read. Of course if they operated in their lives outside the dumb class the same way they do in it, their houses would fall down, their ships would sink, their flowers die, their cars blow up.[24]

What makes the difference is that in their lives outside of schools, compared with their lives inside, teachers are not systematically denied the autonomy that is the precondition as well as the reward for intellectual growth and development. If teachers are to overcome mindlessness, if they are to teach purposefully and intelligently, they must be allowed to work in a context where they do not simply act on the purposes and decisions of others (often unseen others). They must be allowed to formulate their own purposes, initiate their own actions to further those purposes, and then modify their purposes and their practices in the light of the consequences. "To have a mind," argued Dewey, ". . . is to foresee a future possibility; it is to have a plan for its accomplishment, it is to note the means which make the plan capable of execution and the obstructions in the way." To do these things, he adds, is "just what is meant by having an aim or a purpose."[25] And to modify those plans on the basis of experienced consequences is just what is meant by acting intelligently.

Yet educational policy and practice is decided in a manner that precludes the development of intelligent purpose or intelligent practice in this way. For the people who make the decisions about various matters of curriculum and instruction, including textbook utilization, required achievement levels, and school discipline policies, are not the people who must implement and suffer the direct consequences of these decisions. A variety of lay, administrative, and scholarly groups control educational decision-making; but teachers carry out the decisions in classrooms. It is the teachers who must live with the day-to-day consequences, good and bad, of these decisions. This separation of decision-making control from direct and first-hand accountability to consequences, whether in its current institutionalized form or in the form of community control or whatever, is another contributing factor to the failure of mind.

Perhaps in this regard the schools can take a cue from an emerging trend in business. The history of schools is replete with adoptions of business practices by school people in an attempt to improve the operating efficiency and productivity of schools. Recently, cost-benefit analysis, systems analysis, PERT charts, and other business practices have been introduced into the schools in the ongoing search for better education. The value of any and perhaps all of these practices is still to be shown. But there is a trend in business, albeit a fairly limited one to date, whose value is more certain—a trend toward democratizing the factory.

General Foods and Procter and Gamble are presently encouraging employees in at least two of their plants to take almost complete responsibility for their work environment. At a General Foods pet food factory in Topeka, Kansas, the workers come and go as they wish, handle their own scheduling, arrange the tasks that have to be done among themselves, do their own hiring and firing, and generally concern themselves, through their own committees, with all aspects of plant operations—from safety to spare parts to welfare and benefits to recreation. At Procter and Gamble's Lima, Ohio, plant,

60

the workers have virtually complete control of the plant's operations. There are no job classifications, no time clocks, everyone is on straight salary, and the workers have even developed their own pay scales. In both plants, worker morale is high, there is less boredom, and, most important, quality is higher. According to the Lima manager, the Lima plant has the highest productivity of any Procter and Gamble plant in the country.[26]

Given the fairly single-minded way in which school practices are influenced by business practices, perhaps we may soon see a trend toward the democratization of the schools, with similar results.[27]

Mindlessness may be what is mostly wrong with the public schools, as Silberman asserts. But mindlessness cannot be attacked directly. It can be overcome only by creating the conditions in which attending carefully to what one is doing and why makes practical sense. For teachers, as for everyone else, these are the conditions of autonomy and self-governance. What is required, then, are free teaching environments for teachers, where teachers can make decisions and act in accordance with their own understanding of context and consequences, unhampered by prearranged curricula and protected from unwarranted lay and administrative interference in their work. If and when these conditions are established, then the schools will stop making dumb teachers.

NOTES

1. Harry S. Broudy, *The Real World of the Public Schools* (New York: Harcourt, Brace, Jovanovich, 1972), p. 41.
2. Howard K. Beale, *Are American Teachers Free?* (New York: Charles Scribner's Sons, 1936), p. 775.
3. Charles Silberman, *Crisis in the Classroom* (New York: Random House, 1970), p. 10.
4. John Dewey, "The Relation of Theory to Practice in Education," in The Third Yearbook of the National Society for the Scientific Study of Education, Part I: *The Relation of Theory to Practice in the Education of Teachers* (Chicago: Charles A. McMurry, 1904), p. 16.
5. Charles Silberman, *Crisis,* pp. 10-11.
6. Ibid., p. 220.
7. Ibid., p. 374.
8. Ibid., p. 380.
9. Ibid., p. 522.
10. John Dewey, *Democracy and Education* (New York: The Macmillan Company and the Free Press, 1966), p. 107.
11. The use of coercion—strikes, sit-ins, and so on—by teachers against school systems is often regarded, both by teachers and by the general public, as somehow immoral. Teachers are consequently often reluctant to take coercive action to gain greater control over school affairs. This view, however, is based on a confused notion of one's moral obligations to formal institutions. See Donald Arnstine, "The Use of Coercion in Changing the Schools," *Educational Theory* 23 (Fall 1973):277-88; and John Ladd, "Morality and the Ideal of Rationality in Formal Organizations," *The Monist* 54 (October 1970):488-516.
12. John Stuart Mill, *Considerations on Representative Government* (London: Parker, Son, and Bourn, 1861), pp. 46-47.
13. See James D. Koerner, *Who Controls American Education?* (Boston: Beacon Press, 1968).
14. Grasko v. Los Angeles City Board of Education, App., 107 *Cal. Rptr.* 334 (March 26, 1973).
15. The eight states that require at least a majority of the members of the state advisory council on teacher education and certification to be practicing classroom teachers are Alaska, Arkansas, California, Colorado, Connecticut, Illinois, Kansas, and New York. Source: *A Manual on Certification Requirements for School Personnel in the United States* (Washington, D.C.: National Education Association, 1970), pp. 215-21.
In 1952, when the Council of State Governments last surveyed the occupational licensing practices of the various states, all the states required that at least a majority of the members of the licensing boards for physicians, dentists, and lawyers be practitioners in the licensed field; for barbers and beauticians, 42 and 38 states, respectively, required that at least a majority of the members of the respective licensing boards be practitioners in the licensed field. Source: The Council of State Governments, *Occupational Licensing Legislation in the States* (Chicago: The

Council of State Governments, 1952), pp. 84-87.

16. Statewide adoption is practiced in Alabama, Alaska, Arizona, Arkansas, California, Florida, Georgia, Idaho, Indiana, Kentucky, Louisiana, Mississippi, Nevada, New Mexico, North Carolina, Oklahoma, Oregon, South Carolina, Tennessee, Texas, Utah, Virginia, and West Virginia. Arizona, Arkansas, California, and West Virginia adopt state texts only for elementary schools. The other states listed adopt for elementary and secondary schools. Source: *Textbook Adoption Data File*, Part I (White Plains, N.Y., 1971).

17. *Social Education* 36 (November 1972):723-71.

18. John Holt, *How Children Fail* (New York: Dell Publishing Co., 1965), p. 157.

19. Howard K. Beale, *American Teachers*.

20. Ibid., p. 260.

21. Ibid., chapter XIII.

22. These cases and their import for teachers are discussed in David Rubin, *The Rights of Teachers* (New York: Avon Books, 1972), and in Louis Fischer and David Schimmel, *The Civil Rights of Teachers* (New York: Harper and Row, 1973).

23. Dan C. Lorti, "The Balance of Control and Autonomy in Elementary School Teaching," in *The Semi-Professions and Their Organization*, ed. Amitai Etzioni (New York: The Free Press, 1969), p. 10.

24. James Herndon, *How to Survive in Your Native Land* (New York: Bantam Books, 1972), p. 95.

25. John Dewey, *Democracy and Education*, p. 103.

26. David Jenkins, "Democracy in the Factory," *The Atlantic Monthly* 231 (April 1973):78-83.

27. There is already at least some evidence on this contention that greater teacher control over the school program will result in greater gain to children and higher teacher morale. M. Zax and E. L. Cowen found, for example, that when teachers have an important role in the selection and training of teacher's aides, the teachers, the aides, and the children all benefitted more than they did when teachers did not have such control. See Zax and Cowen, "Early Identification and Prevention of Emotional Disturbance in a Public School," in *Emergent Approaches to Mental Health*, ed. E. L. Cowen, E. A. Gardner, and M. Zax (New York: Appleton-Century-Crofts, 1967).

SEMESTER: WEEK FOUR

REQUIRED READINGS

Church

Part II: The Quest for Commonality, 1830-1860,
   Chapter 3: The Common School Movement (29 pp.)

Dye

College of Education, The University of Akron.
   "Objectives" 1980. (02 pp.)

College of Education, The University of Akron.
   "Teaching Competencies: A Working Model"
   1980. (07 pp.)

Florida Council on Teacher Education. "Essential
   Teaching Competencies" 1977. (03 pp.)

Bowers, C. A. "The Messianic Tradition in
   American Education" The Educational Forum.
   V.32, No.2, January, 1967. (07 pp.)

MEETINGS

Monday

Lecture: The Monitorial Tradition

Tuesday

Lecture: Horace Mann

Wednesday

Lecture: Teacher Roles and Compentencies

Thursday and Friday

Small Groups: Book Critique Contracts are due.

64

CHURCH TEXTBOOK STUDY GUIDE: CHAPTER 3

THE COMMON SCHOOL MOVEMENT

1. common school
2. centralization
3. schooling for social manipulation
4. schooling for social control
5. compulsory education

6. compulsory attendance
7. age grading
8. standardized textbooks
9. curricular reform
10. pedagogical reform

11. free school
12. abolition of rates
13. Whig reform efforts
14. Whig political ideology
15. Henry Clay

16. Abbott Lawrence
17. social virtue
18. teaching of morality
19. Horace Mann
20. ills of industrialization

21. ills of urbanization
22. Lowell, Massachusetts experiment
23. Sunday School movement
24. charity schools
25. pauper children

26. mechanics institute
27. lyceum
28. dame school
29. writing school

O B J E C T I V E S

                    College of Education
                    The University of Akron

Students will attain the following:

1. Special experience ...

2. Special knowledge ...

3. Special skills ...

   ...particularly useful for teaching in urban and inner city schools in keeping with the urban mission of The University of Akron.

   ───────────────

4. Knowledge of a major field of inquiry ...

5. Knowledge of related fields of inquiry ...

6. Ability to use this knowledge ...

   ...in explaining the realities of life today.

   ───────────────

7. Knowledge of instructional materials ...

8. Knowledge of new technology ...

9. Skill in recognizing and utilizing instructional tools ...

   ...most suitable for specific purposes.

   ───────────────

10. Knowledge of the social issues relevant to education and to living in a pluralistic society.

   ───────────────

11. Competence to translate implications of changes in society into instructive action as teacher-citizens as well as teacher-scholars.

12. Understanding of the learner.

13. Understanding of the learning processes.

14. Ability to translate these understandings into appropriate teaching behaviors in acting and reacting with students.

15. Appreciation of the values and feelings essential for working with young people and with colleagues.

16. Ability to develop empathic relationships in a wide variety of professional and social roles in the school and community.

17. Skill in the acquisition of inquiry techniques appropriate to generalizing knowledge and choices.

18. Practice in using these skills to inquire into educational problems in rational, defensible ways.

19. Human relations skills.

TEACHING COMPETENCIES: A WORKING MODEL

College of Education
The University of Akron

KNOWLEDGE

Students **WILL DEMONSTRATE** knowledge of:

1. Vocabulary, concepts, principles, and the issues of the subject matter taught.

2. Behavior analysis procedures.

3. Materials, resources, and procedures appropriate to the subject matter taught.

4. Procedures of effective interpersonal communication.

5. Evaluation procedures appropriate to the subject matter taught.

6. Psycho-social dynamics of the classroom.

7. Various leadership roles appropriate to the classroom teacher.

8. Variety of instructional techniques and the type of learning outcomes each generally produces.

9. Techniques of motivation appropriate for students of the age, race, ethnic background, social class, etc., in the teacher's classroom.

INSTRUCTIONAL SKILLS

Students <u>WILL EFFECTIVELY EMPLOY</u> the following skills in their <u>instructional</u> procedures:

10. Identifies and analyzes tasks to be learned.

11. Breaks learning tasks into appropriate learning components.

12. Writes objectives that facilitate learning of components.

13. Designs a variety of instructional activities.

14. Selects content, materials, and resources which contribute to students' efforts to meet the specified objectives.

15. Employs evaluation procedures which are valid measures of the extent to which students have achieved the specified objectives.

16. Individualizes instruction.

17. Displays flexibility in presentation.

Students **WILL EFFECTIVELY EMPLOY** the following skills in their <u>motivational</u> procedures:

18. Gears instruction and materials to the cognitive, affective, social and psychomotor abilities of each individual student.

19. Primarily employs personalized positive reinforcers.

20. Uses positive reinforcement wherever possible;

    seldom uses punishment.

21. Employs social reinforcers.

22. Praises and punishes the behavior of individuals rather than the individual as a person.

23. Gears the workload to the skills and knowledge of each individual student so that each student can experience success in learning.

24. Avoids creating classroom tension by avoiding the use of threats, criticism, sarcasm, etc.

Students **WILL EFFECTIVELY EMPLOY** the following skills in their **evaluational** procedures:

25. Constructs evaluation instruments that are valid measures of student learning.

26. Maintains businesslike atmosphere during evaluation.

27. Provides immediate, personalized feedback which focuses on what students have learned rather than not learned.

28. Employs a variety of evaluation devices throughout the course of instruction.

COMMUNICATION SKILLS

Students **WILL EFFECTIVELY EMPLOY** the following skills in their communication:

29. Utilizes good language.

30. Employs presentations to identify and clarify the major concepts, principles, and issues of the subject matter taught.

31. Encourages students to ask questions.

32. Listens and responds carefully and clearly to students' questions.

33. Provides students with valuable feedback about their learning progress.

34. States the goals and objectives of the course of instruction in clear, concise terms.

35. Communicates feelings as well as facts.

36. Uses a relaxed personal style in communicating with students.

37. Reflects a respect and understanding for the feelings and attitudes of others.

38. Encourages students to communicate in clear, concise terms.

PERSONAL SKILLS

Students <u>WILL EFFECTIVELY EMPLOY</u> the following skills in <u>their personal</u> capacity:

39. Commands the respect of students, parents, colleagues, and administrators.

40. Demonstrates flexibility in handling conflict situations.

41. Can view the world from the student's point of view.

42. Seeks to experiment with and evaluate the teaching-learning process.

43. Prefers dealing with people to dealing with things.

44. Puts others at ease.

45. Demonstrates trustworthiness, dependability, and reliability.

46. Concerned with social problems and issues.

47. Encourages students to put forth their best effort.

ATTITUDES AND VALUES

Students <u>WILL DEMONSTRATE</u> that they <u>possess</u> the following attitudes and values:

48. Accepts each student as a unique, worthwhile individual.

49. Is tolerant of individual differences.

50. Is pleasant, polite, and courteous.

51. Reflects democratic principles and practices in the classroom.

52. Tries to be sensitive to the feelings of others.

53. Is friendly, outgoing, both in and out of class.

54. Is patient, understanding, of the problems of others.

55. Tries to be consistent, yet flexible.

56. Is rational; looks at evidence rather than personal bias.

57. Respects the intellectual ability of others.

58. Displays a sense of humor.

59. Respects the right of the individual to direct his own destiny.

ESSENTIAL
TEACHING
COMPETENCIES

Florida Council on Teacher Education
(1977)

---

1. <u>Demonstrate</u> the ability to orally communicate information on a given topic in a coherent and logical manner.

2. <u>Demonstrate</u> the ability to write in a logical, easily understood style with appropriate grammar and sentence structure.

3. <u>Demonstrate</u> the ability to comprehend and interpret a message after listening.

4. <u>Demonstrate</u> the ability to read, comprehend, and interpret professional material.

5. <u>Demonstrate</u> the ability to add, subtract, multiply, and divide.

6. <u>Demonstrate</u> an awareness of patterns of physical and social development in students.

7. <u>Diagnose</u> the entry knowledge and/or skill of students for a given set of instructional objectives using diagnostic tests, teacher observations, and student records.

8. <u>Identify</u> long-range goals for a given subject area.

9. **Construct and sequence** related short-range **objectives** for a given subject area.

10. **Select, adapt, and/or develop** instructional **materials** for a given set of instructional objectives and student learning needs.

11. **Select/develop and sequence** related learning **activities** appropriate for a given set of instructional objectives and student learning needs.

12. **Establish** rapport with students in the **classroom** using verbal and/or visual motivational devices.

13. **Present** direction for carrying out an **instructional** activity.

14. **Construct or assemble** a classroom test to measure student performance according to criteria based upon objectives.

15. **Establish** a set of classroom routines and **procedures** for utilization of materials and **physical** movement.

16. **Formulate** a standard for student behavior in the classroom.

17. **Identify** causes of classroom misbehavior and **employ** a technique or techniques for correcting it.

18. **Identify and/or develop** a system for keeping records of class and individual progress.

19. <u>Counsel</u> with students both individually and collectively concerning their academic needs.

20. <u>Identify and/or demonstrate</u> behaviors which reflect a feeling for the dignity and worth of other people, including those from other ethnic, cultural, linguistic, and economic groups.

21. <u>Demonstrate</u> instructional and social skills which assist students in interacting constructively with their peers.

22. <u>Demonstrate</u> instructional and social skills which assist students in developing a positive self-concept.

23. <u>Demonstrate</u> teaching skills which assist students in developing their own values, attitudes, and beliefs.

(The research which generated these "essential" teaching competencies was conducted by Charles D. DZIUBAN and Timothy J. SULLIVAN, both of the Florida Technical University, Orlando, Florida, 1977.)

The Messianic Tradition in American Education

C. A. Bowers

RUNNING throughout American educational history is a thread which has largely escaped the attention of many educational historians. This thread is the ubiquitous sense of mission that has shaped the thinking and rhetoric of American educational theorists. During certain periods in United States history it has rendered the pronouncements of the educationist virtually indistinguishable in tenor and content from the revivalism issuing from the pulpit.

Psychologically, this sense of mission has been both a source of motivation and emotional release. Through it educators have expressed what has undoubtedly been a sincere desire to improve society. Yet their naive belief that education alone could bring into being a more ideal social order or raise the individual to a higher level of moral existence has caused them to expect too much both from themselves and from their calling. Intellectually, it has acted as a block to vigorous analysis, leaving many proposals to go unchecked by anything except emotional appeal.

Going back to the early 1800's one finds Horace Mann responding to the alarming amount of dissipation and crime in his day by promising that if all the children could be brought under the "elevating influence of good schools, the dark host of private vices and public crimes which now embitter domestic peace, and strain the civilization of the age, might in ninety-nine cases in every hundred, be banished from the world."[1] Several decades later J. P. Wickersham, who subsequently became state superintendent of schools in Pennsylvania, proclaimed that "American educators hold in their hands the destinies of this nation." Not only did he declare that education had regenerative powers sufficient to re-unite a country torn by civil war, but that educators working in the "unobtrusive quiet of the schoolroom though no eye, save that of God, witness the work, could infuse such a love of country" that the Republic would "stand as firmly as the Egyptian pyramids."[2] Labor unrest in the eigh-

---

C. A. BOWERS *is Associate Professor of Education at the University of Saskatchewan at Saskatoon. His field is the history and philosophy of education in which he did his doctoral work at the University of California. He wrote on "Existentialism and Educational Theory" in* Educational Theory *(July 1965). This article is an adaptation of a talk presented at the annual meeting of the Canadian Association of Professors of Education in Vancouver, B.C., in 1965.*

---

[1] Horace Mann, "Twelfth Report of 1848," *The Life and Works of Horace Mann* (Boston: Lee and Shepard Publishers, 1891), p. 289.
[2] J. P. Wickersham, "Education as an Element

teen seventies and eighties prompted the President of the National Education Association to claim that it "was the good sense of an immense majority of working people, created, fostered, and developed by public education, that has saved us from the terrors of the French Commune."[3] More recently, during the last depression, the most influential disciples of John Dewey set out to replace capitalism with what they called a "collectivist democracy." The manifesto issued by the Progressive Education Association's Committee on Social and Economic Problems declared that as "guardians of childhood, the bearers of culture, the avowed servants of the people," educators would be violating "every trust reposed in them by society" if they did not use the school to build a new social order.[4]

American educational theorists have been so deeply imbued with messianic purpose that they have often lost sight of the fact that the school is only one among many institutions capable of bringing about social improvement. That the power of the school is far more limited than most of these other institutions, say the courts or the legislature, has made little difference to them. For as one educationist stated, giving unconscious expression to the unbounded optimism of the educational theorists, "The power of education, rightly conducted, is almost omnipotent."[5]

Apart from this utopian conception of education which inspired an equally heady prose, the messianic spirit has also been part of the make-up of the two most important professional organizations—the National Education Association and the Progressive Education Association. From its beginning the N.E.A. has approached education as though it were a form of evangelism. Its educational programs, which were often highly political, became a crusade for the faithful. During the nineteenth century, Americanizing the foreign born, checking the spread of socialistic doctrines, and upgrading the level of secondary education each became a special cause; since the turn of the century, it has been freeing the secondary curriculum from the domination of college entrance requirements, and more recently, educating for democracy. These programs in themselves were not always bad, but the religious enthusiasm, and sometimes fanaticism, with which these programs were pursued led to excesses and a general smothering of criticism within the profession itself.

The P.E.A. also had its special mission—to save the child from the pedagogical practices of an unsympathetic adult world. In making a cult of the child, a new idiom was created which contributed to a feeling of "togetherness" in a special undertaking; its special importance was in enabling progres-

---

in Reconstruction," *Proceedings of the National Education Association*, Vol. VII, 1865, p. 549.

[3] M. A. Newell, "The President's Address," *Proceedings of the National Education Association*, 1877, p. 6.

[4] Progressive Education Association, Committee on Social and Economic Problems, *A Call to the Teachers of the Nation*, 1933, p. 6.

---

[5] S. E. Seaman, "High Schools and the State," *Proceedings of the National Education Association*, 1885, p. 176.

sivists to communicate with each other about educational programs without ever having to be specific about the nature of their educational goals. The new methodology could be communicated through the new phrases "the whole child," "learning by doing," and "meeting individual needs." And when referring to the activities and purposes of the Progressive education movement, the phrases "great undertaking," "great message," "its mission," and "its vision" were often used to inspire enthusiasm. The evangelical overtones of their rhetoric was unmistakable and clearly at odds with their commitment to experimentalism.

Of the two, however, only the N.E.A. has a history of combining religion and education. Especially during the nineteenth century, its yearly conventions frequently took on the appearance of revival meetings as delegates presented papers that supposedly dealt with educational matters, but which in fact too often read like sermons. For example, Samuel Greene closed his presidential address to the 1864 convention with the following: "Let our sessions bear testimony to the spirit of earnestness and devotion which animates the leading educators of the land. Let us gather inspiration from personal fellowship, and this interchange of fraternal good will; and let us return to our several fields of labor, moved anew to the gigantic task which lies before us."[6] Not even Russell H. Conwell, the famous Baptist Minister, who proclaimed the Gospel of Wealth, could have improved upon this. Another all too typical example is contained in a paper presented in 1880 by the principal of the Framingham Normal School. She defined the ideal teacher by saying, "Such teachers are in humble measure like Christ, the touch of whose garment was health, and lift their pupils by a divine contagion of virtue. Such are the teachers whom our schools need. It is a sin to entrust the training of God's 'little ones' to any others."[7] And in 1888 a member of the N.E.A. Board of Directors declared that the teacher who "has found his kinship with the divine . . . will be a shining epistle, known and read by all." After attending a N.E.A. convention in the late nineteen-twenties, W. Carson Ryan, Jr., later a president of the P.E.A., was moved to comment on how much it reminded him of a revivalist meeting.[8]

Such religious fervor has tended to shroud educational practices and aims in a cloud of benevolent emotionalism, witness Francis Wayland Parker's statement that "The spontaneous tendencies of the child are the records of inborn divinity." And from G. Stanley Hall, a prominent psychologist, classroom teachers learned that as "The guardians of youth (they) should strive to keep out of nature's way . . . they should feel profoundly that childhood, as it comes

---

[6] Samuel S. Greene, "The Education Duties of the Hour," *Proceedings of the National Education Association*, Vol. VI, 1864, p. 495.

[7] Ellen Hyde, "How Can Character Be Systematically Developed?" *Proceedings of the National Education Association*, 1880, p. 220.

[8] H. E. Buckholz, "The Pedagogues Leap to Save Us," *American Mercury*, Vol. XXVI (July, 1932), p. 333.

fresh from the hands of God, is not corrupt ... Nothing is so worthy of love, reverence, and service as the body and soul of the growing child."[9] But even more important than contributing to the breakdown in effective communication, the messianic tradition has conditioned educationists to view the school as an instrument of social reform. While the Progressive education movement brought about "the transformation of the school," to use Lawrence Cremin's phrase, and with it a number of sharp breaks with the past, it is the educationist's habit of acting as an agent of social reform that provides continuity between the Progressive period and the previous era in education.

During the nineteen-thirties and forties the social reconstructionist faction came to dominate the Progressive education movement with the result that reform of educational methodology became secondary to the goal of building a new society along collectivistic lines. To these followers of Dewey, education became a form of direct political action. Neutrality was no longer to be tolerated; educators, to use the words of George Counts, were to "deliberately reach for power and then make the most of their conquest. . . ."[10] At first glance it would appear that their educational and political program represented a new development in American educational theory. In spite of their radicalism such was not the case. Even though they urged that educators should courageously take their place as the "spiritual leaders of the masses of the people" in the class struggle, they nevertheless had much in common with conservative educationists of the nineteenth century who claimed that a high school education both "detects and exposes the fallacies of socialism" and teaches the poor "that they have an interest in respecting the property of the rich."[11]

One interested in the political views of American educators will note the fact that the social reconstruction group firmly believed that it was impossible to reconcile capitalism's emphasis on the profit motive and competition with their own ideal of a humane social order, while educators in the nineteenth century took the opposite position. But if one analyzes how educators in both periods conceived the purpose of education, it is clear that educational spokesmen in both periods regarded social reform as one of the main purposes of the school. The real difference was one of approach. Whereas the educator in the nineteenth century viewed his social role as one of instituting reform within the established framework of moral and social absolutes, the social reconstructionist of the twentieth century was conditioned to think in terms of changing values. In fact, the latter regarded himself as ideally suited—both as an intellectual and as a student of social change—to understand and anticipate the changes that society would undergo in the future. To

---

[9] G. Stanley Hall, "The Ideal School Based on Child Study," *Forum*, Vol. XXXII (September, 1901), pp. 24-25.
[10] George S. Counts, *Dare the School Build a New Social Order?* (New York: the John Day Company, 1932), p. 28.
[11] Seaman, *op. cit.*, p. 176.

put it another way, the nineteenth-century educator wanted to reform certain elements in society within a framework of an established system of social values, while more recent reformists, on the other hand, wished to overhaul the social system itself. The former performed essentially a conservative role in society, while the activities of the latter group of reform-minded educationists has a socially radical effect. For the student, however, education in both periods was not a liberalizing experience, one that would provide the noetic skills necessary for independent thinking; rather it was a molding process intended to prepare him to live in accordance with the educationists' conception of the good society.

The social reconstructionism of Theodore Brameld, George Counts, John L. Childs, *et al.*, must therefore not be seen as an isolated and somewhat bizarre phenomenon in the history of American educational theory; it represents a continuation of a long tradition of messianic social reformism which has passed as educational theory. Aside from the current educational scene, the only significant departure from this tradition occurred during the early child-centered phase of the Progressive movement. One of the hallmarks of this philosophy of education was that no attempt was made to control the child's development. The curriculum was to be structured in accordance with the child's felt needs and interests. Because the leaders of this movement made a virtue of not having a social philosophy, they were severely criticized and denounced as false prophets of Progressive education. Had this movement been allowed to develop beyond the romanticism and *laissez-faire* attitudes which marred its early beginnings, it might have led to a new and enlightened conception of education, one which treats the student as having the potential for developing his own standards of excellence and goodness.

Aside from a small handful of educators who have opposed using education for partisan purposes by conceiving of it as a humanizing process, the goals of education have largely been articulated by those who have been unable to check the impulse to impose their own social values on the outcome of the educational process. The consequences of this practice and of the messianic tradition, in general, are worth noting, especially since they have exerted a paralyzing effect on the development of public education in the United States.

The notion that education is a potent instrument of reform was not first conceived by educators; such divergent groups as New England conservatives, Jacksonian democrats, and the nascent labor movement championed the idea for their own and often conflicting ends. And they were not the first. From these social groups, and numerous others, educators learned to see in the school an agency for fulfilling social needs. Because their thinking was buoyed by the optimism permeating that era and because of their need to make promises to the social groups from whom they wished to gain support for public education, they quickly outdistanced all others in making claims as to the redemptive powers of education. Thus realistic expectations early became confused with utopian longings.

The unfortunate consequence of this early state of confusion has been the failure on the part of the educational profession to state clearly and publicly what the school can and cannot be expected to do. By claiming that the schools can arrest the spread of vice and crime, develop diligent workers who respect authority, eradicate foreign habits and ideas, and make everybody politically responsible—all claims of the last century—as well as overhaul capitalism, preserve democracy, defeat the Axis powers, and reconstruct the world—all the immodest claims of this century—the educator has contributed to the existence of the popular myth that education is the panacea for every social shortcoming. This myth, which still exists among most educationists and the general public, has resulted in so many responsibilities being placed on the school that the task of liberating minds has never been seriously taken up as the primary goal of education.

A related effect of the messianic tradition is that, until recently, it has prevented educational spokesmen from becoming objective students of society and of their own profession. Generally, they have been so carried away by their own longings to uplift society or to preserve it against evil forces that they have frequently oversimplified social problems and have failed to understand either the structure of the school system, the qualifications and mental disposition of teachers and, most importantly, the purpose of the teacher. During the last century educational leaders insisted upon wearing the mantle of social reformer—which meant using the schools to force errant individuals to conform to existing institutions and values—even though their very commitment to prevailing institutions prevented them from making the analysis necessary for understanding the true cause of social unrest.

Moreover, that the nineteenth-century teacher was unqualified to deal with the social problems taken on by these spokesmen was not even considered. An example from more recent history shows the devotees of Dewey's Experimentalism making the claims that educators could lift the United States out of the depths of the depression and become arbitrators of future social change, if they would only bend themselves to the task. What they failed to understand was a fact commonly known by laymen, that teachers then possessed no real protection from arbitrary dismissal by school boards; nor did they as a group have the understanding, inclination, or power to make socially significant decisions. The mental paralysis induced by this utopian way of thinking was so great they failed to comprehend that it was impossible for society to wait for teachers to organize and educate themselves for their new role before finding a means of ending the social crisis. Events in the thirties simply would not stand still while educators argued about their social responsibilities—government leaders knew this, the unemployed walking the streets were poignantly aware of it, but the experimentalist-minded educators were apparently oblivious to this fact. That these same influential interpreters of Dewey failed to see the rapid growth of specialized skills and knowledge after World War II and that their emphasis on "common learnings" and "life adjustment" education would be in conflict with the new demands of technology is a further indictment of their ability to keep in touch with changing social conditions.

Lastly, the educator's impulse to assume responsibility for those social problems existing outside the classroom and his practice of using the school as an instrument to bring about their correction have both undermined the effectiveness of any argument that might be made to keep other interested social groups from trying to use the schools for the purpose of realizing their own political programs. Because educationists advocated indoctrinating students with a progressive social philosophy during the thirties, it is now very difficult for them to tell such groups as the John Birch Society that it is morally wrong to transform education into indoctrination. The practice of politicizing the educational process by using the student as a means for the realization of specific social ends has thus served as an invitation to other groups, who also feel themselves to be in possession of the truth, to come into the school. As a result the school has too often become a battleground for competing ideologies. Instead of using the schools to foster conformity in accordance with their own social philosophy, educators over the years should have concerned themselves with the problem of providing an educational environment that provides the student with the freedom necessary for raising searching questions about himself and his cultural environment. This non-Instrumentalist approach to education defers commitment on the part of the student until he has the background and skill required for making independent judgments. Should American educators ever take seriously this conception of education, they will find the issue of social reconstruction to be irrelevant and the messianic spirit to be inconsistent with it.

Reprinted from The Educational Forum, Kappa Delta Pi, Volume 31, Number 2, January, 1967.

S E M E S T E R :   W E E K   F I V E

REQUIRED READINGS

Church

Part II: The Quest for Commonality, 1830-1860,
Chapter 4: The Search for a New Pedagogy
(33 pp.)

Dye

Swineford, Edwin J. "Critical Teaching Strategies" The Journal of Teacher Education.
V.22, No.1, Spring, 1971.(08 pp.)

MEETINGS

Monday

Lecture: The Object Teaching Tradition

Tuesday

Lecture: The Herbartian Tradition

Wednesday

Lecture: School Organization: Boards of
           Education

Thursday and Friday

Small Groups: Examination One is
                administered.

CHURCH TEXTBOOK STUDY GUIDE: CHAPTER 4

THE SEARCH FOR A NEW PEDAGOGY

1. pedagogy
2. Professor William Holmes McGuffey
3. McGuffey Readers
4. doctrine of Christian nuture
5. Horace Bushnell
6. Horace Mann
7. nonsectarian morality
8. secular teaching
9. vocal music instruction
10. phrenology
11. Mann's Seventh Report (1844)
12. Johann Heinrich Pestalozzi
13. whole-word method of reading instruction
14. corporal punishment
15. emulation
16. the object method
17. Oswego Normal School
18. Edward Augustus Sheldon
19. learning from sensations
20. sense perception

EDWIN J. SWINEFORD

Critical Teaching Strategies

There are some strategies that are instrumental for successful teaching. These strategies, involving judgment, meaningful experience, and judicious use, have been called "critical teaching strategies" by the author, who has isolated and grouped some of them into ten clusters, each of which is described from an operational level. Spotlighting these critical strategies may alert teacher educators and beginning teachers. The diagnosis of empirically observed teaching ailments may also localize a tender area for in-service and teacher intern growth. In fact, these critical teaching strategies might very well constitute rich curriculum content for interns, since they comprise concepts and skills seldom mastered in the traditional courses or student-teaching experience.

The problems given here were gleaned from a previous study[1] in which over five hundred lessons in English, social studies, mathematics, and science, taught by sixty junior high school student teachers over a four-year period, were observed and immediately reported. An analysis of these reports revealed persistent and recurring problems of teaching strategy. Below is a brief discussion of each of these critical teaching strategy problem areas, with practical, specific suggestions that may be helpful to practitioners, particularly to interns.

1. *Inability To Place the Student in the Center of the Teaching-Learning Process*

   Discussion: This disability appeared frequently with the unsuccessful student teachers; the harder they worked, the more blasé and disinterested the students became. In some cases, the students seemed hypnotized as they watched the busy teachers lecturing, analyzing, writing on the chalkboard, demonstrating, pacing up and down, and assuming entire responsibility and guilt for all the teaching and learning.

   It was impossible to tell what some classes were for; they appeared to be an exhibit of routines and games, the object being to go through the paces without anyone's being hurt or disturbed. This was characterized by a hypocrisy of silence on the part of both students and teacher—if you

---

1. Swineford, E. J. "An Analysis of Teaching-Improvement Suggestions to Student Teachers." *Journal of Experimental Education* 32: 299-303; Spring 1964.

Dr. *Swineford is chairman, Department of Secondary Education, Fresno State College, Fresno, California.*

let us alone, we will not cause any trouble and will play your game. Some students seemed to be especially sensitive to what was coming, and by a series of extremely sophisticated maneuvers, they were able to cop out of the learning situation or to engage in such skillful engineering that the whole class escaped. Teacher and students were engaged in a charade.

Suggestions for improvement:

(1) Be informed of the student's experiential background and start there.
(2) Look critically at the student's learning, not at how hard you worked, how much material you covered, or the dazzling array of educational technology you dragged into the room.
(3) Be zealous about classroom time; set the stage for learning and move the student to it, front and center.
(4) Guide, direct, or turn the flow of experiences so that the student is put into the school teaching-learning frame.
(5) Put on top of the teaching-learning table all the hidden related factors and conditions that may rise up to destroy the teaching-learning process.
(6) Know where you stopped with the class and with individual students, if possible, and start the lesson from this point.
(7) Tell the students your problems in teaching that particular lesson, thus reducing the teaching-learning and student-teacher gap.
(8) Give negative reinforcement to students who "red herring" lessons with calculated deviations and planned distractions.
(9) Plan the lesson for the entire class, not as a reaction to one student's inquiry.
(10) Have a dream; don't settle for cheap, temporary outcomes.
(11) Cause the students to place themselves in the optimum setting for learning.
(12) Hit the students (in terms of teaching and learning) where they live and where a nerve is exposed.
(13) Start preparing a new stage for a new learning while you are polishing off the first one.
(14) Give priority to the immediate teaching-learning setting, placing secondary the bookkeeping and housekeeping duties.

2. *Failure To Establish Clearly the Responsibility for Specific Minimum Learnings for each Member of the Class*

Discussion: This may appear redundant, but it deserves emphasis, particularly in creative and unconventional lessons that fortunately are becoming more numerous. Valuable learnings that might result from creative approaches may be lost because the brilliance of the lesson structure blots out a critical concern—making certain that each student is responsible for specific behavioral outcomes. Even in regular classes, it must be admitted that establishing minimum learnings for each individual is at best a dream, perhaps a myth; as an ideal, it anchors the lesson and facilitates optimum learning.

Suggestions for improvement:

(1) In creative and unconventional lesson patterns, keep your eye on terminal behavioral chang-

es desired, holding the students to these in spite of the temptation to bask in the glow of a satisfying and glittering presentation.

(2) Build specific learnings into the lesson, letting these shape the lesson rather than reacting to temporary and superficial student approval.

(3) Think through your several roles as a teacher, giving priority to being a director of learning.

(4) In long or complex lessons, use some device, perhaps the chalkboard or overhead projector, to capture the attention of all students at the same time in order to define objectives and expected outcomes clearly.

(5) Develop a tool to determine the learnings achieved; in many cases, let the students know in advance how and why they will be asked for a feedback.

(6) Let the most important outcomes come through more strongly than minor outcomes; everything should not sound the same in importance.

(7) Don't be satisfied with favorable reactions to lessons in which students are not required to do anything except listen.

(8) Record and document the extent to which individuals achieve the behavioral outcomes.

(9) Don't undermine student responsibility for learning by taking it all on yourself.

(10) Use pop tests or quizzes to bring the lesson back to substantive learnings when deviations set in.

(11) Avoid the use of "I want," or similar expressions, when setting goals.

(12) Use student names in class to help personalize the lesson.

3. *Tendency To Provide Activity for Its Own Sake and To Work for Narrow Goals*

Discussion: This is characteristic of lessons that tend to go off in all directions at once; a shotgun is used instead of a rifle. The trick is to capture and retain the teacher drive, while at the same time giving direction and purpose to the random activity.

Suggestions for improvement:

(1) Be aware when confusion exists and organize it to achieve educational goals.

(2) Reduce the possibilities for misdirection by paying attention to the freightage of your words and acts.

(3) Recognize that you have limited time and energy and that you must conserve them for precious activities.

(4) Use feedback to check on the productivity of the lesson.

(5) Let your activity result in further student activity.

(6) Know when you are doing busy work.

(7) Plan your deviations and how to get back to the mainstream of the lesson.

(8) Work on concepts, principles, and generalizations rather than trivia.

(9) Do those things in class that can be done there only, protecting those precious teaching-learning moments from nonteaching interruptions.

(10) Be lazy; never do something that other available persons,

including students, could do better, while they profit from the activity.

4. *Difficulty in Diagnosing Learning Problems of Students*

   Discussion: Beginning teachers tend to assume the student's learning slate is wiped clean before they lay on a new lesson. This is compounded by a naïve conception of how the student will perceive the prescribed learning. Further complications set in as additional difficulties in learning develop when the lesson is unfolded. This is a prognosis without diagnosis.

   Suggestions for improvement:
   (1) Assess the total teaching-learning framework before leaping into a lesson.
   (2) Get at the why of nonlearning.
   (3) Don't assume that the class and individuals will cure themselves of learning disabilities.
   (4) Consider whether learning problems are aggravated by your pace, timing, or teaching mixture.
   (5) Neutralize environmental factors that might affect the learning situation.
   (6) React not only to the questions that are asked but also to why they are being asked and what is really being asked.
   (7) Know what to ignore and what to react to as you unfold the lesson.
   (8) Avoid reviewing on top of a previous review lesson.
   (9) Check on student misconceptions, and don't keep going over solved problems.
   (10) Distinguish among lack of ability, laziness, or disinterest.
   (11) Get the students' attention before starting a lesson, and continually check on their attention and interest as the lesson unfolds.
   (12) If the lesson is vague and loosely organized to you, it will be confused and unorganized to the students.
   (13) Monotony and boredom breed learning difficulties.
   (14) Students have a right to fail.
   (15) Stop when you have finished teaching the lesson; further activity or verbalization may be destructive.

5. *Inability To String Learning Experiences Together Toward Significant Long-Range Outcomes*

   Discussion: The ability to tie together and direct learning experiences so as to achieve significant long-range goals is a top-drawer, master-teacher, operational-level activity; it may be asking too much of a beginning teacher. Actually this can be done only by the learner, but the beginning teacher must recognize his responsibility to facilitate this process by at least offering lessons that point in this direction. Wisdom in this area remains the province of the master teacher.

   Suggestions for improvement:
   (1) Don't be caught with piecemeal teaching—if what you teach doesn't extend beyond one lesson, it probably isn't worth presenting.
   (2) Careful attention to the beginning and ending of a lesson will help give integrity to the total string of lessons.
   (3) Systematic overview, review, and homework reinforce the

opportunity to achieve long-range goals.
(4) Know when you are on a plateau in the total sweep toward long-range goals.
(5) Be a director of learning, not a reactor to pupil petulance or whim.
(6) Don't compete with the encyclopedia, computer, or teaching machine.
(7) Protect long-range goals, even at the expense of losing a short-range goal.
(8) Watch your lesson deviations and expansions—they may blur the significant goals.
(9) Use subject matter, not as an end in itself but rather as a means of moving toward the goals or purposes.
(10) Work with the students so that they see the relationship of small learnings in the framework of total goals.

6. *Difficulty in Accepting the Student as He Is*

Discussion: One hesitates to bring this up—it is old hat to students. Before teaching, they may have accepted it as a principle; now they are required to put it into practice, and this is another matter. This principle is a major hurdle in working with the pupils who are socially and culturally different. Unless it is put into practice, it doesn't matter whether the beginning teacher has had course work in this area or not. The teacher must know who he is before he can accept the student as he is.

Suggestions for improvement:
(1) Assess the student in terms of your concerns in a particular class and stop feeling guilty or responsible for what you find.
(2) Know what the student's experiential background is and start there.
(3) Build interests as well as uncovering them.
(4) Reconcile yourself to living and learning among divergent interests and tensions. You are paid to be disliked.
(5) Simple students like simple procedures. Use uncomplicated approaches with difficult classes.
(6) Don't expect all the students to learn all that you know.
(7) Match your idea of expected class outcomes with the raw material in the class.
(8) Remember that you can't pull or push all the students through the same material at the same time and with the same procedures.
(9) Get behind observable behavior. What are they worrying about? What are they thinking? What are their feelings of concern about themselves?
(10) When you accept the student as he is, you also must accept his image of you as a teacher.
(11) Remember that about half the students are different from you —they are a different sex.
(12) Since they are different, and you are different, the setting for learning must be rich and open, and the strategies varied and creative.

7. *Failure To Translate and Give Meaning to Student Behavior*

Discussion: The initial teacher shock of close contact with youth must be followed by an ability to sort out, classify, and give meaning to apparent random student reactions. Observing student behavior was enough in preteaching situations; now the beginning teacher must interpret it and hypothesize in order to decide what is to be done.

Suggestions for improvement:
(1) The mass of student behavior has meaning, is caused, and is capable of being diagnosed, classified, and understood if the teacher uses intelligence and the right tools.
(2) Be a teacher, not a mediator of boy-girl relationships.
(3) Sift out the voluminous mass of give-and-take in the classroom, which stems from the fact you have young men and young women together.
(4) Act on symptoms, especially when the overt act is predictable.
(5) Decide when to suppress a student and when to support him.
(6) Have your hand on the pulsebeat of the total class; know when to give up and start over, what is reasonable, and when learning is taking place.
(7) Translate student behavior into terms of the total school environment and the student's individual life space.
(8) Ask yourself what the student is doing in terms of the situation he is facing with the tools he has to work with.
(9) Listen to the sounds of the classroom, especially the hidden meanings of student laughter.
(10) Modify negative student behavior in the direction of long-range goals, not as an end in itself.
(11) Be sensitive to the ever-present wall of student apathy and disinterest, accompanied by instant student fatigue.

8. *Failure To Capitalize on Rich Learning Experiences That Emerge As the Lesson Develops*

Discussion: In the formal teacher preparation program, the prospective teacher has been taught the value and techniques of long-range, unit, and daily lesson planning. Many have been harassed into making plans for others to read and approve. The result is that few know how to use plans to liberate themselves for artistic teaching.

Suggestions for improvement:
(1) Plan with goals and purposes clearly understood, but with multiple means in mind to achieve them.
(2) Each teacher makes his own little hell with self-imposed restrictions and blinders that cause him to look at learning through a crack.
(3) Philosophize on what you are doing. Stop regularly and take a long, hard look at yourself as you play your role as a teacher.
(4) Remember the seeds of learning you have previously planted; cultivate them and make room for their flowering in your lesson.
(5) Obstacles to learning may be your opportunity for rich teaching.
(6) Work through a core, an essence, a message, welcoming fresh examples and student-centered experiences that reinforce your means toward the goal.

(7) The wisest teachers prepare for spontaneous student contributions.
(8) Run a string through all your lessons; bead it with student-contributed interests and needs.
(9) Your lesson campus is the student's total experiential background and world of fantasy.
(10) Keep your eye on what is happening to your students as the lesson unfolds, not just on what you thought would or should happen.

9. *Lack of Sensitivity to Timing, Pacing, and Transition*

Discussion: These areas, falling outside the province of the science of teaching and into the area of the art of tuition, are seldom taught to beginning teachers but are caught by them as they grow on the job. Those few who are born teachers may already practice sound timing, pacing, transition; if so they should understand and rationalize what they are doing and consciously utilize these hidden ingredients of master teaching.

Suggestions for improvement:
(1) The pause, waiting, silence may sound louder to the learner than anything you might say.
(2) Protect the teachable moment and know when it has arrived.
(3) Capitalize on immediate visual feedback of the lesson in action.
(4) Know when to slow down, speed up, stop, repeat, and overview.
(5) Unload your illustrations, sharp resources, and precious techniques at the time when they can be fully exploited and spent.
(6) You alone are the expert on timing and pacing concerns for your class; you may have to work against administrative and supervisorial lethargy and ignorance in these critical concerns.
(7) A sick or lazy teacher seldom experiences concerns in the areas of timing, pacing, and transition.
(8) Small details of classroom management may wreck timing, pacing, and transition.
(9) In presenting a lesson, decide when to expand or when to contract on the content.
(10) A sensitive teacher knows when to start all over again, when to release students for new learnings, when to cover a little more deeply, when to ask and when to tell, and how long to let the students suffer without answers.
(11) Present honest lessons—don't try to be too clever. Move directly into the lesson.
(12) Don't wonder what happened to your lesson; cause things to happen according to plan.
(13) Plan the transitions from one part of the lesson to another; don't just drift into something new.
(14) Transitions should be logical and psychological. Logical transitions may satisfy you, but students prefer a transition that is natural to them and gives a feeling of fulfillment.
(15) By overview and review connect lessons; these should be brief and sharp, not the whole thing over again.

10. *Poor Judgment in Selecting Subject Matter for All the Students in the Class*

Discussion: Curriculum development by the classroom teacher involves among other things the selection of content for the class. This is necessary even when the school has a detailed curriculum guide. Several misconceptions seem to be common among many beginning teachers on content and content selection; one is that subject matter is an end rather than a means to an end. Instead of the teacher's using subject matter, he is manipulated by it. Another idea that hurts is that the teacher must teach all the subject matter in the discipline; this results in a furious attempt to teach all the students all the teacher knows or can extract from available books. The final misconception is the attempt to teach the same thing to all the students at the same time, in the same way, and with uniform results.

Suggestions for improvement:

(1) Determine your purposes and select subject matter to achieve them.
(2) Teach students the structure, essence, or basic concepts of your discipline.
(3) Be generous and creative in the examples or illustrations you use.
(4) Be a scholar in your discipline, possessing a deep pool of knowledge from which you carefully select content in terms of your specific situation.
(5) The subject matter as you know it from college is too rich in most cases for your students. In stepping it down for them, be certain to retain its scholarship.
(6) The critic of your teaching judgments is the best thinking of your profession, not solely the reactions of a group of students.
(7) Don't depend on the class to stumble onto the key concepts. It is poor teaching to base today's lesson on yesterday's omissions.
(8) Aim not at covering all the material for all the students but at building scholarship in varying degrees in each student.
(9) Remember that students can't be perfect—nor can they be poor—in everything.
(10) Take out your frustrations and dissatisfactions on the subject matter, not the students.

Reprinted from The Journal of Teacher Education, Volume 22, Number 1, Spring, 1971.

S E M E S T E R :   W E E K   S I X

REQUIRED READINGS

Church

Part III: The Retreat from Commonality, 1840-1920, Chapter 5: <u>The Failure of the Common Schools (I): The South</u> (37 pp.)

Dye

Black, Hugh C. "Educational Philosophy and Theory in the United States - A Commentary" <u>Educational Theory</u>. V.20, No.1, Winter, 1970. (10 pp.)

MEETINGS

Monday

Lecture: Rutherford Birchard Hayes

Tuesday

Lecture: Traditions of Black Education

Wednesday

Lecture: Financing Public Education

Thursday and Friday

Small Groups: Examination One results will be distributed.

CHURCH TEXTBOOK STUDY GUIDE: CHAPTER 5

THE FAILURE OF THE COMMON SCHOOLS: THE SOUTH

1. environmentalism
2. hereditarian doctrines
3. hereditarianism
4. power of schooling to solve problems
5. educational crusade
6. National Teachers Association
7. antebellum South
8. unreconstructed South
9. reconstructed South
10. regionalistic point of view p.122
11. poor white native Southerner p.123
12. Southern cultural superiority p.124
13. yeoman farmer p.121, 124
14. independent artisan p.124
15. socialization of the Southerner
16. Bureau of Refugees, Freedmen, and Abandoned Lands p.128
17. Freedmen's Bureau p.128
18. Boston Educational Commission for Freedmen p.129
19. New England Freedman Aid Society
20. Port Royal Experiment p.130
21. abolitionists p.131
22. culture-bound Northern teachers p.133 negative
23. discipline p.135
24. moral training p.135
25. assumption of responsibility of and by the Southern black
26. Ku Klux Klan p.137
27. general decline of Northern educational crusade p.137
28. Edward Everett Hale p.137
29. philanthropists
30. Social Darwinism p.139

31. elevation of the Southern black
32. maintenance of social order
33. keeping the black in his place
34. inferiority
35. industrial training

36. special education
37. Radical Southern state governments
38. New Orleans public schools
39. Southern Democrats
40. Redeemers

41. Wade Hampton
42. redneck politicians
43. demographic conditions in the South
44. dependency rate
45. scattered population

46. shrunken tax base
47. President Woodrow Wilson
48. The New Freedom
49. Southern Education Board. SEB
50. parity

51. literacy test
52. division of tax revenues
53. substantial equality
54. per capita
55. district boards of education

56. county boards of education

Educational Philosophy and Theory in the United States—A Commentary

BY HUGH C. BLACK

IN NOVEMBER 1968 IN AN ELEMENTARY SCHOOL IN A RATHER AFFLUENT NEIGHBORHOOD IN A UNITED STATES CITY OF 250,000 A NUMBER OF SIXTH GRADE PUPILS ORGANIZED THEMSELVES INTO A CLUB CALLED "THE CATS." Meeting at recess and on other occasions outside the classroom, these twelve-year olds pursued the purpose of their club: ways and means to harass their new teacher! They did not *know* the new teacher who two months after the start of school replaced their former teacher. But they made up their minds not to like her and were taking action!

This incident was reported to me at the same time action was being taken in a different part of the country and at a higher educational level: the closing down of San Francisco State College in California and the difficulties of its reopening.

In another shocker just before Thanksgiving 1968, the Associated Press announced that "Broke, without credit and almost without hope, Youngstown's 45 city schools will close their doors," sending home more than 27,000 students with a faint hope that classrooms might be reopened on January 2. Five years ago, Youngstown, the "Steel City" of northeastern Ohio, "boasted one of Ohio's finest city school districts." Today, so the press story put it, "beset by religious, labor and political ills, and a futile attempt at balancing 1963 level income with 1968 costs, the district teeters on the brink of bankruptcy and collapse." "Tax rates have not increased in five years and six new levies have been rejected at the polls."

Also in November 1968 I received a letter from a former colleague reporting directly the experiences of two public school teachers during a year of graduate study in the Eastern United States. Both are intellectually "solid" teachers, the one at the elementary level, the other a secondary teacher of English. Attending different institutions of higher learning, both find their universities "pressing a child-centered, student-directed kind of educational experience." At one of the institutions, the teacher "senses an unbroken chain of affiliation with the Teachers College point of view in the 1930s." "Both places," they report, "are placing a heavy emphasis on the last decade of English school experience, expressing great interest in the Leicestershire 'experiment' in infant and junior school education and in the personal experience approach to English composition." At the smaller school, one of the teachers finds things wearing a bit thin in her "fellowship group." For "the dominant element there is high on feeling and caring, non-verbal communication, and a dogmatism about educational principles but very low

---

HUGH C. BLACK is Professor of Education at the University of California at Davis.

on term papers, responsible discussion, or anything we'd call intellectual." At the larger institution, the other teacher reports that he was not prepared by his public school and western universities experiences for "the iconoclasm, even nihilism, with which problems are approached." His summary of his encounter and his reaction to it is revealing:

> The basic assumption is that present social institutions are corrupt, evil, and irreparable. The public schools are first on the list. The only solution is to destroy and start all over. When one inquires about some reasonable alternative, the answer is that anything would be better than what we now have, so it will all work out (which is another way of saying they don't have a real alternative to offer). Several people I am studying with have shown real signs of strain under the barrage of such a line. I am willing to concede that in a total school experience, a student may meet with considerable boredom, a dose of irrelevancy, and even some experience of emotional assault from insensitive or unhealthy teachers. But I have real trouble conceding their premise that schools are totally evil and that no improvement is possible. I was particularly concerned over the statement of one professor that any attempts to shore up the present system, to provide a stimulating experience for one's own class is an immoral and indefensible attempt to support a corrupt system.... I think I'll go on being an optimist, albeit a blind one possibly.

All four experiences just reported hit me with a jarring impact. For I supposed that in the United States it was common knowledge what the writers of the Declaration of Independence of the Republic of Texas had declared in that document of 1836: "It is an axiom in political science that unless a people are educated and enlightened it is idle to expect the continuance of civil liberty or the capacity for self-government." Now I wonder if those today, who should know what our ancestors discovered through travail, have brought us (through ignorance in the face of available knowledge) to such dire consequences as loss of civil liberty and capacity for self-government. My friend studying in the East went to the heart of his difficulty when he wrote: "We've been unable to put our fingers on any clearcut antecedent for this kind of movement, other than a highly specific dissatisfaction with what had gone on before." And then the public school teacher put it to the philosopher of education: "Do you have any clear picture of the philosophical underpinning for such an attitude in the extreme form we are encountering? We wonder if practice is preceding theory here?"

Gratifying it is to know that responsible public school teachers in the United States such as my friends recognize and react to the philosohical aspects of their encounter. It is challenging to the educational philosopher or theorist to reply meaningfully.

The reply must come from the knowledge we have, and I begin with an event in another November — one of 90 years ago: the ninth annual report covering the year 1878 of John Eaton, United States Commissioner of Education:

> The financial depression noted in several previous reports has continued. The bulwarks of society have not escaped assault either by ignorant, unfortunate, or unprincipled persons. Education has had its share of these attacks. In the midst

of these encounters of sentiment, the thoughtful and patriotic mind has found further occasion for alarm in observing how few, comparatively, of those citizens or statesmen who sincerely desire to maintain our institutions in their purity and vigor have been sufficiently familiar with the history of the questions arising to make that complete defense of our liberties which the facts in our national experience warrant. This has been especially noticeable in the case of certain parts of the public school system, such as the high school, the normal school, supervision, inspection, and adequate salaries. Those who have sowed the idea that anybody is competent, unaided, to decide and act on any educational problem have reaped an abundant crop of absurdities. States, cities, and schools have been seen to blunder back into the errors through which they floundered only a few years before, utterly oblivious of their previous adverse experiences; more frequently still has it been found true that one blunderer has not learned anything from the experience of others, while the discussions as a whole have displayed an utter ignorance and disregard of thorough and far reaching principles. This strain upon our free institutions has tempted not a few, whose moderation would otherwise have restrained them, into measures or expressions of antagonism to our educational instrumentalities. This has been particularly true of those who would modify our present freedom of conscience, and of those who would establish a distinction of classes with a view to a permanent aristocracy, as well as of those who desire to practise some form of destructive communism. Not a few of the steps proposed, if carefully examined, are found to be directly in the return path toward barbarism.[1]

Eaton, I suggest, puts his finger on those frustrating factors in American education which have characterized our blundering swings from one extreme to another during the past one hundred or so years. When my friend studying in the Eastern United States encounters the extreme attitude he describes so well, he is surprised at the challenge at the philosophical level and wonders at practice preceding theory in American education. But I am not surprised, for the history and philosophy of our experiences with education reveal a knowledge we need to be more acquainted with. I suggest that, our people being who they are and holding the values they express, a behavior of extremism is to be expected. I am surprised and concerned that more of our teachers and teachers of teachers do not have this knowledge of how it is in United States education — the realism so well described by Eaton in that November of 1878.

Whether caused by an anti-intellectualism so well-documented by others, I know not. But as I read the American experience of schooling, I find more practice of fads and less exemplification in action of good theory of education. Schooling throughout our history seems to have been constituted of practices arising from practical necessities instituted at a time of crisis, continued until the next crisis (some seemingly continuing on forever) when change occurs by trying-out the newest fad, this in turn being reacted to, and on and on. Most of this development reflects the values of the citizens in a society and culture in which the main-stream is anti-intellectual, anti-humanitarian, and anti-humanism. Rational and "good" theory of education have counted for

---

[1]*Report of the Commissioner of Education for the Year 1878.* (Washington, Government Printing Office, 1880), p. VII.

little in a society in which so much is determined by money, self-seeking lives of "getting ahead," "putting up a good front" (after all, a TV ad reminds us, "It's what's up front that counts!"), power plays of self-aggrandizement, and most of those values Socrates sought to convince his Athenian friends were not worth having. The tragedy, I suggest, is that with all these developments there has been knowledge available which if applied properly might have made a difference. Yet, as Eaton said, we blunder on regardless.

Too often what we have blundered into is the result of our values rather than the best available theory or philosophy. We have talked a good battle, reminding ourselves how necessary education is in a democratic society, saying we value education, and handing our teachers a grand ideal and task of educating all the children of all the people. Our action and commitment have been less than ideal. In the earlier days of our history we had individual instruction of a sort. Since youngsters needed to know how to read, a few were gathered together in a home and taught — the Dame school. But if you are to teach many and at public expense, you go to the opposite extreme and institute the ideas of a Joseph Lancaster and Andrew Bell of England and develop monitorial schools in the United States. In this case it is not the worth of the educational ideas — the theory or philosophy of education — but the cheapness of the means (a money matter) which is the over-riding determiner of school practice. Thus in our early history did we go from one extreme to the other; and it must have become ingrained, for today we struggle with the same problem of extremes in our education.

Space does not permit a detailed documentation of the way of our schools with educational theory and philosophy: from a Colonial America with a child nature considered to be innately evil, through Locke and his discovery of no basis for innate ideas, to Rousseau and an entirely new concept of child nature and what education is, to Pestalozzi and his object-lessons and American elementary education, to Froebel's *The Education of Man* and the kindergarten idea in the United States, to Herbart and the thrilling story of the Herbartian movement in the United States, etc. From this history two examples may be cited to illustrate how our schools have treated educational theory.

The application of the theory and principles of Froebel to kindergarten practices in the United States just before 1900 affords us a fine example of an idea becoming its opposite in practice. When Frederick Eby completed his doctoral dissertation with G. Stanley Hall at Clark University in 1900, Hall thought it was "the most sane and competent presentation of the subject that has been made in recent years in any language" and gave 58 pages of the July 1900 issue of his *Pedagogical Seminary* to printing the condensed results.[2] "As a striking fact of human experience," Eby stated, "the advocates of any truth may, in practice, be exemplifying the corresponding error."[3] In evidence he cited from religious experience the fact that "The Protestant revival could assert the freedom of conscience and yet result in the persecution

---

[2] Frederick Eby, "The Reconstruction of the Kindergarten." *Pedagogical Seminary*, VII (No. 2, July 1900): 229-286. Hall's evaluation appears on p. 150.
[3] *Ibid.*, p. 278.

of its opponents; the Puritans may flee oppression in one land to become its instruments in another; . . . ."[4] And he conjectured that it might be so in education (whether in Europe or the United States): "humanism in Italy may become a worse scholasticism in Germany; the spontaneity of Froebel may be in actual practice the domination of the adult."[5] What he definitely discovered from his own investigations of kindergartens in the United States was that the principle of spontaneity "upon which the kindergarten theory was so strongly entrenched, is almost totally disregarded in real kindergarten practice."[6] He reported:

> In the ordinary kindergarten, there is first of all, a programme for the week, day, and season. This is formulated by the adult, adapted to adult needs, and grows out of the adult conceptions of order and connection. The entire work of the day is directed by the standard set by the adult. The kindergartner regulates the length of time for this play and for that; she selects the order of the daily occupations, she controls the movements of the children down to the minutest details, she even goes so far to the absurdity of a fantastical and puerile regulation of the manner in which the boxes containing the gift building blocks must be handled.[7]

Moreover, he found the play in the kindergarten artificial and unnatural and just the opposite of what Froebel advocated. "In the kindergarten the plays are mechanical, and forced; they exhibit little real spontaneity, little of childlike unconsciousness, nothing of naïveté."[8] Eby further reports that "the very principles of the kindergarten are against all this incessant domination of the infant's interests by those of the adult, and show that it is not educative but mechanizing. These regulations of each successive movement deprives the children of initiative, and robs him of the opportunity for originality."[9] Thus is described the American school way with theory: when sometimes we do pay attention to theory and put it into practice, it becomes its opposite.

Most of the time we pay no attention to theory, and in American education knowledge of educational philosophy counts for very little. The kindergarten story in the United States is another example of how far our practice lags behind theory and what we know. Anyone familiar with the Eby study, the writings of Kate Douglas Wiggin, and the literature knows how long ago we knew how important are the early years in the shaping of the disposition of the child. Yet even today kindergartens are not universally provided for as a part of the public school system, and we accept the "discoveries" of Bloom about the importance of the early years as though they were new! No wonder we blunder our way from extreme to extreme.

The field of comparative education furnishes our second illustration of how we treat theory in the United States. Some of us were amazed indeed

---

[4]*Ibid.*
[5]*Ibid.*
[6]*Ibid.*
[7]*Ibid.*
[8]*Ibid.*, p. 279.
[9]*Ibid.*

in 1957 and 1958 at the results in education of our reaction to the Russian launching of Sputnik I in October of 1957. We saw one effect in the teacher colleges and schools and colleges of education. Hard-pressed by the barrage of school critics lambasting the "fly-casting" and other easy courses, the deans looked for instant "substantial" courses. By the summer sessions of 1958 "authorities" in comparative education were very much in demand, and soon we were to benefit by an active Comparative Education Society and its *Comparative Education Review*. This attention to a field of professional knowledge as though it were new and did have a bearing on what is done in schools amazed some of us. Why? Knowledge of education in other countries has had a long history in the United States, from the annual reports of its commissioners of education, to the journalistic endeavors of Horace Mann and Henry Barnard, to the outstanding writings of I. L. Kandel. Courses in comparative education throughout the nation were a part of the standard "menu" for graduate students in the history and philosophy of education, and they had been for years prior to Sputnik I !! Again we have illustrated the fact that so often when knowledge and theory have been available, the American experience is one of ignoring it until some crisis arises.

As I read the story of our educational history, we seem to have a habit of disregarding or paying only slight attention to that knowledge about which we ought to know most and put into practice. This is certainly true of history and philosophy of education as well as comparative education, a point best illustrated by citing the "Professorships of Didactics or Pedagogics" part of the Report of the Commissioner of Education for the year 1877.[10] In that year John Eaton, the Commissioner, reported:

> The science and art of teaching is surely a subject so important that it may well be included in the curricula of our universities and colleges. The State University of Iowa established a chair of didactics in 1873, made it an elective subject for the senior year, and gives the degree of bachelor of didactics to such of its graduates as have taught two years after receiving this instruction.

Only through bitter experiences did some academic minds from 1958 to the present arrive at the knowledge which John Eaton had in 1877. He saw how education was bound "by the historic customs of our older colleges." The learned men at the head of our colleges were considered the leaders in our educational affairs. But, he noted, "They largely retain the ideas and methods which were brought by the colonists from the mother country, and contemplate the education of a comparatively small number of persons, and this after their minds are measurably mature." "Their methods," he saw, "are poorly adapted to instruct immature minds, have been totally abandoned in all intelligent elementary training, and have been modified in secondary instruction." The leaders in the colleges of the time contended against the teaching of the natural sciences, and "they omitted the philosophy of education from their curriculum, sometimes, indeed, acting as though there were no such subject in the domain of thought." As Eaton saw it, "It is this lack of a really comprehensive philosophy of culture, which should include man in all

---

[10]*Report of the Secretary of the Interior for the Year 1877; Part II — Education* (Washington, Government Printing Office, 1879), pp. LXXIV-LXXV.

his conditions and relations, that has permitted if not promoted foolish prejudices between institutions of learning . . . ." A partial cure, the Commissioner suggested, lay in the various college associations being founded from time to time; but another lay in attention to the philosophy of education! Contrasting the apathy in the United States with the treatment of the philosophy of education by the German universities (fully documented with specific examples), the Commissioner expressed his belief:

> — It is not too much to hope that another result will be a more careful consideration of the philosophy of education and adequate provision for the sound and thorough teaching of it.

And so education courses were begun in the United States on a German model emphasizing history and philosophy of education. Out of this arose a body of knowledge about the human experience of educating the young which was diffused through such men as Paul Monroe at Teachers College, Columbia University, Ellwood P. Cubberley at Stanford, Charles H. Judd and Henry C. Morrison at Chicago, Frederick Eby and Charles F. Arrowood at Texas, and through educators of the stature of Charles DeGarmo, Charles and Frank McMurry, John Dewey, Boyd H. Bode, William C. Bagley, and I. L. Kandel. But over the years new fields of pedagogy and other names came to the foreground. In the preparation of teachers the hours devoted to the basic knowledge so necessary to prevent blundering into "new" ways (already experienced as fruitless) were cut to the minimum. In time even many of the teachers of teachers came to lack that solid knowledge of the history of ideas which could prevent, for example, a John Dewey from becoming an extremist. The situation has not been helped by the battles of the "academicians" vs. "the educationists," which in some institutions have resulted in chairs in history and philosophy of education becoming vacant when some administrator has decided that whatever knowledge in these areas is worthwhile can best be dispensed in the departments of history or philosophy or sociology. Neither has the situation been helped over the years by developments within the professional field itself. Too many deadly dull teachers have killed it for students who never got into it far enough to see the thrilling, exciting, relevant adventure in ideas. If I. L. Kandel is correct,[11] many of the "greats" were sidetracked from their main tasks by the necessity of taking part in the battle of "Traditionalism vs. Progressivism." Many of the younger men, I contend, blind to the limitations of these fields in the experience of general philosophers, have spent too much time worshipping at the altars of existentialism and linguistic analysis. However that may be, there is today in the United States a sad lack of knowledge about educational philosophy and theory. And seldom do our educational philosophers of today face up to the question of the course of study which W. T. Harris said in 1880 was the means for bringing the child into orderly relationship with his civilization and "the most important question which the educator has before him."[12]

---

[11]"Controversy Ended," *Educational Forum*, XXII (January, 1958): 175-181
[12]Lawrence A. Cremin, *The Transformation of the School — Progressivism in American Education 1876-1957* (New York: Random House, 1964), p. 18, quoting from National Education Association: *Addresses and Proceedings,* 1880, p. 174. That part of Cremin's
(Footnote continued)

No wonder neither our teachers nor our teachers of teachers offer much hope in a time characterized by such events as described at the beginning of this article. As my friend studying in the East said of his professors, "they don't know [of any real alternative to offer]."

I contend that we do not know those essentials about which we should most know if we are to approach our problems with any kind of perspective about education. Especially do we not know about the relation of theory to practice in our schools. Already I have illustrated the fact that we often disregard theory or, when we do apply theory, we put into practice its opposite. We also need to know that sometimes laws, such as the compulsory school attendance legislation, affect our schools more quickly, and bring more changes, than do theories. Years ago it was noted that our teachers and administrators take courses, hear lectures and addresses, participate in workshops, serve on committees and in numerous ways expose themselves to ideas and theory but are affected not one whit. Sometimes "movements" catch on: for example, the "life-adjustment" education (not to be associated with Dewey) sponsored by the U. S. Office of Education at the end of World War II.[13] But generally it is what the people want and their values more than the ideas of professional educators which determine what is done in our schools. Events (such as Sputnik I and criticisms leading to federal aid to education under the National Defense Education Act of 1958) and local school board decisions on the prosaic problems of buildings, budgets, busses, bonds, and burgeoning or declining enrollments affect the teacher in the classroom more than do theories of what education is or ought to be.

Our perspective benefits from this knowledge, but we also need to know more of the history of theories in education — a topic which space prevents my doing any more than sampling to indicate a history which I believe to be relevant. This history of theory is mostly one of varying extreme emphases with intermittent attempts to see education "steadily and as a whole" flaring forth from time to time but soon disregarded.

Our first example is Francis W. Parker, who was called by John Dewey "the father of Progressive Education" and labeled by Cremin as "essentially an artist rather than a theorist."[14] His theory developed out of practices — those he observed during European travel and study, those he became famous for as superintendent of the Quincy schools, and those in the practice school of the Cook County Normal School in Chicago. Even so influential a figure as G. Stanley Hall, the founder and editor of no less than four important journals in education and psychology, reportedly visited Cook County annually to set his educational watch by Parker.[15] Our perspective is made better by knowing that that watch was somewhat extreme as educational theories in

---

title which reads *The Transformation of the School* with its implication that Progressivism transformed "the school" bothers me, for he does not offer sufficient evidence to convince me that "Progressivism" actually changed the schools to the extent his title implies.
13See *ibid.*, pp. 333-338, for an acceptable account.
14*Ibid.*, p. 134.
15*Ibid.*, p. 135.

the United States go. For Cremin reports Parker's effort as twofold: "to move the child to the center of the educative process and to interrelate the normal subjects of the curriculum in such a way as to enhance their meaning for the child."[16] Cremin believes, "his philosophy ends up more Rousseauian than anything else."[17]

W. T. Harris' ideas represent an emphasis on factors in education just the opposite of those emphasized by Parker. As superintendent of the St. Louis schools, U. S. Commissioner of Education, and frequent speaker at annual meetings of the National Education Association, this promoter of Hegelian ideas did influence some school practices. But, if we may rely on Cremin for another summary,

> ... the temper of Harris's pedagogy is patently conservative. His emphasis is on order rather than freedom, on work rather than play, on effort rather than interest, on prescription rather than election, on the regularity, silence, and industry that "preserve and save our civil order."[18]

Since the days of Harris and Parker, our story of educational theory has been one of swings between such extremes of emphasis on those dualistic factors in education which Bagley in 1938 pointed out as going back to the Sophists in 5th century B. C. Athens.[19] Few teachers or teachers of teachers today are aware of the other part of the history: attempts to mediate between such extreme emphases and offer alternatives.

When Henry Sabin, State Superintendent of Iowa Schools, addressed the annual meeting of the National Education Association at St. Paul in 1890, his title of "Organization and System vs. Originality and Individuality on the Part of Teacher and Pupil" expressed concretely the fundamental dualism in educational theory in the United States. In the discussion which followed Sabin's address, Charles W. Bardeen of Syracuse, New York, quarrelled with the title, saying: "It reminds me of the old question: 'Will you have meat, or bread?' But why bread *or* meat? Why not bread *and* meat? What we need most is system *and* individuality."[20] And again, in 1914, Charles A. McMurry put his finger on our educational situation in *Conflicting Principles in Teaching — and How to Adjust Them*. But a symposium presentation at the 21st Annual Meeting of the Philosophy of Education Society in New York City on April 11, 1965, indicates that such earlier cries were voices in the wilderness.[21] For these pleas for sanity and rationality in our public schools brought few, if any, changes in school practices. Few paid attention to the 1938 efforts of John Dewey, Boyd H. Bode, I. L. Kandel, and William C.

---

[16]*Ibid.*, p. 131.
[17]*Ibid.*, p. 134.
[18]*Ibid.*, p. 24.
[19]William C. Bagley, "An Essentialist's Platform for the Advancement of American Education," *Educational Administration and Supervision*, XXIV (April 1938): 241-256.
[20]National Education Association, *Addresses and Proceedings* (Topeka, Kansas Publishing House, 1890), p. 234.
[21]Hugh C. Black, "A Four-Fold Classification of Educational Theories," *Educational Theory*, XVI (No, 3, July 1966): 281-291.

Bagley.[22] Still fewer noticed a doctoral dissertation of 1949 with subsequent articles in *Educational Theory* in 1954 and in restated form in 1966 which analyzed the alternative theories of education and urged us to get the controversy on to a new level at least.[23] And today when the educational philosopher with knowledge of these developments attends a student-faculty week-end retreat and hears the views expressed, he is shattered at the realization that the students are again pleading for no more than Progressive Education! Perhaps they may be forgiven for not knowing Robert Holmes Beck's doctoral dissertation in the early 1940s and his 1958-59 articles in *Teachers College Record*.[24] But they do not even know Cremin's *The Transformation of the School — Progressivism in American Education 1876-1957*. So knowledgeable are we about educational theory that we seem fated to repeat the history about which we are ignorant.

Before the present-day extremists do away with the present institution of the school and treat teachers as hopeless, I have a suggestion for students, teachers, and teachers of teachers. To the compassion which we should derive from the Judeo-Christian part of our heritage, let us add the knowledge and understanding which we should value from our Graeco-Roman heritage. Specifically, let us become knowledgeable about educational philosophy and theory and put into practice the valid alternatives we know about already.

The main question about educational philosophy and theory in the United States is this: Will the battle fought in each decade of this century be continued — only this time resulting in the destruction of the public school system as we know it; or will knowledge of educational theory be brought to bear with understanding *and* compassion?

---

[22] John Dewey, *Experience and Education* (New York: Macmillan, 1938); Boyd H. Bode, *Progressive Education at the Crossroads* (New York: Newsome, 1938); I. L. Kandel, *Conflicting Theories of Education* (New York: Macmillan, 1938); and Bagley, *op. cit.*

[23] Hugh C. Black, "The Learning-Product and Learning-Process Theories of Education — An Attempted Synthesis," (Dissertation. Austin, Texas, University of Texas, 1949); "A Way Out of Educational Confusion," *Educational Theory*, IV (April 1954): 113-119; "Practical Implications of a Theory of Education," *Educational Theory*, IV (October 1954): 263-268; and "A Four-Fold Classification of Educational Theories," *op. cit.*.

[24] Cremin cites different dates for Beck's unpublished doctoral dissertation entitled "American Progressive Education, 1875-1930," at Yale University: 1942, on p. 205; 1941, on p. 356. "Progressive Education and American Progressivism," *Teachers College Record*, LX (1958-9), 77-89, 129-37, 198-208.

Reprinted from *Educational Theory*, Volume 20, Number 1, Winter, 1970.

S E M E S T E R: W E E K   S E V E N

REQUIRED READINGS

Church

Part III: The Retreat from Commonality, 1840-1920, Chapter 6: <u>The Failure of the Common Schools (II): The North</u>(38 pp.)

Dye

Cuban, Larry. "Urban Superintendents: Vulnerable Experts" <u>Phi Delta Kappan</u>. December, 1974. (06 pp.)

Riley, Glenda. "Origins of the Argument for Improved Female Education" <u>History of Education Quarterly</u>. V.9, No.4, Winter, 1969.(16 pp.)

MEETINGS

Monday

Lecture: Purposes of Public Education

Tuesday

Lecture: Traditions of Female Education

Wednesday

Lecture: Administering the School Programs

Thursday and Friday

Small Groups:

CHURCH TEXTBOOK STUDY GUIDE: CHAPTER 6

THE FAILURE OF THE COMMON SCHOOLS: THE NORTH

1. early bureaucratization of American schooling
2. nativist
3. Free School Society of New York
4. Public School Society of New York City
5. Bethel Baptist School Society

6. Irish immigration
7. individual weakness
8. individual immorality
9. immigrant slums
10. inculcation of moral values in schooling

11. Whiggish educational reform
12. Governor William Seward, New York
13. local control
14. localism
15. King James Bible

16. Douay Bible
17. Americanization of immigrant populations
18. Bishop John Hughes, New York Diocese
19. diocesan control of local parishes
20. negative liberalism

21. equal rights
22. John C. Spencer, Secretary of State, New York
23. popularly elected boards of education
24. middle class
25. operatives vs. artisans

26. rural middle class values
27. inherited status
28. Lowell, Massachusetts experiment
29. paternalistic labor relations
30. Robert Owen

31. New Lanark
32. self-education
33. self-improvement
34. <u>Lowell Offering</u>
35. drive for culture
36. lyceum
37. cult of true womanhood
38. status anxiety
39. high school education as a badge of status
40. inclusiveness
41. Latin
42. curriculum
43. bureaucracy
44. institutionalization
45. codification
46. the universal redemptive social purpose of education(schooling)
47. standardization of curricula
48. standardization of formal grading
49. standardization of regulations
50. cultural intolerance
51. bias

Larry Cuban

URBAN SUPERINTENDENTS: VULNERABLE EXPERTS

In recent years forced resignations, illness — even mental breakdowns and murder — have cut deeply into the ranks of top schoolmen. Why the increasing turnover rate? Mr. Cuban offers a hypothesis based on a year of study.

> *Just as the sun was coming up, Stuart saw a man seated in thought by the side of the road. Stuart steered his car alongside, stopped, and put his head out.*
> *"You're worried about something, aren't you?" asked Stuart.*
> *"Yes, I am," said the man, who was tall and mild.*
> *"Can I help you in any way?" asked Stuart in a friendly voice.*
> *The man shook his head. "It's an impossible situation, I guess," he replied. "You see I'm the superintendent of schools in this town."*
> *"That's not an impossible situation," said Stuart. "It's bad, but it's not impossible."*
> — E.B. White, *Stuart Little*

Bad but not impossible — a judgment with which many big-city superintendents would nod agreement. Nonetheless, the last decade has been an especially tough one for urban school chiefs, convincing some that perhaps the job is impossible. Certainly it has taken its toll.

The shocking murder of Oakland Superintendent Marcus Foster dramatized in a way that words could not that urban ills have spilled over into previously apolitical schoolmen's domains. Moreover, in the last decade, heart attacks, ulcers, and even mental breakdowns have cut deeply into the ranks of top schoolmen.* Finally, one can add early retirements, shrinking tenure, and forced resignations. For a job that a college president in 1903 called "next in importance to the work of the President of the United States," few informed observers would question now the tough, exacting nature of the urban superintendency. And figures for the 1970s won't bring relief to big-city superintendents.

Consider turnover rates. Between 1960 and 1969 only two large urban school systems held onto their top schoolman. Between 1970 and 1973, of the 25 largest school systems, 23 (92%) appointed new superintendents. While superintendents leave office for many reasons, such wholesale bolting from the job is unusual. Furthermore, there is little doubt that tenure in the position is shrinking. In 1953, for the 25 largest school systems, the average incumbent superintendent served six and a half years; a decade later current tenure slipped to five and a half years; and in 1973 it was just over four years.

Consider job attractiveness. The job of big-city school chief has traditionally been considered the apex of a schoolman's career. Former Superintendent Benjamin Willis spoke of receiving the "call" to head Chicago's schools in 1953. For years presidents of the administrators association were drawn

---

LARRY CUBAN *is the author of* To Make a Difference: Teaching in the Inner City *and* Black Man in America. *A former teacher and administrator in Washington, D.C., he spent 1972-74 in graduate study at Stanford University, where he developed the concepts presented here. Cuban is now superintendent of schools in Arlington, Va.*

*Since less than 1% of superintendents are women, I will use the term schoolman. Currently Washington's Barbara Sizemore is the only female school executive, although Atlanta, Los Angeles, and Chicago have had women serve as superintendents in this century.

from the ranks of big-city schoolmen. So, too, by the early 1970s material rewards made the post attractive. By 1970 salaries for urban superintendents had risen to the mid and high thirties. Fringe benefits ranged from liberal leave provisions to a personal car, often with a chauffeur. Contracts had lengthened to three and four years, the longest in the century.

Yet when Pittsburgh, a school system of 75,000 students, advertised for its top post, only 50 candidates applied. Two hundred miles away, York, Pennsylvania — a school system enrolling 8,000 children — advertised for a superintendent and received over 160 applications. In northern California, an affluent, small district like Los Gatos received over 200 applications for its vacant superintendency while 75 miles away Berkeley, the nationally known liberal showcase of integration and certainly not a big city, mustered fewer than 80 applications. While not a big city, Berkeley had carved out in the public imagination the image of being one. Thus, with salaries reaching levels comparable to mayors, judges, and state officials, with ample fringe benefits and with the longest contracts schoolmen have enjoyed in this century, large urban school systems find it tough to recruit the large pools of candidates they once took for granted.

W hy the shying away? Why the high mortality rate? The answer is complicated. Racial politics, declining school enrollments, large numbers of low-achieving minority children combined with a diminished tax base — put these factors together with a public increasingly reluctant to spend scarce dollars on schools and you have a big part of the answer.

Then there is the cross-cutting, demanding nature of the job itself. An urban superintendent heads an organization composed of hundreds of administrators and thousands of teachers. He is responsible to a board of education and often takes an oath to obey the laws of the state. He may have to offer a public pledge to serve the educational interests of millions of parents without ignoring taxpayer concerns. Around him swirls a perpetual cross-fire of expectations, requests, and demands from board members, middle-level bureaucrats, principals, teachers, students, and civic groups. Yet he sits atop this complex, often disorganized system exercising little control over what happens. For example, different board members may enter and exit. Inflation rates rise while financial resources are inflexible. Principals may ignore or sabotage mandated programs.

Impossible demands are placed upon the superintendent's time and energy. One candidate for an urban superintendency was told by a finger-shaking member of the search committee, "We want you available to us seven days a week, 24 hours a day." The candidate laughed, but a long silence informed him that the committee was dead serious. Even beyond the conflicting expectations and severe demands are the crises. "Catastrophes, disorders, demonstrations, and strikes," veteran Columbus, Ohio, school chief Harold Eibling wrote (shortly before retiring), "all have become part of the new order of reality for the large-city superintendent."

Is it, however, "a new order of reality"? Urban superintendents have consistently come under outside pressure, past and present. The job has been generally acknowledged as a tough one. What has marked the last decade as different has been the high number of schoolmen exiting from the top post.

In one earlier decade, however, an even higher percentage of urban superintendents hastily left office. For example, between 1910 and 1920 Indianapolis hired and fired three superintendents in a five-year period; Chicago appointed and dumped three in four years; Memphis had a new superintendent every two years. The pat explanations for high turnover in the 1960s and early 1970s (i.e., politics of race, financial crunch, declining enrollments, school disorders, etc.) just don't fit the large school systems of the World War I years. Why, then, these periodic high mortality rates for the big-city superintendency?

One way of unlocking this puzzle is to examine the views of leadership that big-city superintendents carry around in their heads and the fit between these views and the times. The match or mismatch between leadership conceptions and the events of the decades may help to explain peak departure rates at certain periods.

Over the last century three basic leadership conceptions have emerged among professional schoolmen: teacher-scholar, administrative chief, and negotiator-statesman.* Consider the intellectual terrain of a big-city superintendent operating under each leadership view. Each one's ideas on decision making, citizen participation, conflict, and change are included. (The first person is used only for stylistic reasons; I am not quoting anyone.)

The Teacher-Scholar — I am the professional educator. Any question that directly concerns children and schools I decide. If it involves other, less important matters, I delegate the decision to my staff. As for outside involvement, what do laymen know? The less outside involvement the better. Nor do I care for conflict. Conflict interrupts the educational process. It upsets children and teachers. I work hard to exclude it from the board, staff, and schools. Cooperation and unity are essential to progress. As for change, if it is instructional or curricular, I direct teachers and principals to begin working on it. I'll provide help to make the change work, but there is no question that it must begin.

The Administrative Chief — A school system is a large organization. System and order are necessary. Good management is essential. After careful study, I make the important decisions. Staff does the gathering and sorting of information and takes care of routine decisions. There are standard procedures for staff, but when the big decisions arrive at my desk, the buck stops there. With respect to external participation in school affairs, a certain amount is probably unavoidable. I try to control the level and direction of the involvement. Too much participation leads to conflict and that's bad. I can't get my job done. Unity among board, staff, and community leads to improved education. Conflict breeds disunity. As for change, I plan it with my staff. Change should come about in an orderly, sequential manner so that it enhances rather than disrupts the organization. All major changes, of course, must be approved by me.

The Negotiator-Statesman — We make decisions cooperatively. Many groups are interested in what happens in schools. On any single issue I have to meet with the board, teachers, parents, civic officials, and even students. We then hammer out a compromise acceptable to all. It's important that each group feels that it has some influence over the final decision. In this process there has to be much outside participation. We don't see folks as outsiders. All

---

*These conceptions are, of course, abstractions drawn from the writings and behavior of urban schoolmen over the last century.

groups should be involved in decision making. That's why conflict doesn't scare me. It's the name of the game. Since there are many divergent interests, conflict is bound to occur. I have to handle it. Similarly, change results from conflicting interests being negotiated and satisfied. It goes on all the time. As conflict is inevitable, so is change.

While these leadership conceptions are presented separately, keep in mind that these views are not mutually exclusive. Shrewd professionals have played out more than one of these conceptions, often unconsciously parlaying them into effective leadership styles. While many juggled these conceptions and acted out variations, nevertheless each man had his center; one conception dominated the others. Perhaps some recent examples will make this clear.

In the long tradition of superintendents as master pedagogues, or teacher-scholars, consider Carl Hansen, who headed Washington, D.C., schools for a decade. Between 1958 and 1967 Hansen clearly played out roles of administrative chief and negotiator-statesman on certain issues, but his achievements (from his point of view) were the Amidon and Four-Track Curriculum plans — determined efforts to overhaul instruction and curriculum — and they were the work of a teacher-scholar. For an obvious example of administrative chief style, one need look no further than Benjamin Willis, Chicago's school chief between 1953 and 1966. Again, Willis played out leadership roles linked to the other conceptions, but his concern for order — managing carefully a corporate organization and being unquestionably in charge — dominated his behavior.

The negotiator-statesman conception of leadership involves bargaining, compromise, and the vocabulary of politics. Due to much patronage in school affairs in the late nineteenth century, dealing with outside partisan groups became a taboo. Of course urban schoolmen developed coalitions, and they negotiated and compromised with other members of the school family, i.e., board members, teachers, principals, etc. But that was seldom seen as politics. The negotiator-statesman conception, then, has lacked the professional stature of the other views, at least until the last few decades. Still, the conception exists with such people as Harold Spears, who was superintendent in San Francisco between 1955 and 1967. Spears demonstrated elements of the teacher-scholar and administrative chief, also, but his center was as negotiator.

Neat as all this sounds, still unexplained is why many urban schoolmen resigned under fire, fled to an early retirement, or simply left during the last decade. Consider the following:

In the 1960s and 1970s most big-city superintendents (like Hansen, Willis, and Spears) had spent at least 50 years of their lives as students and school employees. They had learned the necessary organizational expectations and skills to survive in a school system. Moreover, like these three, most urban schoolmen had made the familiar career trek from farm to city to rural teaching post, small principalship, and central office position to the penultimate job: the big-city superintendency.

In that journey urban school chiefs had absorbed the ideology of the profession. As in any profession, a series of "rights" and "wrongs" — in a word, norms — had developed around the superintendency. Refined and polished by experience, these norms were deposited in codes of ethics and organizational rules; they formed an intricate web of professional expectations. Even had they willed it, few big-city school chiefs could have escaped the embrace of this professional ideology. Key chunks of that ideology appear in the teacher-scholar and administrative chief leadership conceptions.

Consider also the impact of the larger environment in explaining why superintendents exited. "Larger environment" refers to the dominant socioeconomic trends, intellectual climate, and political movements that marked particular times and created a local context within which large urban school systems operated.

If the 1950s, for example, were years of national political conservatism, with population shifts from farm to city and city to suburb, the reassertion of humanitarian concern for racial minorities, and the expansion of schooling, then the 1960s were different. Even if the Kennedy years were not so left of center as initially thought, active federal concern for social issues, the rising tide of popular protest against racial injustice, continued economic prosperity, and the explosion of Great Society programs following Dallas brought different actors, different interest groups, different expectations, and, most important for top school executives, different demands to the urban classroom door.

Save for the Sputnik controversy, the perspective of the 1950s considered schools as an expanding, essential, highly regarded operation. Criticism there was, of course, but the general view of urban schools was positive; belief in schooling as the path to national greatness and personal success remained potent. Typical of the critics was the highly respected James B. Conant, who issued sober national reports on education. These reports pointed out weaknesses, to be sure, but they clearly mirrored affirmative beliefs in the power of public education. For the most part, his recommendations were fervently embraced by schoolmen.

In the early 1960s, however, the situation in urban schools was increasingly defined as critical. Spillover from the civil rights movement and federal interest in the poor made "culturally deprived," "de facto segregation," and, later, "community involvement" the new magic words. More important than anything else, probably, is the fact that increasing numbers of citizens were losing confidence in schools. Once defined as a crisis by the media, the problems of education became still more serious. The public view of the school shifted. Old belief systems came under attack. Education as the "great equalizer" or vehicle for individual success was increasingly questioned. If Conant's studies reflected the faith of the fifties, Ivan Illich's *De-Schooling Society* harvested the growing despair of the sixties.

What faced such nationally respected school chiefs as Hansen, Willis, and Spears were unfamiliar demands, expectations, and groups. The world seemed to have changed on them. What worked for Philadelphia's Allan Wetter, Milwaukee's Harold Vincent, and Detroit's Samuel Brownell in the 1950s seemingly failed a decade later. Remember that Carl Hansen, darling of integrationist liberals in the 1950s, got tagged as a racist a decade later — and by the same integrationist liberals.

As new crises erupted, as outside pressure escalated, urban superintendents steeped in a professional ideology that enshrined teacher-scholars and administrative chiefs as leaders responded in ways that had seemingly worked before; ways they had learned through experience and shared with brother schoolmen; ways they believed in. But their responses were often misinterpreted and sharply criticized. They now seemed inappropriate. When a Harold Spears or Benjamin Willis, for example, rejected a demand from civil rights activists for a racial census — a request that shocked their color-blind version of equality — passions were further inflamed rather than defused. They were saying the right things, pulling the right levers, and pushing the right buttons — except that the expected responses seldom turned up. They had played the game properly, but now, somehow, someone had changed the rules and neglected to tell them. In their terms, the world had gone awry.

Between 1910 and 1920 veteran superintendents must have had the same feeling. They were trained as teacher-scholars, but the cult of efficiency born in that decade triggered demands for a different kind of superintendent, a manager who could scientifically administer a corporate enterprise. As outside pressures pressed upon urban superintendents — a booming immigrant population in schools, fiscal belt-tightening, World War I — responses of teacher-scholar superintendents seldom satisfied critics. What worked during the previous decade now provoked outrage among board members and community. Professional mortality rates soared. The superintendent's world seemed awry in those days too.

Trapped then by complex organizational demands, by the ideology and leadership conceptions of the superintendency, and finally by the particular set of larger environmental forces touching the local school system, the personality, intelligence, and style of urban school administrators in both decades seemingly had little influence on what ultimately happened.

In offering this explanation, I do not argue that big-city schoolmen are wholly programmed by experience and contemporary situations to play out a preordained sequence of moves. Nor do I mean to argue that what did happen *had* to happen. This is not a scenario for a Greek tragedy, minus Mount Olympus. Personal style, leadership role, or some other factor may well have made a difference in survival ratios. After all, while many superintendents were coerced into resigning, some survived the 1960s. Harold Eibling served Columbus, Ohio, schools for 15 years, 1956 to 1971. James Redmond and Paul Briggs, appointed in Chicago and Cleveland in the mid-60s, remain in charge as of 1974.

What may explain the occasional survival is the fact that, in times when sharp external forces strike public schools, and in times when public opinion of school leadership becomes increasingly skeptical (e.g., 1910-1920, 1964-1974), a particular leadership conception and style has survival power. If so, that conception and style is that of the negotiator-statesman.

Teacher-scholar and administrative chief conceptions are bound to ideals, norms, and strategies that minimize conflict and see all problems as solvable. When conflict escalates, especially when it comes from outside the organization, a superintendent, in his efforts to minimize and eliminate it, may seriously misjudge and underestimate the sources and direction of conflict. Quite often this was the case for urban schoolmen in the last decade. The negotiator-statesman conception, at least, embraces the notion that either outside or organizational conflict is inevitable, nay, even basic to human affairs. For the 1960s in big cities this leadership style had more survival power than the others. The same would appear to be true for the rest of the 1970s.*

Contrary to the promotional literature of professional groups, the superintendent is not a man for all seasons. Many big-city school chiefs could not easily adjust to seasonal changes. Too often the fired and retired schoolmen had absorbed an ideology and leadership conception that worked for previous times but became hopelessly out of synch. Describing retired and resigned superintendents such as himself, Carl Hansen laughingly called them "dinosaurs." The fit between the times, the local political context, and the dominant conception of leadership may well determine whether a schoolman can last out his contract. To stretch the metaphor, there are fall, summer, spring, and winter superintendents, but none for all seasons.

---

*Spears retired with full honors from the San Francisco superintendency; he became far more of a negotiator-statesman in his last few years than he was in the early years of his tenure. Briggs, Redmond, Eibling, and others are shrewd school politicians, in the nonpejorative sense of the word. ☐

Reprinted from The Phi Delta Kappan, Phi Delta Kappa, December, 1974.

Origins of the Argument for Improved Female Education

GLENDA RILEY

IN THE 1830's and 40's America was experiencing basic and far-reaching social change derived to a large extent from the revolution wrought by industrialization. One significant area of change, the reformulation of woman's status and capabilities, has been recognized, but is too often ascribed to liberation through her possible or real role as a factory worker. A closer look, however, reveals that the woman who went into the factory as a worker was not liberated but simply shifted her work from home to factory. Her labor had always been absolutely necessary to keep her family economically solvent; where she had woven cloth and produced the necessary family goods at home, she now wove cloth in a factory and used her income to purchase the necessities. This woman lost neither function nor focus in her life. It was rather the middle-class woman who was most seriously affected by industrialization. Machine-produced goods replaced the goods she had once provided for her family and perhaps even deprived her of a pin money sideline "job." Unlike her working-class sister, she could not take a job because incipient social standards demanded her idleness as a status symbol for her husband. As desire for status increased, a man who could afford it even relieved his wife of household duties by hiring domestic servants. All of this increased her financial dependence on her husband, took away her feeling of usefulness to the family, and gave her increased leisure time to reflect on her problems and needs.

What might otherwise have been an intolerable situation for middle-class women was relieved by the fact that at the same time middle-class men were finding themselves compromising their tradi-

---

Mrs. Riley is Assistant Professor of History at the University of Northern Iowa.

tional Puritan ethics to meet the realities of business conditions. To assuage their guilt and protect the morality of America, they began to shift the bulk of their moral burden to the shoulders of women. As a result, women became the guardians of American morality; the last bulkhead to safeguard home, honor, and humanity. It is paradoxical that this newly ascribed "morality" created an escape route *from* the home for women who desired it. They soon learned that their morality could be the justification for almost anything they wanted to do in life. If they wished to escape their homes for a few hours a week to do "charity work" it was their moral obligation to the less fortunate; if they wished to write stories and novels it was their duty to extend their great moral influence through literature; and if they wished to pursue an interest in current affairs it was their moral responsibility so that they might influence male voters and legislators wisely. Women reformers who construed the moral guardian argument in this manner realized that while almost all areas were worthy of development, the crucial area to be opened to women was education. One of the first to advocate improved education of women as a firm first step toward the eventual granting of further concessions was the widowed Sarah Josepha Hale, a well-known author who became editor of the *Ladies' Magazine* in 1828 and of the widely-circulated *Godey's Lady's Book* in 1837. Seeing the potential of the moral guardian argument, she declared early in her career that the only way that women could wield their moral and refining forces effectively was by having their own knowledge and understanding of the world developed and heightened through suitable education.

Although this may seem to be a reasonable line of thought to contemporary observers, it was an extremely difficult point to prove to a generation that had an emotional attachment to the traditional image of women as passive, inferior, and subordinate members of society. Unfortunately, this image was being reinforced in the 1820's and early 30's on the one hand by the current religious revivalism that stressed a return to fundamentalism and the good old days, and on the other, by vague fears about women created by the first stirrings of industrialization which caused people to seek security by reaffirming old beliefs. Those who advocated increased education for women thus had to initiate their campaign by disproving a major belief associated with the traditional image; that women's minds were smaller and weaker than men's, and that women were therefore not educable. Since it could not be empirically demonstrated that women's minds had abilities equal to those of men's, the logical argument was that equality, or the lack of it, could only be proven by giving women the same educational opportunities. This had been suggested as early as 1796 by Mary Wollstonecraft who had argued that women acted like a frivolous and simple-minded sex only because they were trained as such. (1) Mrs. Hale later expanded this point in *Godey's* by challenging the belief that women were nonintellectual and subject to certain faults by their natures. Instead, she claimed, these flaws were due to an environment that blocked women's development. Mrs. Hale firmly believed that if it were not for dissenting public opinion, women in general would soon demonstrate their ambitions and talents. (2) She explained that man's intellect appeared greater because he had more opportunity to attain knowledge and because his time was not largely consumed by domestic duties. (3) Give women "equal advantages," *Godey's* maintained again and again, and women will achieve as much intellectually as do men. (4)

The expression of such sentiments was not limited solely to reformers, but was expressed through fiction as well. In a contemporary novel, *Alone*, a male character similarly argued that a feebler mind does not necessarily belong to a feebler body.

> Do away with this absurd antipathy to clever women; give them our advantages of education, and they will outshine us mentally as they do morally. The mind of a woman is a wonderful thing; like the scimitar of Saladin, it cuts through at a single stroke what our clumsy blades have hacked at in vain. Light, graceful, delicate—it does not lack power because it has beauty. (5)

Although this reasoning seemed at first glance unanswerable, it almost immediately met with a major obstacle. Why should women be given equal educational advantages? What difference would it make if their minds *were* equal to men's since they did not have to use them in the same ways as men used theirs? These traditional questions, which would have squelched reform attempts ten years earlier, now were not merely answered but were negated by the idea of the moral influence of women. In the traditionalist view, mothers had been caretakers who fed, bathed, and dressed their children until they gradually learned to do these tasks for themselves. Now that women's profound morality had at last been realized, mothers were idealized as teachers of reason, virtue, and spirituality. They were far more than caretakers in the physical sense; they were now regarded as the sole molders of the morality and character of future generations. (6)

"Mothers must constantly be employed on what the world terms small or trifling matters," Mrs. Hale declared. "Yet this care, if rightly understood and improved, may be productive of results greater and more beneficial than any which the proud philosophy of learned men have given to the world." (7) She pointed out, for example, that the evils of her time, greed and lust for riches, could be eliminated in a future and better world by mothers who teach their children "right" values. (8) While she did not wish "to see our own sex attempt to emulate the schoolmen's fame," she made it clear that the mother's "mental and moral improvement" was necessary for the true happiness and improvement of her family. (9)

This theme also appeared in fiction, and story after story preached the value of a wise mother's influence. One such story concerned a foolish mother who, after arguing the father into a fashionable boarding school education for their daughter, later found herself deserted by her "fashionable" daughter. The author concluded that the mother had misused her trust by miseducating her daughter, and was only paying the deserved consequences. (10) In another fictional situation, one cousin was reared primarily in domestic virtues while the other had been taught only the fashionable graces. After deciding that they each had but part of the necessary training, the domestic cousin insisted that,

... my daughter shall not only be made acquainted with the particular duties that belong to woman, nor yet acquire them to the neglect of the more important graces of the mind, or at the cost of the elegancies and proprieties of life, which fit us as well to be the companion as the help-mate of man, and as much the instructress as the nurse of his children. (11)

Another young heroine, given up for adoption by her dying mother, grew shallow and worldly. Her defective character development was clearly caused by the lack of a mother's influence, for when her mother, who had not died after all, returned to her after an absence of seventeen years, the evil was quickly remedied. (12)

This kind of thinking was also apparent in novels. A pertinent illustration is again Marion Harland's *Alone* which presented the moral struggle of a girl orphaned when only fifteen. Left to a harsh guardian and boarding school, Ida became headstrong, selfish, and bored. The moral was clearly drawn that any girl deprived of her mother's guiding influence tottered on the brink of moral disaster. Fortunately, Harland's heroine was shocked to her senses by disappointment in love. She drew on her great inner reserves, presumably implanted by her mother during Ida's childhood, and overcame her great handicap so successfully that she matched any well-mothered girl in virtue and morality. (13) Since there were few men or women who were crass enough to find a flaw in this idealistic conception of a mother's relationship to her child it went almost totally unchallenged. It gradually pervaded American thinking concerning women and within a short time motherhood was considered as American as apple pie. The essence of the entire philosophy was best capsulized by Harriet Beecher Stowe's character James, in *The Minister's Wooing*, when he complimented Mary: "And sometimes, Mary, when I have seen girls that, had they been cared for by good pious mothers, might have been like you, I have felt as if I could cry for them." (14)

Another interesting and unique manifestation of this idealization of a mother's benevolent moral influence was a new type of guidebook designed to help mothers fulfill their moral duties toward their children. These guides, which were often in epistolary form, were crammed with sentimental platitudes reiterating a mother's duty to instill some of her own high moral ideals in the minds of her offspring. One of the most typical of these, Mrs. Lydia Sigourney's *Letters to Mothers*, also became one of the most popular because as one reviewer phrased it, "Her precepts to mothers are all based on the law of heavenly and maternal love; and it has been her privilege to perceive the obligation imposed on women to cultivate the young mind in the right way." (15) Even the enthusiasm of the guidebooks was surpassed by another manifestation of the deification of motherhood; the tendency to attribute the deeds of great men to their mother's unending influence. Founding Fathers, presidents, statesmen, and Americans of any stature were reassessed in terms of their mothers' morality as a basis for their own great achievements. The epitome of this movement was the monument built to George Washington's mother at Fredericksburg. When it was dedicated not only did crowds of officials, several bands, and hundreds of onlookers attend the great ceremony, but the President of the United States himself was present to dedicate the statue. (16)

In case there were any dissenters who dared raise objections to this overwhelmingly popular idealization of motherhood, the argument was broadened to include the welfare of men as well as children. Like the case for educated mothers, it asserted that since women were the moral shapers of men, they could be much more effective if they had enough knowledge to understand the situations which men faced. An unsigned article in *Godey's* stated it succinctly:

> God created the woman as a *help-meet* for man in every situation; and while he, in his pride, rejects her assistance in his intellectual and moral career, he never will succeed to improve his nature and reach that perfection in knowledge, virtue and happiness, which his faculties are constituted to attain. (17)

Mrs. Hale, naturally a leading advocate of this theory, sagely concluded that "Men will never be wise while women are ignorant." (18) In a later issue, she became bold enough to add that "In education, literature, religion, she is the companion, in truth, often the mentor, of the stronger sex. . . . The destiny of the human race is thus dependent on the condition and conduct of women." (19)

If, at this point, someone objected that while it might be true that more education increased women's moral influence on men and children it might also decrease their abilities as housewives, the reformers were ready with another answer. "*A well balanced mind*," Catherine Beecher explained, "is the greatest and best preparation for her varied and complicated duties. Woman, in her sphere of usefulness, has an almost equal need of all the several faculties." (20) *Godey's* added that "Learning versus Housewifery" was a specious debate because in reality the two were complementary. For example, it was argued that a knowledge of chemistry was very helpful both in planning a family's nutrition and in the actual cooking of food. It was concluded that,

With candour and seriousness, we must say that we cannot entertain a very favorable opinion of the intellect of those men who would restrict the acquirements of females to those branches of knowledge which were thought sufficient for them forty or fifty years ago. The change of public sentiment on this subject, we consider one evidence that the world is advancing to a perfect state of civilization. (21)

Godey's also considered "Intellect versus Affection" an invalid dichotomy. The educated woman actually had more love to give her family because she not only used knowledge as a "means of sustaining her inward life," but she also learned that "the gift of life is a holy responsibility, that it is a germ from which it is her duty to cultivate a plant worthy of being transplanted to an immortal garden." (22) The educated wife could also provide for more than the physical welfare of her family as was demonstrated by the fictional case of the uneducated young wife who saw her husband turn to her more educated sister for advice, sympathy, and conversation. After some serious study, the wife was able to become more than just a housekeeper and to gain her place as her husband's intellectual companion. (23)

On the practical level, *Godey's* maintained that the house of an educated woman was usually very well managed because she wasn't busy displaying her fashionable accomplishments but was quietly and modestly efficient in the interests of the true happiness of her family (24) Furthermore, it was argued that education trained and regulated a woman's mind and that "a well-regulated mind can find time to attend to all." (25) Thus, rather than becoming a poorer housewife, an educated woman would be both efficient and modest in her domestic achievements. Mrs. Marvyn of *The Minister's Wooing* characterized just such an ideal wife and mother figure. She had been "one of the handsomest girls" her husband knew. After marriage she "brought him a thriving family of children" and in all her household arrangements was known for her "thrift and order." But, Mrs. Stowe adds,

In her bedroom, near by her work-basket, stood a table covered with books, —and so systematic were her household arrangements, that she never any day missed her regular hours for reading.... History, biography, mathematics, volumes of the encyclopaedia, poetry, novels, all alike found their time and place there,—and while she pursued her household labors, the busy, active soul within travelled cycles and cycles of thought.... (26)

Mrs. Stowe implied that far from harming the Marvyn family, this had helped them, for "her children had grown up successively around her, intelligent and exemplary." (27)

As the arguments for Mrs. Marvyn's type became more and more popular, the education of women in the United States was gradually changing. In the late summer months many newspaper ads appeared soliciting students for young ladies' seminaries and boarding schools, (28) among which Emma Willard's Troy Seminary and Catherine Beecher's Hartford Seminary were clearly the outstanding leaders of reform in women's education. As early as 1819, in her famous address to the New York legislature, Mrs. Willard had deplored the fact that female education had been left to "chance" and expressed the hope that publicly supported female seminaries "would constitute a grade of education, superior to any yet known in the history of our sex...." (29) Although this plan was unsuccessful, both she and Miss Beecher worked to inform the public of abuses and wastes in female education and to suggest alternative plans of action. (30)

Unfortunately, much of the reform energy in the United States was dissipated in the unending debate over what girls should be taught. In 1837 Auguste Carlier commented that,

Ideas in America do not yet seem to be sufficiently settled in reference to the range of women's education. This is often superficial; at other times it embraces the Latin language, mathematics, trigonometry, algebra, etc. (31)

Many reformers felt that too much time was given to training a young woman in the "superficial attainments" and that more effort should be given to making her a mature and responsible individual, (32) but there was little agreement on how this goal could best be achieved. While one author argued that "There is no incapacity in the female mind for exertion in the highest departments of literature and science," (33) another felt that women's formal education should be even better than men's because of the great and varied demands placed on a mother. (34) The Albany Female Academy believed that the inclusion of "natural sciences" such as "Physiology, Natural History, Astronomy and Philosophy" would produce "better women and better mothers,—mothers who could reply intelligently to the questionings of the little child concerning the ordinary phenomena of nature...," (35) while Catherine Beecher argued that the major defect in female education was its lack of emphasis on domestic training thus overlooking a woman's duties in favor of her intellect. (36) Another author maintained that women's education should consist primarily of training in the home since "The best schools in the world, can never supply the want of nursery culture,—of early moral and intellectual training," (37) while a female educator suggested that women's education should be pursued through public schools so that formal training could be properly supplemented by home influences. (38) Perhaps the only point they did agree upon was delineated by a contributor to the *Female Companion* who wrote,

... the influence which [woman] rightfully has to exercise over her husband and her children should be a cultivated and rational influence, sustained by the best motives and based upon the best foundation. Without education, this is difficult indeed; with education this is easily attainable. The days are past in which a sampler and a shirt, jointly with household matters and cares, formed the staple education of a lady. (39)

In addition to the confusion regarding the best methods to achieve this general goal, another major hurdle to meaningful reform was fear of the American male's reaction. One very frank article warned young women that although men may not be superior, they liked to think they were, and since women depended on men for support, the educated lady must acquire knowledge with great modesty while "looking up" to men. (40) A similar essay admitted the superiority of men, and warned girls to show dependence in everything as gratitude for any support they might receive from men. (41) Yet another wrote that,

We are grateful for our heightened privileges. We hope that those who have bestowed them, will be no losers by their liberality. Still we believe that an increase of benefits may be made profitable both to giver, and receiver. (42)

Even one of the most liberal female educators publicly announced that her reforms were not directed toward making her young ladies into *"learned* women." (43) *Godey's* shared this fear of the male ego to the extent that it assured men that the education of women would not cause them to compete with men for honor or renown, but rather would be used to attain "happiness in private life." (44) By 1844 the argument for educating women seemed to have made some progress for the *Ladies' Repository* exclaimed that "The importance of educating the female mind is now so generally acknowledged in every intelligent, Christian community" that it seems useless even to discuss it. (45)   Yet, less than a year later, Margaret Fuller Ossoli's *Woman in the Nineteenth Century* leveled a bitter attack against men for blocking improvement in women's education. "Men," she charged,

> ... will not help this work, because they are under the slavery of habit. We only ask of men to remove arbitrary barriers. Ye cannot believe it, men; but the only reason why women ever assume what is more appropriate to you, is because you prevent them from finding out what is fit for themselves. (46)

While men provided convenient scapegoats for the problems of reform in women's education, many realized that the hesitancy of women themselves would have to be overcome. Mrs. Hale constantly admonished women that reform and improvement in their education would not come from "without." Women, she wrote, must unite in their own behalf and turn their charity toward themselves. (47) She advised them to prove women's capabilities and desires for education by beginning a systematic course of reading and study which would remedy some of the defects in their knowledge. (48)   She followed this with lists of recommended titles, and with suggestions urging women to find a learned correspondent, to write brief sketches of everyday events, to jot down their thoughts, and to keep a commonplace book, all in order to keep their minds alert and to clarify their thoughts. (49)   Mrs. Ossoli similarly enjoined women, "It is my belief that something effectual might be done by women, if they would only consider the subject, and enter upon it in the true spirit, a spirit gentle, but firm, and which feared the offence of none." (50)

The situation regarding female education in general might best be summed up by another comment of Mrs. Ossoli's.

Thus vaguely are these questions proposed and discussed at present. But their being proposed at all implies much thought and suggests more. Many women are considering within themselves, what they need that they have not, and what they can have, if they find they need it. Many men are considering whether women are capable of being and having more than they are and have, *and*, whether, if so, it will be best to consent to improvement in their condition. (51)

Those who desired changes were encouraged that there was so much discussion and thought on the subject of female education by both men and women, but they also realized that although some female seminaries were being founded, the issue was still too abstract. In an attempt to achieve more concrete progress, the argument was broadened to support the involvement of women directly in education as teachers. The conception of women as moral guardians was ideally suited to justify this idea. It was pointed out that since children's minds were unformed they should be shaped only by the pure and delicate sense of a woman teacher, (52) a line of reasoning which was particularly relevant to a generation whose schools were still church-oriented and thus very much concerned with achieving the greatest degree of "morality" possible in education. (53)

Supporters of women as teachers emphasized that, unlike men, women had an innately high character which suited them for teaching the young. (54) Not only was woman "constitutionally fitted by her Creator for the duties of a teacher," (55) but it was really her mission to educate since her sphere of living embraced all areas of knowledge and thus fitted her by experience for teaching. (56) Furthermore, she had a capacity for affection that would make the students anxious to respond to her, and she had maternal instincts which would allow her to build a greater familiarity and rapport than would be proper for the "other sex." (57) It is not surprising that the new heroines of literature, the indispensable women, often numbered among their activities a competency in teaching. Gerty of *The Lamplighter*, for example, an indispensable woman from eight years of age on, somehow managed to work in an education which prepared her for school teaching. This did not blunt her femininity or her moral example, but heightened her inspirational effect on those around her. (58)

Since there are no employment figures available for this period it is impossible to determine the actual increase in the number of women teachers, but it was not uncommon to see newspaper advertisements placed by female teachers desiring teaching positions. (59) Mrs. Hale either believed they were increasing or wished to make her readers believe it, for time after time she rejoiced that "the station of instructress is constantly gaining, in importance and respectability, on the public mind." (60) She was delighted when a leading male educator, Horace Mann, advocated female teachers on the basis of their moral influence. "The great advantages of employing female teachers in preference to men are beginning to be understood," she wrote. "Horace Mann ... has given his opinion thus: 'Females govern with less resort to physical force, and exert a more kindly, humanizing and refining influence upon the dispositions and manners of their pupils.'" (61) Mrs. Hale's views were also shared by another educator, Henry Barnard, who worked zealously to establish women as teachers. His teachers' institutes did much to elevate the position of women and he proudly claimed that the "introduction of a large number of female teachers, in winter as well as in summer, has greatly improved the discipline, moral influence, and *manners* of the Rhode Island public schools." (62) Female teachers were further advocated by the woman educator, Mary Lyon, who believed that,

Teaching is really the business of almost every useful woman. No woman is well educated who has not all the acquisitions necessary for a good teacher. She needs thorough mental culture, a well-balanced character, a benevolent heart, an ability to communicate knowledge and apply it to practice, an acquaintance with human nature, and the power of controlling the minds of others. (63)

With the efforts of such enthusiastic reformers behind them it is not surprising that many women appeared to enter the teaching profession during the 1830's and 40's. (64) Mrs. Hale confidently attributed this trend to the influence of *Godey's*. In 1846 she claimed that the *Lady's Book* had

... been the pioneer of all these improvements in female education, and the steady advocate for this enlarged sphere of female talent and influence. Very few females were employed as teachers in the schools in Boston, even, when we first began to advocate the plan: now they are employed, not only there but throughout the state, during winter as well as summer, in the proportion of nearly two female teachers to one of the other sex. (65)

If women teachers were "fast becoming the fashion" as she claimed, (66) it is probably more valid to attribute it to the willingness of men to give up a profession that offered neither wealth nor respect for a more rewarding position in industry. Men also seemed hesitant to go into barely settled frontier areas as teachers, thus creating opportunities for women. Missionary and other societies were formed for the specific purpose of recruiting and sending female teachers westward and their efforts were enthusiastically supported by female reformers. (67) It has also been suggested that when the financial panic of 1837 forced destitute "ladies" to support themselves, they found teaching ideal since they usually had some education. Their financial need absolved them of strong-mindedness or feminist aggressiveness, so that their entry into teaching tended to cast a glow of respectability over all women teachers. (68)

The significance of the employment of women as teachers is not only what caused it, but how it changed American beliefs about women. As more and more women became teachers and proved themselves willing and capable, many Americans accepted teaching as part of woman's sphere. Not only was she now considered educable, but she could enter, with public approval, a profession which had always been dominated by men. By the 1840's many Americans agreed, consciously or unconsciously, with the female educator who had said,

The profession of teaching is, then, one which is open to those of our sex who are disposed to gain for themselves an honorable standing and support, to be useful to the world, and to cultivate the talents which God has given them. (69)

The import of this change in attitude is heightened by the realization that it was a major step toward the organized women's rights movement of later years. Not only did the drive for improved female education provide women with knowledge, organizational techniques, and awareness, but it helped create a public image of American women as intelligent, competent individuals who desired, and perhaps even deserved, broadened horizons, and who were capable of striving toward them on their own behalf.

Notes

1. Mary Wollstonecraft, *A Vindication of the Rights of Woman* (London: Walter Scott, 1891), p. xxxvi.
2. "Female Education," *Godey's Lady's Book*, XIV (June 1837), 252.
3. "Importance of Female Education," *Godey's Lady's Book*, XX (February 1840), 92.

4. Mary W. Hale, "Comparative Intellectual Character of the Sexes," *Godey's Lady's Book*, XX (June 1840), 273.
5. Marion Harland, *Alone* (Richmond: A. Morris, 1855), p. 128.
6. "Woman," *Godey's Lady's Book*, XXI (July 1840), 34.
7. "Editor's Table," *Godey's Lady's Book*, XXXI (September 1845), 128.
8. Mrs. Sarah J. Hale, "Cause and Cure; or, Conversations by the Fireside," *Godey's Lady Book*, XXIV (February 1842), 112-15.
9. "Editor's Table," *Godey's Lady's Book*, XXII (December 1841), 294-97.
10. "The Fashionable Daughter and Unfashionable Parents," *Godey's Lady's Book*, XXXII (March 1846), 109-17.
11. "Reminiscences," *The Knickerbocker*, II (January 1838), 21.
12. Henry F. Harrington, "The Childless Mother," *Godey's Lady's Book*, XXVI (April 1843), 175-83.
13. Harland, *Alone*.
14. Harriet Beecher Stowe, *The Minister's Wooing* (New York: Derby and Jackson, 1859), p. 70.
15. Review of *Letters to Mothers*, by Mrs. Lydia H. Sigourney, *The Knickerbocker*, XII (October 1838), 369-70.
16. "Monument to the Mother of Washington," *The Knickerbocker*, II (July 1833), 72-73.
17. "Maternal Instruction," *Godey's Lady Book*, XXX (March 1845), 108.
18. "The Ladies' Mentor," *Godey's Lady's Book*, XIV (May 1837), 229.
19. "Editor's Table," *Godey's Lady's Book*, XXIII (August 1841), 94.
20. Catherine Beecher, *Suggestions Respecting Improvements in Education, Presented to the Trustees of the Hartford Female Seminary, and Published at Their Request* (Hartford, Conn.: Packard and Butler, 1829), p. 42.
21. "Learning vs. Housewifery," *Godey's Lady's Book*, XIX (August 1839), 95.
22. "Intellect vs. Affection—In Woman," *Godey's Lady's Book*, XXXIII (August 1846), 86.
23. Mrs. Mary H. Parsons, "The Wife and Sister," *Godey's Lady's Book*, XX (January 1840), 27-32.
24. "Intellect vs. Affection—In Woman," *Godey's Lady's Book*, XXXIII (August 1846), 86.
25. Mrs. Lydia H. Sigourney, *Letters to Young Ladies* (New York: Harpers, 1841), p. 81.
26. Stowe, *Minister's Wooing*, pp. 102-03.
27. *Ibid.*, p. 105.
28. See for example the *New York Tribune*, August 28, 1841, p. 1.
29. Mrs. Emma H. Willard, *Address to the Members of the Legislature of New York Proposing a Plan For Improving Female Education* (Middlebury: J. W. Copeland, 1819), pp. 1-46.
30. Beecher, *Improvements in Education*, p. 4.

31. Auguste Carlier, *Marriage in the United States* (Boston, Mass.: DeVries, Ifarra and Company, 1837), p. 75.
32. Mrs. Lydia H. Sigourney, "Superficial Attainments," *Godey's Lady's Book*, XXI (July 1840), 29-31.
33. "Education," *The Knickerbocker*, V (June 1835), 515.
34. Caleb Atwater, "Female Education," *Ladies' Repository*, I (January 1841), 10.
35. Quoted in Clifton J. Furness, ed., *The Genteel Female* (New York: Alfred A. Knopf, 1931), p. 291.
36. Beecher, *Improvements in Education*, p. 58.
37. "Education of Young Ladies," *The Knickerbocker*, VI (November 1835), 381.
38. Mrs. Lincoln Phelps, "Remarks On The Education of Girls," *Godey's Lady's Book*, XVIII (June 1839), 253-55.
39. Quoted in Furness, *Genteel Female*, p. 217.
40. "Thoughts on the Happiness of Woman as Connected with the Cultivation of Her Mind," *Godey's Lady's Book*, XV (November 1837), 204.
41. Mrs. Elizabeth Sanford, *Woman, In Her Social and Domestic Character* (London: Longman, Brown, Green, and Longman, 1842), pp. 14-15.
42. Sigourney, *Letters to Young Ladies*, p. 10.
43. Mrs. Elizabeth Sandford, *Female Improvement* (London: Longmans, 1836), p. 204.
44. "The Ladies' Mentor," *Godey's Lady's Book*, XV (July 1837), 46-47.
45. J. S. Tomlinson, "Address On Female Education," *Ladies' Repository*, IV (August 1844), 246.
46. Margaret Fuller Ossoli, *Woman in the Nineteenth Century* (New York: Greeley and McElrath, 1845), pp. 51, 107, 158.
47. "The Ladies' Mentor," *Godey's Lady's Book*, XV (August 1837), 93-94
48. "Editor's Table," *Godey's Lady's Book*, XVI (March 1838), 143.
49. "Editor's Table," *Godey's Lady's Book*, XVI (April 1838), 190.
50. Ossoli, *Woman in the Nineteenth Century*, p. 153.
51. *Ibid.*, p. 19.
52. "The Ladies' Mentor," *Godey's Lady's Book*, XV (July 1837), 46.
53. See Timothy L. Smith, "Protestant Schooling and American Nationality, 1800-1850," *The Journal of American History*, LIII (March 1967), 679-95.
54. Catherine E. Beecher, *The Evils Suffered by American Women and Children* (New York: Harper and Brothers, 1846), p. 11.
55. "The Ladies' Mentor," *Godey's Lady's Book*, XIV (April 1837), 185.
56. "The Ladies' Mentor," *Godey's Lady's Book*, XV (November 1837), 230.
57. Beecher, *Improvements in Education*, p. 50.
58. Maria Cummins, *The Lamplighter* (Boston, Mass.: J. P. Jewett and Company, 1854).

59. See for example the *New York Tribune*, April 16, 1841, p. 3.
60. "Editor's Table," *Godey's Lady's Book*, XXVII (September 1843), 142.
61. "Editor's Table," *Godey's Lady Book*, XXXII (June 1846), 284.
62. Quoted in Ralph C. Jenkins and Gertrude Chandler Warner, *Henry Barnard: An Introduction* (Hartford, Conn.: The Connecticut State Teachers Association, 1937), p. 45.
63. Quoted in A. E. Winship, *Great American Educators* (New York: American Book Company, 1900), p. 76.
64. Robert M. Smuts, *Women and Work in America* (New York: Columbia University Press, 1959), p. 19.
65. "Editor's Table," *Godey's Lady's Book*, XXXIII (November 1846), 236.
66. "Editor's Table," *Godey's Lady's Book*, XXXVI (April 1848), 247.
67. Beecher, *Evils Suffered by American Women and Children*, p. 12.
68. Patricia Thomson, *The Victorian Heroine: A Changing Ideal, 1837-1873* (London: Oxford University Press, 1956), pp. 37-39.
69. Mrs. Almira H. Phelps, *The Female Student, or Lectures to Young Ladies on Female Education* (New York: Leavitt, Lord, and Company, 1836), p. 420.

Reprinted from The History of Education Quarterly, Volume 9, Number 4, Winter, 1969.

SEMESTER: WEEK EIGHT

REQUIRED READINGS

Church

Part III: The Retreat from Commonality, 1840-1920, Chapter 7: <u>Training the Hand: The Rise of Special Education</u> (35 pp.)

Dye

Gersman, Elinor Mondale. "Progressive Reform of the St. Louis School Board, 1897" <u>History of Education Quarterly</u>. V.10, No.1, Spring, 1970. (19 pp.)

Johnson, Ronald M. "Politics and Pedagogy: The 1892 Cleveland School Reform" <u>Ohio History</u>. V.84, No.4, Autumn, 1975. (11 pp.)

MEETINGS

Monday

Lecture: William Torrey Harris

Tuesday

Lecture: Calvin Milton Woodward

Wednesday

Lecture: Legal Concerns in Schooling

Thursday and Friday

Small Groups:

CHURCH TEXTBOOK STUDY GUIDE: CHAPTER 7

TRAINING THE HAND: THE RISE OF SPECIAL EDUCATION

1. special education
2. common schooling
3. differentiated schooling
4. hand training
5. manual training
6. dexterity training
7. vocational training
8. industrial education
9. generic term
10. reform school
11. moral rehabilitation
12. Charles Loring Brace
13. preventative industrial training
14. New York Children's Aid Society
15. Horatio Alger stories
16. moral disinfection
17. inculcation of industriousness
18. assimilation to American values
19. truancy
20. vagrancy
21. neglected children
22. the dangerous populations
23. American kindergarten
24. blackness as a crime
25. blackness as a defect
26. Samuel Chapman Armstrong
27. Hampton Institute
28. Morrill Act (1862)
29. lack of moral strength and industrial energy
30. black teacher as a model of moral character

31. Booker T. Washington
32. Tuskegee Institute, Alabama
33. Atlanta Compromise (1895)
34. Peabody Fund
35. Slater Fund

36. Atticus C. Haygood
37. J. L. M. Curry
38. Anna Jeannes Fund
39. Phelps-Stokes Fund
40. Julius Rosenwald Fund

41. black accomodationist view
42. W. E. B. DuBois
43. talented tenth
44. Calvin Milton Woodward
45. The Manual Training School of Washington University

46. William Torrey Harris
47. Felix Adler
48. New York Ethical Culture Society
49. domestic science
50. home economics

51. self-discipline
52. will power
53. coordination of hand and eye
54. coordination of hand and mind
55. hand, heart, and head

Progressive Reform of the St. Louis School Board, 1897

ELINOR MONDALE GERSMAN

THE PROGRESSIVE IDEA of reform developed through years of experimentation in St. Louis and achieved success in the 1897 School Board reorganization. (1) As early as 1877 the tendency to treat the city as a separate entity became apparent when a new charter separating the city from the county was effected. Previously there had been both a city and a county government in the same area, each with two legislative houses and the power to tax. The "dual double-headed system then in force," one critic argued, "was anomalous and absurd." The two bodies, both of which levied taxes, did not really represent the people, since neither was elected at large. (2) The new charter, although retaining the two-house City Council, required one house to be elected at large; efficiency was increased through extended terms for most officials and an increase of administrative powers for the mayor. (3)

Reform intentions were stated in a series of editorials in the *Missouri Republican*, which argued that the charter ensured a representative council because the upper house was to be elected at large. It also ensured "a better class of men in the council, for who will assert that our ordinary type of alderman could be elected by the general vote of the city?" It would abolish "the execrable system of ruling the city by ward representatives" and reduce city expenses by substituting a compact economical system in place of the previous bungling caused by a lack of central authority. (4) Not everyone liked the new charter. Although the *Republican* said it was framed in the interests of all taxpayers, others said it discriminated in favor of the rich. (5) An interesting feature of the discussion

---

Mrs. Gersman is Assistant Professor of Education at Wagner College.

Reprinted from The History of Education Quarterly, Volume 10, Number 1, Spring, 1970.

was the explicit belief that a businessman, experienced in handling a large office force, would make the best official. Having a businessman in charge of an office guaranteed "thorough practical efficiency and at the same time guarded against political influence and abuse of the power committed to it." (6)

Until 1887 representation on the St. Louis School Board was based on ward elections; in that year the Missouri legislature passed a law requiring fourteen members to be chosen from school districts of two contiguous wards each, and seven members to be elected from the entire city. This change attests the success of the at-large method of election in gaining representation for the upper class and increasing efficiency. The reformers wished to remove German and other curricular innovations from the elementary schools for reasons of economy and needed a majority on the School Board. The *St. Louis Post-Dispatch*, a barometer of reform sentiment, claimed that the organizational change was endorsed by leading educators of the city and "is antagonized only by the small ward interests which are disturbed by it." Marshall S. Snow, professor of history at Washington University, agreed that the bill ensured freedom from that "bane of good administration of city affairs in any branch of its government—the ward politician." (7)

A "Citizens' Ticket" won at the polls, seventeen of their twenty-one candidates being elected, including all of those who ran at large. The members of the new board, particularly those elected at large, displayed a noticeably greater social prominence than the former members, prominence being measured by occupation, education, residence in the outlying, large-area wards and in the fashionable West End, honorary biographies in books about prominent St. Louisans and listings in *Gould's Blue Book*, which was the social register of the day. Of the 1886 School Directors, 32.1% had been listed in *Gould's*, 10.7% were the subjects of honorary biographies and 21.4% lived in the West End; of those with known occupations 10.7% were employees, 60.7% owned small businesses, 3.6% were large businessmen and 21.4% were professional men with some higher education. In the 1887 board the percentage of small businessmen increased to 66.7%, partly because the number of professional men decreased to 14.3% and partly because the number of employees dropped to 4.8%; big business representation increased to

14.3%. *Gould's Blue Book* listed 52.4%, there were honorary biographies of 14.3% and 38.1% lived in the West End. According to the reform theory men elected from the entire city should have been of higher status than the board as a whole. The percentages for the at-large members taken alone show this to be true: 57.1% were small businessmen, 28.6% were big businessmen, 14.3% were professional men and none were employees. The at-large group had 85.7% listed in *Gould's Blue Book*, 28.6% in honorary biographies and 42.9% living in West End residences.

F. N. Judson, who was a writer of the reorganization legislation, leader of the Citizens' Ticket and president of the new board, stated the reform position. The electoral mandate, he said, had approved keeping politics out of public school management, providing room for every child without raising taxes, observing rigid economy in construction and teaching no other language than English in primary and district schools. Both of his reports as president emphasized that business techniques were being adopted, especially the hiring of experts to execute school affairs efficiently, since board members served without compensation and could give only such time as might be spared from their business affairs. The new board also introduced the Australian ballot for School Board elections. (8)

While St. Louisans sought an acceptable arrangement for administering their public schools, changes were taking place across the country. During the late nineteenth century the American public school, like other American institutions, was unable to keep pace with the rapid urbanization and industrialization. As a result public education was subject to frequent criticism; one of the most influential critics was Joseph Mayer Rice, a pediatrician, who had studied pedagogy in Germany. He wrote a series of articles based on his observations in thirty-six cities which appeared in *The Forum* during the winter of 1892-1893 and later in a book. Rice was highly critical of political influence in the schools. Advocates of local control, he said, argued that it provided the opportunity for local people to improve the schools; they forgot that it also left the schools at the mercy of local politicians. He praised school boards with few members for their efficiency, the ease of placing responsibility and the fact that they were usually removed from politics. He recommended, in particular, a recent change adopted in Cleveland. (9)

The school board reorganization in Cleveland became widely known in education circles through the efforts of Judge Andrew S. Draper, the first superintendent under the system. The *American School Board Journal* reprinted the Ohio law legalizing the change; (10) and Draper wrote an explanatory article which appeared in *The Forum*, the *Educational Review*, and the *American School Board Journal* in 1893. The law provided for a school council of seven men elected from the entire city for two years, a school director to handle business matters and a superintendent appointed by the director with the approval of the council. (11) The National Educational Association promptly made Draper a member of its Committee of Fifteen on current school problems. The committee made Draper head of the subcommittee on organization of city school systems; Draper's report duly advocated adoption of as much of the Cleveland plan as local conditions permitted. (12)

The Draper Report established a number of guidelines for school boards wishing to reorganize but not able to achieve a plan similar to Cleveland's. The report specifically opposed ward representatives' seeking advantages for their own sections while the common interest suffered. Appointment of board members was recommended as the best way to remove politics from school affairs; the best person to make the appointments was the mayor, who, having been elected at large, could be held directly responsible by the entire city for the quality of his appointees. Election at large was an acceptable alternative if appointment was not possible. In either case, the members should be nonpartisan so that the board might stay completely out of politics. The board should perform only legislative functions; executive functions should be divided between two salaried men, one in charge of education and the other in charge of business. Both board members and officers should have secure terms of office, the longer the better. Even the name of the new board received attention; "Board of Education" was believed to have the proper aura.

This plan became an ideal for reform-minded educators during the 1890s and the early twentieth century. The acceptance of Progressive ideals and of the need of upper-class participation is evident in the report. In 1898 an anonymous article written by three superintendents appeared in the *Atlantic Monthly*; the third section, apparently written by L. H. Jones, who had succeeded Draper in Cleveland, made the purpose clear. The change in election methods made it possible for good men to get in office, but there was a further difficulty. "Businessmen of unusual ability, and of large business interests of their own to look after, cannot afford to accept positions on a school board under existing conditions. The only way to secure the services of such men is to require of them only the direction of the general policy and work of the schools." (13)

This discussion among educators was not lost on St. Louisans because it confirmed their own experience, and in 1897 a second reorganization of the School Board completed the change to direct election of members from the entire city, decreased the number of members to twelve and made the board a legislative body. However, local problems made the change possible. At the beginning of 1896 eleven directors of the School Board were up for reelection. This board was no less socially prominent than the one elected in 1887. The listings in the social *Gould's Blue Book* had dropped to 33.3% and West End residence to 19.1%, while the number of employees increased to 14.3%; but these changes were balanced by increases in big business representation to 28.6%, in higher education to 19.1% and in honorary biographies to 28.6%. The at-large members continued to be above the overall board level in important categories: big business, *Gould's Blue Book* and honorary biographies each showed 42.9%, while 57.1% now lived in outlying, large-area wards including the West End.

Years later this board was described by a panel of educators as "a typical city school board of that period, and even of the present period, endowed with large discretionary powers." (14) The board could determine the amount of money it needed, levy taxes within limits set by the legislature, and distribute the money as it saw fit. It made its own procedural rules but was not bound by them, and it directed and controlled its own elections. The abuse of these powers consolidated opposition to the board during 1896 and gave reformers the upper hand. (15)

As the election in March 1896 neared, a nonpartisan ticket of four candidates for the at-large positions entered the field sponsored by "some of the best-known and most influential men of both parties locally." The candidates, representing large businesses and divided between the two parties, were strongly endorsed by the *Post-Dispatch* and the Democratic City Central Committee because they would "redeem the schools from political influence and corrupt ring-rule." (16) The previous board was believed to have been unduly influenced by the Republican machine, despite its apparent social quality. Therefore the Republican convention to select a ticket caused a cry of outrage when it adopted a resolution saying:

Resolved, That all candidates nominated in this convention be instructed to enter a caucus of the Republican members of the School Board and be guided by the decision of the caucus in matters pertaining to the shaping of the public school system, in accordance with the Republican principle, and candidates accepting nominations of this convention so pledge themselves. (17)

The campaign was complicated by charges of duplicity and corruption; an investigation of the charges, despite promises of honesty and thoroughness, proved to have been an attempt at whitewashing and added fuel to already leaping flames of suspicion. (18) Despite the adverse publicity the Republican ticket won, apparently because of public apathy; only 28,558 ballots were cast out of an estimated 148,000 qualified voters. The Republican *St. Louis Globe-Democrat* said of the election, ". . . The Republicans carried four members at large and three out of eight district members. It was not quite as big a victory as we expected, but it will do." (19)

The new board showed a decided drop in social status, apparently because of political manipulation and public apathy. None of the newly elected directors were included in biographical collections on well-known St. Louisans, and no director is known to have had any kind of higher education, the only professional person on the board being an architect who admitted having planned only one house during the previous eight years. (20) The category of employees included 28.6% of the newly constituted board, small business men 47.6% and big business only 9.5%; other categories showed little change. It is of importance to note that even in this situation the at-large members were above the board average in some categories: 14.3% were in big business, 57.1% were listed in *Gould's Blue Book* and 42.9% lived in large-area wards including the West End. Nonetheless the election crystallized the opposition of the so-called "better" people against the "machine" by exposing the strength and intentions of the Republican party organization while pointing up the reformers' need to organize and rally public opinion.

The actions of the new board did nothing to allay reform anxieties. The first problem facing the new board was the election of officers; after a week of well publicized deadlock and the airing of unsavory tales from his past, Henry Bus was made president. There was a question of whether Bus, who was also a deputy sheriff, was legally a director; and it was discovered that one new member, H. H. Rebenack, had not fulfilled the legal requirement of paying a school tax, although he had paid a merchant's license tax. The cases of Bus and Rebenack were laid before the Missouri Supreme Court, and Bus quickly resigned his post in the sheriff's office, hoping that this would solve his problem. (21) The *Post-Dispatch* pointedly wondered why a man without private resources would drop a salaried post in order to keep an unsalaried one. Until recently, it said, school directors had usually been men of means who could meet the financial requirements of the position. This remark was accompanied by a statement attributed to Louis J. Holthaus, a member of the former board, that a poor man could easily make $5,000 a year out of a board membership. (22)

Having chosen a president, the board had to take steps to arrange an election in the Tenth District, where the representative had resigned. The district was normally Democratic, and it was believed that John P. Kelleher of the Democratic City Central Committee would win. At the behest of the board's Republican caucus, the election committee of the board, consisting of six Republicans and one Democrat, chose only Republicans as judges and clerks for the polls. Since the committee refused to listen to protests, the Democrats of the Tenth District filed a petition in the state Supreme Court for a writ of mandamus, giving them equal representation in each precinct. After the Republican directors tried with a notable lack of finesse to appoint pseudo-Democrats, the Supreme Court postponed the election and summoned the board to appear and show reason why it should not be cited for contempt of court. The entire board appeared on May 11 before the Court, which ruled that eight

Republicans, all members of the caucus, were to spend ten days in jail and pay a $25 fine plus $200 in court costs. The election was to be arranged with all possible speed, after which the directors would serve their jail sentences. The Democratic poll representatives were chosen and the election was held on May 26; Kelleher won. The jail terms were served in June, forcing the directors to miss the national Republican Convention, which was held in St. Louis that year. (23)

During the summer the Supreme Court ruled that Henry Bus's holding the positions of deputy sheriff and school director did not incapacitate him for either; but Rebenack's seat on the board was declared vacant because he had not qualified. An election was held in September, and Republican Robert Paulus, a contractor, was elected. (24)

In 1895 St. Louisans had established a Civic Federation as a permanent organization for civic reform; its charter proclaimed it to be nonpolitical and nonsectarian, embracing all interests in the city for the purpose of "promoting the honesty, efficiency and welfare of its citizens...." (25) In fact the federation appears to have been composed mainly of businessmen and professional men; in July 1896 it was organized for action under the leadership of Dr. W. W. Boyd, minister of the socially prominent Second Baptist Church. (26) This group planned to combat the philosophy of men like Henry Bus, who said of himself: "I always take care of my friends. I care nothing for my enemies. When a man votes with me, I take care of him." (27) To Bus this was an attitude of integrity, but it enraged the reformers who felt that the only basis for awarding a position should be merit. Two different moral philosophies as well as two social classes confronted one another.

For its first project the federation chose to investigate the heating contracts that the school directors were negotiating with the Peck-Williamson Company. The federation's historian noted, "The first step taken by the Federation was to call upon the courts to declare void a contract which had been let in violation not only of the rules of the board, but of the plainest dictates of business sense." The case became known as A. L. Berry vs. the School Board, because Berry, the federation treasurer, took action in his own name. (28) A circuit court judge declared, in ruling on the case, that no rule of the board was binding on it under the terms of its charter. This was not new information, but the *Post-Dispatch* played up the possible results of such power in the hands of the kind of men who made up the School Board. "Re-doubled efforts are to be made by the Civic Federation for the reform of the School Board, on account of Judge Valliant's decision in the Peck-Williamson injunction case," the paper said. (29)

The case of Berry *vs.* the School Board was appealed to the Supreme Court, which ruled in favor of Berry in May 1897. By that time the heating system provided by Peck-Williamson was already in use, but the federation's use of the case to arouse public interest through exposure of the board's business methods and the characters of the directors had also achieved success. In November 1896 the federation appointed a committee of nine men, "all gentlemen of unquestioned probity, high talent and specially fitted by past experience for the work they have on hand," to draft a bill for reorganizing the School Board. (30) Several members had worked on the 1887 law, and several were former board members; the committee was headed by F. N. Judson. This committee wrote to cities all over the country for information and opinions, and, in its final report of December 27, 1896, said:

The bill which we have unanimously agreed upon is based upon the recommendations of the National Educational Association, with modifications to conform to our local conditions. It provides for a separation of the business from the educational department of the system, vesting each in a responsible official, with an honorary supervisory board of twelve members appointed by the Mayor of the city, to be known as the Board of Education. The head of the educational department is the Superintendent of Instruction, who is responsible for the condition of the schools and has powers fitted to his responsibility. (31)

The similarities between this brief description and the Draper Report's recommendations are clearly apparent.

This Civic Federation bill was introduced in the house of representatives of the Missouri legislature on January 14, 1897. A number of other School Board bills were filed later, but the Civic Federation bill had the advantage of being written by lawyers and backed by men with the means and the will to spend as much time in the state capital as was necessary to guide the bill through the legislature. Furthermore, as the *Globe-Democrat* pointed out, the legislature, mainly Democratic, would not object to changing the structure of the predominantly Republican School Board. (32)

Although it was a Republican paper, the *Globe-Democrat* took a stand against the School Board during the fall of 1896 as the unsavory details of the heating contracts were exposed. However, the paper strongly opposed the appointive clause in the Civic Federation bill, and in this it expressed the popular will. (33) After nearly going down to defeat because of the section requiring appointment of board members by the mayor, the Civic Federation bill was amended, in accordance with the alternative recommended by the Draper Report, so that the board members would be elected in a citywide contest. Reformers had liked this feature of the bill because they felt it would be possible to pressure the mayor to appoint good men, but it was rejected by most people, and, probably more important, the Democratic legislature was unwilling to give appointive functions to the usually Republican St. Louis mayor. A. L. Berry, interviewed after a week at the state capital, said fourteen Republican representatives from St. Louis had opposed the appointive feature of the bill; this had looked very bad to the legislators, who had moved to postpone the bill indefinitely. In order to save the bill, Berry had changed the appointive feature to election at large, despite contrary orders from the Federation. (34)

The law, as it was passed and signed by the governor on March 23, 1897, required the election at large of twelve members to a "Board of Education" which would have the power to control school property and levy such taxes as might be needed within limitations set by the state. The members must be at least thirty years old, citizens and residents and taxpayers for three years, and must hold no other office; they must take an oath that these things were true, and they were to receive no compensation. They would hold office for six years, four being elected at municipal elections every second year. Vacancies within the board would be filled by the mayor until the next election. Four main officers were to be appointed, a superintendent of public instruction, a commissioner of school buildings, a secretary and treasurer and an auditor. All rules and by-laws of the board would be binding on it until altered. Janitors and building engineers were to be chosen by competitive examination, while teachers were to be appointed for merit. Both the superintendent of instruction and the commissioner of buildings were to be appointed for a term of four years and were, within legal restrictions, to have complete power of administration within their own areas. (35)

This law carried out the purpose of the Cleveland plan and the Draper Report in spirit if not in letter. It centralized authority by decreasing the size of the board and making it responsible to the entire city while separating business functions from educational ones, and legislative functions from executive ones. These separations, with the appointment of officials, reduced the time a member must devote to board business, clearing the way for busy men to serve. The terms were long, giving the board stability, and the rules of the board would be binding on it. The board would continue to levy taxes separately from city taxes, as was recommended by both Draper and James C. Boykin, the city expert of the U.S. Office of Education. The law combined national Progressive ideas with local experience and practical necessity.

The law required an election within sixty days, and the Civic Federation prepared for action. Since the parties had little time, neither of them chose to go through the necessary processes to put their names on the ballot; the main effort of all groups centered on selection of an appropriate ticket. Prominent men and women worked to have "fit" men elected, and there was talk, as there was in every school election, of the eligibility of women for the School Board. Dr. Boyd, leader of the Civic Federation, hoped that an arrangement such as existed in Kansas City might be made whereby each party nominated half of the candidates, so that the board would be effectively nonpartisan. (36) The Civic Federation, however, realistically assessed the political situation in St. Louis and decided to make up a ticket of seven Republicans and five Democrats taken from a list of men believed to be acceptable to the Federation's central council. Since the support of the parties was necessary if such a ticket were to succeed, the council appointed two committees to confer with each of the parties.

As Dr. Boyd told the story later, the Democratic Party agreed to the division and to a ticket of the federation's choosing. The Republicans under Chauncey I. Filley, the party leader in Missouri,

155

met with a federation committee of three men led by Professor Calvin M. Woodward of Washington University. Filley evidently persuaded them to accept a named ticket of eight Republicans and four Democrats chosen by Filley and Woodward from the approved federation list. However, to the concern of the federation, it soon became known that Filley had, on his own initiative, changed four names among the Republicans. When this ticket was finally approved by the Civic Federation central council by a vote of five to four, Boyd announced his withdrawal from the federation; its principles had been compromised, he said. In an interview he added that Woodward should be suspended because he had allowed himself to be placed on the ticket.

Boyd was especially bitter because the organization had agreed to endorse the Woodward-Filley ticket out of friendship for Woodward. However, Boyd's report of the discussion shows practicality to have been the deciding factor. F. N. Judson, a member of the central council, realized that Republican cooperation was essential if the purpose of the law were to be realized. "He [Judson] said the Democratic party amounted to nothing, being rent by factions, while the Republicans have thoroughly organized and could elect whom they pleased. The presence of eight good men insured a good Board." (37) The *Post-Dispatch*, although it disapproved any connection with Filley, found very little to criticize in the Woodward-Filley ticket, known as the Nonpartisan Ticket, while the *Globe-Democrat* was pleased at the turn of events. The Democrats refused to accept the ticket, saying that it did not have the agreed-upon division and that Filley had chosen the four Democrats who were on it. They chose their own ticket, known as the Citizens' Democratic Ticket, made up entirely of Democrats and including one woman.

A number of women who were disappointed at the presence of only one woman on the Democratic ticket filed a Women's Ticket which, for lack of signatures, failed to get on the ballot. Two other tickets were filed: the Liberal Ticket and the Peoples' Ticket both had a number of old board members on them and had borrowed candidates from the Nonpartisan Ticket without their approval. (38) A comparison of these tickets shows that only the Nonpartisan Ticket can be said to have represented the professional and large business men by more than one or two token candidates. This situation must have given the Nonpartisan Ticket an advantage, since there was only one ticket for reform supporters to choose; the opposition was divided among the other three tickets.

The campaign engendered a great deal of interest because of the issues and because, since there were no official party tickets, it was possible, even for party faithfuls, to consider scratching names. Up to the last moment the *Post-Dispatch* predicted that Filley would switch his allegiance from the Nonpartisan Ticket; but he did not, and all members of the Nonpartisan Ticket were elected. The total vote was 43,000, the largest ever cast in a school election although less than half the number cast in the mayoralty election of the previous month. Candidates on the Nonpartisan Ticket received between 16,000 and 28,000 votes, with those who had been on more than one ticket receiving the larger amounts. (39)

A comparison of the social status of the new members with that of the old board bears out the Hays thesis that Progressive reform was a means of achieving power for the upper class. Only three new board members are not known to have had some college education, nine of them (75%) appeared in *Gould's Blue Book* and seven (58.3%) had been mentioned in honorary books. Although there were still many socially prestigious areas near the city center, five of these men (41.7%) lived in the fashionable West End. Occupational categories show 58.3% were professional men, 25% were large business men and 16.7% were small business owners. All new members met the legal qualifications except one, D. C. Ball, who was out of the city on business thirty days later, evidently through a misunderstanding, and could not technically qualify. In accordance with the law, the mayor appointed a replacement, John Schroers, the business manager of the *Westliche Post* and a Republican, thereby changing the board politically but not occupationally.

In later elections the system of bipartisanship, or nonpartisanship, was improved and maintained by "general consent," as each party nominated two candidates for each election and supported the combined slate of four on the ballots of both parties. This practice lasted until 1909 and was continued intermittently thereafter; it was said to have received the approval of the voters but not the politicians. (40)

Throughout the campaign and after the election, the reformers were singleminded in their criticism of the old board and in their campaign promises. Efficiency and bookkeeping were their concerns, and they insisted also that appointments be on merit alone. Efficiency had become the dominant morality in the drive for organization as Wiebe and Hays have elaborated it. The success in carrying out their proposed program shows that the St. Louis reformers were wise in choosing the School Board as their first project. The qualitative change in administration was effected by a tightening of procedures and rules and an application of business methods, the latter supported by a required oath. (E. C. Eliot, a member of the new board, who had helped write the law, explained the importance of the oath. ". . . An honest man has no excuse for yielding to religious or political solicitation or to personal considerations, when he can point to his oath of office, controlling him to the contrary." (41)

The Board of Education proceeded to put the proposed reforms immediately into effect. Board business meetings were conducted with careful attention to parliamentary rules and exemplary efficiency, the latter aided by the decision to hold committee meetings behind closed doors. The *Post-Dispatch,* alarmed by the authoritarianism of the decision, reminisced about the old method when "over in the old Polytechnic building a daily bulletin of committee meetings was hung up in the secretary's office, so that persons having business to transact with the board could know when to appear." (42)

Another new rule forbade any board member's interfering with or entertaining applications for subordinate positions. The Department of Buildings, source of most scandal, was thoroughly reorganized under William B. Ittner; applicants for janitorships had to pass competitive examinations in reading, writing and the ability to do small repairs. At the same time, in accordance with new economy measures, janitorial salaries were reduced from $100 and $125 per month to $50 and $75. (43)

Trade unions were displeased by several economy measures: requiring janitors to make repairs, removing the union labor clause from construction contracts and discontinuing free textbooks to school children unless need were proven. The secretary of the

Building Trades Council wrote a long letter demanding that these changes be rescinded because many artisans were out of work; and, he said, it was not right that working men be stamped as paupers if they could not afford school books for their children. The only argument eliciting a positive response from the board was the one relating to free books. (44) The discontinuance of free books, the *Post-Dispatch* pointed out, was a disservice to the community because it affected children belonging to the classes for whom school was of the greatest advantage. According to a compromise "free books without restriction are recommended for the first four grades. Above these grades books are to be supplied to needy pupils who prove their inability to pay." The board economized by keeping the books in the schools and requiring a careful count. (45)

For some time there had been a surplus of teachers, and in 1897 about 600 Normal School graduates were on a waiting list. A resolution to close the Normal School until demand caught up with supply had failed of passage for several years; the new board passed it. Board president Paul Coste was pleased that, despite an increase of 1,455 children enrolled in 1897-1898, only seven more teachers had been hired because of "a more economic distribution of work, and the withdrawal of extra teachers from schools where their services could be dispensed with." (46)

The need for more schoolrooms in St. Louis had reached crisis proportions during 1896. The population of the city as a whole had increased 28% since 1890, and the number of school children had grown proportionally. The difficulty of accommodating the increase was aggravated by a tornado on May 27, 1896, which did severe damage to many school buildings; by November of that year it was estimated that at least sixty new rooms were needed immediately. The 1897 Board of Education, prevented by law from raising taxes or making long-term loans, made heroic efforts to meet this need. Nonetheless the board's view of city welfare seems unnecessarily narrow. It was epitomized by board president Coste: "We must economize somewhere, and our first duty is to provide more space for children rather than to increase the number by increasing free books." (47) This comment emphasizes the reform hierarchy of values which were in reality business values. Balancing the books and improving capital assets were given priority over social welfare. This is also evident in the treatment of teachers and unions. As Hays has said, Progressive reform aimed at putting a new class in power; it was not necessarily a democratic change.

At the end of a year Coste's annual report showed the results of the new system of management. In the finance department, the deficit of the previous year had been wiped out, and there was a large balance on hand to meet unexpected bills. Revenues had been increased through close attention to collection of taxes and rents, while expenditures, especially for supplies and repairs, had been substantially reduced. Books and accounts were up to date. Teachers were more efficiently distributed; better textbook contracts had been obtained. Tremendous savings had been effected through rigid inspection of all work; better bidders on construction work had been attracted by the distribution of copies of specifications in advance, and eighty-nine new schoolrooms, all fireproof, were under contract. Eliot wrote that the virtue of the new law was its efficiency:

There is no doubt that at all times a portion of the community would prefer to have public action go by chance or favor, rather than in accordance with abstract justice. For the perpetuation of the system the better sense of the people must assert itself in this regard. (48)

The struggle for power by the upper, business-oriented class had been won, in accordance with the Hays thesis. Legislative changes had evolved experimentally, hindered by public opinion from becoming autocratic. Eliot clarified the reasons for reform acceptance of at-large elections:

A city is an entirety for all executive purposes. No system of representation local in character can operate successfully unless the political unit is small enough to be locally manageable. The ward and borough are now simply devices for the suppression of the popular voice at the dictation of bosses. . . . The necessity of large cities, with shifting populations, is to devise a basis of representation which will in fact determine the will of the people. Until such is found the election at large is the safest method. (49)

The main concern of the St. Louis reformers was, overtly at least, with finances; "reform" was synonymous with "business efficiency and economy" in their eyes; and the at-large method of election was a device to help them gain power in order to put their beliefs into effect. The reformers had learned the methods and developed experience that would direct further changes during the Progressive Era.

Notes

1. Samuel P. Hays, "The Politics of Reform in Municipal Government in the Progressive Era," *Pacific Northwest Quarterly*, XXXXXV (October 1964), 157-69; Robert H. Weibe, *The Search for Order 1877-1920* (New York: Hill and Wang, 1967).

    Recent interest in the Progressive Era has centered on the sources of reform sentiment. Wiebe argues that many segments of society, especially the new middle class, desired centralization of power and an increased orderliness in government, business, and community life. Samuel P. Hays identifies the reform groups as a new upper class; migration to newly fashionable, outlying areas, he says, had given this group an interest in the city as a whole while tending to disfranchise it. Both men identify the reformers as business and professional men interested in the rationalization and systematization of modern life; both identify them as people who had risen to social position from newly created wealth or in professions. The difference between the "new middle" and "new upper" classes to which these men refer would seem to be one of terminology, in the main. For purposes of clarity the reform group will be referred to as "upper-class" in this paper.

    The city political "machines" based on ward organizations had given lower and middle-income groups, including immigrants, what seemed to reformers an undue influence on city government. The upper-class reformers, in order to minimize their own geographic and social distance from city government, made the ward system their special target in the battle to gain political power. The characteristics marking this movement, which Hays dates between 1901 and the Great Depression, were a desire to model government on efficient business enterprise rather than on the New England town meeting, a revolt against ward politics in favor of narrowing centers of power, and a disdainfulness toward the waste and inefficiency of customary government. In order to accomplish their political goals, the reformers believed such changes as direct city-wide election of the city council and school board were essential. The change to election at large did achieve the desired results in some known cases, Hays says. For example, in 1911 Pittsburgh changed to city-wide representation for both the city council and the school board. In the new government professional men and large business dominated. Of the newly elected members, none were small businessmen or white-collar workers, and each body had only one man designated as a representative of labor.

2. *Missouri Republican Editorials: During the Years 1875 and 1876 Regarding the Separation of the City of St. Louis from the County of St. Louis* (St. Louis: Board of Freeholders, 1925), p. 26.
3. Marshall S. Snow, "City Government of St. Louis," *Johns Hopkins University Studies in Historical and Political Science,* V (Baltimore, 1887), 151. See also Dwight M. Collier, "The Freeholders and the Scheme and Charter, address delivered to St. Louis Commercial Club (February 17, 1894), p. 11.
4. *Missouri Republican Editorials,* pp. 28-29.
5. *Ibid.,* p. 33.
6. *Ibid.,* pp. 21-22.
7. *St. Louis Post-Dispatch,* February 19, 1887, p. 4.
8. *Ibid.,* November 23, 1887, p. 1. See also "Report of the President," *Annual Reports of the Board of Education of the City of St. Louis,* 1887-1888 and 1888-1889.
9. "Our Public School System: A Summary," *The Forum,* XV (June 1893), 512. See also J. M. Rice, "A Plan to Free the Schools from Politics," *The Forum,* XVI (December 1893), 500. For a discussion of Rice, see Lawrence A. Cremin, *The Transformation of the School: Progressivism in American Education, 1876-1957* (New York: Vintage Books, 1964), pp. 4-6.
10. *American School Board Journal,* IV (April 1892), 1.
11. "Plans of Organization for School Purposes in Large Cities," *Educational Review,* VI (June 1893), 10-12. For other discussions of this change, see James C. Boykin, "Organization of City School Boards," *Educational Review,* XIII (March 1897), 243, and L. H. Jones, "The Politician and the Public School," *The Atlantic Monthly,* LXXVII (June 1896), 820.
12. Andrew S. Draper, W. B. Powell and A. B. Poland, "Committee of Fifteen: Report of the Sub-Committee on the Organization of City School Systems," *Educational Review,* IX (March 1895), 304-322.
13. "Confessions of Three School Superintendents," *Atlantic Monthly,* LXXXII (October 1898), 652.
14. Charles H. Judd *et al., Survey of the St. Louis Public Schools* (St. Louis: Board of Education, 1917), p. 48.
15. *St. Louis Post-Dispatch,* December 29, 1895, p. 7; November 10, 1896, p. 7; Boykin, *op. cit.,* p. 242.
16. *St. Louis Post-Dispatch,* February 18, 1896, p. 6; February 27, 1896, p. 7.
17. *Ibid.,* February 15, 1896, p. 2; February 17, 1896, p. 4.
18. *Ibid.,* February 23, 1896, p. 15; February 24, 1896, pp. 2, 3.
19. *St. Louis Globe-Democrat,* March 4, 1896, p. 6.
20. *St. Louis Post-Dispatch,* March 14, 1896, p. 8.
21. *Ibid.,* March 5, 1896, p. 6; March 10, 1896, p. 3; March 11, 1896,

p. 10; March 12, 1896, p. 8; April 13, 1896, p. 2; April 16, 1896, p. 8.
22. *Ibid.,* March 14, 1896, p. 8.
23. *Ibid.,* March 28, 1896, p. 5; April 15, 1896, p. 4; April 27, 1896, p. 3; May 12, 1896, p. 2; May 13, 1896, p. 4; May 26, 1896, p. 7; June 21, 1896, p. 5.
24. *Ibid.,* June 30, 1896, p. 3; July 15, 1896, p. 1; September 8, 1896, p. 2.
25. William Hyde and Howard L. Conard, eds., *Encyclopedia of the History of St. Louis* (New York: The Southern History Company, 1899), I, 389-90.
26. *St. Louis Post-Dispatch,* July 7, 1896, p. 8. *See also* Hyde and Conard, *Encyclopedia,* I, 393.
27. *St. Louis Post-Dispatch,* August 12, 1896, p. 2.
28. Hyde and Conard, *Encyclopedia,* I, 391.
29. *St. Louis Post-Dispatch,* November 24, 1896, p. 7.
30. *Ibid.,* November 22, 1896, p. 16.
31. *Ibid.,* December 27, 1896, p. 10.
32. *St. Louis Globe-Democrat,* November 6, 1896, p. 12.
33. *Ibid.,* September 9, 1896, p. 6; March 2, 1897, p. 6; March 4, 1897, p. 6.
34. *St. Louis Republic,* March 5, 1897, p. 12.
35. William F. Woerner, *The Revised Code of St. Louis, General Ordinances* (St. Louis: Sam'l F. Myerson Printing Co., 1907), pp. 191-99.
36. *St. Louis Post-Dispatch,* April 8, 1897, p. 9; April 18, 1897, p. 20; April 24, 1897, p. 3.
37. *Ibid.,* April 28, 1897, p. 9; May 8, 1897, p. 5; May 9, 1897, p. 4.
38. *Ibid.,* May 1, 1897, p. 3; May 2, 1897, p. 5; May 4, 1897, p. 6.
39. *Ibid.,* May 19, 1897, p. 2; May 20, 1897, p. 4.
40. Edward C. Eliot, "School Administration: The St. Louis Method," *Educational Review,* XXVI (December 1903), 467; David Mahan, "The Influence of the Efficiency Movement on Public Education in a Large Urban School System: A Case Study of the St. Louis Public Schools" (Dissertation for Ph.D., Washington University, 1968), p. 111.
41. Eliot, "School Administration," p. 467.
42. *St. Louis Post-Dispatch,* June 15, 1897, p. 3.
43. *Ibid.,* June 27, 1897, p. 8; July 14, 1897, p. 5.
44. *Ibid.,* August 23, 1897, p. 4; August 26, 1897, p. 2.
45. *Ibid.,* October 12, 1897, p. 10. Also, *Annual Report of the Board of Education,* 1897-1898, p. 20.
46. *Annual Report of the Board of Education, 1897-1898,* pp. 17-18.
47. *St. Louis Post-Dispatch,* July 9, 1897, p. 5.
48. Eliot, "School Administration," p. 475.
49. *Ibid.,* p. 466.

Politics and Pedagogy: The 1892 Cleveland School Reform

RONALD M. JOHNSON

On May 25, 1892, a large crowd gathered at Cleveland's Stillman Hotel. The occasion was the announcement of Andrew S. Draper as the city's new school superintendent. The assembled group listened attentively as H. Q. Sargent, the school director, introduced Draper, a prominent New York educator. Sargent dwelt momentarily on the recently reformed school system, which had led to the creation of his own office. Draper followed with a brief statement. He praised Clevelanders for a "unique plan" of school administration. He urged all "to act in harmony to the end that the desired results may be attained," promising that in "attempting the reorganization I will do the right, with malice toward none."[1] Many early advocates of the reorganization, including Edwin J. Blandin, a former municipal judge, were at the Stillman that day. In 1887, Blandin had first called for school reform. He was ready to witness the fruition of his original effort.[2]

The story of the Cleveland school reform is significant for a variety of reasons. The event is illustrative of Cleveland history between 1870 and 1900. During that period, the city expanded at an accelerated pace, growing in population from 92,829 to 381,768. Once a secondary Great Lakes commercial terminus, the city became a major manufacturing center. The social consequences of this change were enormous. Even as members of founding Connecticut families formed the Early Settlers' Association, an urban-industrial society emerged that contained great wealth and extreme poverty. The contrast was evident in John D. Rockefeller's mansion on 40th Street and Euclid Avenue and the dilapidated shanties of laborers in the industrial "flats" along the Cuyahoga River. In this setting, a new political order unfolded. Politics revolved around a clash between the business-dominated Republican party and an increasingly immigrant-oriented Democratic organization. The latter slowly gained new strength from spreading working-class neighborhoods. By the early 1890s, the Republican hold on city government was threatened as Democratic ward organizations increased in number and influence.[3]

---

1. *Cleveland Leader*, May 26, 1892.
2. For an early assessment of the reform, see Samual P. Orth, "The Cleveland Plan of School Administration," *Political Science Quarterly*, XIX (1904), 402-416.
3. The political history of Cleveland for this period is discussed most fully in James B. Whipple, "Cleveland in Conflict: A Study in Urban Adolescence, 1876-1900" (unpublished doctoral dissertation, Western Reserve University, 1951), 337-349. A later phase of political development has been covered by Thomas Campbell, "Background for Progressivism: Machine Politics in the Administration of Robert E. McKisson, Mayor of Cleveland, 1895-1899" (unpublished thesis, Western Reserve University, 1960). Additional analysis of Cleveland politics can be gleaned from Samuel P. Orth, *A History of Cleveland*, 3 vols. (Cleveland, 1910), and Philip D. Jordan, *Ohio Comes of Age, 1873-1900* (Columbus, 1943).

Dr. Johnson is Assistant Professor of History at Georgetown University.

The 1892 school reform occurred as part of this sustained political battle. The close relationship between municipal politics and school reform has often been overlooked or deemphasized. Urban historians have stressed mayoralty races, councilmanic elections, and party organization; educators, the role of professional schoolmen, institutional bureaucracy, and pedagogical theory.[4] Too few studies link these historical developments together. The 1892 Cleveland school reform offers such an opportunity. Both its origins and the Draper superintendency reveal the intermingling of political and pedagogical concerns.[5]

Public school enthusiasts throughout the nation praised the Cleveland school reorganization. In June of 1892, Joseph M. Rice, an early muckraking journalist, wrote a series of articles for *The Forum* on conditions in urban school systems. He depicted most as creatures of political interference and inefficient management. Rice alluded hopefully to Cleveland. He saw the recent reform as a new breakthrough to improve the schools.[6] Three years later, the National Educational Association endorsed an urban school plan based largely on the Cleveland system. In 1897, St. Louis reorganized its schools under the direct influence of the Cleveland experiment. By the turn of the century, urban reformers in New York, Boston, Philadelphia, Chicago, and San Francisco had looked carefully at Cleveland in restructuring their own school systems.

From the beginning, public education had reflected the growth of the city. Schools existed in early Cleveland, but not until 1837 did the city council establish the first system of public education. The first two decades involved steady but manageable growth.[7] A three-member school committee initially governed the schools. In 1849, a state law passed which required Cleveland to have a six-man school board and a school superintendent. For almost a quarter century, this system was followed. In 1873, the Ohio legislature again altered the Cleveland school system. The state stipulated that two representatives from each ward in the city had to serve on the school board, a step taken to encourage greater popular representation. When this policy led to constantly enlarging school boards, the Ohio Assembly, a decade later, limited school boards to twenty members in Cleveland and Cincinnati, the two cities affected by the earlier legislation.[8]

After the Civil War, Cleveland's rapid influx of population resulted in larger numbers of school-age children. By 1880, the city contained 49,256 such children, a number that grew to 64,550 seven years later for a thirty-one per cent increase. Student enrollment rose only twenty-seven per cent for that same period, up to 33,150 from 24,262. Between 1887 and 1891, the gap widened. The number of potential students rose to 80,745, up twenty-five per cent but enrollments showed

---

4. Many of the best monographs on the history of urban education, such as Michael B. Katz, *Class, Bureaucracy and Schools* (New York, 1971), still deal essentially with professional schoolmen. Sol Cohen, *Progressives and Urban School Reform* (New York, 1964), is a solid example of educational history placed in a broader context. Another is David B. Tyack, *The One Best System* (Cambridge, 1974), but his primary concern is with administrative structure and pedagogical developments.

5. Two important articles which represent fresh efforts to see educational history as part of a larger process are Samuel P. Hays, "The Politics of Reform in Municipal Government in the Progressive Era," *Pacific Northwest Quarterly*, LV (October 1964), 157-169 and Robert H. Wiebe, "The Social Function of Public Education," *American Quarterly*, XXI (Summer 1969), 147-164.

6. Joseph M. Rice, "Our Public School System: A Summary," *The Forum*, XV (June 1892), 512.

7. Orth, *History of Cleveland*, I, 522-524. For a fuller coverage of this period, see William J. Akers, *Cleveland Schools in the Nineteenth Century* (Cleveland, 1901).

8. Nelson L. Bossing, "The History of Educational Legislation in Ohio from 1851 to 1925," *Ohio Archaeological and Historical Quarterly*, XXXIX (1930), 180-182.

only 38,314, or a thirteen per cent expansion over four years earlier.[9]

At the same time, enrolled children faced overcrowded classrooms and understaffed facilities. Old school buildings, suffering from long use, and the few structures built since the Civil War no longer could handle the numbers coming into the schools. The instructional staff, even with annual additions from Cleveland Normal School, were overworked. In addition, increasing numbers of teachers gained positions without basic pedagogical training. These appointments resulted from ward representatives intervening on their behalf before the school board. Administratively, these conditions caused a series of turnovers, specifically in the superintendency. In the past, strong personalities, such as Harvey Rice and Andrew S. Rickoff, had held the post. In 1882, Burke A. Hinsdale, a highly respected Michigan educator, assumed the office. The school board hoped that he, as an experienced individual, might restore the schools to take their earlier stability.

In 1886, his sudden departure raised new questions about the schools. These doubts did not dissipate when Cleveland school supervisor, L. W. Day, succeeded Hinsdale. An Ohio-born schoolman, Day had logged sixteen years in the Cleveland school system. A local rather than national entity, Day was not of the same stature as his predecessor. He did pride himself on having close relations with the school board, including its Democratic members. After a year in office, Day came under sustained criticism from the *Cleveland Leader*. The newspaper attacked the superintendent for tolerating improper procedures by the school board in awarding text-book contracts and illegal use of school building materials. The *Leader* also chastized Day for his slow response to the Thomas Whitehead incident. This involved Whitehead's alleged misuse of school funds for private loans. Indicted by a grand jury and forced to resign as school board treasurer, Whitehead was not criticized sufficiently by Day, according to the *Leader*.[10]

The *Cleveland Leader's* reaction to Day involved a wider concern about the entire municipal structure. Since the early 1880s, business and professional men had sought to reverse the growing influence of Democratic ward organizations on city government and public schools. Their complaints included allegations of "rings and combinations" in the rewarding of city contracts. They attacked the excessive number of ward-level patronage jobs and general inefficiency in the operation of the government commissions. At first, any attempt at reform was limited to the efforts of individuals. In 1885, for example, Myron T. Herrick, a vice president of the largest bank in Cleveland, ran successfully for a term on the city council. He overcame opposition from Sixth Ward Democratic politicians in this bid. He later recalled the motives for his actions. "Educated and well-to-do people," he stated, "not only in Cleveland but in a great many towns everywhere, had begun to realize that they had some civic duty besides making a contribution to the campaign funds and paying their taxes."[11]

During his term on the council, Herrick helped launch an organized reform movement. On January 12, 1887, the Board of Trade called a meeting to discuss municipal problems. A large crowd met at the Board's offices. They heard Edwin Blandin condemn the breakdown in government and the schools. Born in New

---

9. The statistics on school-age eligibility and enrollment come from the *Annual Reports, Cleveland Public Schools*. The low percentage of enrolled students was partly due to the limited range of Ohio's 1877 compulsory attendance law which applied only to children from 8 to 14 and then only for 12 weeks of each academic year. In 1899, this law was strengthened to cover 20 weeks, with 10 to be in succession. Finally, the Cleveland schools did not hire their first truant officer until 1888. For additional commentary on this question, see Whipple, "Cleveland in Conflict," 392-398.

10. See Daniel W. Lothman, "Cleveland Educators I Knew," Clipping File, Education Section, Cleveland Public Library.

11. T. Bentley Mott, *Myron T. Herrick: Friend of France* (New York, 1929), 31.

York, but a resident of Cleveland for over a decade, Blandin had recently served two years on the Court of Common Pleas.[12] His experience in that post made him concerned over the general social conditions in the city. He contacted Edwin Cowles, the *Leader's* outspoken publisher, about revising the city charter. Out of this collaboration came the Board of Trade meeting.

The focus of Blandin's criticism was the decentralization of local government. He rejected the traditionally limited mayoralty as an anachronistic administrative approach, increasingly ineffective in a period of rapid urban growth. A stronger civil government would not only be more efficient, he argued, but could begin to deal with the social problems facing the city. He called for all commission heads to become appointive posts, their offices, such as finance, police, fire, public works, charities and correction, and legal affairs made strictly accountable to the mayor. As for the schools, he desired an appointed school commissioner, who would handle business matters and select the school superintendent, and a smaller school board of five or seven members.[13] This approach was, as Melvin Holli found in Detroit, an attempt "to change the structure of municipal government...and to introduce the business system of the contemporary corporation into municipal government."[14]

Soon labeled the "Federal Plan," the Blandin proposal sparked a struggle to revise both Cleveland's municipal and school charters. Throughout early 1887, the reformers laid the groundwork for this effort. First, the Board of Trade established a Municipal Reform Committee. The Committee incorporated Blandin's general ideas into a specific statement. Such a document would help publicize the proposed changes and could be used to approach the state legislature which held final authority over all charter revisions. A month later, the Committee oversaw the creation of the Board of Industry and Improvement as a permanent vehicle of reform.

The membership of the new Board agreed to the creation of a Committee of One Hundred. In addition to Herrick, Cowles, and Blandin, this group included such "prominent businessmen and professional gentlemen" as Mark Hanna, Norman A. Gilbert, John Hay, George W. Gardner, Andrew Squire, John H. Wade, Jr., and Orlando J. Hodge. Also active Republicans, these men epitomized the reform leadership. The Committee contained a small number of Democratic businessmen, including Tom L. Johnson. The dominant reform view appeared in a *Leader* editorial which referred to the Board of Industry and Improvement as "essentially of a business character, and in its conduct it will be actuated by the sole desire to promote the business interests of this city."[15]

Between 1887 and 1892, the Cleveland reform movement pressed for acceptance of the Federal Plan. The *Leader* emerged as an energetic advocate of the reform. On April 2, 1888, for example, the *Leader* charged Democratic ward leaders and Catholic diocesan officials of conspiring to create "a Democratic machine out of the public school system."[16] Many Clevelanders agreed with the *Leader* and some joined the reformers, such as Cleveland Normal President El-

---

12. For a brief profile of Blandin, see William R. Coates, *A History of Cuyahoga County and the City of Cleveland*, 3 vols. (Cleveland, 1924), I, 459.
13. *Cleveland Leader*, January 13, 1887.
14. Melvin G. Holli, *Reform in Detroit* (New York, 1969), 162.
15. *Cleveland Leader*, March 1, 1887. Of the three major newspapers, the *Leader* provided the fullest coverage of reform activities. Because of Cowles' involvement and the newspaper's strong editorial support of the reform, the extent of reporting was much greater than that found in either the *Plain-Dealer* or the *Press*.
16. *Cleveland Leader*, April 2, 1888.

roy M. Avery, also founder of the Logan Club, a Republican organization. Educator, writer, and inventor, Avery brought added prestige to the movement. Other important city figures became involved including William J. Akers, businessman and influential member of the Tippecanoe Club, another Republican body; John S. Covert, who succeeded Cowles as the *Leader's* editor after the latter's death in 1890; and Hiram C. Haydn, pastor of the Old Stone Presbyterian Church. All shared with Avery a desire for educational reform. Haydn played a critical role in bringing the Civic Federation into the campaign. Composed of leading Protestant clergy and Western Reserve University academics, the Federation stressed greater morality in government. Founded in 1890, this organization supported the Federal Plan as necessary to encourage the participation of principled men in local civic affairs.

During this period of agitation, the reformers faced both internal difficulties and strong opposition. In 1888, for example, the indictment of Thomas Axworthy, Cleveland city treasurer, dimmed much of the early support for the movement. Axworthy was the vice-president of the Board of Industry and Improvement and his embezzling of $500,000 in city revenues temporarily undermined public confidence in the reform leadership. A more serious problem was the hostility of the *Cleveland Plain-Dealer*. This newspaper accepted the need for change but remained suspicious of reformer motives. Owned by L. E. Holden, the *Plain-Dealer* assumed a Democratic position on most political issues. Between 1889 and 1892, the newspaper often questioned the veracity of the reformers and charged them with advancing Republican party interests. The *Plain-Dealer's* concern was shared by many Democratic politicians, such as former City Clerk Charles P. Salem. He early rejected the Federal Plan as an attempt to establish through government centralization "one supreme ring to control and manipulate the entire machinery of municipal administration." As an alternative Salem proposed the standard Democratic view that a strengthened city council would adequately meet most reformer complaints.[17]

The *Catholic Universe Bulletin* also criticized the municipal and school reformers. In early 1892, this diocesan weekly characterized the reformers as "a few men who surreptitiously got together and purpose to create some partisan offices, which they hope themselves to fill or control. . . ." It added that school board reform would mean "fresh, fat offices for prominent reformers, and the schools can go—to the lower order of spoilsmen."[18] The leadership of the Board of Industry and Improvement, as well as that of the Civic Federation, denied all such accusations.

Both municipal and school reorganization eventually passed the Ohio legislature within the space of a year. On March 16, 1891, the state assembly incorporated the basic tenets of the Federal Plan into a city charter for Cleveland.[19] Shortly thereafter, Republican William Rose won the mayoralty under the plan. This success encouraged those in the reform movement still pursuing educational reorganization. For most of the next year, the reformers increased the number of delegations to Columbus lobbying for the measure. Blandin, Avery, and Gilbert, among others, argued for passage of a school reform bill.[20] Their efforts were finally successful. On March 5, 1892, the state legislature revised school systems in cities of "the second grade of the first class," a category which applied only to

---

17. *Cleveland Leader*, January 27, 1887.
18. *Catholic Universe Bulletin*, February 25, 1892.
19. The Federal Plan has received little scholarly attention. For a participant's view, see Elroy M. Avery, "Federal Plan of Municipal Government as Illustrated in the City of Cleveland," *Leigh Quarterly*, V (June 1892), 3-15.
20. *Cleveland Leader*, March 2, 1892.

Cleveland. "The new type of school government was an innovation," wrote Nelson L. Bossing in his history of educational legislation. He noted that "the ordinary school board of the other districts gave way to a group known as the School Council and a School Director. This council was composed of seven representatives who were divided into two classes, of three and four members each. These classes were elected biennially in alternate years, to serve for a period of two years."[21] Under the Cleveland charter, the school director appointed the superintendent and held extensive veto power over council legislation. In addition, the school council members were to be elected at-large, so that the candidates able to muster a large city-wide vote were favored to win.

The Cleveland election board set the initial school election for the first Tuesday in April. At this point, the Republican influence among the reformers led directly to a coalition between them and the party. The reformers persuaded H. Q. Sargent, a successful photo manufacturer, to run for school director. He was viewed as "a gentleman of the old school," an individual of "sagacity and commercial honor." The Republican city convention endorsed Sargent. The Republicans put forth a school council slate of five downtown businessmen and two lawyers. The group was advertised as a "Citizens' Ticket." To oppose this effort, the Democrats organized a slate of predominantly neighborhood businessmen who represented wards with the strongest party support. Of Bohemian, German, and Irish extraction, the Democratic candidates included an undertaker, cigarmaker, oil-firm manager, and brewer. The party nominated August Zehring, their German-American central party chairman, for the school directorship.

The campaign proved vigorous and intense. The Republicans understood well their advantage under the school charter. Still able to marshal a city-wide plurality, they anticipated a clean sweep with their slate. To achieve this goal, party operatives worked through a network of political clubs. Besides the prestigious Logan and Tippecanoe organizations, there were the Garfield, Cambria, and Fremont Clubs. Black Republicans worked through the Foraker, Harrison, and Morton Clubs. The German Central Republican Club sought to secure the Protestant-German vote. Throughout March, Republican and Democratic ward organizations prepared for election day.[22]

When voter apathy appeared to threaten Republican strategy, the *Cleveland Leader* sought to stimulate the Protestant voters into action. Under Covert, the newspaper raised the spectre of a "Popish" conspiracy undermining public education. Covert charged that a Democratic victory would result in a city-supported parochial school system. The *Leader* effort led many Protestant clergy to deliver election-eve sermons on the threat of possible Catholic intrigue. The *Leader* carried the texts of these sermons under such headings as "The Public Schools: The Foundation of the Republic" and "Our Public Schools—The Duty of the Hour." Hiram Haydn, for example, warned his flock at Old Stone Church of growing "chicanery," "jobbery," and "priestcraft" in the school system. The Reverend D. E. Leavett of Plymouth Congregational Church asked his parishioners to "realize the extent of the Roman Catholic population" in Cleveland. He focused on the "hierarchy at the center, skillful, secret, combined, unwearying in its efforts to make a vast political ecclesiastical machine...."[23]

---

21. Bossing, "The History of Educational Legislation," 182-184. The full text of the new law is contained in *Ohio Laws*, LXXXIX, 74.
22. The Republican party in Cleveland had earlier suffered internal dissension because of a clash between Cowles and Hanna. Cowles' death, however, resulted in a five-year period of dominance by Hanna. See Herbert Croly, *Marcus Alonzo Hanna: His Life and Work* (New York, 1912), 127. Also see Jordan, *Ohio Comes of Age*, 206-212.
23. *Cleveland Leader*, April 4, 1892.

Andrew S. Draper. WESTERN RESERVE HISTORICAL SOCIETY

On April 8, 1892, all Republican candidates won narrow victories over their Democratic opponents. Sargent gained the school directorship, but with only 50.4 per cent of the vote. While far short of a popular mandate, an exclusively Republican slate had won control of a highly centralized school system. The *Leader* proclaimed that the reform would prove "as satisfactory to the tax-payers of Cleveland as the splendid record of economy and efficient administration which has been made by the municipal government."[24]

The decision to seek a nationally-known schoolman for the superintendency came partly out of the close margin of victory. An established figure would be effective, the reformers hoped, in developing wider support for the new plan. The choice of Andrew Draper, whose reputation was known among Ohio schoolmen, assured the Cleveland reformers of such a man. A former schoolmaster, lawyer, state legislator, and federal judge, Draper had turned to educational administration in 1886. For the next six years, Draper served as New York state school superintendent, winning a formidable reputation as a school administrator.[25] His identification with the Republican party in that state led to his dismissal when a

---

24. *Cleveland Leader*, April 20, 1892.
25. For biographical treatments of Draper see Harlan H. Horner, *The Life and Work of Andrew Sloan Draper* (Urbana, 1934), and Ronald M. Johnson, "Captain of Education: Andrew S. Draper, 1848-1913; An Intellectual Biography" (unpublished doctoral dissertation, University of Illinois, 1970).

Democratic majority was elected to the state legislature. Contacted by Sargent at that point, Draper accepted the Cleveland superintendency, but saw it as a temporary assignment at best. His arrival in late May, and the attention given his speech at the Stillman Hotel, marked a critical phase in the Cleveland school reform.

Draper acted decisively from the outset. He released all but one of the existing supervisors. He claimed "their ways were not my ways, and they would not readily come into sympathy with me." To assist him, Draper hired Jay D. Stay of Cleveland Normal School as an assistant superintendent. One of Draper's earliest acts was to call together the school principals. He told them the central issue under his administration would be to improve the instructional level. He insisted this effort would not be based on partisan or sectarian standards. Nevertheless, Draper alerted all involved in the school system. "No matter with what party he trains," he declared, "no matter with what church he worships, or indeed whether he worships at all, no matter how brokenly he speaks the English language, or whether he must express himself in a tongue I do not understand...I seek his friendship and I will be the friend of every one in Cleveland who is the friend of the Cleveland public schools."[26] That he would even raise the question of religious, ethnic, and political backgrounds, or condition his trust of an individual on being a "friend," alarmed many principals and teachers.

To strengthen his hold on the school staff, Draper organized a Principals' Round Table. This group was to meet regularly and discuss the needs of each school. At the initial meeting Draper emphasized that the majority of teachers need not fear for their jobs. To develop a collective profile of the faculty he asked the principals to fill out a form on each teacher under their authority. These questionnaires included sections on educational training and previous work experience. They also contained an oath requiring each teacher to affirm his support of the "healthful growth of the public school system."[27] During the two years he served as superintendent, this system of teacher evaluation led to the dismissal of, in Draper's estimate, "upwards of an hundred" supposedly inadequate teachers.[28]

The effort by Draper to improve the Cleveland schools involved other steps designed to stimulate better teaching. One teacher later recalled his brief administration as an "epoch" in the system's history. Writing four decades later, Daniel W. Lothman remembered Draper because

> he held frequent teachers' meetings that were led by the superintendent or a supervisor; he urged the teachers to form clubs for pedagogical study and self-improvement; he organized a class in university extension work; he had a teachers' reading room fitted up at school headquarters where there were on file leading educational periodicals of this country and countries abroad; he invited teachers to make a written report to him at the close of the year of what they had done for professional advancement; he encouraged travel because of its broadening influence; in short he overlooked no means for developing a strong teaching force.[29]

The administrative approach Draper took reflected the new freedom guaranteed the superintendent by the reform. He attended school council meetings, but

---

26. *Cleveland Leader*, June 1, 1892.
27. *Ibid.*
28. Andrew S. Draper to Mrs. J. Elliot Cabot, January 31, 1900, Andrew S. Draper Papers, Record Series 2, 3 4, Box 6, University of Illinois Archives.
29. Daniel W. Lothman, "Early Schools of Cleveland," Clipping File, Education Section, Cleveland Public Library.

did not feel bound to any request concerning his administrative duties. He recognized Sargent as his immediate superior. Draper remained close to the school director, later thanking him for having "never interfered with the superintendent." Free to do as he saw fit, Draper widened the exercise of bureaucratic responsibilities. He relied on Stay to keep educational activities on schedule. He utilized primary, elementary, and secondary grade supervisors to check out the daily routine of classroom work. The Principals' Round Table proved a valuable asset in identifying and remedying inadequacies in the fifty individual schools, specifically in the physical points. His administrative effort satisfied the school director and council. Sargent confirmed that when he praised Draper for a "most desirable reorganization" which had "gone forward steadily, quietly and effectually."[30]

The primary objective of Draper at Cleveland was a revitalized educational process. He assumed that, under the watchful eyes of professional administrators, public schooling was "the only safeguard of the Republic." He emphasized that schools must turn out "young men and women" with "intellectual powers so trained that they will have both the ability and desire to acquire more and more; with some moral sense and some love for the good and the beautiful, and with the emotional powers so active that they will continually strengthen; with character set for intelligent, honest, patriotic citizenship."[31] To effect these goals, Draper made a series of changes in the pedagogical realm. He instituted a liberal method of annual student promotions, based primarily on teacher evaluations. He also modified the disciplinary code, an "old-fashioned, over-reaching military system of managing children," by forbidding corporal punishment and establishing separate classes for children with behavioral problems. The "new education" Draper brought to the Cleveland schools also involved the dissemination of industrial training to all levels, including the elementary grades. He laid the basis for the first public kindergartens, which by 1896 numbered twelve in operation.

By early 1894, the reform mandate had been largely fulfilled. Ward influence on the administration of the schools, particularly from Democratic spokesmen, had been virtually ended. The school bureaucracy had been restructured so that the personnel policies and teaching function were now effectively controlled by the superintendent. On March 7, 1894, Edwin Blandin praised the Draper administration for having accomplished new "directness in administration," reduction of per-student cost, increased professionalism among teachers, and improved classroom work.[32] Most of all, Draper's effort had increased school enrollments. Almost 4500 more students were in school than when he had arrived. In the following years, the numerical gains continued. By the fall of 1896, the total number of eligible students swelled to 93,861, up thirteen per cent over 1892. School enrollment increased twenty-six per cent for the same period, rising from 39,813 to 50,454. Thus, while only forty-eight per cent of those eligible actually enrolled in Cleveland schools in 1890, eight years later that number totalled fifty-five per cent.

In May of 1894, Draper resigned the superintendency to become the president of the University of Illinois. He had never intended to remain in Cleveland long and, by this juncture, felt that "I have done about as much as I can do for this system." The close relationship between the Republican party and the reformers also worried him. Earlier in the spring both had pressured him into speaking out for the Republican school board slate. Draper agreed reluctantly. In a letter to an

---

30. H. Q. Sargent to ASD, Draper Papers, Record Series 2/4/5, Box 1.
31. *Fifty-Eighth Annual Report, Cleveland Public Schools* (Cleveland, 1894), 66.
32. *Cleveland Press*, March 7, 1894.

associate he expressed fear of becoming "a smaller and weaker man every year I should remain in a city suptc'y."[33] The Republicans won the spring election, and Draper accepted the Illinois post the following month.

As he prepared to depart, Draper observed that "thoughtful people of other large cities" had inquired of the reform. Such individuals saw him as a spokesman for urban school reform. In 1893, the Cleveland Department of Superintendence had created a special unit to investigate city school organization, curriculum, and teacher certification. The Department membership voted Draper on the task force, which became known as the Committee of Fifteen. Draper was elected chairman of the sub-committee on city school organization, a five-member group studying city school systems throughout the nation.[34]

In 1895, Draper returned to Cleveland to attend the National Educational Association. He presided over the session where the majority report for the sub-committee on school organization was discussed. His influence on the report appeared in the call for small school boards, business managers, and strong school superintendents. Subject to considerable debate, the report was endorsed by the National Education Association. Later that year, the Chicago Civic Federation contacted Draper about the report and his involvement in the Cleveland reorganization. Other inquiries followed as well as invitations to address various reform groups. Between 1897 and 1903, Draper traveled widely to speak on urban school reform, addressing reform groups in San Francisco, Chicago, Boston, and Philadelphia. His influence on the St. Louis school reorganization, for example, was extensive. As recorded by Elinor M. Gersman, the reformers in that city relied heavily on "the Draper report."[35]

The resignation of Andrew Draper had no real effect on the continuation of the Cleveland school reform. He was succeeded by Lewis H. Jones, former Indianapolis school superintendent, whose views on politics and schooling were similar to Draper's. Jones believed that the "end of modern education requires that one become able to think clearly, to aspire nobly, to drudge cheerfully, to sympathize broadly, to decide righteously and to perform ably; in short, to be a good citizen."[36] Throughout his eight years in the office, Jones maintained the policies established by his predecessor. For most of that time, Jones could rely on the experience of Sargent, who served as school director until 1900. The Republicans kept control of the school board, never losing an election under the reform charter. In 1904, the reform came to an end when the Ohio Supreme Court ruled all existing school charters invalid. The Court had found too many differences among the various systems and directed the state legislature to create a new, uniform state law.

In the years following passage of the reorganization bill, the original reform coalition persisted but experienced some internal realignment. In 1893, the business leadership had founded the Chamber of Commerce as a successor to the Board of Industry and Improvement. This organization became their voice for

---

33. ASD to Charles W. Bardeen, April 4, 1894, published in the *School Bulletin*, XXXIX (May 1913), 200.
34. "Department of Superintendence, Secretary's Minutes," February 21-23, 1893, *Proceedings and Addresses of the National Educational Association, Thirty-Second Annual Meeting* (New York, 1893), 252-256.
35. Elinor M. Gersman, "Progressive Reform of the St. Louis School Board, 1897," *History of Education Quarterly*, X (Spring 1970), 3-21.
36. *The Centennial Celebration of the Founding of the City of Cleveland and the Settlement of the Western Reserve* (Cleveland, 1896), 188.

social, political, and industrial improvement in the city. Dominated by "self-made men who have by their industry and ability elevated themselves," the membership of the Chamber continued to concentrate on needed civic development, school and library needs, and municipal service problems.[37] The clerical and academic reformers remained generally aloof from this development, still preferring to work through the Civic Federation. In 1896, however, they launched the Municipal Association of Cleveland. Through this body, they worked for "good government" on a non-partisan basis, rejecting in 1899, for example, the Republican mayoralty of Robert E. McKisson as a "machine."[38]

Under the Cleveland reform, the public school system underwent significant improvement. A more responsive administrative structure replaced an antiquated and diffused form of school management, increasingly subject to school board interference. The reform granted greater independence to the superintendent, and Draper was instrumental in assuring that theory became fact. He centralized authority in himself while decentralizing the actual administration of the schools. The Cleveland school reform appeared to Draper as a critically important experiment which, if successful, would affect future developments in public school administration.[39] A second major gain for the Cleveland schools came in improved teacher efficiency. Again, Draper was a major factor in this change. He pushed the teaching staff hard, to the point that as Daniel Lothman recalled, "they were all afraid of him." Instructional preparation increased, and teachers became more fully involved in their work under the Draper administration. Finally, the reform succeeded in bringing larger numbers of disaffected, or plainly truant, children into the schools.

These gains were not achieved without several unfortunate developments that accompanied the mixing of politics and pedagogy. The socially-conscious and efficiency-minded reform movement succumbed to partisan election tactics. As a result of the reform, and the kind of campaign waged in behalf of the Republican slate, a politically balanced school board was reshaped into a single-party forum. The Democratic ward members, who represented immigrant and laboring interests, were eliminated. Instead of reducing "politics in the schools," the reform led to a Republican entrenchment in public education for over a decade. As Democratic school critic Charles Salem had warned earlier, the school reform established a "despotism," a "municipal aristocracy."

The reform also convinced the Catholic Diocese of Cleveland to press on with its plan to build a private school system. At the same time, the reformers had deepened old-stock Protestant suspicion of Roman Catholicism. These developments detracted from the positive achievements that came with the reform. In the end, the Cleveland school reorganization was only a partial success, creating a new administrative system while intensifying old partisan and sectarian conflicts.[40]

Reprinted from Ohio History, Volume 84, Number 4, Autumn, 1975.

---

37. Whipple, "Cleveland in Conflict," 71-74.
38. Campbell, "Background for Progressivism," 84.
39. *Fifty-Seventh Annual Report, Cleveland Public Schools* (Cleveland, 1893), 183.
40. For the origins of Catholic education in Cleveland, see Paul J. Halliman, "Richard Gilmore, Second Bishop of Cleveland, 1872-1891" (unpublished doctoral dissertation, Western Reserve University, 1963), and Thomas J. Murphy, "History of Catholic Education in Cleveland" (unpublished doctoral dissertation, Western Reserve University, 1944).

SEMESTER: WEEK NINE

REQUIRED READINGS

Church

Part III: The Retreat from Commonality, 1840-1920, Chapter 8: <u>The Rise of the University: Special Education at the Top</u>(24 pp.)

Dye

Arnstine, Donald. "The Use of Coercion in Changing the Schools" <u>Educational Theory</u>. V.23, No.4, Fall, 1973.(12 pp.)

Snook, I. A. "Neutrality and the Schools" <u>Educational Theory</u>. V.22, No.3, Summer, 1972,(08 pp.)

MEETINGS

Monday

Lecture: Educational Settings, Educational Bureaucracy, Educational Issues

Tuesday

Lecture: American Higher Education

Wednesday

Lecture: Critical Contemporary Concerns in American Public Education

Thursday and Friday

Small Groups:

CHURCH TEXTBOOK STUDY GUIDE: CHAPTER 8

THE RISE OF THE UNIVERSITY: SPECIAL EDUCATION AT THE TOP

1. creation of research
2. dissemination of research
3. academic graduate school
4. Ph.D.
5. elitist

6. intellectual preparation
7. inculcation of social duty
8. inculcation of social responsibility
9. improvement of American society
10. Francis Wayland

11. Brown University
12. disillusionment with common school reform
13. William Marcy Tweed
14. Charles Eliot Norton
15. Nation

16. North American Review
17. redirection of American society
18. method of problem solving
19. methods of scientific research
20. elective system.

21. free election of coursework
22. methods of scholarly inquiry
23. majors
24. minors
25. disciplinary concentrations

26. specialization of university faculty
27. taking the question out of politics
28. German university

The Use of Coercion In Changing the Schools*

By Donald Arnstine

I. INTRODUCTION

Public and professional concern for the education of America's children has led to a wealth of proposals for making schools more effective. But few of the proposed changes are put into practice, apart from occasional classroom innovations and a scattering of short-lived "free" schools. I want to discuss this apparently odd situation, in order to show what can justifiably be done to get changes under way more readily.

When they work on their own initiative, teachers find it difficult to institute changes in schools. The reason for this is that teachers do not act wholly on their own. Consciously or not, they make their decisions in accord with the rules, customs, and pervasive climate of the school. These rules and customs depend, in turn, on a school principal who himself abides by constraints set by higher level administrators who are bound by the rules, values, and opinions that are influential within the community. Within the school system, then, decision-making is hierarchically organized. With occasional exceptions, and without the precision that characterizes the military, decisions flow downward: from the superintendent, through his staff, to the building principals, and from them through department heads to teachers, who finally convey to schoolchildren the original decisions in a transformed and often unrecognizable form.

When decisions in a formal organization are made in this way, the organization is to that extent a bureaucracy. Bureaucracies are often maligned for being impersonal and inhumane, and deprecated as being the source of unnecessary red tape. But these are only features of malfunctioning bureaucracies. On the contrary, bureaucracies are intended to promote the efficient operation of complex organizations of people. As such, a bureaucracy may be defined as "an institutionalized method of organizing social conduct in the interest of administrative efficiency."[1]

Not all human groups are bureaucratically organized, nor do they need to be. Families, clubs, small businesses and shops, some performing groups, and neighborhood volleyball teams can all operate without bureaucratic organization. Educational institutions, too, can operate informally and on a face-to-face basis, although this is seldom found today except in an occasional rural school or independently financed "free" school. In contrast, most school systems today fit the standard identifying criteria for bureaucracies that were elaborated by Max Weber and later expanded on by other writers.[2] Thus not only are school personnel organized in a hierarchy, but most of them are also highly specialized, and nearly all of them were appointed to their posts after

---

Donald Arnstine is Professor of Education at the University of California, Davis. He served as President of the Philosophy of Education Society for 1972-73.

---

* Presidential Address at the Twenty-ninth Annual Meeting of the Philosophy of Education Society, April 16, 1973, Monteleone Hotel, New Orleans, Louisiana.
   1. Peter M. Blau, *Bureaucracy in Modern Society* (New York: Random House, 1956), p. 60.
   2. See Max Weber, "The Essentials of Bureaucratic Organization: An Ideal-Type Construction," in Robert K. Merton, *et al.* (eds.), *Reader in Bureaucracy* (New York: The Free Press, 1952), pp. 21-22; and Blau, *op. cit.*, pp. 18-19.

having been certificated on the basis of technical qualifications. Salaries are usually fixed for each position, and they increase by standard increments which an employee receives through a regularized system of promotion that depends more on seniority than it does on measured ability. Finally, most decisions made within school systems are bounded by codified rules and regulations. It is these impersonal rules, rather than informal agreements, emotional ties, or trust, which govern relations among people within the formal organization.

While bureaucracies are intended to maximize administrative efficiency, I do not wish to evaluate them as such; instead, I want to assess their value for explicitly educational undertakings. In the discussion that follows, I hope to make clear three major points. The first is that bureaucracy is an inappropriate decision-making structure for schools in a democratic society. The second point is that the only reasonable way to effect significant changes in educational bureaucracies is through some form of coercion, and the third point is that the only people capable of initiating and sustaining this coercion are schoolteachers.

II. WHY BUREAUCRATIC ORGANIZATION IS INAPPROPRIATE FOR EDUCATION

There are two principle reasons why a bureaucratic structure is an inappropriate form of organization for schools. First, bureaucracy can facilitate administrative efficiency only when the goals of the organization are clear, relatively unchanging, and accepted by all. I will try to show that educational goals in a free society lack these characteristics, and that therefore a bureaucracy cannot well serve educational goals. Second, studies of the impact of bureaucracies upon those who work within them consistently show considerable psychological damage. This damage is a calculated risk in industries that produce socially needed goods and services. But the damage cannot be justified in this way in a school system, which is intended to benefit those who work within them. I will try to elaborate in a little more detail each of these reasons for rejecting a bureaucratic form of school organization.

First, educational goals are not of the right sort to be implemented by a bureaucratic organizational structure. Bureaucracy is intended to promote efficiency, and an organization can be efficient only when its goals are relatively fixed and very clear. The manufacture of cars and the operation of the postal service are obvious examples of enterprises with clear-cut goals. As such, they appropriately lend themselves to organizational forms that will make their operation more efficient.[3] But it is just the nature of educational goals that they are often vague (and legitimately so), often shifting, and seldom agreed upon by all who are expected to carry them out and benefit from them.[4]

There has been much political concern lately to reduce expenditures for schooling by eliminating ineffective programs and personnel. In order to reach this goal, the precise measurement of educational achievement is called for, and this measurement in turn presupposes the postulation of very explicit and fixed educational objectives. Educators have met this demand by trying to make educational goals explicit and fixed by stating them in behavioral terms. While such statements are often helpful in planning and

---

3. Blau, *op. cit.*, pp. 22–23.
4. Dewey summarized this feature of aims in education in the following way: "... it is well to remind ourselves that education as such has no aims. Only persons, parents, and teachers, etc., have aims, not an abstract idea like education. And consequently their purposes are indefinitely varied, differing with different children, changing as children grow and with the growth of experience on the part of the one who teaches." In John Dewey, *Democracy and Education* (New York: The Macmillan Company, 1916), p. 125.

evaluating classroom activities, they do not obviate the necessity for more general and less precise goal-statements. For without general and flexible conceptions of educational goals, we should have no basis for drawing up our lists of specific, behavior objectives. It makes sense, for example, to maintain that citizenship is an educational goal, but it is foolish and politically dangerous to suppose that such a goal can be translated into a single list of explicit behaviors.[5] Citizenship, social sensitivity, and aesthetic taste are only a few of many goals that are open-ended—i.e., subject to continuous reinterpretation. As such, these kinds of goals simply do not lend themselves to efficient bureaucratic administration.

It may be argued that at least some educational goals, like competence in reading, are relatively fixed and clear-cut. As such, they might lend themselves to behavioral statement, precise measurement, and efficient bureaucratic organization. While I cannot explore this suggestion in any detail here, I believe it is mistaken. For example, if reading were *simply* a mechanical skill, it *could* be precisely measured, and reading instruction could be organized to produce this skill efficiently. Indeed, when this is attempted we produce children whose reading skill, limited to the vocal utterance of printed words, is quite mechanical. That is, we produce poor readers who do not read critically, interpretively, selectively, or with pleasure. If these latter characteristics of reading are expected to be included among the outcomes of reading instruction, then goals in this area are as complex, open-ended, and thus interpretable as goals in the area of citizenship. Since reasonable people can disagree about what constitutes both good citizenship *and* good reading, then instruction in these areas does not appropriately lend itself to the efficient organization that bureaucracies are intended to promote.

The other main reason why bureaucratic structures are unsuited to educational organizations lies in the fact that most people suffer psychological damage when their lives are regulated by a bureaucracy. Extensive studies in industry indicate that apathy and immaturity in workers is directly proportional to their distance from the top of the decision-making hierarchy.[6] Teachers working within bureaucratically organized school systems have been observed to display similar symptoms, e.g., in their infrequent and sparsely attended teachers meetings,[7] in their reluctance to assert or defend their opinions in school,[8] and in their willingness to submit to inflexible routines.[9]

Some workers react to bureaucratic organization not with apathy, but with a zealous, almost slavish adherence to rules and regulations. This formality, which multiplies the amount of red tape so often associated with bureaucracy, appears to increase as authority becomes more centralized and less well understood at the lower echelons. Thus the behavior of many schoolteachers in highly centralized, urban school systems is similar to that of the civil servants in Hitler's Germany who apparently

---

5. This point is elaborated in Donald Arnstine, "The Language and Values of Programmed Instruction, Part II," *The Educational Forum* (March, 1964), pp. 340–341. A somewhat different type of argument has been forcibly offered by Leonard Waks, who concluded that "exhaustive behavioral conditions for most mentalistic aims cannot be stated." See Waks, "Philosophy, Education, and the Doomsday Threat," *Review of Educational Research*, Vol. 39. No. 5 (December, 1969), pp. 615–618.

6. See Chris Argyris, *Personality and Organization* (New York: Harper and Brothers, 1957), pp. 60–66.

7. See Myron Lieberman, *The Future of Public Education* (Chicago: University of Chicago Press, 1960), p. 192.

8. See Harmon Zeigler, *The Political Life of American Teachers* (Englewood Cliffs, N.J.: Prentice-Hall, 1967).

9. A striking example is furnished in Gerald E. Levy, "Acute Teachers," in *Ghetto School* (New York: Bobbs-Merrill Co., 1970), reprinted in Glenn Smith and Charles R. Kniker (eds.), *Myth and Reality* (Boston: Allyn and Bacon, Inc., 1972), pp. 215–225.

preserved their sense of security by the ever more anxious and rigid observance of procedural rules.[10]

A very typical response of workers in bureaucratic organizations is to set standards of production lower than those set by management.[11] This is commonly called goldbricking, and the least popular worker in any shop is the "rate-buster"—the man who conforms to the standards of management rather than to those of his peers. Goldbricking workers have their counterparts in schools. Both teachers and children are subject to rules and standards set by the central and local school administration, and neither teachers nor children have any greater attachment to those standards than factory operatives have to the standards set for production lines.[12] Like their counterparts in industry, teachers and students find themselves in a position where it does not pay to produce any more than the minimum that is tolerable. Thus plant managers, school administrators, and teachers come to believe that their charges—whether workers, teachers, or schoolchildren—are "naturally" lazy, apathetic, careless, and materialistic.[13] The logical status of this belief is similar to that of racist beliefs about blacks, for it characteristically mistakes an effect for a cause. The victims of a type of social organization are accused of inherently possessing the personality traits which were a consequence of that social organization.

Since a bureaucracy withholds the power of making significant decisions from most of its personnel, interest in the job comes to rest solely in the paycheck and in the fringe benefits. This is normally true of industrial and office workers, and it is becoming increasingly true of teachers as schools become more bureaucratized. But it is particularly characteristic of students, for whom the grade is a kind of surrogate paycheck. Peter Drucker describes a factory in terms that precisely fit many school settings:

> For the great majority of automobile workers, the only meaning of the job is in the paycheck, not in anything connected with the work or the product. Work appears as something unnatural, a disagreeable, meaningless, and stultifying condition of getting the paycheck, devoid of dignity as well as of importance. No wonder that this puts a premium on slovenly work, on slowdowns, and on other tricks to get the same paycheck with less work.[14]

All that is needed is to change the terms "work" to "study," "paycheck" to "grade," and "automobile workers" to "students," in order to get an apt description of typical schools.

To summarize the foregoing, a bureaucratic form of organization is not appropriate for schools or school systems. There are two reasons for this claim. First, the open-ended nature of educational goals does not lend itself to administrative treatment that aims at efficiency. Second, unlike an industrial plant, an educational system turns out no "product," the utility or importance of which justifies the psychologically harmful

---

10. See Frederick S. Burin, "Bureaucracy and National Socialism: A Reconsideration of Weberian Theory," in Merton, *op. cit.*, p. 43.

11. A classic example of this may be found in F. J. Roethlisberger and W. J. Dickson, *Management and the Worker* (Cambridge, Mass.: Harvard University Press, 1946), pp. 379-548.

12. The similarities between schools and factories, and the unfortunate consequences that result, are discussed in Murray L. Wax, "How Should Schools be Held Accountable?" in P. A. Olson, *et al.*, *Education for 1984 and After* (Washington, D. C.: U.S. Office of Education, n. d.), p. 60, and in Samuel Bowles, "Unequal Education and the Reproduction of the Social Division of Labor," in Martin Carnoy (ed.), *Schooling in a Corporate Society* (New York: David McKay Company, 1972), p. 50.

13. See Argyris, *op. cit.*, p. 123.

14. Peter F. Drucker, *The Concept of the Corporation* (New York: The John Day Company, 1946),

impact that bureaucracies have on the people who work within them.[15] If it is thus understood why school bureaucracies systematically undermine what teachers and students are trying to do, I will now try to show why coercion is the only sensible way of altering the organizational structure of schools.

III. CHANGING THE SCHOOLS

I wish to use the terms "coercion" and "coercive" to refer to any action undertaken with the intention to compel an overt action in response. Thus a person or group against whom coercive action has been taken does not consider himself at liberty, nor is he so considered by others, either to ignore the coercive action or merely to respond with an utterance that indicates no action on his part. "Fly me to Havana or I'll blow your head off," is a paradigm case of coercion, but there are many other kinds of instances, e.g., a student sit-in that threatens to be maintained until tuition is lowered; a strike to gain higher wages; a threat of dismissal unless an employee follows administrative rules; a consumer boycott of products until a manufacturer changes its employment practices; the withdrawal of federal funds from agencies that investigated illegal activities of federal officials. As a means of initiating action, coercion is to be contrasted with requests, pleas, rational argument, and moral suasion. Coercion continues to dominate men's relations in economic and political life, although its use by one person against another is often deplored. But in our consideration of educational changes, we are not concerned with relations between persons as such, but rather with the relations between persons and formally organized bureaucracies.

I will try to show that individuals have no moral obligations whatever to bureaucracies, that people are therefore free to act toward them in their own interests as effectively as they can, and that such action will often turn out to be coercive. To see why people may justifiably act toward formal organizations in just the manner that those organizations act upon them, we must re-examine the process of decision-making in bureaucracies.

When an official of a formal organization (or bureaucracy) makes a decision, he does so in terms of the objectives of that organization. Insofar as his decisions exclude all considerations unrelated to those objectives, they are said to conform to the "ideal of rationality"[16] — that is, they maximize efficiency of means without making any judgments about the value of the goals. Thus as he acts for the organization, the official perceives his decision as ethically neutral, since "morality as such must be excluded as irrelevant," just as it is to a move in chess.[17]

Someone outside the organization may take a quite different posture, and judge the official's decision or the objective of his organization as morally right or wrong. But the official considers only whether the decision enhances or obstructs the organizational objective. If in his official capacity he considered the moral dimensions of his decisions, he could no longer operate efficiently, and his role in the organization would become jeopardized. For the bureaucrat, this may be a source of continual discomfort. While his

---

15. More extended discussion of both theses may be found in Donald Arnstine, "Freedom and Bureaucracy in the Schools," in Vernon F. Haubrich (ed.), *Freedom, Bureaucracy, and Schooling* (Washington, D. C.: Association for Supervision and Curriculum Development, 1971), pp. 13-23.

16. See Yehezkel Dror, *Public Policymaking Re-examined* (San Francisco: Chandler Publishing Company, 1968), p. 336.

17. John Ladd, "Morality and the Ideal of Rationality in Formal Organization," *The Monist* (October, 1970), p. 498. This discussion of rational decision-making in formal organizations owes much to Ladd's argument.

career is dependent upon unhesitating action in behalf of organizational goals, his emotional life may be disrupted by a personal sense of values in conflict with his official actions. To make matters worse, action directed against the bureaucracy of which he is an official may cause him additional personal distress. One might suppose that the only means by which a bureaucratic official could protect himself from these discomforts would be the development of a set of attitudes and dispositions so focused on the importance of organizational goals and his own role in implementing them that moral considerations would remain wholly unperceived. Such a disposition might not only preclude feelings of guilt, but might even result in a feeling of righteous indignation when the bureaucracy was criticized or attacked.

Earlier in this discussion I claimed that educational processes had many goals, and that these goals were necessarily open-ended and subject to change. Under these conditions, it might seem difficult for school officials to undertake the sort of bureaucratic decision-making that must necessarily be predicated on a few relatively fixed, clear-cut objectives. Yet this difficulty disappears when we make a distinction between educational goals, which *are* manifold and open-ended, and the current goals of schools, which are far more clear-cut and amenable to bureaucratic implementation. For as school bureaucracies grew in size and thereby demanded a clear-cut goal on which to focus, such a goal gradually emerged: that of retaining as many students in school as long as possible.[18] By "students" I mean anyone from a pre-schooler to a college student, and by "school" I mean anything from a nursery to a reform school.

Although their official policies seldom declare that schools intend to retain as many of their students as they can for as long as possible, our assumption that this is so helps us to understand many otherwise mystifying decisions and judgments. For example, a school system is judged to be "good" if it includes a pre-school program and it sends many of its high school graduates to college. Schools are thought to be "good" if their dropout rates are low, and "poor" if they have high dropout rates.[19] The dropout himself is regarded as morally unwholesome and urged to return to school. Guidance counselors who find him without academic talent or aspirations can then find some vocational track, or vocational or continuation school, for him to attend. Disadvantaged children and slow learners are treated to more school, either at an earlier age or in summer, and children whose test performance is high are counseled to stay in school longer. On educational and moral grounds, these policies do not always make sense. But they make perfectly good sense if we understand them as implementing the single, clear-cut goal of the educational bureaucracy: to keep children in school as long as possible.

Given the existence of so straightforward an objective, and adding to it some secondary goals, such as the more recent political concern to operate schools as cheaply as possible, and the goal of raising pupils' test scores as much as possible, the point of a school bureaucracy can be better understood. At the same time, it must be kept in mind that the administrative efficiency promoted by the school bureaucracy, like that of any bureaucracy, is to be understood as independent of moral considerations. It might be wondered whether it is better for a child, on educational and moral grounds, to do

---

18. The extension of schooling downward and the extension of the compulsory attendance age upward has resulted in what Ivan Illich calls a virtual monopolization of education by schools. Correlatively, other institutions which historically have performed important educational functions, such as family, church, politics, work, and leisure, are discouraged from doing so. See Ivan Illich, *Deschooling Society* (New York: Harrow Books, 1972), p. 11.

19. The dropout causes a reduction in school attendance figures, and this in turn reduces state and federal financial aid. Hence the method of financing schools results in strong pressures to keep enrollments up.

something other than attend school. But this is a question that no school official seriously raises. John Ladd reminds us how mistaken we would be to expect bureaucratic conduct to be moral:

> We cannot and must not expect formal organizations, or their representatives acting in their official capacities, to be honest, courageous, considerate, sympathetic, or to have any kind of moral integrity. Such concepts are not in the vocabulary, so to speak, of the organizational language-game.[20]

Despite this mode of bureaucratic conduct, individual persons are often advised to conduct themselves according to standards of ordinary morality toward the organizations that serve or employ them. They should be honest, fair, and loyal.[21] Yet it is commonly understood that people are hired and fired by organizations on the basis of efficiency, quite apart from considerations of honesty, fairness, or loyalty. To soften the harshness of this supposedly ethically neutral system, jobs are protected by seniority. But seniority, too, is allegedly ethically neutral, and it therefore protects the competent and the incompetent equally, and discriminates against the young without regard to competence, needs, or virtues. The old, for their part, are retired at an arbitrary age without regard to personal needs or abilities. Given these modes of bureaucratic behavior toward individuals, it would be nonsense to speak of a person's having a moral obligation to a bureaucratic organization.

Since they do not recognize moral obligations, formal organizations cannot be expected to exercise any initiative in acting upon the values, needs, and interests of individuals:

> It is fatuous to expect an industrial organization to go out of its way to avoid polluting the atmosphere ... or to desist from wire-tapping on purely moral grounds.[22]

The moral grounds to which a citizen might appeal in opposing industrial waste are analogous to the educational grounds to which a teacher appeals in trying to initiate educational change. But it would be just as fatuous to expect an educational bureaucracy to desist, on purely educational grounds, from closely regulating the academic lives of students and teachers.

Thus the only way to make the rights and interests of individuals relevant to organizational decision-making is to translate them into pressures of one kind or another. In the examples just mentioned, it is worth noting that Gulf Oil *will* take pains to stop spilling oil in San Francisco Bay if the resulting bad publicity should result in a consumer reaction that reduces sales. The government *may* desist from wire-tapping if those who order it are prosecuted and subsequently disciplined. And officials in school systems may grant greater autonomy in classrooms when teachers and pupils stop showing up for class. In each of these cases, significant changes are made possible by some form of coercion.

Since the mode of decision-making in bureaucracies prevents officials from recognizing moral obligations, they cannot in their official capacities claim any moral

---

20. Ladd, *op. cit.*, p. 499.
21. Bonnie and Clyde wouldn't have agreed, and it is noteworthy that they have achieved the status of modern folk heroes, even though they were not noted—as Robin Hood was—for giving their plunder to the poor. It may take some time for moral philosophy to catch up with public opinion.
22. Ladd, *op. cit.*, p. 508.

rights. Thus however distasteful coercion may seem to those who consider only the relations of individuals to one another, it follows that

> there can be nothing morally wrong in exercising coercion against a formal organization. ... Hence ... it would be irrational for us, as moral persons, to feel any moral scruples about what we do to organizations.[23]

The upshot of all this is that the tactics of initiating change in education must themselves continue to change. Responsible people have traditionally presented to school officials new ideas that were based on carefully thought-out educational and moral grounds. But if the history of education can be believed,[24] this tactic has typically failed to reach its objective. It may not be necessary to mention here that the reason for anyone's proposing an educational change must be relevant to some conceived benefit to students or the society. But such reasons cannot be expected to make any practical difference in the decisions made by the officials of educational bureaucracies.

If a change is wanted, then the bureaucracy must simply be compelled to make it or allow it. And since no individual person or small group can expect to succeed in coercing an extensive formal organization, it behooves those who desire change to identify others who might also stand to gain from the change, to convince them of their stake in the situation, and to join with them in exerting pressure on the bureaucracy.[25] This, of course, is what working people have had to do to achieve their objectives, despite charges of unethical conduct levelled at them by their employers, by the press, by the courts, and by the public.

The point of this discussion has been to show that there is nothing unethical, and much that is practical, in the use of coercion as a means of educational change. Indeed, the only question to raise is how to organize it effectively in particular situations. Now I would like to suggest who it is that can and cannot be expected to initiate and carry out significant changes in education.

IV. CHANGE AGENTS

If we exclude from our consideration pressure groups whose efforts are confined to particular educational issues, we are left with about a half-dozen categories of people that represent potential agencies of change in education: school boards, local communities served by schools, the pupils themselves, school administrators, federal and state political and educational agencies, and schoolteachers. I will try to show why only teachers,

---

23. Ladd, *op. cit.*, p. 508. But it should also be noted that the officers of bureaucracies, as individuals, must still be treated as moral agents. Many of our most difficult ethical choices focus on when to treat a person as an individual, and when to treat him as a representative of an organization. In order to promote organizational goals, the officials themselves capitalize on our hesitation and present themselves as "just plain folks."

24. I have especially in mind some more recent contributions to the history of American education, e.g., Michael B. Katz, *The Irony of Early School Reform* (Boston: Beacon Press, 1968); and Katz, *Class, Bureaucracy, and Schools* (New York: Praeger Publishers, 1971).

25. To the contrary, John Walton claims that "it would be impossible to maintain our educational attainments without complex organizations and the bureaucracy that is an integral part of their nature. It would, therefore, be extremely foolish to advocate the elimination of bureaucratic organization [the reference here is to Paul Goodman's *Community of Scholars*], or even to assume that it will diminish." See Walton, *Introduction to Education: A Substantive Discipline* (Waltham, Mass.: Xerox College Publishing, 1971), p. 24. Walton does allow that some human enterprises might be less amenable to bureaucratic organization than others, but he does not entertain the possibility that educational activities might be more appropriately organized in forms other than bureaucratic ones.

among all these groups, have any hope of effecting significant changes. The other groups are powerless.

Traditionally, boards of education have been perceived as the most likely and the most legitimate change agents in American education. Originally established when professional teachers were either scarce or non-existent, school boards were given legal responsibility for overseeing education. Today, influential educators like James B. Conant continue to address their proposals to school board members.[26]

Such expectations are hopeless. While legally responsible for the education of most American school children, school boards simply lack the means of effecting significant changes in schools. The decisions of local board members are hemmed in by externally dictated spending guidelines and limitations, by state education laws, and by whatever latitude for choice is allowed by local school professionals. Ten years ago, Stephen Bailey and his associates examined the constraints on school boards and concluded that, "in a highly interdependent, technological world, the myth of local control of educational policy is increasingly unrealistic."[27]

While school boards in smaller districts may exert some influence on educational policy, boards of education in large and middle-sized cities and in metropolitan suburbs have become virtually helpless; the evidence supporting this conclusion is already voluminous.[28] Time forbids a detailed account of all the reasons why this is so, but it may be worth noting that one of the major tasks of school administrators is the gradual and effective indoctrination and co-optation of each new person who becomes a school board member. Eventually, the latter comes to believe that the schools are doing as well as could be hoped for under the circumstances, and that the superintendent offers wise counsel on technical matters. If the board as a whole should reject these beliefs, it will hire a superintendent who will make them believe it. Thus school boards

> perform the function of *legitimating* the policies of the school system to the community, rather than *representing* the various segments of the community to the school administration, especially with regard to the educational program.[29]

Most school board members would probably deny this powerlessness. They will also probably be the last to realize it.

If school boards cannot reasonably be expected to promote educational change, the local communities they nominally serve are even less able to do so. The local citizenry is further removed from the intricacies of running schools than the school board is, and although parents are often concerned about what their children are up to in the

---

26. See James B. Conant, *The American High School Today* (New York: McGraw-Hill, 1959), p. 9.
27. Stephen K. Bailey, *et al.*, *Schoolmen and Politics* (Syracuse: Syracuse University Press, 1962), p. 11.
28. For an analysis of the role of school boards in New York City, see Marilyn Gittell, *Participants and Participation* (New York: Frederick A. Praeger, 1967); for an analysis of Boston's School Committee, see Peter Schrag, *Village School Downtown* (Boston: Beacon Press, 1967); for Chicago, see Joseph Pois, *The School Board Crisis: A Chicago Case Study* (Chicago: Educational Methods, Inc., 1964). Summaries and comparisons of the roles of school boards in the cities of New York, Boston, San Francisco, and Chicago, can be found in Alan Rosenthal, *Pedagogues and Power* (Syracuse: Syracuse University Press, 1969). For analyses of the roles of school boards in smaller school systems, see Roscoe C. Martin, *Government and the Suburban School* (Syracuse: Syracuse University Press, 1962), and Arthur J. Vidich and Joseph Bensman, *Small Town in Mass Society* (Princeton: Princeton University Press, 1958), pp. 171-197. Each of these studies clearly indicates the powerlessness of local boards of education.
29. Norman D. Kerr (pseudonym), "The School Board as an Agency of Legitimation," in Alan Rosenthal (ed.), *Governing Education* (New York: Doubleday and Company, 1969), p. 139.

classroom, they are seldom concerned enough to bother voting, let alone campaigning, in school board elections.[30] Disagreements within local communities are often enough to keep them from acting effectively, even when sensitive issues are prominent. In the relatively few cases when community members agreed with one another about what changes they wanted, the educational bureaucracy has been effective in obfuscating issues, retaining power, and impeding action.[31]

Romantics have from time to time expressed the hope that students themselves might serve as the impetus to educational change. But while students are the immediate victims of schools, they seldom have much of an idea of what the trouble is, and even less idea of what to do about it. Those students who finally do reach some consciousness of changes that are needed are usually too close to graduation—and too close to some of the other promised rewards—to risk pressing for any changes. Like prison inmates on the verge of being paroled, they cannot be expected to engage in serious (and coercive) efforts at reform.[32]

School administrators are often perceived as a promising source of change in education. This is about as likely as the Pentagon's becoming the chief architect of peace. Just as the business of generals is to plan for war, the business of administrators is to maintain an institutional *status quo*. While it may be an oversimplification to claim that the role of *all* school personnel is to maintain the educational *status quo*,[33] historical research strongly suggests that, in their efforts to promote efficiency,[34] administrators have been far more effective in retarding than in promoting educational change.[35]

People often mention dedicated principals and superintendents who led their staffs to the frontiers of educational change, and protected those of their teachers who had the courage to experiment. Such men do exist. They are about as typical as air force generals who publicly condemn bombing as a means of reaching political objectives. The appearance of an occasional change-agent among administrators no more justifies our *expecting* changes to originate in this group than the appearance of an occasional Marcus Aurelius justifies our expecting emperors to be benevolent or democratic. Just as the concept of emperor implies ruling an empire, the concept of administrator implies administering an institution—not changing it.

Whatever organization is needed by educational institutions may best be perceived by those who work in them and who are directly served by them. Thus effective school administration might be attained when teachers and citizens can hire, on a contract basis, teams of administrators sponsored by management firms.[36] But until then, the dedication of school administrators to the maintenance of established institutional procedures will constitute only an obstacle to educational change. The same can be said for state and federal governmental and educational agencies. They only multiply the

---

30. See F. M. Wirt and M. W. Kirst, *The Political Web of American Schools* (Boston: Little, Brown and Company, 1972), pp. 61–67.

31. See Joseph Featherstone, "Wiping Out the Demonstration Schools," *The New Republic* (January 10, 1970), pp. 10–11. Featherstone recounts the sad history of unsuccessful efforts of local citizens to promote educational change in the Ocean Hill-Brownsville district of New York City.

32. That students cannot reasonably be depended on to risk coercive action on behalf of educational change is poignantly illustrated in Patricia Michaels, "Teaching and Rebellion at Union Springs," *No More Teachers' Dirty Looks* (January, 1971), pp. 262–266; reprinted in Smith and Kniker, *op. cit.*, pp. 37–46.

33. See, for example, Ralph W. Larkin, "Pattern Maintenance and Change in Education," *Teachers College Record* (September, 1970), pp. 111–119.

34. See, for example, Raymond E. Callahan, *Education and the Cult of Efficiency* (Chicago: University of Chicago Press, 1962).

35. See Katz, *Class, Bureaucracy, and Schools, op. cit.*

36. See Charles H. Wilson, "School Administration by Contract," *School Management* (March, 1971), pp. 11–13.

inefficiencies of local administrative units and add to them the ignorance of educational affairs that is characteristic of elected officials and the entrepreneurs and civil servants who staff the agencies.

Of all of the groups of people broadly concerned with education, only schoolteachers have the potential for initiating change. The training and experience that teachers can bring to bear upon the insight gained from daily contact with children makes them far more qualified to initiate changes than those who try it from administrative and legislative offices. Equally important, teachers directly undergo the consequences of change. If an experiment was ill-advised, they will be the first to hear about it and the most concerned to do something about it. This distinguishes teachers from people whose only conception of the value of a proposed change is based on how much they liked the original idea, and how much it costs to act on it.

I am not claiming that all teachers are wise, and that everyone else who cares about education is foolish. But I am claiming that among those who teach, there are many who *could* effect significant changes in classrooms and schools if they were not discouraged from acting by the existing educational bureaucracy. To find the impetus and the freedom to act on their own ideas, these teachers, acting not alone but in well organized groups, will have to confront and overcome the bureaucratic inertia and vested interests which cannot respond to mere requests. Thus the first change that is needed is a political one, and political changes do not just happen unless coercive pressures are exerted by seriously committed people.

I would like to close with an observation about the role in educational change that might be played by people trained in educational theory. Theorists still need to teach about what can be learned, about how things are learned, and about what is worth learning. Without this kind of study, education is only a trade.[37] But without the study of *more* than this, I doubt that education will ever be a profession. Students and teachers want to know *how* to put their ideas into action, but their professors are often silent on this point. It is not surprising that many students have unpleasant memories of their exposure to educational theory.

Educational theorists can meet this problem by bringing their theories to bear upon the situations that teachers face.[38] Prospective teachers need to study school methods and aims in the context of examining not only classroom situations, but also the politics and the political philosophy of education.[39] Similarly, the in-service education of

---

37. See Harry S. Broudy, "Teaching—Craft or Profession," *The Educational Forum*, vol. 20 no. 2 (January, 1956), pp. 175-184.

38. For further discussion of this approach to the use of theory in teacher education, see B. Othanel Smith, *et al.*, *Teachers for the Real World* (Washington, D. C.: American Association of Colleges for Teacher Education, 1969), p. 51; and John I. Goodlad, "The Reconstruction of Teacher Education," *Teachers College Record*, vol. 72 no. 1 (September, 1970), p. 68; and Donald Arnstine, *The Humanistic Foundations in Teacher Education* (Washington, D. C.: ERIC Clearinghouse on Teacher Education: January, 1972), pp. 34-49.

39. See Joe R. Burnett, "Changing the Social Order: The Role of Schooling," in Donald Arnstine (ed.), *Philosophy of Education 1969: Proceedings of the Twenty-fifth Annual Meeting of the Philosophy of Education Society* (Edwardsville, Ill.: Studies in Philosophy and Education, 1969), p. 241. This task may not be so easy. For example, while the state of California does not require prospective teachers to study *any* educational theory, it requires all of them to study pharmacology. Legislators apparently hoped that this would enable teachers to deal intelligently with drug addicts. Needless to say, if the universities comply with state curriculum mandates, higher education will come increasingly to resemble what is offered in the lower schools. Many universities may have to choose between breaking the law or abandoning their traditional commitments to academic freedom and professional autonomy. Since most universities have become as bureaucratically inert as most public school systems, they may not be capable even of making the choice. Thus passivity leads to a gradual deterioration that is noticed only by a few scholars and political activists. Totalitarianism, like the end of the world, comes not with a bang, but a whimper.

practicing teachers needs to focus on the means and ends of change in educational bureaucracies. Theory and practice might even be more intimately joined when theorists work in on-going consulting relationships with school staffs that are trying to institute changes. Finally, professors can test the value of their theories by establishing consulting relationships with teacher organizations, for the latter's efforts to secure greater power can obscure the goals and the interests for which that power was initially sought.

In order to operate effectively in settings like these, theorists will have to convince school staffs and organized teachers that they have something practical to offer. But the challenge of doing this raises a serious question: what if educational theorists *didn't* have something practical to offer? I have argued that significant change in education is dependent on the use of coercion in overcoming the inertia of educational bureaucracies, and I have suggested that only schoolteachers have the potential to do this job. But there is no way of knowing whether any changes thus made will be for the better or the worse. If we can count on teachers' being wise, then perhaps the changes will be for the better. But our schoolchildren would be less victimized by circumstance if theorists did have something practical to offer.[40]

---

40. The other option for theorists is, in Maxine Greene's words, "to play a role like that of the 18th century blue-stocking lady, drawing her skirts around her and retiring from the leaking gutters and confusion of the streets to talk philosophy in her salon." See Greene, "Morals, Ideology, and the Schools: A Foray into the Politics of Education," in D. B. Gowin (ed.), *Philosophy of Education 1967: Proceedings of the Twenty-third Annual Meeting of the Philosophy of Education Society* (Edwardsville, Ill.: Studies in Philosophy and Education, 1967), p. 145.

Neutrality and the Schools*

BY I. A. SNOOK

One of the boasts of educators in democratic countries is that their schools and universities, unlike those in totalitarian states, are politically neutral. In periods of social tranquility the boast is accepted at face value. When there is social unrest and disharmony, the claim is challenged by those who assert that the schools are not really neutral, or more strongly still, that neutrality is impossible. Such attacks were very much in evidence in the United States during the Depression years. After a period of comparative calm, they have emerged again, this time in the writings of the New Left. It is very interesting to notice the striking similarities between the arguments of the Social Reconstructionists of the 1930's and those of the New Left today. George S. Counts wrote:

> Any defensible educational programme must be adjusted to a particular time and place, and the degree and nature of the imposition must vary with the social situation.[1]

Anthony Arblaster writes:

> The content of our education is determined by what people have thought to be the purposes of education, and those purposes can never be socially or politically neutral.[2]

In each case the purpose of the argument is the same, to advocate a different bias from the one currently in evidence.[3] To argue that the schools are in fact not neutral is insufficient for this purpose since it is open to the counter argument that the solution to the problem is for the schools to become neutral. The much stronger claim that schools *cannot* be neutral is required to support the argument that they should cease to support, say, the forces of reaction and begin to support the liberal position.

There are, then, three questions which need to be distinguished and, if possible, answered:

(1) Are schools neutral?

(2) Can schools be neutral?

(3) Should schools be neutral?

I. A. Snook is Senior Lecturer in Education at the University of Canterbury, New Zealand.

*Paper read at the second annual conference of the Philosophy of Education Society of Australasia; Adelaide, August 1971.

[1]George S. Counts, *Dare the Schools Build a New Social Order?* New York: John Day, 1932, p. 18.

[2]Anthony Arblaster, "Education and Ideology" in David Rubinstein and Colin Stoneman (eds.), *Education for Democracy*. Harmondsworth: Penguin Books, 1970, p. 50.

[3]This was, of course, ably shown by Robert H. Ennis in his "Is it Impossible for the Schools to be Neutral" in B. Othanel Smith and Robert H. Ennis (eds.), *Language and Concepts in Education*. Chicago: Rand McNally, 1961, pp. 102-111. Subsequent events have provided ample reinforcement for this view.

The first question is largely an empirical question and is, therefore, outside the scope of this paper. However, it is important to recognize that it is an empirical question. Many on both sides of the debate fail to recognize that their position needs to be argued: they assert or deny that the schools are neutral without feeling bound to present evidence for their claim. Of course, the question cannot be answered until the meaning of 'neutral' is specified and hence this paper is not irrelevant even to the empirical question.

The second question is a logical matter and requires a conceptual analysis and a consideration of arguments such as those of Arblaster and Counts quoted above.

The third question is an ethical question and requires a discussion of the nature of education. The latter two questions are closely connected, of course, since if schools cannot be neutral, it is futile to insist that they should be.

In Section I, I attempt a preliminary analysis of the term 'neutrality' as it is used in educational discourse. In Section II, I tackle the question 'Can schools be neutral?' and in III, I discuss whether it is desirable that schools be neutral.

I

In educational discussion, 'neutrality' is used in the following ways:
(1) A teacher is neutral if and only if he has no firm convictions on anything that matters.

(2) A teacher is neutral if, regardless of his personal convictions, he does not reveal them in his teaching.

(3) A teacher is neutral if he does not allow his enthusiasms to show when he is presenting material in the classroom.

(4) A school (or school system) is neutral if its curriculum consists solely in the 'safe' subjects — e.g. spelling, writing, reading, mathematics, science. It is non-neutral whenever it teaches history, politics, religion or economics.

(5) A school (or teacher) is neutral if it (or he) does not take sides on a disputed issue.

(6) A school (or teacher) is neutral if it (or he) takes sides on a disputed issue only to the extent that the evidence warrants it.

It is clear that the concept of neutrality is polymorphous. It is not surprising therefore to find that the case against neutrality is very easy to sustain, for some forms of neutrality are clearly unacceptable in an educational institution. The ever-present danger is, however, that in rejecting one form of neutrality, a theorist believes that he has shown all the others to be absurd, incoherent, impossible, or undesirable. The first point of clarification required of anyone discussing neutrality is: which meaning of 'neutrality' do you have in mind?

A second distinction which must be made is that between teachers and schools. Arguments quite frequently move from 'teachers cannot be neutral' to 'schools cannot be neutral'. Even if in this context 'schools' means 'the totality of teachers' the move is still illegitimate. This can be shown by considering the move from 'a politician cannot present an unbiased view' to 'Parliament cannot present an unbiased view'. When we have said that a person is not neutral, we have said nothing about the direction of his partiality. Hence it is quite conceivable that several biased individuals can make up a neutral group. I shall show later that this distinction is of great importance for answering the question 'is neutrality desirable in education?'.

It needs to be said at the outset that some forms of neutrality are impossible in an educational institution. No school worthy of the name can be 'neutral' towards truth and falsity, aesthetic standards, logical coherence, styles of writing or expression, or conventions needed for the smooth running of the school. No teacher worthy of the name can be a person without beliefs, values and convictions and to teach without enthusiasms is to teach with little hope of success. Such statements are so obviously true that those who have defined neutrality in these ways have had no difficulty in showing that neutrality is either logically impossible or completely undesirable in education.

What then is the concept of neutrality which many have thought worth defending or attacking? It might be stated in this way: *in matters on which experts differ substantially, the school should not use its power and authority to favour one side or the other.* This general statement can apply to many areas: morals, politics, religion, history, literature, economics. In this paper I am concentrating on the political implications of this principle of educational neutrality.

II

When stated in this way it would seem that the principle may be undesirable, or difficult to implement, but is certainly logically coherent. James E. McClellan, however, has mounted a radical attack on the principle on the grounds that it is logically impossible for schools to be politically neutral.[4] I want now to examine his argument in some detail because he presents in its most sophisticated manner the argument which undercuts all the claims of neutrality and all the rhetoric designed to encourage teachers to aim for it. For, if it is logically impossible for schools to be neutral then *no* school is neutral and no school ever could be. The principle must vanish from the educational literature and educators must face the burden of acting on their preferences.

McClellan argues:

> Yes, it is clearly possible for a particular teacher to be neutral in a class election; yes, it may be possible for a particular school to be neutral on the issue of public vs. private ownership of electrical power systems. Indeed, unless one could find

---

[4]James E. McClellan, "The Politicizing of Educational Theory: a Re-evaluation" in *Proceedings of the Philosophy of Education Society, 1968*, pp. 94-105.

certain clear cases where a school or a teacher is politically neutral, then the rest of my argument would be senseless. It isn't self-contradictory or meaningless to say that a teacher or a school is neutral on a particular issue. It is clearly true in many instances. But that truth is only one pole of the dialectic. The other pole now has to be constructed.[5]

The 'other pole' is constructed in the following way: the intention to be politically neutral is not in itself an educational intention since it is compatible with never teaching anything at all. It becomes an educational intention when linked to the intention to teach something. That is to say, it is a codicil added to an educational intention e.g. "I am going to teach the students about the American Constitution, and preserve political neutrality in the process." This codicil, he argues, is inconsistent with some educational intentions and gratuitous with others. If added to "I am going to teach the class that the American business corporation is the most noble institution conceivable by the mind of man" it would be inconsistent. Added to "I am going to teach them the alphabet" it would be gratuitous.

The policy of political neutrality, then, is one in which it is the policy "to frame only those educational intentions to which the codicil of neutrality can be added without inconsistency and to add the codicil of neutrality to every statement of educational intention when, in context, that codicil would be relevant."[6] He adds: "There is nothing self-contradictory about such a policy."

What, then, is the problem? The problem arises when we come to justify this policy. For "to justify a policy, one must be prepared to advance arguments that appeal both to the universalized rationality and also to the particular interests of those who constitute the polity for that decision.... It is obvious that any such argument would be, by definition, a political argument."[7] That is to say, at the policy level it is not possible to be politically neutral. The decision to be politically neutral is itself a political decision, a non-neutral decision.

As I have already said, this is a powerful argument. I believe, however, that it is fallacious although I am not completely confident that I can show that it is. But, I shall try.

McClellan's argument derives its cogency from the use of the words 'political' and 'justify' and it is in terms of these that it has to be attacked. It can be agreed that the decision to be neutral is a policy decision. If every decision about a policy is a political decision, then clearly McClellan's argument must stand. That he does make this equation is implied in his paper which we are discussing and is made explicit in his book.[8] He says "As I am using the term, a problem or issue belongs in the realm of politics only if there is more than one real or genuine interest involved",[9] and "The term

---

[5] *Ibid.*, p. 98.
[6] *Ibid.*, p. 101.
[7] *Ibid.*, p. 102.
[8] James E. McClellan, *Toward an Effective Critique of American Education.* New York: J. B. Lippincott, 1968.
[9] *Ibid.*, p. 9.

policy may be considered as a derivative from 'politics'."[10] His position then is clear. A policy is any attempt to reconcile divergent beliefs or values in the interests of action and all such attempts are political activities. In his own terms, his argument is sustained. But is this the normal meaning of 'political' and, more importantly, is it the meaning which it has when we talk of the schools being politically neutral or non-neutral? The answer, I submit, is no.

We can agree that a policy is a decision to act in a certain way on certain specified issues or in certain specified circumstances: 'my policy is to give money to anyone who solicits help'; 'the policy of the government is to build up overseas reserves'; 'the policy of this school is to admit all without distinctions of academic attainment'. If a policy is a rational one, those who decide the policy should be able to give reasons for the policy, that is to *justify* the policy. This justification can take many forms, not all of which can reasonably be called 'political'. The decision to restrict good medical care only to the wealthy is very likely a political decision to be justified in terms of a social theory. The decision to give a certain rare drug only to those who have a particularly painful disease is a medical decision to be justified in terms of medical knowledge. (This is not to deny that there are ethical elements in these decisions, but only to deny that the term 'political' is appropriate.) Once we have established that there can be policy decisions based on non-political considerations, the way is open to thrust into the heart of McClellan's argument.

The second prong of my attack is directed at the term 'justify'. To talk of justifying a decision or a point of view is ambiguous. On one level it is simply to produce good reasons for acting or good grounds for believing. A justification is appraised formally in terms of the amount of evidence, the validity of the argument, the cogency of the reasons. A claim or decision can be justified regardless of whether anyone accepts the justification or not. On another level, however, the note of success is written in. To justify a claim or decision to someone is to succeed in convincing him that the claim is true or the decision correct. On this level, he must accept the reasons as good reasons, follow the argument and so on. It follows that one can justify X to person P even when X has not really been justified. In other words people do accept inadequate evidence, faulty logic, and insufficient reasons. The two uses of 'justify' are, then, distinct. I can formally justify a policy although the justification is not accepted and I can justify a policy to A even though the justification is formally invalid.

McClellan's argument depends on the successful use of 'justify'. It becomes a tautology to say that if we are going to justify X to person A, A must accept that our reasons do justify X. McClellan, however, makes an even stronger claim than this. He says "To justify a policy, one must be prepared to advance arguments that appeal both to the universalized rationality and also to the particular interests of those who constitute the polity for that decision."[11]

---

[10]*Ibid.*, p. 10.
[11]"The Politicizing of Educational Theory", p. 102.

Now it may be the case that people will not favour, adopt, or approve a policy unless they see it to be in their own interests but this is an empirical not a logical claim. It certainly is logically possible for people to accept the validity of a decision which is not in their interests and I believe it does happen.

To pull together the strands in my critique of McClellan:

(1) Not all policy decisions are political decisions and not all forms of justificatory arguments are political arguments: there are, for example, medical arguments.

(2) A policy can be justified even if people do not accept the justification.

(3) It may be the case that if we are to get our policies accepted, we shall have to use political arguments. But even this is not obviously true.

To conclude this section and to anticipate the next, let me state the force of my argument so far. The answer to the question 'Is it possible for the schools to be politically neutral?' is 'yes' since it is logically possible to have a justification of the policy of political neutrality which is not a political justification. In the next section, I want to try to construct such a justification and to see what it does justify.

III

I would argue that a decision is political if it is made for political reasons i.e. in terms of some particular interest group, and an argument is a political argument if it is couched in terms which are meant to appeal to a particular interest group. Defined in this way, decisions based on scientific findings and decisions based on high-order ethical principles (e.g. justice, equality) are not political decisions. Similarly, arguments based on science or ethics are not political arguments. In McClellan's terms they are based on 'universalized rationality' and not on 'particular interests'. I believe, similarly, that it is possible to justify some educational decisions on educational grounds. If 'neutrality' (in some sense) can be so justified, we will be able to say that McClellan's argument fails and we will have a firm base for the policy of political neutrality in schools.

It seems to me self-evident that whenever we set out to educate people we are concerned to develop their rationality. We want them to know what is true rather than what is false and to do what is reasonable rather than what is unreasonable. That is to say we are concerned with rational beliefs and rational action. It is, of course, easy to say this but when the whole spectrum of the educational endeavour is being viewed, 'rationality' is extremely elusive. A teacher used to dealing only with mature scholars at a post-graduate level might see the development of rationality as a comparatively simple task for he inherits a group of people who are more or less rational and more or less committed to rationality. But this is not true of the parent of the young child nor the teacher in a primary or secondary school. Children are not born rational and rationality does not develop as the bodily organs develop. It is the outcome of social living and the gradual incorporation of minds into traditions of critical thought. Hence, the problem of developing rationality is a twofold one. It involves teaching pupils those traditions in which rationality is defined and it involves encouraging them to use their skills and understandings in wider and more inclusive ways. To put it another way, what is involved are the methods of critical thinking and the dispositions to use them.

It is easy to see, then, the complete absurdity in the view that the teaching of any body of knowledge violates the principle of neutrality. For educational neutrality only makes sense in relation to teaching something and is valuable only because rationality is valuable. Yet without bodies of knowledge with their critical standards, rationality itself is impossible. To argue that all teaching is non-neutral is to obscure the situations in which neutrality is obviously breached — e.g. when a particular view of history is presented in the interests of a political or religious ideology. That this is often done on behalf of capitalism as well as socialism, democracy as well as totalitarianism, Christianity as well as Communism, is not denied. What is denied is that such a state of affairs is logically necessary.

In the development of reason, schools must teach certain bodies of knowledge. Those with carefully defined standards of truth and falsity present no real problem. Those subjects in which there are no clear standards present the difficulties. These are the matters on which the evidence and the weight of authorities does not overwhelmingly favour one side. The principle of neutrality, I have suggested, means that in these areas the school shall not add the weight of its authority to the scale.

I see no reason why this should be an *impossible* ideal although I think it is in practice difficult. What I want to consider now is whether this neutrality is desirable. That it might be politically desirable or undesirable is, I submit, not the point. What I want to ask is whether it is educationally desirable and this must be determined by reference to rationality. Once the development of reason is placed firmly in the centre of the stage distinctions between 'schools', 'school systems' and 'teachers' become important. In discussions of neutrality, these distinctions have often been ignored or blurred.

(1) It seems to me evident that school systems should be neutral. A school system should have no orthodoxy beyond that of commitment to the evidence and logic inherent in various forms of knowledge. If a school system puts its authority behind one political system or ideology, the inevitable result will be a diminution in the overall commitment to rationality. Teachers and students will have an area which they are not free to explore rationally: an area closed off to free inquiry.

(2) When we consider teachers, the situation is a little different. I would argue that teachers should not always be neutral in the presentation of controversial issues. The reason is that their commitment is not to neutrality as such but to the development of rationality. In their prudent judgment, this will sometimes necessitate the presentation of a particular point of view very strongly. For example, if a teacher faces a class of rather conservative pupils, he may judge that they need to face up to a more liberal point of view. A class of children indoctrinated in anti-Communism may need for the develop-

ment of reason an injection of a sympathetic view of Communism. The criterion, it should be noted, is not what the teacher himself believes or values (this *is* irrelevant to the education of the child) but what is required by the commitment to develop the rationality of the pupils. Naturally, many particular judgments are required in practice, e.g. the age of the child, his degree of knowledge and understanding, perhaps even his intelligence. The question, then, should teachers be neutral requires the answer 'no'. Teachers should aim for the development of reason and this will sometimes demand neutrality, sometimes non-neutrality. Non-neutrality, however, is nothing more than a pedagogical device to preserve the overall neutrality of education and the rationality of the students.

(3) Should individual schools be neutral is the most difficult question of the three. In one way, schools are like school systems: they involve many teachers and a large number of pupils. On these grounds we are inclined to say that schools, like school systems, should be neutral. In another way, schools are like teachers: they handle a particular group of children, drawn perhaps from a particular area, social grouping or religious denomination. On these grounds we are inclined to say that schools, like teachers, should not be neutral but should adapt their point of view to rationality.

On balance, I would argue that schools are more like school systems than they are like teachers and should, in fact, be neutral. The reasons for this are: (a) If a school has a policy of partiality there is bound to be some limiting of the freedom of teachers to critically examine issues. (b) The school (i.e. those who make school policy) is not in the same position as the teacher to know what in fact pupils already do accept or value. (c) The development of reason is essentially an individual matter, best left to the teacher. (d) In many schools, especially at secondary and tertiary levels, there are differences in competence between teachers. The history teacher, for example, is expected to know more about what is in fact well established about the past. A school policy of non-neutrality ignores these distinctions.

In summary, neutrality, as defined, is possible and overall is desirable, because necessary for the development of reason. This general commitment to neutrality, however, does not require that the teacher always be neutral: his decision in a particular case is dependent on a judgment about the situation and his general commitment to develop his pupils' rationality. Schools and school systems should be neutral in the sense I have defined it for only then is rationality adequately safeguarded. To overthrow my basic argument, one would need to show that rationality is itself a position logically dependent on a particular political view. I would then have to argue that rationality is a basic human value. But that would be another paper.

SEMESTER: WEEK TEN

REQUIRED READINGS

Church

Part IV: School and Community: Progressivism in Education, 1890-1940, Chapter 9: <u>Educational Reform in the Progressive Era</u> (37 pp.)

Dye

Bagenstos, Naida Tushnet. "The Teacher as an Inquirer" <u>The Educational Forum</u>. V.39, No.2, January, 1975. (07 pp.)

Spring, Joel. "Education and Progressivism" <u>History of Education Quarterly</u>. V.10, No.1, Spring, 1970. (19 pp.)

Wirth, Arthur G. "The Deweyan Tradition Revisited" <u>The Washington University Magazine</u>. 1971. (05 pp.)

MEETINGS

Monday

Lecture: Corporate Education: Goodyear Industrial University and P. W. Litchfield

Tuesday

Lecture: Transition: Manual Training to Vocational Education, Canton City Schools

Wednesday

Lecture: John Dewey

Thursday and Friday

Small Groups: Examination Two will be administered.

CHURCH TEXTBOOK STUDY GUIDE: CHAPTER 9

EDUCATIONAL REFORM IN THE PROGRESSIVE ERA

1. individual intellectual achievement
2. individual moral achievement
3. individual social contribution
4. community service ideal
5. the school as community agent

6. educational reform
7. Progressive Era
8. progressive education
9. Frederick Jackson Turner
10. frontier thesis

11. democratic experiment
12. conflicts over distribution of limited resources
13. Herbert Spencer
14. Lester Frank Ward
15. liberal progressive reformers

16. social justice
17. conservative progressive reformers
18. social order
19. President Theodore Roosevelt
20. New Nationalism

21. John Dewey
22. The Laboratory School of the University of Chicago
23. Johann Heinrich Pestalozzi
24. Friedrich Froebel
25. Johann Heinrich Herbart

26. Francis Wayland Parker
27. Cook County Normal School, Chicago
28. dualisms
29. dichotomy
30. child-centered education

31. subject-centered education
32. school or society
33. cooperative learning
34. hand training
35. teaching the occupations

36. interdependency
37. new education
38. settlement house movement
39. Jane Addams
40. Hull House, Chicago

41. Charitable Organization Society
42. friendly visitors
43. social democracy
44. socialized school
45. socialized education

46. Public Education Association of New York City
47. visiting teacher movement
48. Julia Richman
49. Public Education Association Committee on Visiting Teachers
50. casework approach of visiting teachers

51. take the school out of politics

The Teacher as an Inquirer

NAIDA TUSHNET BAGENSTOS

THE position in this article is that developing a teacher education program which will produce "teachers as inquirers" as the term is used by Schaefer[1] and others (e.g., Joyce)[2] is a worthy task *if* a central dilemma is dealt with directly. The dilemma is that teachers are *not* independent professionals free to act on the results of their inquiry but are, in fact, bureaucrats with prescribed roles and powers. What will be argued is that the trainers of teacher-inquirers should accept that fact and work within the constraints of the situation. At the same time, teachers can deal with pushing at the limits of their prescribed role in ways that do not cause the bureaucracy to crush them.

This article is organized first to defend the position that schools represent bureaucratic organizations and to describe within them the role of the teacher. Secondly, after defining the term inquiry, the author will spell out the implications and limitations which the bureaucracy places on teacher-inquirers. The final section will deal with a rationale for inquiry within these limits.

THE SCHOOLS AS BUREAUCRATIC ORGANIZATIONS

Presthus,[3] following the Weberian tradition, lists the following characteristics of bureaucracy:

Naida Tushnet Bagenstos is a research assistant and graduate student in the Graduate Institute of Education at Washington University, St. Louis, Missouri.

1. fixed and official jurisdictional areas, which are regularly ordered by rules;
2. principles of hierarchy and levels of graded authority;
3. administration based upon written documents;
4. administration by full-time officials who are thoroughly and expertly trained;
5. administration by general rules which are quite stable and comprehensive.

The following discussion will apply each of the points to schools in reverse order.

Administration by general rules. In American schools rules abound. Perhaps the most significant are those concerning compulsory attendance. These are promulgated at the state level, and the procedures for implementing them are developed within the local school system. Both remain stable over time and, despite the ideology of local control, are quite similar throughout the nation (e.g., school leaving age, number of days school must be open). Indeed, some critics[4] contend that compulsory attendance is *the* crucial fact about schools and the rules governing attendance are (both in terms of state law and intra-building attendance-taking procedures) the key rules.

Administration by trained full-time officials. It is sufficient to point out that teachers, principals, school nurses, etc., are all *certified* by the state. Their certificates indicate that they have completed requisite training programs, and although specific requirements differ from state to state, there is enough commonality among states to indicate the existence of a *national* training program. In addition, the National Council of Accreditation of Teacher Education (NCATE) certification is recognized in twenty-eight states. A final point is that training is specifically for schools—*school* administrators receive different training from hospital or business administrators; *school* social workers are required to have courses in the field of "education" along with their MSW. Such certification is in line with Weber's idea of "technical competence." It sets the *minimum* levels of competence for work within the bureaucracy. A persistent problem is that there are few rewards for higher achievement within the schools.

Administration based upon written documents. Such documents exist on the level of state and federal law, "guidelines" written by state departments of education, and internal school memoranda. The experience of receiving, yearly, "bulletins" concerning how to open and close school (which was later read aloud at a faculty meeting!) is part of this author's memories of her years within the bureaucracy.

Principles of hierarchy and levels of graded authority. The typical American school system exemplifies the hierarchical structure—from teachers (or students) through department chairpersons, assistant principals, principals, upward to the superintendent.

Fixed and official jurisdictional areas, which are already ordered by rules. As Max Abbott[5] puts it:

> . . . the school organization has clearly been influenced by the need for specialization and the factoring of tasks. The division of the school into elementary and secondary units; the establishment of science, mathematics, music, and other departments within a school; the introduction of guidance programs and psychological services; indeed, the separation of the administrative function from

the teaching function, all represent responses to this need.

In teaching, broad jurisdictional areas are defined. However, teachers have a degree of freedom within their area. For example, the conventional wisdom speaks of a teacher's isolation "after she closes the door," and this isolation presents an opportunity for experimental approaches to teaching. (The isolation also can have negative consequences,[6] but this article will not deal with them.) An elementary school teacher can, behind her door, experiment with combining reading and science lessons, role play, or use other creative ideas. On the secondary level, the textbook becomes in one way a definition of what the jurisdiction of the course is, particularly if other materials are not available, but a teacher can use a text in different ways.

The determination of what areas are open for creative teaching in a school hinges around the boundaries of a teacher's jurisdictional areas, and the role expectations within those boundaries. If the boundaries are vaguely defined in a given system, the teacher has more chance to be an innovator. Further, if it is expected only that she exercise "control," she has a clear field so long as she convinces her class to be quiet. Obviously, the boundaries and role expectations are more rigid in some systems than in others. Kozol, for example, reports being fired from the Boston schools for teaching two poems, one not on the district wide "approved" list and the other belonging to a different grade level. The teacher-inquirer, then, must determine what the boundaries and expectations in her setting are.

Schools fulfill the definition of bureaucracy developed by Presthus. However, the individual teacher does have some room to maneuver. She is, in short, a special kind of bureaucrat whose role is not fully proscribed by rules. The argument here is that inquiry *can* operate within the limitations of a teacher's bureaucratic office.

DEFINITION OF INQUIRY AND RATIONALE

Robert Schaefer defines inquiry as the production of new knowledge. An inquiry-oriented school is one which is "more than a place of instruction. It must also be . . . a producer as well as a transmitter of knowledge."[7] While such an aim is laudable and even necessary, it is clear that an inquiry-oriented teacher cannot fully achieve it within the bureaucratic framework. The goal for teachers is more modest—to "search for meaning and rationality in (their) work."[8] The search for meaning may not take a teacher to the "cutting edge" of educational research. It will, however, be characterized by constant questions of the nature "What am I doing? What are my reasons? What effects do my actions have upon my students?" Inquiry-oriented teachers are those who have the skills to analyze what they are doing and the habit of mind to do so. Such teachers then choose among alternative approaches. Inquiry is "a process that moves in cycles from experience to conceptualization, from conceptualization to practice, and from practice to an evaluation that produces the data necessary for the step back to experience, thus repeating the cycle."[9] The implication is that the step back to experience will be different, based on what is learned from the first attempts. As will be argued below, however, teachers are seldom in a position to act fully on what they have learned.

In some ways, arguing for the importance of inquiry-oriented teachers approaches arguing for the importance of love. In most educational circles it is considered "a good thing." However, the reasons for preparing teachers in this mode go beyond either their own personal fulfillment (i.e., "the unexamined life is not worth living") or "a questioning attitude is good in itself" approach. First, teachers are role models for students and, as such, should exemplify a mode of thinking and behaving which deals in some way with the intellectual dimension of life. Also, approaching the job of teaching as an inquirer can make it an exciting endeavor and, if the thinking and decisions are the teacher's own, increase his personal commitment to the tasks. Finally, inquiry is good for teachers because they need to confront, in their daily work, the current attacks on the schools and to be aware of which of those they cannot deal with in their professional role.

Inquiry teachers have an important function in the socialization of students. Within our society schools are the main centers for intellectual endeavor. What this means for children is that teachers are the major (if not only) adults who can serve as models of an intellectual life. Socialization refers to the "processes by which (is developed) a . . . self, with its characteristic values, attitudes, knowledge, and skills. Socialization takes place primarily through social interaction with people who are significant for the individual."[10] Teachers are, or can be, significant for students. Kimball and McClellan maintain that a commitment to continuous learning "is a requirement of everyone who would not be a slave to the society he serves."[11] Of all the adults with whom students come into contact, teachers have the special responsibility for teaching students how to learn. "Schools fulfill their responsibilities in the modern world only when students are encouraged to make systematic inquiry into the substance and meaning of their subjects." As models for students, then, teachers themselves should be inquirers. "How can youngsters be convinced of the vitality of inquiry and of discovery if the adults with whom they directly work are mere automatons?"[12] If one goal of teaching is to create independent thinkers, then teachers should be independent thinkers themselves, and this involves both knowing the processes of thinking (inquiry) and pursuing them.

A second reason for developing inquiry teachers relates to the job of teaching itself and is, in a sense, an "unexamined life" argument. As Schaefer states: "When divorced from appropriate scholarship . . . teaching resembles employment as an educational sales clerk and ceases to be more than a humdrum job."[13] It is difficult to imagine a U.S. history teacher communicating excitement, relevance, or importance, for example, to the controversy surrounding Jackson and the Bank of the United States year after year unless he was involved in questions concerning the historical issues involved or the pedagogical questions raised by the existence of the topic in the syllabus. The technique and answers a teacher arrives at need not be purely original. The act of invention itself is frequently what is exciting and makes for a richer classroom. Further, if teaching is to develop into a profession, there must be an "enrichment of practical knowledge"[14] on which to base professional courses. According to Everett Hughes,[15] a profession is both "a culture and a technique." The commitment to and methods of inquiry are the "culture" of education, and the technique is still being developed, and will continue to be developed out of the accumulation of the work of teacher-inquirers. The argument here is that teachers need to be inquirers both to sustain their own excitement and commitment to teaching and for the development of a profession of teaching.

Recent literature, both popular and scholarly, has raised questions about the purposes and effects of public schools. One set of arguments is that differences among schools have little to do with variations in pupil achievement. Silberman[16] argues that schools are "mindless." Other critics see schools as dull, lifeless, anti-creative, anti-intellectual places. Another group emphasizes the processing and certifying functions of schools[17] which make them anti-democratic and oppressive to students. Finally, students themselves have been in rebellion against both school and society, attacking the schools as institutions (e.g., Birmingham,[18] Libarle and Seligman[19]). In short, schools have been seen as fulfilling a custodial function which has little intellectual effect.

The image of an inquiry teacher seems to answer some of these attacks, particularly the question of mindlessness. Such a teacher asks, for example, what effects the reading of a particular novel has on high school students. Can it increase their ability to read and analyze literature? Does it raise questions relevant to their lives? Does it give a view of books which is positive? The teacher as inquirer asks, in addition, *how* to approach the teaching so as to have more positive than negative effects on students. Finally, she is able to view her classroom and her students objectively and analyze the procedures and effects (immediate and long-range, at least in a tentative way) so she can choose among alternative strategies.[20] In this way, a teacher-inquirer is speaking, in her daily work, to the criticisms raised.

What all of this means for the training of teachers is that the entire teacher-education program must have built into it opportunities for critical analysis of curricula and teaching. Both through reading and observation, pre-service students should deal with models of such analysis. Their own teaching and curriculum decisions should be subjected to such an approach. (For one model of such training see McIntosh, 1968.[21]) Finally, problems of "craftsmanship" in teaching should be directly addressed.

LIMITS OF INQUIRY AND IMPLICATIONS FOR TRAINING

The argument for inquiry-oriented teachers seems to assume that an individual teacher will be free to inquire and to act on the results of his inquiry. Contrary to such a view, Wayland argues that ". . . the teacher is a functionary in an essentially bureaucratic system. As such, he is a replaceable unit in a rationally organized system and most of the significant aspects of work are determined for him. Any areas in which he makes decisions are those which are given to him and are not inherent in his role as teacher."[22] For example, "*Whom he will teach; what he will teach; where, when, and for how long he will teach; how he will evaluate the work of the student; and (in a measure) how he will teach* are determined for the teacher."[23]

A further limitation on inquiry which arises from the particular bureaucracy is that the stated goals and rules for her jurisdictional area may not be the real ones or that a number of the stated goals might be in conflict. For example, schools have as goals both that students gain certain knowledge (e.g., reading skills) and that they attend for stated periods of time. The most efficient way of accomplishing the first goal might be to release from school or class those students who know how to read and concentrate resources on those who do not. However, teachers who attempted to do this would soon be in trouble with the community, which does not want students in the streets. Teachers need to be aware of the limits of their own decision-making. Such awareness involves understanding the sometimes unclear limits to their roles.

An understanding of the ascribed role can help a teacher manipulate the bureaucracy and push at the outer reaches of the role. An example of this might be a teacher who wants to take her class on an off-beat but educationally exciting field trip. Getting a principal's permission might prove difficult if the teacher emphasizes the educational aspects of the trip. Fighting for the idea on these grounds might well prove psychologically exhausting for the teacher. Even if she "won," the excursion could be less than satisfying for both students and teacher. However, if the problem were addressed in terms that the principal could accept (e.g., dealing with potential control problems), the teacher would, in all likelihood, receive permission with less strain.

An important factor for the survival of inquiry teachers in the bureaucratic schools may be that they have a peer group or reference group which supports their efforts. Herndon, who was fired from one school and made a positive impact on another, illustrates this point.[24] A key difference between the settings was the existence of a like-minded group of teachers in the second school. A training institution can help create a reference group by two methods. First, it can encourage its graduates to apply to schools in the same district, perhaps by concentrating student teacher placements. Second, it can create an informal alumni organization which meets regularly, but not necessarily frequently, to serve as a social function and as a forum for the exchange of ideas, complaints, and insights.

The suggestion here is that the training of teachers should involve the issue of bureaucratic constraints on performing as a teacher-inquirer. Pre-service teachers aware of the limitations will either know better how to deal with them or choose not to teach at all. This component of training involves dealing with questions of power, norms of the school, teacher and student status, and the function of schooling. In short, pre-service teachers should gain the tools of analysis which enable them to determine the boundaries of their jurisdictions and the roles they are expected to occupy within the system in which they work. The further role of the teacher training institution is to create an informal support mechanism which continues its role after the student becomes a teacher.

CONCLUSION

The argument has been that schools are bureaucracies and teachers are not free to inquire and act on the results of their inquiry in many aspects of their professional life. However, there is enough room within the ascribed role of the teacher for an inquiry approach to be valuable both for her and her students. Further, if a teacher is prepared to inquire into the nature of the bureaucracy and its constraints, she will be able to enhance the area over which she has control, particularly if the training institution continues to play a supporting role through the creation of an informal reference group.

NOTES

1. Robert J. Schaefer, *The School as a Center of Inquiry* (New York: Harper & Row, 1967).
2. Bruce Joyce and Marsha Weil, *Perspectives for Reform in Teacher Education* (Englewood Cliffs, N.J.: Prentice-Hall, 1972).
3. Robert Presthus, *The Organizational Society* (New York: Random House, 1962).
4. Ivan Illich, *Deschooling Society* (New York: Harper & Row, 1971).
5. Max Abbott and John T. Lovell, eds., *Change Perspectives in Educational Administration* (Auburn, Ala.: School of Education, Auburn University, 1965), p. 44.
6. Dan C. Lortie, "Teacher Socialization: The Robinson Crusoe Model," *The Real World of the Beginning Teacher* (Washington, D.C.: NEA National Commission on Teacher Education and Professional Standards, 1965).
7. Schaefer, *School,* p. 1.
8. Ibid., p. 3.
9. Ad Hoc Committee on Undergraduate Teacher Education, "Report," mimeographed (Washington University, 1970).
10. Robert K. Merton, George G. Reader, M.D., and Patricia L. Kendall, eds., *The Student-Physician* (Cambridge, Mass.: Harvard University Press, 1957), p. 287.
11. Solon T. Kimball and James McClellan, Jr., *Education and the New America* (New York: Random House, 1962), p. 295.
12. Schaefer, *School,* p. 3.
13. Ibid.
14. Lortie, "Teacher Socialization"
15. Everett Hughes, *Men and Their Work* (Glencoe, Ill.: The Free Press, 1958), p. 35.
16. Charles E. Silberman, *Crisis in the Classroom: The Remaking of American Education* (New York: Random House, 1970).
17. Martin Carnoy, *Schooling in the Corporate Society: The Political Economy of Education in America* (New York: David McKay Company, Inc., 1972).
18. John Birmingham, *Our Time Is Now: Notes from the High School Underground* (New York: Praeger, 1970).
19. Marc Libarle and Tom Seligson, eds., *The High School Revolutionaries* (New York: Random House, 1970).
20. A. P. Coldarci, "The Teacher as Hypothesis-Maker," *Journal of Instructional Improvement,* (1959), pp. 3-6.
21. Robert Gordon McIntosh, "An Approach to the Analysis of Clinical Settings for Teacher Education," Address to the Association for Student Teaching, February 15, 1968.
22. Sloan R. Wayland, "The Role of the Teacher," in *Curriculum Crossroads,* ed. A. Harry Passow (New York: Bureau of Publications, Teachers College, 1962), p. 43.
23. Ibid., p. 48.
24. James Herndon, *How to Survive in Your Native Land* (New York: Simon & Schuster, 1971).

Education and Progressivism

JOEL SPRING

A MAJOR PROBLEM with Lawrence A. Cremin's *The Transformation of the School* is the neglect of one aspect of progressive political ideology and one stream of educational thought during the pre-World War I period. The neglect of these two movements was probably caused by a failure to give a coherent statement as to the nature of educational reforms during this period and the use of a rather vague definition of progressive political and social change. What Cremin calls "progressive education" during the pre-World War I period appears to be a conglomeration of educational changes with no particular common bonds except that they represented something new. This lack of clarity gives the impression that a strange combination of people were called "progressive educators." Under the roof of this title is mixed the free atmosphere of Marietta Johnson's Organic School with the well ordered air of the platoon system of the Gary Public Schools. The title also houses the educational elitist and test-oriented Edward L. Thorndike with Caroline Pratt's Play School. This confused picture of educational change is a function of an equally obscure definition of progressive political and social change. Cremin vaguely defines "American Progressivism writ large" as social and political change designed to improve the lives of individuals, a valueless definition since it literally includes everyone.

What I would like to do in this paper is to clarify some of these relationships by suggesting one possible link between the social and political movement called "progressivism" and educational reform. In doing this I will attempt to be more specific about the goals of

Mr. Spring is Assistant Professor of Education at Case Western Reserve University.

educational and political reformers by exploring the type of society and individual they hoped would result from their work. I believe that if the problem is approached in this manner, meaningful differences will become apparent. Certainly, the Organic School and Gary, or Thorndike and Pratt, were attempting to produce different types of individuals and by implication different versions of the good society. The same argument holds for political reformers. It is not enough to say that they wanted to improve social conditions. One must give some indication of the direction in which they were headed. Only then can one discern the common elements of a political and social movement. When the elements of a movement become sharply defined, then decisions can be made about similarities of purpose.

The two parallel streams of social and educational thought that Cremin neglects had in common the vision of a corporate society dependent upon specialization and cooperation. What distinguished this group of progressive reformers from others who adopted the progressive label was the belief that industrial combination and organization was beneficial and represented the wave of the future. In strictly political terms this meant opposition to antitrust legislation and to attempts to restore traditional American values by destroying large corporate combinations. Politically these progressives supported government regulation of the economic system. For educators this goal meant an attempt to educate the child in a specific economic skill and to develop character habits suited for this type of social organization. Large corporate businessmen and labor leaders supported this progressive movement because it rationalized the social and economic system and assured the recognition of their place in society. The educational and political aspects of this movement were to provide the basis for the major developments in American education and American liberalism in the twentieth century.

What the vision of a corporate society meant for these reformers was that traditional notions of rugged and independent individualism had to be replaced with the ideal of the socialized, cooperative man who worked for the good of the whole society. It also meant that the concept of an atomistic society with everyone working as an independent unit had to be replaced with one of an interdependent society in which each man did his specialized job in cooperation with the entire social system. One concise statement of this view of the well working social system was given by sociologist Edward Ross in a book published in 1901. Ross wrote that "success in social organization implies that each man, whether watched or unwatched, sticks to his appointed work, and interferes with no else in his work." For Ross this meant that each man must do his special task, "trusting that others will do certain things at certain times, in certain ways, and will forbear from certain other things." (1) A similar view of society and man was expressed by educator William C. Bagley in 1904 when he wrote that the goal of education should be social efficiency. Bagley described the socially efficient man as one who performed his specialized productive task for society, interfering "as little as possible with the efforts of others . . . sacrificing his own pleasure when this interferes with the productive efforts of his fellows . . . [and] when its gratification will not directly or indirectly lead to social advancement." (2)

The first goal of the educators and the social reformers who adopted this vision of the well ordered society was to change the basis of human motivation from desire for economic gain to unselfish interest in working for the good of society. The rapid growth of urban areas after the Civil War was partially responsible for creating this goal. Urbanization presented the American public with the ugly picture of rapidly sprawling slums and the innumerable problems connected with municipal government. Many reformers felt that the closeness of urban living required the development of individual social responsibility. If the problems of the city were to be solved, people had to learn how to cooperate and sacrifice their own interests for the welfare of the community. One writer stated in 1901 that if Americans wanted a livable, beautiful and moral physical environment in their cities they could not allow "each individual to assert what he believes to be his economic interests. . . ." (3)

The concentration of wealth, the problems of poverty, and labor struggles also made many people question the laissez-faire doctrine of a marketplace governed by the natural laws of individual self-interest. There was concern during the pre-World War I period about the possibility of some form of class warfare. Jacob Riis warned

America in his popular book published in 1890, *How the Other Half Lives*, that the slums were splintering American society and creating the "Man with the Knife." Riis's man with the knife was a poverty-stricken individual who, while standing on a busy New York street watching the affluent on their way to spend in an hour of shopping an amount that would have kept his family from want for a whole year, suddenly flung himself into the crowd and wildly slashed with his knife. Riis wrote that this symbolized what would happen if something was not done about the gap between the rich and the poor. The man with the knife represented the anarchist who was raising "the danger-cry of which we lately heard in the shout that never should have been raised on American soil— the shout of 'masses against the classes'—the solution of violence." (4) A similar warning was issued by a socialist to a gathered audience of labor, business and political leaders in Chicago in 1893. He reminded the audience of the way Chicago treated the worker by describing how policemen were used to drive assembled laborers from the Lake Front into the tenement districts so that visitors to the World's Fair would not see their misery. "Do you believe," he asked the meeting, "that under these social conditions here in this free country there are no anarchists, no bombs, no dynamite? Do you believe some desperate man, under the load which you allow to rest on him, will get uneasy and will revolt?" Upon hearing these words the crowd rose in angry protest and then settled back and tried to do something by organizing the Civic Federation of Chicago. The leadership of the organization would provide a common meeting ground for cooperative municipal improvement. Within just a few months the organization had expended $135,000 on the city's homeless. (5)

It was hoped by many progressive reformers that these problems could be solved if people placed society's interests above their own. One of the most forceful statements of this position was given by Herbert Croly in his *The Promise of American Life*. Croly's book, published in 1909, was important as a statement of progressive theory and because of its supposed influence on Theodore Roosevelt and the 1912 Progressive Party campaign. In this work, Croly stated that the promise of American life consisted of improved economic conditions for all people. In the past this promise had been achieved through the free play of economic self-interest. Croly wrote, "The fulfillment of the American Promise was considered inevitable because it was based upon a combination of self-interest and the natural goodness of human interest." This marketplace philosophy had resulted, he argued, in a concentration of wealth and power in the hands of a few, who had in turn closed off the traditional workings of the free market. In essence this meant that self-interest as a working economic philosophy was self-destructive. Croly wrote that this philosophy had to be abandoned "precisely because the traditional American confidence in individual freedom has resulted in a morally and socially undesirable distribution of wealth."

What Croly proposed as a replacement for laissez-faire doctrines was an economic system that provided government regulation of industry and labor. Economic self-interest as a motivation to work was to be replaced by a desire to work for the common good. Croly hoped to achieve this by showing the individual the value of his work to the collective endeavor. Croly wrote that "when a nation is sincerely attempting to meet its collective responsibility, the better individuals are inevitably educated into active participation in the collective task." Within Croly's system an individual gained his individualism not through the amount of money he accumulated while pursuing his self-interest, but rather in terms of the job he performed for society. Croly wrote, "A man achieves individual distinction, not by the enterprise and vigor with which he pursues an exclusive interest—an interest usually, but not necessarily, connected with his means of livelihood." This Croly believed was a much more meaningful definition of individualism. (6)

Educators labeled this idea of creating a cooperative individualism, social education. In 1909 Michael V. O'Shea, a leader of the social education movement and professor of education at the University of Wisconsin, summed up the objectives of this educational process as bringing the individual "into harmony with the customs, ideals and institutions of present-day society. Intense individualistic feelings and actions must be brought under control, and cooperation must largely take the place of original tendencies to opposition and aggression." (7) To accomplish this goal educators argued that the competitive atmosphere of the classroom had to be changed. One writer in the *Educational Review* in 1902 argued that if the social ideal of mutual cooperation and dedication to the common good were to be accomplished all prizes, awards and competition would have to be removed from the classroom. He claimed that these stimulants to competition were just concessions to modern commercialism. The competitive spirit in the classroom, he wrote, should be replaced by a "functional pleasure in acquiring and using knowledge, and the gratification which always comes from successful cooperation toward a worthy end." (8) The same concern was voiced by Samuel T. Dutton in *Social Phases of Education in the School and the Home*, published in 1899. This book consisted of a series of lectures that Dutton, as superintendent of schools in Brookline, Massachusetts, had given at the Chicago, Harvard, and Boston universities. Dutton asked his audiences, "Is the acquisition of knowledge of such tremendous importance that the social code is to be constantly violated in the schoolroom?" According to Dutton the social code and the teaching of social cooperation should assume a higher place than the mere acquisition of knowledge. The problem with the usual classroom recitation, Dutton felt, was that "a few brilliant pupils are permitted to do all the work, and that, too, with an air of superiority which is the highest degree unsocial." (9)

One widespread solution to the problem of classroom competitiveness was the organization of group activities. The Francis Parker School in Chicago devoted its first yearbook in 1912 to explaining how the school had attempted to replace selfish individualism with cooperative group ideals. The goal of the Parker School was to find some other method of motivation besides that of the reward system. The solution was to devote the majority of school time to group dramas, projects, and games. The school aimed to create an atmosphere where "competition is ruled out as a force in the school work, personal aggrandizement is done away with in every form and in its place is brought in the social motive. . . ."(10) The social motive became such an overriding factor at the Parker school that according to John and Evelyn Dewey the school came to believe, "Studying alone out of a book is an isolated an unsocial performance; the pupil may be learning the words before him, but he is not learning to act with other people. . . ." (11)

The organizational medium for spreading the idea of group activities and social training was the Social Education Congress organized by Colin Scott in 1907. The stated objective of the association was: "To emphasize the fact that the fundamental purpose of education should be to prepare the child for a useful service as an active and creative member of the social organism." (12) Colin Scott had been campaigning for social education for many years before organizing the Social Education Congress. Working in the West and in Boston he had developed a theory of classroom activities based upon group activities. Scott believed that the ideal social organization was one based on groups with shared responsibility. He wrote in his book *Social Education*, published in 1908, that he wanted groups "in which each individual in the various groups to which he may belong, finds himself in contact with others whose weaknesses he supplements or whose greater powers he depends upon." Scott's particular method of handling classroom organization was that of turning all activity and direction of the class work over to the students. Working in groups they were to initiate all classroom activity with just the title of the course as a guide. (13)

The Social Education Congress did not devote all of its time to promoting Scott's self-initiated group activities. The Congress touched on a variety of ways of training people for social cooperation and service to the common good. These ranged from E. A. Filene's description of how his department store in Boston organized group activities to teach their employees that "when work is for the common weal, then work is worship, work is prayer," to discussions by librarians on the value of using open shelves to direct their patrons to particular books on pressing social issues. (14)

The social atmosphere of the classroom was not the only point of concentration. School subjects were changed to make students more aware of social problems and the need for cooperation. The curriculum that was offered to accomplish this end was usually called social studies, and in general it was designed to introduce the student gradually to the complex interdependency of society. For instance, one course of study proposed in 1914 called for introducing the child in the first grade to immediate community relationships and then progressing to the point of studying local and county government in the seventh and eighth grades. The proponent of this curriculum plan began his article in the *American Journal of Sociology* with the comment, "The recent developments in our country have abundantly shown that much of the abuse which has arisen in our political and industrial affairs has taken place because of the one-sided and exaggerated individualism which has been fostered in our educational and political system." (15)

Educators also turned to the organization of the school as a means of teaching cooperation. One result of attempting to integrate a social spirit into school life was the development of a tremendous emphasis upon extracurricular activities, such as clubs, team games, and other group activities. The man who probably did the most to point out the value of the educational training when the school functions as a social community was John Dewey in his *School and Society* lecture. While Dewey's lecture was often quoted by educators, many of his ideas underwent some strange transformations in the process. For instance, one principal wrote that his school had been organized around "Dewey's principle that 'the school cannot be a preparation for adult social life except as it reproduces within itself situations typical of social life'—'purified and idealized,' he adds somewhere else—is to be followed." (16) What educators tended to get out of Dewey's lecture was the idea that it was their responsibility to organize and direct student activities so that traits of selfish individualism would be eradicated.

The idea of social activities as an educative tool rested on the assumption that the school's job included regulation of the social life of the student. W. B. Owen, dean of the University of Chicago High School, wrote in an often quoted article in 1907, "It is a common saying that education is not a preparation for life; it is life. This can be made true only on condition that the school cares for all the interests which govern the child's life while he is under the influence of the school." What Owen proposed was a "programme of enlargement of the functions of the school to include the general social training of the child, so far as the life of the child in the school affords opportunity." (17) Not all educators were willing to accept these added duties. One teacher in 1899, in a paper given before the Michigan Schoolmaster's Club, argued, "There is no necessity for a high school in a city to take upon itself the establishing of social functions. Our greatest trouble is not in furnishing to our pupils sufficient social life, but in restraining them from the over abundant opportunities offered in the outside surroundings. . . ." The speaker went on to state her concern that the school by involving itself in the social life of its students was treading on dangerous ground. The school could never fully understand what it might accomplish by institutionalizing social relationship. "For my part," the speaker said, "I am unwilling thus to risk tangling the threads of fate." (18)

The schools, of course, did not heed this warning and rapidly developed extensive programs to teach people how to cooperate. For instance, sports were stressed because they created social loyalty and gave the students a sense of interdependence. As one writer put it, "In the boy's mind, the football team is not only an aggregation of individuals organized to play, but a social instrument with common needs, working along common lines, and embodying a common purpose." (19) Even school newspapers began to flourish both as a method of teaching English and because the "Press Association, usually composed of all the students in the school, meets an important demand. It is a unifying organization, and is therefore a wholesome factor if properly directed. Its purpose is to edit a school paper through which a school spirit may be awakened and nourished." (20) After-school groups and clubs served the same function of bringing the students together for social training. As one writer stated, "The extracurricular activities fix the youth's attention on mutual cooperation for the good of the whole." (21)

The second goal of this social and educational movement was the establishment of a highly organized and interdependent social structure. This meant that the socialized man would also have to have an occupational specialization. Both the social educators and their progressive counterparts selected as their model the large industrial organizations that had developed after the Civil War. The key organizational terms for these new corporate structures were specialization and cooperation. It was the acceptance of these new industrial developments that distinguished these progressive reformers. Four representative figures in this progressive movement were George W. Perkins, Samuel Gompers, Theodore Roosevelt and Herbert Croly.

Perkins began his career as a very successful corporate organizer, first for New York Life Insurance, and later for the House of Morgan. He later became involved in politics and helped organize the Progressive Party in 1912. During the campaign of 1912 he served as Roosevelt's right-hand man and acted as chairman of the executive committee of the Progressive Party. Perkins brought to the progressive movement a belief in the value of corporate organization that he had gained while helping to organize for the House of Morgan two of the largest industrial combinations, U. S. Steel and International Harvester. He was in fact primarily responsible for the existence of International Harvester. In 1902 Perkins brought together the two leading manufacturers of farm implements, the McCormicks and the Deerings, to form a joint corporation which immediately issued preferred stock worth $120,000,000. The formation of International Harvester was of course designed to reduce competition and give the company control of the market. For Perkins these features were of great social value because the end of competition would lead to more efficient industrial practices and the production of cheaper and better goods. (22)

It was on the attitude toward corporate organization that Perkins and Theodore Roosevelt joined forces to organize the Progressive party in 1912. (23) Perkins summed up the general economic philosophy he had developed through his experience in business to the Southern Commercial Congress in Atlanta, Georgia in 1911. Perkins told the group that some alternative had to be found to antitrust legislation. The large modern corporation, he emphasized, was not only going to remain, but it would also provide the most efficient way of organizing the industrial system. The alternative, he told the group, "would seem to lie through the medium of cooperation, with federal supervision. By cooperation I mean a system of doing business by which all parties interested will enjoy the benefits of the business." This meant that conflict and special interests had to be removed from the social system. Perkins stated, "I mean by this, cooperation in any given line of business will fail unless it is cooperation between labor and capital, between company and government." (24)

Samuel Gompers, the president of the American Federation of Labor, shared Perkins' view on industrial organization. When

Gompers, in the early part of the twentieth century, was invited to dine with Charles R. Flint, a man who claimed he organized the first American trust, he reported that he told his host that "the trust or centralized control over production was a natural development of industry, and legislation to curb this development was really a limitation on the industrial and commercial development of the United States." Gompers was, of course, arguing from a position of self-interest. The antitrust laws had been used against labor. In Gompers' opinion the ideal industrial situation was large industrial combinations bargaining with large labor organizations. Gompers told his host "that labor organizations were also voluntary associations for production and distribution, and whatever restrictive or prohibitive legislation was enacted was always used more drastically against associations of workers than against associations of employers." What Gompers suggested to Flint was that labor and business work together to end antitrust legislation. (25)

Theodore Roosevelt arrived at a similar belief in economic organization after many years of trying to avoid the image of being an enemy of business. In his early career as governor of New York, Roosevelt expressed his concern about the differences between the rich and poor but warned that any attempt by the government to interfere would result in a fettering of the "freedom of individual action, [and] would be injurious to a degree far greater than is the evil aimed at." (26) By the time of his Presidential address in 1902 Roosevelt was willing to adopt the position that the government must be more active in the eradication of "evil" from business. By "evil" Roosevelt meant not large corporate organization, but those "trusts" that acted in a "bad" manner. Roosevelt told Congress in 1902 that "we can do nothing good in the way of regulating and supervising these corporations until we fix clearly in our minds that we are not attacking the corporations, but endeavoring to do away with any evil in them." (27) In 1910 at Osawatomie, Kansas in his famous speech for a "New Nationalism," a speech that became a rallying call for the Bull Moose campaign, he clearly stated his belief that the economic system should be highly organized and regulated for the good of the entire society. He told the gathered crowd, "The right to regulate the use of wealth in the public interest is universally admitted. Let us admit also the right to regulate the terms and conditions of labor, which is the chief element of wealth, directly in the interest of the common good." (28)

It was exactly this government regulation that Herbert Croly advocated in *The Promise of American Life*. Croly believed that the best and most efficient society was one organized around large corporate structures and combinations of labor. These conditions, he argued, required occupational specialization for industrial workers, businessmen and politicians. For Croly specialization meant that even more emphasis had to be placed upon social cooperation. He believed that specialization had broken down the homogeneity of interests and goals that had held the community together during the pre-Civil War period. Croly hoped that this unity could be replaced in the modern world by an allegiance to a common social ideal. This common ideal was working for the good of the social whole. (29)

Acceptance of this corporate vision of society led educators to advocate both training for social cooperation and training for a special slot in society. Edward Krug in his *Shaping of the American High School* has called this movement social efficiency and has shown the impact of this idea on education. (30) Some of the major results of social efficiency ideology were vocational guidance, the junior high school, and the 1918 *Cardinal Principles* report.

The goal of vocational guidance was to increase efficiency in the social order by matching individual talent with an appropriate job. Frank Parsons, the father of vocational guidance, stressed the importance of this task when he wrote that a "sensible industrial system will .... seek ... to put men, as well as timber, stone and iron, in the places which their natures fit them,—and to polish and prepare them for efficient service with at least as much care as is bestowed upon clocks, electric dynamos or locomotives." (31)

The philosophy of the early vocational guidance leaders reflected a strong desire to create a highly organized and cooperative society. Parsons' opening of the first vocational bureau in Boston in 1908, and his death in the same year, climaxed a career devoted to reform and the spreading of his philosophy of mutualism. His career before 1908 included the study of engineering, the teaching of law at Boston University, the authorship of books on reform in municipal government and an attempt to establish a college devoted to research into social and economic problems. The goal of Parsons' philosophy of mutualism was the creation of a paradise of brotherly love. He argued that by gradual establishment of public ownership of the means of production and the creation of a guaranteed annual income men could be conditioned to think in terms of working for the good of all. In Parsons' ideal state no external controls would be required to maintain a blissful existence of brotherly love and mutual service. Parsons was not a revolutionary and therefore sought very gradual and practical ways of achieving a rationalized economic system. (32)

Another pioneer of vocational guidance, Eli Weaver, also hoped to rationalize the system. Weaver, as chairman of the Students' Aid Committee in New York City, organized between 1905 and 1910 committees of teachers to work with students in planning their careers. His work was the basis of a plan to establish a central government bureau that would function as a commodity exchange market for human resources. Weaver proposed that a central vocational bureau be established that would determine the type of training and character needed for each occupation. The bureau would relay this information to the schools for development of appropriate courses of study. The bureau would also maintain records of talents and training so that proper placement could be made. To avoid industrial inefficiency caused by manpower shortages and surpluses the bureau would have the added function of encouraging and discouraging training in particular occupational fields. Weaver wrote that his proposed guidance bureau would "facilitate the exchange of labor between the workers and employers as the exchange of other commodities is now assisted through the standardizing operations of other exchanges." (33)

Vocational guidance people were also very concerned about the type of social character possessed by their clients. Efficiency in corporate organization required not only specific talents for a specific job, but also personality traits that would contribute to the smooth working of the social organism. For instance, Parsons believed that it was the job of the guidance worker to mold and shape character. In his book on mutualism he wrote, "Life can be moulded into any conceivable form. Draw up your specifications for a dog, or man . . . and if you will give me control of the environment, and time enough, I will clothe your dreams in flesh and blood." (34) At the Vocation Bureau in Boston he would give his clients a questionnaire which told them to "Look in the glass. Watch yourself. Get your friends to . . . tell you confidentially what they think of your appearance, manners, voice. . . ." (35)

Within the school systems vocational guidance worked with a general program of social education to produce individuals with a cooperative character who would function in their particular social slot. One school that became an early model for combining social education with vocational guidance was the Grand Rapids Central High School in Grand Rapids, Michigan. The popularity of this system among the guidance leaders was attested to by the fact that the first meeting of the Vocational Guidance Association was held there in 1913. The principal of the Central High School, Jesse B. Davis, was elected the first secretary of the association and the following year became its president. The whole social life of the Central High School was organized to train the students for a corporate structure. Student groups were organized into a pyramid of activities. At the base were clubs, athletics and student government. Above these activities in ascending order were a Boys' and Girls' Leadership Club, a Student Council, an Advisory Council and the principal. Davis, the principal and founder of the system, believed that organization of all school activities into a social whole would demonstrate to the students the value of system and combination of effort. This type of organization he felt reflected the realities of an organized industrial system. He compared his position as principal to that of a general manager, and called the advisory council of teachers a board of control. Davis stated that "the ideals upon which honest living and sound business stand, are the ideals of the public schools." While these industrial traits were being learned in the social life of the school, class work was aiding the student to choose a job. Topics in English composition were assigned in progressive steps to help the individual understand himself and the type of career he should follow. In the ninth grade students at the high school analyzed their own characters and habits. In the eleventh grade they chose a career and investigated the type of preparation that they would need. In the twelfth grade the students made "a special study of the vocation with respect to its social obligations, its peculiar opportunities for human service, and responsibilities . . . [to] the community." Davis believed that people should enter an occupation with the idea that "it was the best means by which they, with their ability, might serve their fellow man." This belief he placed in the historical context of the development of social interdependence. (36)

One important assumption made by the guidance movement was that each student should follow a particular course of study, depending upon his vocational destination. The job of the counselor was to help the student match his interests and abilities with an occupation and then plan a school program that would help the student achieve that goal. Edward Krug has shown that this view of curriculum construction was intimately linked with the concept of a specialized society. He has shown that educators argued for a differentiated curriculum in terms of the need for the schools to turn out citizens with a particular type of training. Krug points out that it was within this context that the junior high school developed. The junior high school "put forward as advantageous features . . . the advancement of practical subjects, the provision for early differentiation, and the fostering of socialized aims." (37)

The junior high school embodied all of the features of the educational reforms under consideration. The junior high movement got into full swing after national publicity was given to its development in Berkeley, California in 1910. It was hoped that early differentiation in the junior high would provide for future social specialization, while social education would provide for social unity and cooperation. One writer in the *Educational Review* stated that a new spirit would prevail in the junior high. "This spirit will be the spirit of cooperation, the spirit of service and of sacrifice for the common good." (38) One example of a highly publicized junior high school that organized around the principles of differentiation and social education was the Ben Blewett School of St. Louis, Missouri. Principal Philip Cox, organizer of the school in 1917, stated that his junior high was guided by two basic principles. One was that the school "must not lose sight of its responsibility to each child as an individual, and to society, whose agent it is for leading the children as individuals and as groups toward the goal of social efficiency." The other principle was that the school was a community. Beginning in the seventh grade each child at the Ben Blewett school spent 150 to 200 hours in advisory periods. The advisory periods were the basis for the organization of the total school social program. The advisory period was also designed to help the child choose a future career. In the eighth grade students made a tentative vocational choice and were programmed into three tracks. Students in each track were separated according to intellectual ability. To avoid the loss of social cohesion and training caused by the differentiation the school established "m, n, o groupings" which were "intended primarily to bring about, in social activities, cross sections of the other two types of groupings." It was claimed that in actual practice they were superfluous because "spontaneous and natural associations of playground and extracurricular activities apparently break indiscriminately across intellectual and vocational groupings." (39)

The question of early differentiation in the junior high school was one of the major problems discussed by what one might call the official statement of this educational reform movement, the *Cardinal Principles of Secondary Education*. This report was issued in 1918 after five years of labor by the Commission on the Reorganization of Secondary Education of the National Education Association. The *Cardinal Principles* report became one of the most popular documents for spreading the idea that the purpose of education was to socialize the individual and place him in his social niche. The commission report stated that "education in a democracy, both within and without the school, should develop in each individual the knowledge, interests, ideals, habits, and powers whereby he will find his place and use that place to shape both himself and society toward ever nobler ends." The report also agreed with Croly that individualism now had to be conceived of in terms of what one did for society. The report stated, "The purpose of democracy is to so organize society that each member may develop his personality primarily through activities designed for the well-being of his fellow members and of society as a whole."

While the *Cardinal Principles* report did not support differentiation in the seventh and eighth grades it did support it in the upper grades. One of the problems raised by this support of differentiation was the problem of promoting social unity and cooperation. There had been considerable pressure, particularly from David Snedden, to establish separate schools for each vocational track. The commission rejected this idea and supported differentiation only in the context of a comprehensive high school. "The ideal of democracy," the report stated, "involves on the one hand specialization whereby individuals and groups of individuals may become effective in the various vocations . . . and on the other hand unification whereby the members of that democracy may obtain those common ideas, common ideals, and common modes of thought, feeling, and action that make for cooperation, social cohesion, and social solidarity." (40)

The *Cardinal Principles*, the comprehensive high school, vocational guidance, and the junior high school represent, of course, the main stream of education in the twentieth century. In the same way the progressive counterpart that centered around the activities and ideology of Theodore Roosevelt's New Nationalism has provided the bases for American liberalism in the twentieth century. (41) It is the case that American liberalism has defined as its goal the accommodation and regulation of the corporate system by a strong, centralized government. American liberalism has stood firmly against socialism but at the same time allowed for the growth of large industrial empires and labor organizations. This system has made the large corporation and union the dominant factors in our economy. Since the major changes in the American public school system have been geared to the liberal rhetoric, one wonders if some of the people who called themselves progressive educators in the 1920s were not in fact offering a radical and meaningful alternative to American education. Maybe the liberal views of most educational historians have hindered their ability to see some of the real issues in education.

Notes

1. Edward Alsworth Ross, *Social Control: A Survey of the Foundations of Order* (New York: The Macmillan Company, 1922), p. 11.
2. William Chandler Bagley, *The Educative Process* (New York: The Macmillan Company, 1924), pp. 62-64.

3. L. S. Rowe, "Social Consequences of Cities," *Yale Review*, 10 (November 1901), 298-312.
4. Jacob A. Riis, *How the Other Half Lives* (New York: Hill and Wang, 1957), p. 200.
5. Ray Ginger, *Altgeld's America* (New York: Funk & Wagnalls Co., 1958), pp. 248-50.
6. Herbert Croly, *The Promise of American Life* (New York: Capricorn Books, 1964), pp. 1-26, 399-421.
7. Michael V. O'Shea, *Social Development and Education* (Boston: Houghton Mifflin Co., 1909), p. 272.
8. Ira W. Howerth, "Education and the Social Ideal," *Educational Review*, 24 (September 1902), pp. 150-65.
9. Samuel T. Dutton, *Social Phases of Education in the School and the Home* (New York: The Macmillan Company, 1899), p. 22.
10. "The Social Motive in School Work," *The Francis W. Parker School Year Book* (Chicago, 1912), p. 7.
11. John and Evelyn Dewey, *Schools of Tomorrow* (New York: E. P. Dutton & Co., 1962), p. 92.
12. Social Education Association, undated announcement.
13. Colin Scott, *Social Education* (Boston: Ginn and Co., 1908).
14. *Social Education Quarterly*, I, 1907.
15. John M. Gillette, "An Outline of Social Study for Elementary Schools," *American Journal of Sociology*, 19 (January 1914), 491-501.
16. Philip Cox, "The Ben Blewett Junior High School: An Experiment in Democracy," *School Review*, 27 (May 1919), p. 346.
17. William B. Owen, "Social Education Through the School," *School Review*, 15 (January 1907), 11-26.
18. Florence Lilner, "School Management from the Side of Social Life," *School Review*, 7 (April 1899), 215-16.
19. V. K. Froula, "Extra-Curricular Activities: Their Relation to the Curricular Work of the School," *National Education Association Proceedings* (1915), pp. 737-42.
20. D. E. Cloyd, "Student Organizations in City High Schools," *Education*, 31 (September 1910), 17-20.
21. Froula, "Extra-Curricular Activities," p. 739.
22. John A. Garraty, *Right-Hand Man: The Life of George W. Perkins* (New York: Harper, 1957).
23. See Garraty, *Right-Hand Man*, pp. 243-309, and George E. Mowry's *Theodore Roosevelt and the Progressive Movement* (New York: Hill and Wang, 1960), pp. 256-304.
24. George W. Perkins, "Modern Industrialism" (address given before the Southern Commercial Congress, Atlanta, Ga., March 8, 1911).
25. Samuel Gompers, *Seventy Years of Life and Labor* (New York: E. P. Dutton & Co., 1948), II, 110-12.

26. "Annual Message to the State," *The Works of Theodore Roosevelt, Memorial Edition* (New York: L. Scribner's Sons, 1925), XVII, 46-47.
27. "Second Annual Message," *ibid.*, XVII, 162-66.
28. "The New Nationalism," *ibid.*, XIX, 10-37.
29. Croly, *The Promise of American Life*, pp. 100-40.
30. Edward Krug, *The Shaping of the American High School* (New York: Harper and Row, 1964), pp. 249-84.
31. Frank Parsons, *Our Country's Need* (Boston, 1894), p. 69.
32. *See ibid.* and Parsons, *The Drift of Our Time* (Chicago, 1898).
33. Eli W. Weaver, *Wage-earning Occupations of Boys and Girls* (Brooklyn, 1912).
34. Parsons, *Our Country's Need*, p. 2.
35. Frank Parsons, *Choosing a Vocation* (Boston, 1909), p. 32.
36. Jesse B. Davis, *Vocational and Moral Guidance* (Boston: Ginn and Co., 1914), and "Vocational and Moral Guidance in the High School," *Religious Education*, 7 (February 1913).
37. Krug, *The Shaping of the American High School*, p. 330.
38. Thomas Gosling, "Educational Reconstruction in the Junior High School," *Educational Review*, 57 (May 1919), 384-85.
39. Cox, "The Ben Blewett Junior High School," and R. L. Lyman, "The Ben Blewett Junior High School," *School Review*, 28 (January 1920), 26-40.
40. *Cardinal Principles of Secondary Education* (Washington: Bureau of Education Bulletin, 1918), p. 35.
41. *See* Eric Goldman's *Rendezvous with Destiny* (New York: Vintage Books, 1962), pp. 248-68; and Gabriel Kolko, *The Triumph of Conservatism* (Chicago: Quadrangle Books, 1963), pp. 279-305.

Reprinted from The History of Education Quarterly, Volume 10, Number 1, Spring, 1970.

THE DEWEYAN TRADITION REVISITED

By ARTHUR G. WIRTH
Professor of Education

There has been a moratorium on the use of John Dewey's name in recent years. There are hazards in referring to him. To mention Dewey is to flaunt the fact that you are over thirty, and the young have made clear how much confidence they have in persons of such vintage. In addition, you demonstrate that you are hopelessly out of touch with current professional terminology: educational hardware-software, modulation, simulation, the "teacher and his staff" processing "teacher-proof materials," and much more.

The moratorium extends even into the conclaves of the philosophers of education. At their 1967 convention in New Orleans there was a session on "Critiques of Recent Literature in Philosophy of Education." The four main areas reviewed were: (1) Analytic philosophy, (2) Catholic philosophy, (3) Existential philosophy, and (4) "Is there any other?" That is quite a switch from the days not long ago when the name of Dewey was much in the air at these meetings.

Why the silence? There is no doubt that an opprobrium came to be attached to Dewey's name in the years after Sputnik I. The tendency was to assume some causal connection between Dewey and whatever weakness one was worried about in American education. In the public media Dewey was equated with progressivism and progressivism was equated with anti-intellectualism, soft-pedagogy, unruly children—perhaps even a vague subversive-ism.

Whatever the reasons, I am one who happens to think that there is merit to the moratorium. A turning away from revered figures seems to be in vogue in various fields. (One thinks of the advice coming from avant-garde spokesmen in theology.) A substantive case for the decline in talk about Dewey is that we had arrived at a point where the terminology associated with his name—reflective thinking, problem-solving, democratic process, etc.—had taken on the quality of incantation. Tired terminology can mesmerize its users so that they get encapsulated and lose contact with reality. Bombardment from outside is then not only inevitable but salutary.

So I am not bothered by the moratorium. On the other hand, I simply feel that important aspects of Dewey's point of view have not lost their relevance to American culture and American education. If that notion is presently not fashionable, I am not disturbed. I shall give several examples of Dewey's thought that continue to have staying power. If we lose sight of these and others simply because he is out of style, *we* will be the real losers.

I want to give examples that grew out of my study of Dewey's work at Chicago *(John Dewey as Educator: His Design for Work in Education, 1894-1904).* My purpose in returning to this period was to get behind the clichés and to re-check what Dewey stood for when he founded and directed his own Laboratory School. I wanted to analyze the kind of thinking about education he was doing at the one point in his career when he was directly involved as a practicing educator.

My first example has to do with the curriculum rationale of his Laboratory School. This feature of his work was relatively neglected in the period of his popularity when the progressives concentrated on methodological innovations. The curriculum was based on Dewey's sense that twentieth-century men were entering a new stage of human development. A primary task of formal education was to help the young develop insight into events that were transforming the human situation. From this thesis Dewey located integrating themes which he hoped would give coherence to the curriculum from the kindergarten to the university. Recently, of course, this kind of concern for coherence has been lacking as we have worked by reform projects on separate bits of the curriculum (although we may be seeing a revival of interest in integrated plans as the systems analysts are getting involved). If, as I am arguing, Dewey's educational rationale was aimed at helping men adjust to a new stage of human experience we must ask the questions: What is the new stage of man? What are man's critical needs in entering it?

For answers to these questions I shall not use Dewey's words, but those of several perceptive contemporary com-

Reprinted from The Washington University Magazine, 1971.

Portrait of John Dewey, noted American philosopher of education.

mentators who are representing *now* the point of view expressed by Dewey at the opening of this century. I refer to Kenneth Boulding, economist and social philosopher, at the University of Michigan and Elting Morison of the California Institute of Technology.

Boulding, in *The Meaning of the Twentieth Century*, begins by saying "The twentieth century marks the middle period of a great transition in the state of the human race." He holds that we are beginning to leave a stage of civilization that gradually took shape from the Renaissance to about the beginning of the twentieth century. It culminated in producing revolutionary change agents: science, technological inventions and innovations, and the combination of these with organized research and development operations—all of which, in turn, are leading to global social change and invention. The result, according to Boulding, is that "the technical changes introduced by the scientific revolution are so great that we are passing into *a new state of man*. . . . *This is the meaning of the twentieth century.*"

He refers to this emerging era as the stage of the "technologically developed society": a stage where the workings of man's mind—as represented in the explosive power of scientific knowledge and modes of inquiry, harnessed now through research and development processes—become *the fundamental agents for transforming* the quality of life on this planet—and beyond it into surrounding space. This theme is sounded also by Elting Morison in *Men, Machine, and Modern Times,* in which he agrees with Boulding that the paramount tasks of our time are: (1) to give men insight into the nature of the transition we are in, and (2) to provide the temper of mind and skills to enable men to cope with the new order of world realities.

"The most important invention for the future lies [in] the way we are to deal with all the new conditions produced by the new machines and ideas." The rate of change accruing is placing enormous strains on individuals and human institutions. Morison argues that to avoid a variety of disasters the paramount problem is to develop the attitudes and skills that will enable men to face this radical change without feeling overwhelmed by it—while learning to assess consequences so that change can be directed toward humane ends. As he puts it, the critical task is "to create a mood and means that will enable the members of society to explore new instruments and procedures by designed experiments while pondering alternatives and reserving judgments until the returns are in.

"In all the areas of difficulty and doubt—transport, the organization of cities, the control of traffic, the intelligent, indeed, the loving care of the sick, the process of education, the structure of existing institutions, and the like—in all these areas the development of a series of small experiments, with the means available for observing the evidence produced and analyzing the results, would produce a set of alternative solutions and the data necessary both for fuller understanding of the nature of new situations and for intelligent selection among alternatives." If we can create such an experimental or hypothetical mood in the society at large, then "members of the society can have a direct part in the decisions affecting the shape of the society; by offering the possibility of reasoned change, it may measurably reduce the natural human resistance to changes not fully understood."

We had an example of such a style of thinking in the St. Louis area when Professor Barry Commoner of Washington University proposed to a sub-committee of the U.S. Senate that a pilot program be instituted to find technical, economic, and administrative solutions to the air pollution problem. Note that he did not propose a surefire panacea, but a pilot program in which possible solutions would be put to a test, evaluated, and modified or elaborated as feedback comes in.

While a couple of quotations cannot give a clear indication of the thesis to which whole books are devoted, I hope that they convey something of the conviction of these authors that the twentieth century is ushering us into a new stage of human experience. Science, the modes of inquiry represented in science, and technological inventions tied to it are the great transformers. No area of the globe now is unaffected.

THIS IS, OF COURSE, the point of view that Dewey took as his departure point in designing the program of his Laboratory School—and it was a major theme in his philosophical work in general. As he saw it, the great task, as we came into the twentieth century, was to foster the attitudes and skills of experimental inquiry combined with a concern for democratic values. He did not offer the curriculum of his Laboratory School as *the* answer. It was, however, an imaginative curriculum effort integrated around the theme of providing insight into the critical events in the human past that had led to this twentieth-century moment. The approach was essentially anthropological. Dewey chose to focus on what he called the "occupations," i.e., the basic modes for producing life necessities, as basic items of inquiry. His thesis was that basic changes were effected in the total pattern of culture when the form of the occupations or activities required to produce the necessities of life, like food, fuel, etc., were changed. Thus in the early elementary grades there were units in which children studied the interrelated consequences that developed when men passed from primitive hunting and gathering societies, to pastoral, then to agricultural, and to commercial stages.

Always attention was centered on critical factors that were change-producers, such as the domestication of animals, the introduction of new metals, and on the complex interactional effects following these for the total pattern of social life. Thus, in Phoenician culture the changes when men entered a commercial stage were studied—changes in modes of transportation, in the political, economic, and religious patterns, and the impetus given to symbol systems, both alphabetical and numerical. Later units explored the effects on man's experience that derived from the expansion of Europe and the consequences of cultures interacting on each other.

As study in the upper elementary grades shifted to this country, extensive units were concerned with a study of the changes that occurred in human life in one geographical region—the Chicago area. There were early units on the culture of the Plains Indians, then analyses of the conflicts of culture which followed when the European explorers and fur traders entered the area. A sequence of units traced what happened as this stage gave way to pioneers, farmers, and new commercial ventures; what happened when water and wagon transportation gave way to the railroad, and packing plant complexes required new supplies of cheap immigrant labor. While the Dewey School did not continue long enough to work out the details, the stage was set to show how the complex problems of industrialism, urbanism, and commercialism required that men learn how to learn at levels never required before. This required, for one thing, the establishment of university campuses as research centers to advance knowledge and techniques, and the need to put the lower schools in touch with the modes of inquiry generated there. Chicago, of course, gave birth to the University of Chicago in the 1890's which within a half century was to produce the research that released the energy of the atom.

235

Pivotal to the curriculum rationale of Dewey's school was the "web of culture" concept. The goal was to help students to see how the aspects of a society were interrelated—economic, technological, political, aesthetic, intellectual, spiritual—and to learn that when fundamental change-factors were introduced, the whole pattern of relationships was transformed and human experience entered into new stages.

Parallel to these historical units were studies in the sciences which dealt with man's understanding of his natural environment—how this understanding led to an increase in the ability to control the forces of nature which, in turn, transformed social and cultural life.

All of this was to aid the gradual realization that previous history had led men to the point where the human mind—as now represented in the modes of thinking in science and the harnessing of knowledge to techniques—has become the radical planetary change agent. If the curricular orientation was to provide this kind of perspective, the *methods* were to give students experience and insight into grasping the new attitude on which science was based. By engaging in a series of inquiries in shops, laboratories, gardens, and in studies in the "occupations," children were to develop the tentative, critical attitudes that go with the experimental temper of mind.

A SECOND MAJOR ASPECT of Dewey's philosophy was his concern with the meaning of the new turn of events for *democratic values*. A distinctive feature of his thought was his conviction that the educational objective of developing the experimental and critical attitudes and skills was to apply to *all* children—not just to an intellectual elite in the society. There were at least two reasons for this: One was a functional reason—a society that was to move into "the next stage of man." The scientific-technological-change-oriented stage had to have available throughout its population the quality of mind needed to make such a society viable. An anecdote told by Professor F. S. C. Northrop illustrates the point. He underscored the difficulties of introducing new technologies into cultures whose peoples have not been steeped in the modes of thought related to science with an anecdote about Asiatic peasants who could see no point in periodic lubrications of new tractors since the machines had been "anointed" the first time. It is futile or dangerous to introduce the products of science and technology into a society unless its peoples are being helped to acquire the conceptual and attitudinal values that are intrinsic to the culture of science.

A second reason was related to Dewey's concern about whether the values of free men could still apply in a complex, science-oriented, big-system kind of society. There is the possibility that such a system will, in fact, require an elite of brains and power which will scientifically engineer not only the physical and energy aspects, but the human material as well—everyone will be measured and conditioned to fit into the slot which is efficiently right for him. Soma pills or some other happy gumdrop will keep us in a continuous smiling, euphoric state while we perform according to plan. Dewey resisted this. He insisted that the attitudes and skills of the mode of experimental inquiry had to be made widely available to children of all classes and groups to make it possible for them to be responsible participants in a change-oriented society. And he operated from the faith that, with proper educational aid, such attitudes and skills could be acquired by the majority of men.

Dewey was aware of the evils of manipulation that could come from the creation of huge impersonal megalopolises and rigid bureaucracies. There was the possibility that men would feel overwhelmed and powerless and lose meaningful freedoms. The dangers were real. It was not Dewey's style, however, to react with anguished hand-wringing, nor with self-serving bleats about the need to drop out. The perilous and the threatening were not new in human experience. History does not assure us that answers will always be found. Dignity comes, however, from persistently trying to apply intelligence, imagination, even courage on problems which seem intractable.

If the participatory values of free men were to have a chance, Dewey insisted that they had to be learned in living communities. Schools, where the young were nurtured, could perhaps be created into communities where the tough problems of implementing the techniques of free, responsible participation could be confronted in practice. Those schooled in such experiences later might be able to bring imagination to bear in creating arrangements for fulfillment and democratic involvement even in the huge communities in which twentieth century men are destined to live. If Boulding and Morison are right, this is still the paramount task as we approach the last three decades of the twentieth century and it applies now to people all over the globe.

Thus, three major themes in Dewey's school are: (1) to provide students with a mode for understanding the evolution in human experience which has led us to our present period of transition, (2) to develop both the attitudes and skills of the experimental mood and method which are indispensable for meaningful participation in the emerging reality, and (3) to learn to weigh the consequences of change in terms of its harm or support for human values.

These relate to a fourth point. In Dewey's epistemological theory the process of inquiry was characterized by continuing interplay between conceptual-theoretical work and the check of ideas against the stuff of reality. This had implications for his pedagogical theory. He accepted the fact that the major function of the school is to provide conceptual training. It necessarily has as its business the teaching of the heritage which is contained in verbal and mathematical symbols. But this inescapable duty poses also a constant danger. Whenever the work of the school becomes exclusively abstract the school is in danger of becoming isolated from the real world. Students (some at least) will sense sterility and will rebel or cut out. Dewey, therefore, reached for pedagogical devices at the elementary level—occupations, field trips, school gardens, cooking, etc.—to give children a sense of the functional relation between knowledge and ideas and the everyday-ongoing life of men. His theory at the secondary and higher educational levels endorsed the design of educational approaches that tried to place youth into some meaningful relation to the out-of-school community. (The Antioch plan, for example, was influenced by Dewey's frame of reference.)

This is not the place to elaborate the point, but I think it is becoming clear that we are going to have to reconsider this emphasis. We are developing a post-Sputnik hangover. There is a clear case for academic excellence, but we also see some of our most interesting kids at the secondary and college levels rebelling against the effort to monopolize their lives with the academic grind. They resent the isolation of education from life that Dewey warned against. When a society places its entire youth population in classrooms until they approach age twenty, it is fair to ask if schools become agents for alienating the young from their society. Our youth are hungry for genuine participant roles in the off-campus community as well as within it. Some of them are refusing to sit still for the endless game of exam taking and mark collecting. One of our most pressing tasks will be to develop programs that will enable youth to be meaningfully related to the out-of-school world and to learn how to use such experiences to advance theoretical and conceptual studies.

We need to examine imaginative projects being tried here and there. We need to re-think uses to be made of summer programs in which cross-sections of our youth could be put to work on neglected but vitally needed social tasks, in reclamation projects in mountain areas, clean-up projects in urban slums, etc., or as the Russians do in polytechnical education: give their promising secondary and college age students experience in industrial laboratories or experimental gardens, without forcing them to wait until they get their Ph.D.'s.

FINALLY I REFER to Dewey's pioneer plan to transform school-keeping into a teaching profession that would be experimental and inquiry-centered in mood and practice. He had a responsibility in this area as he was chairman of the combined Departments of Philosophy, Psychology, and Education at Chicago.

Operationally, Dewey argued that a profession is dependent on basing practice on a body of theory as opposed to empirical, rule-of-thumb practice. In his view this meant that educators had to be committed to building, slowly and progressively, a more sophisticated body of theory and practice that would grow out of inquiry. Specifically, he proposed a triadic pattern of collaboration. At one level would be investigators working at the abstract conceptual level, trying to clarify understanding of such basic factors as motivation, the nature of human learning, etc. A second group of people, middle-level theorists, would work in collaboration with people in the classroom and those doing research at the more abstract levels to develop series of hunches or hypotheses relevant to pressing problems of the schools. These hypotheses would be dependent on the collaboration of classroom teachers. These teachers, who themselves would be prepared in skills and attitudes for investigation, would try the ideas; they would provide feedback to the researchers at the other levels. In addition, they would also be the source of providing their own kinds of hypotheses for defining problems that require joint collaboration in seeking solutions.

The most important thing in this plan is that Dewey was taking an approach to education that would present us with a defense against the diseases of ideological thinking or faddism. Instead of constantly having to struggle to remain at the crest of whatever is the lastest new wave, Dewey was arguing that, in effect, we should admit the large areas of our ignorance and insist on having the right to approach problems of the profession in the spirit of experimental inquiry. This would mean that ideas for change, instead of being regarded as the "new gospel," would be treated as ideas to be tested and evaluated. Practice would provide feedback and correctives for modification, for rejection, or for acceptance. To come to the job in this spirit might relieve us all from the pressures of having to keep up with the Joneses in the next school district. An alternative to being nervously "on the make" is to work from a sense of being an honest workman. It can bring a refreshing sense of self-respect. In the Graduate Institute of Education we would hope, however imperfectly, to make a contribution to supporting such attitudes and skills.

An insistence on applying the modes of experimental inquiry to the work of the profession has new relevance and urgency today. We have entered the era when the giants of the communication industry—R.C.A., I.B.M., Xerox—have discovered that education is big business. Great issues for educators are at stake which can't be discussed here. The profession is on the spot. It will be taking significant action even if it decides "to go along" to find out what "they" come up with—or if we all rush off to join 'em by jumping into the flesh pots. It is just possible that the profession might take another stance—move to insist that professional standards and safeguards be applied before schools are flooded with hardware and software

It may even be time to revive the Laboratory School idea, this time, perhaps, supported by regional labs and universities. In such schools the profession might ask the corporations to subject the technological and curriculum innovations to experimental scrutiny. The value questions regarding consequences for human beings—as well as functional results—would be included in inquiry designs. Since our level of sophistication in research techniques has advanced since our earlier experience with laboratory schools, we might insist that this time they not be primarily *demonstration* schools, which could become merely advertising centers for corporation products, but that the emphasis be truly experimental, with the hard and honest questions to the fore. If that happens the vitality of the tradition of John Dewey will be demonstrated.

SEMESTER: WEEK ELEVEN

REQUIRED READING

Church

Part IV: School and Community: Progressivism in Education, 1890-1940, Chapter 10: The High School in the Progressive Era (28 pp.)

Dye

Hunt, Thomas C. "The American High School in Crisis: A Historical Perspective" The Educational Forum. V.37, No.1, November, 1974. (12 pp.)

Wirth, Arthur G. "Charles A. Prosser and the Smith-Hughes Act" The Educational Forum. V.35, No.2, March, 1972. (07 pp.)

_____. "John Dewey's Philosophical Opposition to Smith-Hughes Type Vocational Education" Educational Theory. V.22, No.1, Winter, 1972. (09 pp.)

MEETINGS

Monday

Lecture: American Vocational Education

Tuesday

Lecture: The Cardinal Principles of Secondary Education

Wednesday

Lecture: Teacher Employment

Thursday and Friday

Small Groups: Book Critiques are due.

CHURCH TEXTBOOK STUDY GUIDE: CHAPTER 10

THE HIGH SCHOOL IN THE PROGRESSIVE ERA

1. <u>Report of the Committee of Ten</u> (1893)
2. <u>Report of the NEA Commission on the Reorganization of Secondary Education</u> (1918); The Cardinal Principles of Secondary Education
3. increased secondary school enrollment
4. greater numbers of secondary school teachers
5. increased specialization of secondary school teachers
6. development of professional secondary school educators
7. social engineering function of schooling
8. The NEA Committee of Ten
9. James H. Baker
10. University of Colorado
11. Nicholas Murray Butler
12. Columbia University
13. Charles W. Eliot
14. Harvard University
15. college admissions examinations
16. accreditation
17. North Central Association of Colleges and Secondary Schools
18. central examination boards
19. College Entrance Examination Board, CEEB
20. William Torrey Harris
21. United States Commissioner of Education
22. terminal secondary school student
23. to prepare for the duties of life
24. articulation
25. Carnegie Fund for the Advancement of Teaching

26. Carnegie unit
27. limited secondary school elective system
28. introduction of modern secondary subjects
29. classicist opposition to the <u>Report of the NEA Committee of Ten</u>
30. development of professional schools of education

31. <u>Report of the Massachusetts Committion on Industrial and Technical Education</u> (1906), The Douglas Commission Report
32. National Society for the Promotion of Industrial Education, NSPIE
33. educationists
34. educators
35. inculcation of industrial intelligence

36. the German threat
37. the dropout
38. secondary vocational training
39. vocational guidance movement
40. Frank Parsons

41. Vocation Bureau, Boston
42. efficient utilization of manpower resources
43. counselors
44. <u>Smith-Hughes Act</u>(1918)
45. Commission on the Reorganization of Secondary Education of the NEA, CRSE

46. Clarence D. Kingsley
47. theme of social efficiency
48. David S. Snedden
49. ideal of the efficient democratic society
50. Charles A. Ellwood

51. University of Missouri
52. eugenics
53. comprehensive high school

Reprinted from *The Educational Forum*, Kappa Delta Pi, Volume 37, Number 1, November, 1974.

The American High School in Crisis: A Historical Perspective

THOMAS C. HUNT

THE American elementary school has a rudimentary task—the teaching of the "three Rs." As fundamental as this assignment is to the individual and society, the elementary school has escaped, to a large extent, the controversy which has beset the American high school. Whether in a time of social upheaval or national emergency, the curriculum of the elementary school, indeed the school itself and its personnel, have been spared the pressures to which their high school counterparts have been subjected.

As we behold the confusion and controversy which surround the high school of the 1970s, its nature, function, and task, we might do well to look for historical precedents to the present crisis. Not that these precedents caused the current turmoil nor that they are identical with it, but the American high school, due to its role in society, has an existence which cannot escape recurring crisis.

The United States of America is a nation of immigrants. Immigration has brought about evolutionary, at times almost revolutionary, changes in American society. One of the greatest periods of immigration was around the turn of the twentieth century.

Thomas C. Hunt is an assistant professor in the College of Education at Virginia Polytechnic Institute and State University.

TABLE 1.[1] AMERICAN IMMIGRATION, 1860–1920

Period	Total	North & West Europe Number	Percent	South & East Europe Number	Percent
1861–1870	2,314,824	2,031,624	87.8	33,628	1.4
1871–1880	2,812,191	2,070,373	73.6	201,880	7.2
1881–1890	5,246,613	3,778,633	72.0	958,413	18.3
1891–1900	3,687,564	1,643,492	44.6	1,915,486	51.9
1901–1910	8,795,386	1,910,035	21.7	6,225,981	70.8
1911–1920	5,735,811	997,438	17.4	3,379,126	58.9

This is so, not simply because of the numbers of immigrants who landed on America's shores, but also because of the cultural traits of these people, which were so different from their predecessors. Table 1 illustrates that, beginning with the last decade of the nineteenth century, the majority emigrated to the United States from southern and eastern Europe.

American society, faced with the influx of multitudes of people so different from "native" white Americans, considered the recent arrivals to be "undesirable." It girded itself to make "Americans" out of those who were already in the country and who had the potential of joining the American mainstream. The nation looked to its institutions to accomplish this task. Foremost among the country's socializing agencies were the public schools, including the newest of America's educational institutions, the public high school. The high school was summoned to meet its responsibilities.

In 1890, 2,526 public high schools enrolled 202,963 pupils, of whom over half (57.6 percent) were girls. By 1900 there were 6,005 public high schools with a total enrollment of 519,251 students, 58.4 percent of whom were girls. Not nearly as many graduated from high school as entered, however. In 1890, 10.7 percent of the number enrolled graduated, and by 1900 this figure rose slightly to 11.9 percent.[2] By 1910, 915,061 pupils were reported to be in public high schools.[3] The percentage of graduates reached 12.1 percent of the total enrollment that year.[4]

As early as 1890, concern about the secondary education of the children of the "masses" had been expressed in meetings of public educators. For instance, at the 1890 meeting of the National Education Association (NEA), E. A. Steere of Butte, Montana, estimated that five of every six pupils in high school were from the working classes. He proclaimed that the high school had a good influence on these youngsters by lifting the curtain from their minds which their social class had imposed on them.[5] A scant seven years later the state superintendent of New York's schools told an NEA audience that the children of the "plain people" were crowding the schools so that, as a consequence, in a few years the "children of the masses and not of the classes will rule us."[6]

This prospect was not at all endearing to native American whites. They viewed the rapidly increasing numbers of southern and eastern European immigrants in their midst with growing alarm. As early as 1882 legislation was passed which excluded lunatics, convicts, and idiots from entering the country. The American Protective Association, a Protestant group which opposed the swelling ranks of Catholics in the country through immigration, was organized in 1887 to combat Catholic influence and to instill patriotic nativism. In 1891 one writer editorialized that the industries of the urban North were "in a state of perpetual siege by an army of semi-savages."[7] That eminent stalwart of public education, Ellwood P. Cubberley, described this horde and the pernicious effect it had on American society as follows:

> These Southern and Eastern Europeans were of a very different type from the North and West Europeans who preceded them. Largely illiterate, docile, lacking in initiative and almost wholly without the Anglo-Saxon conceptions of righteousness, liberty, law, order, public decency, and government, their coming has served to dilute tremendously our national stock and to weaken and to corrupt our political life.... They have created serious problems in housing and living, moral and sanitary conditions, and honest and decent government, while popular education has everywhere been made more difficult by their presence. The result has been that in many sections of our country foreign manners, customs, observances, and language have tended to supplant native ways and the English speech, while the so-called "melting pot" has had more than it could handle. The new peoples, and especially those from the South and East of Europe, have come so fast that we have been unable to absorb and assimilate them, and our national life, for the past quarter of a century, has been afflicted with a serious case of racial indigestion.[8]

Many of these immigrants settled in the metropolitan areas of the northeastern United States. They worked at low-paying jobs in America's rapidly expanding industrial machine. Cities became industrial jungles, their districts sharply cordoned off by extremes of wealth and poverty. Living conditions for the immigrant families of the laboring class were so dismal that by 1900 they were comparable to the worst European slums.[9]

The Immigration Restriction League was formed to combat the evils of unrestricted immigration. This group was fearful of the mixing of "races." According to the nativistic point of view, there were four European races: "Teuton," "Nordic," "Alpine," and "Mediterranean." The first two were deemed far superior to the latter two.[10] Consequently, they should not mix with each other. The league's literature asserted that southern and eastern Europe were dumping large numbers of "illiterates, paupers, criminals, and madmen" into the country.[11] The nation, its character, and its way of life were endangered.

The situation was thought to be so critical by some elements of American society that in 1895 Senator Henry Cabot Lodge and Representative McCall, both of Massachusetts, proposed in Congress that a literacy test be given potential immigrants. All those over fourteen years of age who could not read and write some language would not be allowed to enter the United States.[12]

Granville Stanley Hall, the child psychologist and president of Clark University, held little hope of educational success for the children of immigrant families. They formed, in his words, an "army of incapables," for whom the schools could do very little. Unable to profit from any advanced form of education, these children should be placed in a "dullard school" and taught to be good citizens and docile servants.[13]

Not all educational figures were so outspoken as Hall. The majority, however, viewed the school as a social institution ready to do society's bidding and "Americanize" these immigrant youngsters. Since the high school enrolled many children of the working class, it was called upon to join in the missionary effort. The schools were to civilize the "undisciplined and uncouth hordes of foreigners," whose only "hope of salvation" lay in the schools.[14] For some, "Americanization" meant teaching the immigrants English. Some who advanced this position discouraged the use of foreign languages, especially in school. (Some parochial schools sought to maintain the native European tongue and customs and sometimes taught subjects in that language as well as teaching the language itself. Therefore, these schools were opposed by public school advocates.) Others, intentionally or not, used the school as a wedge between the children and their parents. World War I, with the prospect of American involvement, made foreign languages and loyalties more menacing and the task of Americanization correspondingly more urgent. Cubberley was in the forefront of those who advocated that American society in general and its schools in particular eradicate these foreign attachments and implant American values in these youngsters:

> ... to break up these groups or settlements, to assimilate these people as a part of our American race, and to implant in their children, so far as can be done, the Anglo-Saxon conception of righteousness, law and order, and popular government, and to awaken in them a reverence for our democratic institutions and for those things in our national life which we as a people hold to be of abiding worth.[15]

The immigration of southern and eastern Europeans and the industrialization of the cities caused the demand for "practical" subjects to be taught in high schools. The high school was supposed to prepare the students to be good citizens in America's democratic society and to prepare them to make a living. The vocational education movement contended that high schools should prepare students for life, not for college. The National Society for the Promotion of Industrial Education, organized in 1906, was an offshoot of this movement. The report of the Douglas Commission in Massachusetts in 1905 gave considerable impetus to the vocational movement in education. This report described the evil consequences which would befall the United States on the world market due to the scarcity of trained mechanics. It recommended that vocational schools be founded separate from public schools and operated by an independent authority.[16] The high schools, some argued, had failed to meet society's and students' needs. Their curricula were too liberal and they failed to provide a broader range of subjects. Susan M. Kingsbury, special investigator for the commission, noted in her subreport that some 25,000 youngsters between the ages of fourteen and sixteen in Massachusetts were not attending school. The blame for this, she stated, lay not with industrialists who used child labor, nor with parents who failed to insist that their children stay in school, but with the antiquated, irrelevant curriculum and policies of the schools.[17]

The cause of vocational education was assisted by the President of The United States, Theodore Roosevelt. In his annual message to Congress on December 3, 1907, he stated:

> Our school system is gravely defective in so far as it puts a premium upon mere literacy training and tends therefore to train the boy away from the farm and the workshop. Nothing is more needed than the best type of industrial school, the school for mechanical industries in the city, the school for practically teaching agriculture in the country. The calling of the skilled toiler of the soil, the calling of the skilled mechanic, should alike be recognized as professions, just as emphatically as the callings of lawyer, doctor, merchant or clerk. The schools should recognize this fact and it should equally be recognized in public opinion.[18]

A short time later, in a talk to the nation's school superintendents, President Roosevelt reiterated his support for practical vocational training, asserting that education should be "directed more and more toward training boys and girls back to the farm and shop."[19]

An essential task still remained—someone had to identify the boys and girls who were to enroll in vocational education courses. Accordingly, a new field, vocational guidance, developed. Vocational counselors were appointed and given the authority to select pupils for vocational courses on the basis of aptitudes the students had displayed in elementary school. This field organized in 1913. Under the leadership of Charles A. Prosser, secretary of the National Society for the Promotion of Industrial Education, the National Vocational Guidance Association was formed.[20] According to Prosser, vocational guidance would harmonize with efficient school administration and with early curriculum differentiation, subordinating the individual's needs to society's needs. Fourteen was the most critical age for students, Prosser maintained. It was then that students had to decide whether to stay in school or to drop out. If they remained, they had to choose the kind of school or course in which to enroll. The assistance of vocational guidance personnel in this decision was necessary, Prosser held, because the school served "as the agent of the state for the welfare of childhood."[21]

The vocational movement was important in American secondary educational circles by 1910, but it had its opponents. To understand the opposition of individuals such as John Dewey and groups like the American Federation of Labor, it is necessary to understand the relationship of social class to vocational education. Some advocates of the vocational movement advocated early curriculum differentiation (by the seventh grade). Ostensibly, this program would keep youngsters in school, would be suited to their interests and needs, and would give them the opportunity to develop skills in order to get a better job upon graduation. In practice, this plan too often meant that the sons and daughters of the laboring class were "differentiated" early and channeled into the vocational curriculum on the basis of socioeconomic class.

The vocational movement in secondary education arose at an opportune time. It fit snugly within the confines of the dominant movement in education and in society in the first quarter of the twentieth century—social efficiency. Briefly, social efficiency may be described as the process of subordinating the individual to society (social) with as little waste as possible (efficiency). Applied to education, social efficiency would enable the schools to turn out "products" according to predetermined number and specification, as set by society's needs and interests. It would do this with little waste, at a very low cost per pupil. In the practical realm, social efficiency devotees advocated the early channeling of students (why waste time and money on students who could not profit from the "academic" subjects?) into areas which society needed (vocational education). These areas would meet their needs, abilities, and interests, and from which, therefore, they would profit (match lower socioeconomic class students with the "practical" subjects).

William C. Bagley coined the term "social efficiency" in 1905. The idea's existence in society predated its naming. Social control, one severe form of social efficiency in the early twentieth century, had its impact on education. This doctrine was advanced by "progressive" sociologists, such as Edward A. Ross. Ross submitted to class bias. For instance, he argued that "The cheap stucco manikins from Southeastern Europe do not really take the place of the unbegotten sons of the granite men who fell at Gettysburg and Cold Harbor."[22] This latest immigration, he maintained, brought to the country an inferior breed of humans, and they would remain thus, and so hamper the nation's advance:

The flood of immigration now flows from different sources, and taps lower human levels than the earlier tide. Over-persuaded, from Croatia and Dalmatia and Sicily and Armenia, they throng to us, the beaten members of beaten breeds, often the more aboriginal men that have been elbowed aside or left behind in the swayings of the mightier European races. Do these Slovaks and Syrians add so much to the strength of the human piers that support our civilization as Scotch-Irish or Scandinavians? As undersized in spirit, no doubt as they are in body, the later comers lack the ancestral foundations of American character, and even if they catch step with us they and their children will, nevertheless, impede our progress.[23]

Ross believed in the superiority of the industrial society then existing in Europe and the United States and that industrialization would expand over the entire earth. He believed in the supremacy of the white man, who, in his words, "spreads his economic gospel, one hand on a Gatling, the other on a locomotive."[24] What role did Ross assign to the school? It should manipulate and indoctrinate; it should promote order; it should, in fact, serve as an economic system of police, replacing religion as "the method of indirect social restraint."[25] The task of the school and its staff was of extreme importance to society, even if that importance was only lately recognized. As he phrased it:

To collect little plastic lumps of human dough from private households and shape them on the social kneadingboard, exhibits a faith in the power of suggestion which few peoples ever attain to. And so it happens that the role of the schoolmaster in the social economy is just beginning.[26]

Another influential devotee of social efficiency in education was David Snedden, a pupil of Ross'. Snedden held that institutions of society should be examined with society's welfare as their measure of worth. The school, as a social institution, must be subjected to this criterion. Snedden, the first state commissioner of education in Massachusetts, felt that the school played an important role in the task of reconstructing society. One reason for this elevated position, according to Snedden, was the fact that the school, unlike other social institutions, was completely under state control.[27] All subjects, he maintained, had to prove themselves socially useful. There was no intrinsic value of learning or knowledge in itself. The curriculum, the way the subjects were to be taught, the aims of teachers, and the subjects were to be socialized, according to the demands of society.

Another educational movement which developed in the second decade of the twentieth century, and which also harmonized with social efficiency, was the new "science" of educational administration, called scientific management. The educators provided the "scientific"; business was responsible for "management." Existing concurrently with the time-motion study movement in industry, scientific management was to be the administrative means by which education would be directed, as industry was, in an efficient manner. No institution, the president of the NEA proclaimed in 1912, could survive unless it used "twentieth-century business methods."[28] The public high school became the center of attraction for scrutinization in this regard. The subjects earned their right to survival by how efficiently, i.e., with as little waste and as low cost per pupil, they contributed to socialized aims. The high school principal, no longer the "master teacher," was to be the educational plant's "scientific manager," responsible for the implementation of efficiency in the individual school.

This was the social and educational atmosphere out of which the report of the Commission of the Reorganization of Secondary Education (CRSE), called the Cardinal Principles, emerged. The immediate source out of which the CRSE originated was the NEA Committee on Articulation of High School and College. Its chairman was Clarence D. Kingsley. It was absorbed into the CRSE at the summer meeting of the NEA in 1913.[29]

The reviewing committee of the CRSE consisted of twenty-six members, sixteen of whom were chairmen of committees and ten were members-at-large. Its chairman, Kingsley, although having taught in college, was a secondary school man. The sixteen committee chairmen held the following positions: four education professors, one dean of an art school, three high school representatives, one president of a business college, one from a normal college, two people from the United States Bureau of Education (one of these was a woman), one person from the Extension Division of The University of Wisconsin, one music director, and one Y.M.C.A. director. The ten members-at-large were drawn from the ranks of: the United States commissioner of education, three college education professors, one college president, one normal school president, two high school representatives, a Y.M.C.A. secretary, and one person from an ethical culture school.[30]

The backgrounds of the following chairmen are of interest because they reflect the status and role of the high school at the time. The classical languages chairman was a high school teacher, the English chairman came from a normal school, the mathematics chairman was an education professor, the modern languages had a chairman from the high school ranks, sciences were represented by an education professor and director of the Lincoln School in New York City, and social studies was chaired by a representative of the United States Bureau of Education. An agriculture education professor was the chairman for agriculture; art education, business education, and music were chaired by men from schools specifically organized for those purposes. Household arts took its chairwoman from the United States Bureau of Education, an extension person chaired industrial arts, and an associate superintendent of schools held the leadership of vocational guidance.[31] Not only were there entirely new content areas for secondary schools such as household arts and industrial arts, but even where the content areas were traditional, such as English and mathematics, the chairmen were drawn mainly from people directly associated with high schools or engaged in the preparation of teachers. Liberal arts professors from the "subject matter" areas were not involved in leadership positions in the CRSE. The memberships of the various committees reflect the same emphasis. For example, English had eight high school people, a school superintendent, an English supervisor, a state department of education person, and three college English professors. The membership of the committee on social studies, ancient languages, and modern languages show this emphasis to a greater degree than English.[32] Within four decades after it became a major American educational institution, the public high school leadership had changed from college academicians to high school people and pedagogues. This leadership change points out the change in direction which the institution itself had undergone.

The chairman of the Cardinal Principles report was Clarence D. Kingsley. He was a former theology student who had taught mathematics at Colgate University and in New York high schools. Kingsley had been a social worker before becoming high school inspector for the state of Massachusetts.[33]

The recommendations of the Cardinal Principles report spring not only from the temper of the times in which they were written and from the ideology of its leaders, but also from the tasks given the group. The Cardinal Principles committee perceived its tasks to be the formulation of a comprehensive program of reorganization of secondary school education, and the adoption of this program in all the secondary schools of the country.[34] To accomplish this it set forth seven objectives, toward which all efforts in secondary education were encouraged to be directed and by which the subjects would be evaluated. The main objectives of secondary education were said to be: (1) health, (2) command of fundamental processes, (3) worthy home membership, (4) vocation, (5) citizenship, (6) worthy use of leisure, and (7) ethical character.[35] These aims were stated in terms of the effect schooling had on students, rather than as processes by which students master subject matter content. The committee apparently believed that the current needs of society determined what

250

secondary education should be. It asserted that substantial changes had occurred in American society which necessitated a different form of high school education than had existed previously.[36] The school, the committee felt, had to be more concerned with social change and its effects, because other agencies, for example the Church, were doing less in the field than hitherto.[37]

The Cardinal Principles committee had sixteen "subject" committees. Many of these were new, and not even considered by another important NEA committee, the Committee of Ten on Secondary School Studies in 1893. Among the new fields were agriculture, art education, articulation of high school and college, business education, household arts, industrial arts, music, organization and administration of secondary education, physical education, and vocational guidance.[38] These new areas reflected not only the belief of the committee that the needs of society determine curriculum content, but also the changes in American society, and hence the high school, which had occurred since the report of the Committee of Ten in 1893.

The main report of the Cardinal Principles did not consider the academic subjects, except to mention them in brief fashion. The subcommittees did, however, and the way they did is worthy of consideration. Latin had to show it was "practical" in order to survive in a school in a democracy.[39] English was to be taught for "training for efficiency."[40] The overriding aim of social studies was "good citizenship." The social studies committee believed its field had "peculiar opportunities" to contribute to the goal of training the individual to be a worthwhile member of society. Regardless of the subjects' value to a person, the committee stated, "Unless they contribute directly to the cultivation of social efficiency on the part of the pupil they fail in this most important function."[41] Civics would be rejuvenated, becoming "a study of manner of social efforts to improve mankind."[42] History was to be called for an accounting, for it, too, "must answer the test of good citizenship."[43]

The CRSE was concerned with the goals of education in a democracy. The seven main objectives would determine constants in the curriculum, variables would be according to vocational goals of students. All subjects were to be "practical," the criterion of importance. The committee believed that democracy would be endangered unless the high schools sought the development "in each individual of the knowledge, interests, ideals, habits, and powers whereby he will find his place and use that place to shape both himself and society toward even nobler ends."[44] This was to be done, the committee decreed, in a democratic society whose purpose "is to organize society that each member may develop his personality primarily through activities designed for the well-being of his fellow members and of society as a whole."[45] As for the individual, the committee referred to his dignity and his "potential and perchance unique" worth.[46]

In order that the high school fulfill its goal of socializing youth into a democratic society, the committee went on record favoring compulsory education for all American youth until the age of eighteen in a comprehensive high school. While the students would be separated according to their post-high school destinations in the curriculum, assemblies and other cocurricular offerings would provide the opportunity for the mixing of all pupils, regardless of their destinations.

In the event a young person demonstrated that he could not profit from an all-day school, the committee was willing to allow him to go to school half days (called a continuation school), provided he participated in assemblies.[47]

To implement the seven objectives in a high school, the CRSE advocated the formation of a Principal's Council, with a director for each major objective.[48] The committee placed the auditorium in a position of new-found esteem, based on the unifying, democratic role it was to play in the thrust of the high school.

The Cardinal Principles report was generally well received throughout the educational world. It had responded to American society's changed needs, and was indeed an attempt to reorganize secondary education. The NEA endorsed the seven objectives as a means of evaluating the school and all of its activities, including the subjects of the curriculum. It satisfied most backers of the social efficiency movement, an exception being David Snedden. He complained that the report "almost completely" missed the significance of vocational education, was too academic, and that secondary education's problem could be answered only by specialized, not comprehensive, high schools.[49]

The Department of Superintendence attempted, a decade later, to appraise the report's influence. Accordingly, they surveyed 1,228 high school principals. Of the principals contacted, 689 (56.1 percent of those replying) said that they had tried to organize the programs of their schools around the Cardinal Principles. Two hundred and fifty-five, mostly from small schools, stated that the report had never been called to their attention, and nine said they were not in sympathy with it.[50] That same year the National Congress of Parents and Teachers (PTA) adopted the seven objectives for their national platform. They called them "The Sevenfold Program of Home and School."[51]

While the PTA spoke of educating "the whole child" as the Cardinal Principles report did, there was a notable difference between them. The PTA conceived of the educational program as taking place in home and school, whereas the CRSE envisioned it as exclusively a school function. The Cardinal Principles report reflects the position of Herbert Spencer, that the school should prepare its students for "complete living." The report may be seen as an attempt to educate the whole man, mind and body. The high school, in this philosophy, takes on a more comprehensive and consequently more important function in the education and life of its students. Given the crucial position of the high school, and given the social realities of the age, this changed and expanded role of secondary education should not be unexpected. In the second decade of the twentieth century, American society faced perplexing and threatening events. It had a large immigrant population, somewhat illiterate, which held to their respective native languages and customs. These people were not as yet assimilated to the American mainstream to the satisfaction of native white Americans. This was especially critical before 1917 because of the possibility of participation in global war, and the nation was not sure of the loyalties of its recent arrivals. Also, the country was beset by rapid industrialization, with all of its social ramifications. In light of this, the nation had to look to its schools for assistance. For the high schools, this entailed a new and different kind of program. It was a time of crisis for the nation, thus a time of crisis for the nation's schools. The Cardinal Principles report was born in this period of national emergency and social upheaval. With it, the American public high school not only reorganized itself and its program, but also met the needs of society. In so doing it managed to survive its second major crisis in its relatively brief history, and continues to exist as one of American society's vital institutions.

NOTES

1. R. Freeman Butts and Lawrence A. Cremin, *A History of Education in American Culture* (New York: Holt, Rinehart and Winston, 1953), p. 308.
2. Edward A. Krug, *The Shaping of the American High School 1880-1920*, vol. 1 (Madison: The University of Wisconsin Press, 1969), pp. 167-72.
3. Ibid., p. 284.
4. William M. Alexander, J. Gaylen Saylor, and Emmett L. Williams, *The High School Today and Tomorrow* (New York: Holt, Rinehart and Winston, 1971), p. 83.
5. E. A. Steere, "The High School as a Factor in Mass Education," *National Education Association, Journal of Addresses and Proceedings, 1890* (Topeka, Ks.: Clifford C. Baker, 1890), p. 646.
6. Charles R. Skinner, "The Best Education for the Masses," *National Education Association, Journal of Addresses and Proceedings, 1897* (Chicago: The University of Chicago Press, 1897), p. 53.
7. "Editorial," *Education* 11 (May 1891):573.
8. Ellwood P. Cubberley, *Public Education in The United States* (Boston: Houghton Mifflin Company, 1919), p. 338.
9. S. Alexander Rippa, *Education in a Free Society: An American History* (New York: David McKay Company, 1971), p. 160.
10. David B. Tyack, ed., *Turning Points in American Educational History* (New York: Blaisdell Publishing Company, 1967), p. 233.
11. John Higham, *Strangers in the Land: Patterns of American Nativism 1860-1925* (New York: Atheneum, 1970), p. 103.
12. Ibid.
13. Granville Stanley Hall, *Adolescence*, vol. 2 (New York: D. Appleton and Company, 1905), p. 510.
14. "Editorial," *Education* 26 (October 1905):116.
15. Ellwood P. Cubberley, *Changing Conceptions of Education* (Boston: Houghton Mifflin Company, 1909), pp. 15-16.
16. *Report of the Massachusetts Commission on Industrial and Technical Education* (Boston: Wright and Potter, 1906), pp. 18-23.
17. Ibid., pp. 87-88.
18. Theodore Roosevelt, "Annual Message, December 3, 1907," *Congressional Record, Sixtieth Congress, First Session*, vol. 42 (Washington: Government Printing Office, 1908), p. 74.
19. Theodore Roosevelt, "Address," *The Educator-Journal* 8 (April 1908):382.
20. Krug, *Shaping*, p. 242.
21. Charles A. Prosser, "Practical Arts and Vocational Guidance," *National Education Association, Journal of Addresses and Proceedings, 1912* (Ann Arbor, Michigan: The Association, 1912), p. 650.
22. Edward A. Ross, *Foundations of Sociology* (New York: The Macmillan Company, 1905), p. 342.
23. Ibid., pp. 392-93.
24. Ibid., p. 365.
25. Edward A. Ross, *Social Control* (New York: The Macmillan Company, 1912), pp. 174-76.
26. Ibid., p. 168.
27. David Snedden, "Educational Tendencies in America," *Educational Review* 39 (January 1910):24.
28. Edward T. Fairchild, "President's Address," *National Education Association, Journal of Addresses and Proceedings, 1913* (Ann Arbor, Michigan: The Association, 1913), p. 35.
29. Krug, *Shaping*, p. 300.
30. National Education Association, *Cardinal Principles of Secondary Education* (Washington: Government Printing Office, 1918), p. 6.
31. Ibid.
32. National Education Association, *Preliminary Statements by Chairmen of Committees of the Commission of the National Education Association on the Reorganization of Secondary Education*, U.S. Bureau of Education Bulletin no. 41 (Washington: Government Printing Office, 1913), pp. 16, 27-28, 40, 58.
33. Krug, *Shaping*, pp. 265, 300-301.
34. National Education Association, *Cardinal Principles*, p. 8.
35. Ibid., pp. 10-11.

36. Ibid., p. 7.
37. Ibid., pp. 7-8.
38. Ibid., p. 6.
39. Walter E. Foster, "Statement of Chairman of the Committee on Ancient Languages," *Preliminary Statements by Chairmen,* pp. 31-33.
40. Commission for the Reorganization of Secondary Education, *Reorganization of English in Secondary Schools,* U.S. Bureau of Education Bulletin no. 2 (Washington: Government Printing Office, 1917), p. 26.
41. Commission for the Reorganization of Secondary Education, *The Social Studies in Education,* U.S. Bureau of Education Bulletin no. 28 (Washington: Government Printing Office, 1916), pp. 1-2.
42. Thomas Jesse Jones, "Statement of Chairman of the Committee on Social Studies," *Preliminary Statements by Chairmen,* pp. 16-17.
43. Ibid., pp. 17-18.
44. National Education Association, *Cardinal Principles,* p. 9.
45. Ibid.
46. Ibid., p. 32.
47. Ibid., pp. 24-26.
48. Ibid., p. 28.
49. David Snedden, "Cardinal Principles of Secondary Education," *School and Society* 9 (May 3, 1919):522-23.
50. William M. Proctor and Edwin J. Brown, "College Admission Requirements in Relation to Curricular Revision in Secondary Schools," *The Development of the High School Curriculum,* Sixth Yearbook (Washington: NEA, The Department of Superintendence, 1928), pp. 173-76.
51. National Congress of Parents and Teachers, *Jubilee History: 50th Anniversary 1897-1947* (Chicago: The Congress, 1947), pp. 95-96.

Charles A. Prosser and the Smith-Hughes Act[*]

ARTHUR G. WIRTH

As THE United States entered the twentieth century it faced the fact that it had become an urban-industrial society. New processes of technology and corporate, bureaucratic organizational forms were changing the world of work and the life-style of Americans. The capacity to survive under the new conditions was dependent on education as never before in history. Many sectors of the public—farmers, industrialists, workers, and progressive reformers like settlement house leaders and women suffragettes—looked at the public schools and found them wanting.

The criticism of public schooling was strident and complex. It included groups as diverse as proponents of progressive education who wanted a new schooling to "free children and reform society" to those who pressured school-men to meet the business efficiency criteria which presumably marked the operations of industry and commerce. I shall make no effort to confront the total range of the debate, and shall limit my comments to one of the strong pressures of the time—the demand for a more practical schooling which would serve the new skill needs of industry and business. This movement for vocational education culminated in the passage of the first federal legislation to aid pre-collegiate education—the Smith-Hughes Act of 1917.

The acknowledged leader of the coalition which formed to lobby for such legislation was Charles A. Prosser, Executive Secretary of the National Society for the Promotion of Industrial Education and the effective author of the Smith-Hughes Act. He was a proponent of the social efficiency philosophy. I shall attempt to show how the features of Prosser's philosophy of education left their marks on the American approach to vocational education in the decades after 1917. General educators tend to be less informed about vocational education than any other aspect of the system. A look at the concept of vocational training represented in Prosser's orientation may help explain the relative isolation of vocationalism in the American pattern of schooling.

Charles A. Prosser came from a fam-

---

[*] This article is based on material for a chapter in *Education in the Technological Society* (Scranton, Pa.: Intext Educational Publishers, 1972). For the biographical details the author is indebted to John Gadell of Wright State University who is doing doctoral research on Prosser at Washington University.

An interesting perspective on the current controversies about the shortcomings of the public schools is provided by the views of the man who is the subject of this paper, Charles A. Prosser. ARTHUR G. WIRTH *is Professor of Education at the Graduate Institute of Education, Washington University, St. Louis. He has written extensively on the educational theories of John Dewey and on education in the technological society.*

ily of steel-workers in New Albany, Indiana. As a student and young professional, he was noted for his "get-up-and-go," a quality which later enabled him to win success when he moved to New York and the East. In 1898, while teaching physics, chemistry, and literature in the New Albany High School, Prosser succeeded in completing two years of legal training in one at the University of Louisville Law School. He won the honors of both classes and all the prizes for which he competed. The following year he was appointed Superintendent of New Albany Schools. While serving in that post (1900-1908), he became President of the Indiana State Teachers Association, "the youngest man ever elected to the position." He left Indiana to begin doctoral study at Teachers College, Columbia University. There he became a student under David Snedden and developed his first interest in vocational education. His dissertation was *A Study of the Boston Mechanic Arts High School*. He obviously impressed his mentor, for Snedden, when he became Massachusetts Commissioner of Education, invited Prosser in 1910 to fill the new post of Deputy Commissioner for Vocational Education. Prosser's meteoric rise was capped two years later (1912), when he became the full-time Executive Secretary of the prestigious National Society for the Promotion of Industrial Education. In this capacity he became involved in the whirl of events which led to enactment of the Smith-Hughes law.

The Smith-Hughes Act was passed after years of preparation and political maneuvering. The final draft won the approval of groups as divergent as the National Association of Manufacturers and the Chamber of Commerce, the American Federation of Labor, the major farm organizations, settlement house leaders, and the National Education Association. The coming together of such ordinarily feuding factions is a rare event. It is even more remarkable to find them agreeing on so controversial a matter as the introduction of federal power into the operation of public schools. Many men contributed to this agreement; but there is general agreement that the one individual most responsible for it was Prosser.

By the time Prosser received his appointment from N.S.P.I.E., the Society had decided to promote its cause by securing action through federal and State legislatures. Prosser immediately became active in helping to draft a bill by Senator Page of Vermont which, in fact, became the legislative source for both the Smith-Lever and Smith-Hughes Acts. (The Smith-Lever agricultural extension bill was passed first in 1914, as a concession to farm interests, in return for a promise from farmers to support vocational education later). In January of 1914, Congress approved a joint resolution authorizing President Wilson to appoint a Commission to study national aid for vocational education. The Commission was conveniently composed of a group of Congressmen and citizens who had been ardent advocates of industrial education. Among them was Dr. Prosser. The Commission's two-volume final report[1] contained a section on "proposed legislation" which, with minor changes, became the text of the Smith-Hughes Act. Dr. Prosser's son, William, recalls seeing his father write the "proposed legislation" at their dining room table.[2]

Prosser was instrumental in working out the final wording of Smith-Hughes to satisfy groups like the N.E.A. and the A.F. of L. After Congress approved the bill (1917), Prosser was named Executive Director of the newly created Federal Board for Vocational Education. His vigorous leadership was manifest as every state in the Union accepted the provisions of the Act within a year. As the first chief administrator of the Act, Prosser saw to to it that the bare bones of the law were filled in with operating procedures consistent with the principles he had built into the legislation.

We turn briefly, then, to examples of Prosser's theories of vocational education as they were reflected in Smith-Hughes.

Grant Venn pointed out that the Smith-Hughes Act established the pattern for nearly 50 years of Federal aid in the field of vocational education. "In fact, its major provisions remained untouched by amendment until 1963."[3] The great strength of the Act was that it was designed directly to meet a compelling need of the new America—the need to provide American industry with the complicated work skills required in a technological society. The genius of Charles Prosser lay in his capacity to focus energies unwaveringly on creating functional programs to accomplish this task.

Yet from the beginning, there were doubts in some quarters about the educational orientation of the Act. Its strengths in securing quick short-term gains were also the source of its fundamental flaws.

A Commission appointed by President Franklin D. Roosevelt to review the effectiveness of the Act expressed misgivings in a report issued in 1938.[4] The Chairman, John D. Russell of the University of Chicago, stressed the point that the Act was marked by a specificity of prescription for programs and administration which was a feature of no other federal legislation for education, such as the Morrill or Smith-Lever Acts. This specificity, said Russell, tended to limit imaginative experimentation with curricula and led to interference with institutions of higher education by prescribing details of teacher education. Narrow concentration on skill training resulted in almost total neglect of the cultivation of broad social and economic insights in students. The law seemed to foster a restricted quality of mind, as reflected in the type of leadership found in the federal office of voca-

---

[1] *Report of the Commission on National Aid to Vocational Education*, 2 vols. (Washington: Government Printing Office, 1914).

[2] Interview with William L. Prosser, Saint Louis, Missouri, September, 1967.

[3] Grant Venn, *Man, Education, and Work* (Washington: American Council on Education, 1964), p. 112.

[4] John D. Russell and associates, *Vocational Education: Staff Study No. 8* (Washington: U.S. Government Printing Office, 1938), pp. 25-40, 210-220 *et passim*.

tional education. The Chairman thought he detected an inbred, parochial quality in the office and a tendency toward isolation from the mainstream of American education.

A look at some of the principles cherished by Dr. Prosser may help to explain both the strengths and weaknesses of the Act.

One of its cardinal tenets was the definition of vocational education so that it would accommodate only specific job training programs. Prosser was fond of quoting a friend, Charles R. Allen: "The purpose of vocational education is to help a person secure a job, train him so he can hold it after he gets it, and assist him in advancing to a better job."[5] Vocational education was, in brief, "training for useful employment," and nothing else.

Prosser insisted that all vocational content must be specific and that its source was to be found "in the experience of those who have mastered the occupation." The content must come from the minds of competent workers, and it will have "little or nothing in common with corresponding content in any other occupation. In setting up its program, therefore, the [all] day vocational schools must provide as many specific courses or groups of courses as there are occupations for which it proposes to train."[6] Prosser was convinced that to produce trained workers ready for useful employment, vocational programs had to be managed not by general educators but by those qualified and committed to advance "real vocational education." He pushed hard for "the dual system": for vocational education administered separately from general education.

Throughout his long career, Prosser repeated endlessly the arguments for his position. Traditional scholastic education, he maintained, aimed to prepare the citizen for the worthy use of his leisure time. Traditional schoolmen, committed to the task of fostering "leisure culture," operated from the psychological tradition of faculty psychology and formal discipline. This, they thought, would lead to general mental training and "cultural appreciations." There were several clear reasons why new programs of vocational training could not be entrusted to such men. "Culturists" were cut off from the practical world of work, and their outmoded theory of learning made them incapable of managing genuine skill training programs. "Vocational education," Prosser argued, "only functions in proportion as it will enable an individual actually to do a job . . . Vocational education must establish habits: habits of correct thinking and of correct doing. Hence, its fundamental theory must be that of habit psychology."[7] The new scientific psychology pioneered by Edward Thorndike, said Prosser, assumed that the mind is a habit forming machine. There was an obvious fit between this psychological theory and vocational education,

---

[5] Charles A. Prosser and Thomas H. Quigley, *Vocational Education in a Democracy*, revised edition (Chicago: American Technical Society, 1950), pp. 454-455.
[6] *Ibid.*, pp. 286-287.

[7] *Ibid.*, pp. 215-220 *et passim.*

when the latter was conceived as "essentially a matter of establishing certain habits through repetitive training both in thinking and doing."[8] In contrast to the theory of general mind training of the discredited faculty psychology, Thorndike's theory taught that "all habits of doing and thinking are developed in specific situations." Prosser deduced correlatively that the content of vocational training should be determined by "the actual functioning content" of a given occupation. "If you want to train a youth to be an efficient plumber, you must select the actual experiences in the practice of the plumbing trade that he should have and see that he gets these in a real instead of in a pseudo way."[9] Furthermore, general studies like mathematics or science should ideally be broken into short units which would bear "directly on specific needs of workers in the performance of specific tasks or operations." They should, when possible, be taught by the craftsman-teacher skilled in the task, rather than by general mathematics or science teachers.

A prototype of the plan favored by Prosser was established in the short unit courses which he developed while Director of the Dunwoody Institute in Minneapolis. "In garment making, one unit might deal with kimonos, one with underwear, and another with house dresses."[10] Training should be done either on the job, as in cooperative-work programs, or in settings which duplicated as closely as possible the environment of the workshop itself. At the Dunwoody Institute, units were programmed in great detail to lead students step by step through the skill development cycle. Students punched in on time-clocks and instructors behaved like shop foremen rather than public school teachers. A no-nonsense attitude prevailed. If students were not punctual, orderly, and efficient, they were asked to leave. (This Spartan regimen was made possible because Dunwoody was a private training school.)

If this brief description of Dunwoody conveys a feeling of Prosser's orientation, some of the features he favored in Smith-Hughes can readily be understood. Approved programs had to meet the criterion of "fitting for useful employment" persons over fourteen but under college age who were preparing for work on farms, in trades, in industrial pursuits, and the like. Federal funds were given only for support of vocational training classes. General education costs were to be borne by the States and local school districts. At least 50 percent of subsidized instruction had to be devoted to "practical work on a useful or productive basis." Funds for the training of teachers were restricted to those who "have had adequate vocational experience or contact in the line of work for which they are preparing."[11]

Since his rationale excluded general educators from the management of vocational training, Prosser fought as long as possible for a separately administered type of vocational education. In the final

---

[8] *Ibid.*, p. 216.
[9] *Ibid.*, p. 228.
[10] *Ibid.*, p. 291.

[11] *Smith-Hughes Act of 1917*, in U.S., *Statutes at Large*, XXXIX, Part I, 929-936.

politicking prior to 1917, he had to make some concessions; but in the main, he created a framework which permitted vocational programs to stand apart. The Smith-Hughes Act did establish a Federal Board for Vocational Education, separate from the U.S. Office of Education, and responsible only to Congress. The seven member Board consisted of the Secretaries of Labor, Commerce, and Agriculture and three citizens representing labor, agriculture, and manufacturing and commerce. The Commissioner of Education was added partly to allay the anxieties of the N.E.A. Philander Claxton, Commissioner of Education, helped to secure a separate board for vocational education by maintaining that the U.S. Office of Education staff was not properly constituted to administer the provisions of the Act.[12]

Prosser was immediately appointed Executive Director of the Federal Board and served in that office in its first two crucial years. He established the initial tone of administration. States were given the option of setting up separate boards, or of administering vocational education under the aegis of their general Boards of Education. In actuality, both the language of Smith-Hughes and the administrative style of Dr. Prosser assured that vocational education would function largely as a separate aspect of education within the States.

Vocational education became firmly established and expanded in the years ahead. By the time John F. Kennedy became President and the Russians launched their first Sputniks, some of the shortcomings of Smith-Hughes had become apparent. The feeling of urgency grew as discontented urban minorities faced job obsolescence as a result of their inferior education and training. Review procedures were established, and the first fundamental revision of vocational education legislation was readied for President Johnson's signature in 1963.[13] Detailed analyses of evolving economic conditions and recommendations for procedural changes in vocational training appeared in profusion. We shall mention a few of these shifts in orientation which could eventually lead to major philosophical and power changes in American education.

The critics of the 1960's identified two central failures of vocational education: (1) its lack of sensitivity to changes in the labor market, and (2) its lack of sensitivity to the needs of various segments of the population. Critics charged that Smith-Hughes programs had been confined to a very narrow part of the spectrum of work activities and had failed to make imaginative adaptations to the demands of a fast changing economy. By concentrating on the job

---

[12] Melvin Barlow, *History of Industrial Education in the United States* (Peoria: Charles A. Bennett Company, 1967), pp. 114-115.

[13] See, for example, U.S. Department of Health, Education, and Welfare, "Education for a Changing World of Work," Report of Consultants on Vocational Education, 1963. For a comprehensive overview of shifts in policies and evaluation of their effects, see United States Senate, *Notes and Working Papers Concerning the Administration of Programs Authorized Under Vocational Education Act of 1963*, prepared for Subcommittee on Education of the Committee on Labor and Public Welfare (U.S. Government Printing Office, March, 1968). Hereafter referred to as *Working Papers*, 1968.

requirements of industry and by restricting its efforts to secondary school age students, Smith-Hughes also failed to give priority to the vocational needs of all groups in the community.

The 1963 Act announced as its aim the development of vocational education for persons of all ages in all communities. This was to be accomplished with a unified concept of vocational education, rather than by sharply separated programs for vocational, agriculture, home economics, trade and industries, or distributive education. Special attention was to be paid to the needs of disadvantaged persons who had dropped out of school, lacked basic education skills, or needed re-training.

Several of the basic "operational principles" of the revision of the sixties illustrate dramatically the departure from Prosser's preferences.

Vocational education cannot be meaningfully limited to the skills necessary for a particular occupation. It is more appropriately defined as all of those aspects of educational experience which help a person to discover his talents, to relate them to the world of work, to choose an occupation, and to refine his talents and use them successfully in employment....

The objectives of vocational education should be the development of the individual, not the needs of the labor market....

It is no longer possible to compartmentalize education into general, academic, and vocational components. Education is a crucial element in preparation for a successful working career at any level.... Culture and vocation are inseparable and unseverable aspects of humanity....

The practice of structuring teacher education along the traditional occupational category lines perpetuates fragmentation of vocational education, severs it further from general education and hinders adaptation to labor market conditions.[14]

The 1968 evaluators also suggested that pedagogical techniques inherent to vocational education, such as opportunities for multi-sensory experiences and the relation of classroom study to out-of-school experience, might also enliven general education. They suggested that studies which relate learning to the world of work could be important at all levels, from the elementary school on.

Clearly, important aspects of Charles Prosser's concept of vocational education had become inadequate by the 1960's. We are at a moment when the relations of pre-vocational and vocational studies to general education are ripe for reconsideration.

[14] *Working Papers*, 1968, pp. 47-50, 37-39, *et passim*.

John Dewey's Philosophical Opposition to Smith-Hughes Type Vocational Education*

BY ARTHUR G. WIRTH

The question of industrial education is fraught with consequences for the future of democracy. Its right development will do more to make public education truly democratic than any other one agency now under consideration. Its wrong treatment will as surely accentuate all undemocratic tendencies in our present situation, by fostering and strengthening class divisions in school and out.[1]

Dewey was writing on the subject of industrial education as the century opened; he stepped up his efforts as state and federal legislation for vocational education was being readied prior to 1917. Dewey's strategy was to describe the possibilities for imaginative educational uses of industrialism and to contrast these with wrong tendencies in the vocational education movement. In a 1916 article, "American Education and Culture," Dewey said,

To transmute a society built on an industry which is not yet humanized into a society which wields its knowledge and its industrial power in behalf of a democratic culture requires the courage of an inspired imagination.

I am one of those who think that the only test and justification of any form of political and economic society is its contribution to art and science—to what may be called culture. That America has not yet so justified itself is too obvious for lament. . . . To settle a continent is to put it into order, and this is a work which comes after, not before, great intelligence and great art. . . . It means nothing less than the discovery of a method of subduing and settling nature in the interests of a democracy that is to say of masses who shall form a community of directed thought and emotion in spite of being masses. That this has not been effected goes without saying. It has never been attempted before. . . . That the achievement is immensely difficult means that it may fail.[2]

Dewey assumed that the twentieth century would be a testing period revealing how Americans would respond to the pressures of an emerging

---

Arthur G. Wirth is Professor of History and Philosophy of Education, Washington University, St. Louis, Missouri.

---

*Based on research completed for the U.S. Office of Education: "The Vocational-Liberal Studies Controversy Between John Dewey and Others (1900-1917)," September 1970 (Project # 7-0305). This article is to be a part of a chapter in the author's *Education in the Technological Society* to be published by the International Textbook Co., Scranton, 1972.

[1] John Dewey, "Some Dangers in the Present Movement for Industrial Education," *Child Labor Bulletin,* I, (February, 1913), p. 70.

[2] John Dewey, "American Education and Culture," *Characters and Events,* II, 1929, p. 500. (Originally in *The New Republic,* July 1, 1916.) One is reminded of a comment by John Smith in *The Spirit of American Philosophy*: "The candor, the concern for fact, and the unwillingness to abandon an ideal merely because it is difficult to realize are traits which we must associate at once with the mind of Dewey."

technologism. Some, he said, would retreat to asylums and hospitals; some would be caught in "the meshes of a mechanical industrialism;" and others would commit themselves to the long fight to "subdue the industrial machinery to human ends until the nation is endowed with soul."[3]

1906 was a year in which proponents of federal aid for vocational education began to marshal their forces. The National Society for the Promotion of Industrial Education was founded and an influential report was issued in Massachusetts, a report by the Commission on Industrial Education created by Govenor Douglas. In that year Dewey published an assessment of the new stirrings over vocational education. The time had arrived, he said, to face not the question of "What shall the school do for industry?" but of "What shall industry do with the school?"

Business, said Dewey, was the dominating force in American life, affecting everything and everyone, whether educators were aware of it or not. The ideals and methods that controlled business "take possession of the spirit and machinery of our educational system." Pressures were strong to put the schools in the service of business interests — to introduce industrial education to promote the cause of American economic supremacy (to which end an emulation of German vocational education was urged); to create a stable group of workers who would produce efficiently while becoming passive and contented under the reward of higher wages.[4]

These trends were reinforced, Dewey said, by the habitual ways in which business and educational leaders thought about education. They still thought in terms of a European tradition which from the time of Aristotle, distinguished "education" for the directive and leisured classes from "training" for the menial, servile masses. At present, said Dewey, the vast majority of children leave school at the end of the fourth or fifth grade —a pattern which until recently served industry's need for a large supply of unskilled labor. The school drop-outs were taught little more than reading, writing, and figuring — a schooling which made them into nothing more than economically useful tools. They entered jobs which were routine, repetitive, and demeaning; and after a short while they became unfit for further special training. They were, furthermore, relatively helpless to protest their plight, since they had been denied the kind of education which would equip them with "initiative, thoughtfulness, and executive force." Many businessmen were quite content with this arrangement, said Dewey. They demanded that schools stick to the three R's and attacked "fads and frills" — knowing full well that their own children would receive enriched experiences which they deplored for the masses.[5] The new trend in favor of vocationalism, Dewey maintained, derived from the fact that more complex industrial processes required a better trained work force.

3*Ibid.*, p. 501.

4See also John Dewey, "The Need of an Industrial Education in an Industrial Democracy," *Manual Training and Vocational Education,* XVII, (February, 1916), pp. 409-414; and "A Policy of Industrial Education," *The New Republic,* I, (December 19, 1914), pp. 11-12.

5See John Dewey, "Learning to Earn," *Education Today* (New York: G.P. Putnam and Sons, 1940), pp. 126-132. Originally in *School and Society* (March 24, 1917), V, pp. 331-335, based on an address to the N.E.A.

From time to time, Dewey pin-pointed specific dangers as the focus of his criticism. In an article for the *Child Labor Bulletin* written in 1913, he pointed to abuses arising from the new enthusiasm for vocational guidance. The tendency, he said, is to use a high-sounding phrase like "vocational guidance" for what is nothing more than a plan to find jobs for children under sixteen. These plans become mischievous or worse when they actually encourage young people to leave school to fill job openings in local industries.

Vocational guidance enthusiasts, he said, should encourage children to stay in school to get an education they could build on later; they should work to modify school programs by providing opportunities for students to have study experiences connected to the out-of-school environment; and they should seek to establish supplementary centers where young people could get advice and further educational experience after they took jobs.[6] He called for an alliance between educators and Settlement House workers to counteract pressures for narrow training orientations. They should advocate community schools which might serve as centers for each neighborhood's social, artistic, and educational life. Such schools, open day and night, should offer avenues for exploration of personal interests or "callings," or for vocational self-improvement; they should stimulate the thinking and the skills necessary for social action.

As late as 1928, Dewey reported to the N.E.A. that a study of statements on education by the National Association of Manufacturers revealed that organization's inclination to give many reasons why large numbers of children should drop out of school. They pointed to the increases in high school enrollments in terms of escalating costs. They charged that many of the public schools and colleges promoted socialism or Bolshevism. Some manufacturers concluded that the best way to protect workers was to get them early into the factories, where they would be protected from subversive ideas.[7]

Dewey also followed closely the vocational education bills that were being considered by the state legislatures. In 1915, for example, he described an Indiana law as "a wrong kind." He endorsed comprehensive features of the law which included provision for agricultural and domestic education as well as industrial training; and he felt provision was rightly made for evening school programs and "continuation" schools. The latter provision was spoiled, however, by limiting state aid to instruction which was connected with a man's regular employment. The consequence, said Dewey, was that workers were denied the chance to change their minds, or to seize other work opportunities. Furthermore, provisions for full-time vocational schools specified that vocational programs would be open only to those who were already in that field of work or who indicated their intention to enter employment related to the specific training programs. The law was written to deny aid to schools giving general industrial or pre-vocational courses designed to help students explore

---

[6] John Dewey, "Some Dangers In the Present Movement for Industrial Education," pp. 69-70.

[7] John Dewey, "The Manufacturers' Association and the Public Schools," *Journal of the National Education Association*, XVII, (February, 1928), pp. 61-62.

career alternatives or to lay a broad base for future vocational decisions. Dewey said that the Indiana law was an object lesson in the kind of absurdity which could result when legislators rushed hurriedly into specific educational details without consulting intelligent school men.[8] The defensible alternative, Dewey argued, was for the states to pass statutes with only the broadest provisions, so that state Boards of Education could exercise discretionary powers in their execution. Such laws would permit necessary experimentation and could prevent the hobbling of schools by inflexible legislative prescriptions in a period of rapid social change.

A. The Fight Against "The Dual System"

In the years immediately prior to enactment of the Smith-Hughes law, Dewey concentrated his criticism on efforts to pass state and federal legislation which would establish separate systems of vocational schools alongside the general common school.

One of the most notable battles was the struggle against the Cooley Bill in Illinois. It was formally presented to the legislature in 1914 and 1915 and triggered a bitter controversy before finally being defeated. Dewey joined educators, labor and Settlement House leaders, and other progressives in a concerted resistance to this bill. Support for the measure came from powerful segments of the business and manufacturing community and from vocational education leaders active in the National Society For the Promotion of Industrial Education.

The Cooley Bill proposed a separate State Commission of Education to administer all forms of vocational education for youth over age fourteen. Dewey quoted Mr. Cooley, an ex-Superintendent of Chicago Schools and a spokesman for the Chicago Commercial Club, as saying that the proper task of vocational schools was to provide "the direct training in vocational life of the youth who must leave the ordinary school at fourteen," and that "vocational education must be shaped to dove-tail with the industry in which the group of pupils happened to be."[9] With this definition of vocational education, it is not surprising, said Dewey, to find Mr. Cooley arguing that the enterprise requires "different methods of administration, different equipment" from those of the unified school system.

Dewey said that proponents of the bill denied that the plan was designed to serve the interests of employers and argued that separate vocational schools would be more effective in meeting the needs of youth forced to leave school at fourteen. The plan, it was claimed, would raise the general level of industrial efficiency and thus benefit the whole community. Further, the interests of labor would be protected because labor representatives would sit on local and state advisory boards. One could assume the best of intentions in supporters of the bill, said Dewey, but still conclude the measure should be resolutely opposed.

---

[8] John Dewey, "Industrial Education — A Wrong Kind," *The New Republic*, II, (February 20, 1915), pp. 71-73.

[9] John Dewey, "Splitting Up the School System," *The New Republic*, II, (April 17, 1915), p. 284.

The real issue, he insisted, was whether the school system would be split so that "a sharp line of cleavage shall be drawn as respects administrative control, studies, methods and personal associations of pupils, between schools of the traditional literary type and schools of a trade-preparatory type."[10] Dewey predicted a series of evil consequences if the bill were passed. It would, he said, divide and duplicate administrative machinery and thus lead to frictions and wastes of funds.[11] Secondly, at a time when industrialism was already polarizing class divisions, the separation of pupils along these lines would accentuate this tendency.

One of the ironies of the Illinois situation, Dewey thought, was that the Cooley law would split the schools just when urban education had begun to come alive under the leadership of Ella Flagg Young.

> More than half of the pupils in the high schools of Chicago today are engaged in "vocational" work. There are industrial centers in twenty elementary schools; were there funds they would have been established in twenty-six more. Under unified control, the pupils are kept in constant personal association with youth not going into manual pursuits; the older type of school work is receiving constant stimulation and permeation. Technical subjects are taught by practical men and women whose horizon and methods are broadened by contact with wider educational interests, while the teachers in more theoretical subjects are brought into living touch with problems and needs of modern life which in the isolated state they might readily ignore.
>
> In short, a complete education system preserving the best in the old and redeeming the heritage of lively association with studies, methods, and teachers representing newer social needs, is in active development.[12]

It would not be surprising if a closer look revealed that Dewey, in the heat of argument, had given a rosier picture of Chicago's schools than the facts warranted. His statement does reveal, however, the aspirations he had for public school work.

Cooley, in a tempered reply, denied that his bill would interfere with reform movements in the public schools; after all, it did not involve elementary education.[13] These new schools, said Cooley, would encourage the development of character, civic responsibility, and joy in work — absolute essentials for the happiness and self-respect of the individual. The decision to propose dual administration was made upon primarily practical grounds; experience had shown, Cooley said, that the people who had already allowed public education to become ineffectual were not capable of providing the leadership required for a reformed system. He concluded that "while I dislike to differ with Dr. Dewey on any question, I must insist that the argument is against him in this case."

---

[10]*Ibid.*
[11]John Dewey, "Some Dangers in the Present Movement for Industrial Education," pp. 70-71.
[12]*Ibid.*
[13]Edwin G. Cooley, "Professor Dewey's Criticism of the Chicago Commercial Club and Its Vocational Education Bill," *Vocational Education*, III, (September, 1913), pp. 24-29.

David Snedden, who had been a student and colleague of Dewey at Columbia University, was stung to a sharper reply. Snedden began a two-page letter to *The New Republic* as follows:

> Sir: Some of us school men, who have profound respect for the insight of Dr. Dewey where the underlying principles of social organization and of education are under discussion, are somewhat bewildered on reading the contributions which he has recently made to *The New Republic*. Those of us who have been seeking to promote the development of sound vocational education in schools have become accustomed to the opposition of our academic brethren, who, perhaps unconsciously, still reflect the very ancient and very enduring lack of sympathy, and even the antipathy, of educated men towards common callings, "menial pursuits" and "dirty trades." We have even reconciled ourselves to the endless misrepresentations of numerous reactionaries and of the beneficiaries of vested educational interests and traditions. But to find Dr. Dewey apparently giving aid and comfort to the opponents of a broader, richer, and more effective program of education, and apparently misapprehending the motives of many of those who advocate the extension of vocational education in schools designed for that purpose, is discouraging.[14]

Snedden went on to say that, in his opinion, the question of so-called unit or dual control was not fundamental at all. A decision concerning the administration of vocational education was "merely one of securing the greatest efficiency." In order to decide the issue it was important to have a clear definition of vocational education: "vocational education is, irreducibly and without unnecessary mystification, education for the pursuit of an occupation."[15] Young people had a right to the same kind of specific training which universities gave to those headed for professions. A boy of fourteen, said Snedden, will already have had a general education. He "should be able to concentrate his efforts largely in learning the occupation selected. It is not desirable to blend so-called liberal and vocational education in this period, it being always within the possibilities of the youth to continue in the regular or general elementary or high school if he so selects."

Snedden said that it was incredible that men acquainted with economic conditions should think that state-supported vocational education would be beneficial chiefly to employers. It was, in fact, designed for the hitherto neglected majority. Vocational programs would tend to their needs, and the whole society would benefit. Snedden said that candor required admission of the fact that business men were suspicious of the "so-called academic mind." "They feel assured neither of the friendliness nor of the competency of our schoolmasters in developing sound industrial education. For that reason they often favor some form of partially separate control, at least at the outset of any new experiment." To get best results, said Snedden, it is better to admit that "school men, however well intentioned, are apt to be impractical and to fail to appreciate actual conditions."[16]

---

[14]David Snedden, *The New Republic*, III, (May 15, 1915), p. 40.
[15]*Ibid.*, p. 41.
[16]*Ibid.*, p. 42.

If Snedden thought his letter would mollify Dewey, he was doomed to disappointment. Dewey replied that Snedden had simply failed to meet the heart of his argument, and he attempted to repeat it in one sentence: "I argued that a separation of trade education and general education of youth has the inevitable tendency to make both kinds of training narrower, less significant and less effective than the schooling in which the traditional education is reorganized to utilize the industrial subject matter — active, scientific, and social of the present day environment."[17]

Snedden's insistence on a narrow definition of vocational education designed for a specific segment of students was at loggerheads with Dewey's highly complex model aimed at a reformed education for all. He refused to accept an identification of "vocation" with certain trades that could be learned before eighteen or twenty; and he rejected any conception of vocational education which did not have as its "supreme regard the development of such intelligent initiative, ingenuity and executive ability as shall make workers, as far as may be, the masters of their own industrial fate."[18]

Dewey said that his difference with Snedden was not so much narrowly educational as it was profoundly social and political.

> The kind of vocational education in which I am interested is not one which will "adapt" workers to the existing industrial regime; I am not sufficiently in love with the regime for that. It seems to me that the business of all who would not be educational time-servers is to resist every move in this direction, and to strive for a kind of vocational education which will first alter the existing industrial system, and ultimately transform it.[19]

He challenged Snedden to indicate whether he favored substituting the dual features of the Cooley bill for the kinds of efforts to integrate liberal and industrial studies that were going on in Chicago and Gary. For whatever reasons, Snedden did not reply. The goals of the two educators were disparate, and it was probably just as well to let the issue rest.

B. DEWEY AND THE SMITH-HUGHES BILL

Dewey's misgivings about the Smith-Hughes bill were related to his growing doubts about proposals of the state legislatures for vocational programs. Dewey commented on these developments in an article entitled, "A Policy of Industrial Education."[20]

Dewey urged a "go slow" policy. The case for federal aid for vocational education was based, he said, on an ill-digested set of reasons aimed at serving needs of various interest groups. These included the demands of employers for more skilled workers; the fear of dropping behind in international commercial competition; the need to find a substitute for declining apprentice

---

[17] *Ibid.*
[18] *Ibid.*
[19] *Ibid.*
[20] John Dewey, "A Policy of Industrial Education," *The New Republic,* I, (December 19, 1914), pp. 11-12.

training; and the need for a more "vital" kind of instruction. The temptation to copy Germany's dual school system was strong, but to do so would be a fatal mistake. American businessmen might envy the German arrangement, said Dewey; but they should recognize that such a school system perpetuates class divisions and eventually leads to an increased class conflict.

There were important reasons, said Dewey, why we should reject federal policies for education that were designed primarily to improve industrial efficiency rather than general education. Even the practical arguments put forward for special trade training ignored significant features of industrial development. The main problem was not to provide workers for the skilled crafts. These trades already had effective unions, with organized training programs and the strong resolve to avoid an over-supply of workers. The revolutionary factor and the heart of the problem, said Dewey, was the introduction of automatic machines, which reduced labor to highly specialized operations.

This meant, Dewey continued, that the only defensible approach was to incorporate a new kind of industrial education as part of general education reform whose aim would be to cultivate "industrial intelligence" throughout the population. Dewey's personal definition of "industrial intelligence," a term popular at the time, was: the "initiative and personal resources of intelligence" which would enable the American worker to infuse existing industrial arrangements with democratic values. While we did not yet know fully how to accomplish this, Dewey said, preliminary efforts had been made in school systems like those of Gary and Chicago. The aim has not been to turn schools into preliminary factories supported at public expense, but to borrow from shops the resources and motives which make teaching more effective and wider in reach."[21]

A general education designed to promote industrial intelligence would provide a genuine alternative to German dualism:

> Instead of trying to split schools into two kinds, one of a trade type for children whom it is assumed are to be employees and one of a liberal type for the children of the well-to-do, it will aim at such a reorganization of existing schools as will give all pupils a genuine respect for useful work, an ability to render service, and a contempt for social parasites whether they are called tramps or leaders of "society".... It will indeed make much of developing motor and manual skill, but not of a routine or automatic type. It will rather utilize active and manual pursuits as the means of developing constructive, inventive and creative power of mind. It will select the materials and the technique of the trades not for the sake of producing skilled workers for hire in definite trades, but for the sake of securing industrial intelligence—a knowledge of the conditions and processes of present manufacturing, transportation and commerce so that the individual may be able to make his own choices and his own adjustments, and be master, so far as in him lies, of his own economic fate. It will be recognized that, for this purpose, a broad acquaintance with science and skill in the laboratory control of materials and processes is more important than skill in trade operations. It will remember that the future employee is a consumer as well as a producer, that the whole tendency of society, so far as it is intelligent and wholesome, is to an increase

---

[21] *Ibid.*, p. 12.

of the hours of leisure, and that an education which does nothing to enable individuals to consume wisely and to utilize leisure wisely is a fraud on democracy. So far as method is concerned, such a conception of industrial education will prize freedom more than docility; initiative more than automatic skill; insight and understanding more than capacity to recite lessons or to execute tasks under the direction of others.[22]

Neither congress nor the people were of a mind to heed such talk. By 1917, the urgent need to increase military production provided the special motivation required to spur federal action. Congress and the President gave the proponents of the Smith-Hughes bill the measure for which they had worked so long and hard.

---

[22] John Dewey, "Learning to Earn," pp. 131-132.

SEMESTER: WEEK TWELVE

REQUIRED READINGS

Church

Part IV: School and Community, Progressivism in Education, 1890-1940, Chapter 11: Progressivism and the Kindergarten, 1870-1925 (27 pp.)

Dye

McFarland, Mary A. "A Consideration of Educational Decision-Making" The Educational Forum. V.40, No.1, November, 1975. (05 pp.)

O'Connor, James J. "Teaching: A Questionable Career" The Educational Forum. V.37, No.2, January, 1973. (05 pp.)

MEETINGS

Monday

Lecture: The Junior High School and Middle School Programs

Tuesday

Lecture: The Child Study Movement

Wednesday

Certification Orientation Program in Education

Thursday

Certification Orientation Program in Education

Friday

Certification Orientation Program in Education

CHURCH TEXTBOOK STUDY GUIDE: CHAPTER 11

PROGRESSIVISM AND THE KINDERGARTEN, 1870-1925

1. Friedrich Froebel
2. kindergarten
3. Froebelian gifts
4. occupations
5. kindergartners
6. Froebelian creative activities
7. creative play
8. Mrs. Carl Schurz, Watertown, Wisconsin
9. Elizabeth Palmer Peabody, Boston
10. Mrs. Quincy Adams, Boston
11. Susan Blow, St. Louis
12. American Froebel Union
13. International Kindergarten Union, IKU
14. NEA Kindergarten Department
15. free kindergarten associations
16. Women's Christian Temperance Union, WCTU
17. social reform mission of the kindergarten
18. by teaching the children, one teaches the parents
19. kindergarten as alternative to the public school
20. kindergarten as appendage of the public school
21. G. Stanley Hall
22. child study movement
23. John Dewey's criticism of the kindergarten
24. efficiency
25. habit formation in the kindergarten
26. economic justification of the kindergarten
27. unification scheme
28. primary department
29. Edward Lee Thorndike
30. Teachers College, Columbia University

31. connectionism
32. stimulus-response psychology
33. S-R Bond Theory
34. learning as habit formation
35. Thorndike's law of exercise
36. Thorndike's law of effect
37. William Heard Kilpatrick
38. project method
39. Patty Smith Hill
40. Kindergarten-Primary Department, Teachers College, Columbia University
41. the teacher as a guide, not a dictator
42. Agnes Rogers
43. habit inventory
44. conduct curriculum

A Consideration of Educational Decision-Making

MARY A. MCFARLAND

PICTURE this—a class of thirty quiet students awaiting instructions from the teacher standing in the front of the room.

The teacher speaks, "For tomorrow read pages 200 to 207 in the text and write answers for the five questions at the end of the chapter."

The students have heard such assignments before; they have done such assignments before; and they now turn their attention to the task at hand because the teacher has decided that the class should do this assignment and so it must be right.

Is the above a vision of the future? No, it is a phantom of the past—thirty accepting, conforming, unthinking puppets who bear little resemblance to today's American students who often ask, "Why?" "Why do I need this course?" "Why is this topic important?" "Why is this activity beneficial?" Students want to know "Why?" and they deserve an answer from a teacher who has made conscious, rational, deliberate decisions as to "Why?"

Could the teacher have made the above decision (assigning pages to read, questions to answer) consciously, rationally, and deliberately to achieve a specific objective? Certainly such an assignment might meet an objective profitable to students. The teacher may have reached a reasoned decision to make the assignment—but possibly

---

Mary A. McFarland is instructional coordinator of social studies, K-12 in the Parkway School District, St. Louis County.

Reprinted from The Educational Forum, Kappa Delta Pi, Volume 40, Number 1, November, 1975.

he did not. Such a decision cannot be left to chance, since rational decision making represents a central responsibility of the teacher—the responsibility to know "why" students are asked to engage in certain activities and to help the students themselves realize "why."

Knowing Why. Research studies of decision-making have led to significant findings. Richard J. Shavelson asserts that "any teaching act is the result of a decision—sometimes conscious but more often not."[1] Although Shavelson believes that decision-making is *the* basic teaching skill, it receives little attention in teacher education.[2] Emory and Niland have found that most people use only a fraction of the decision-making ability they possess, but through training and development can improve the utilization of the potential that they have.[3] An in-service project in Maryland directed at training teachers in a decision-making model specified nineteen distinct—but interrelated—decision-making skills.[4] A report by Hill and Martin of the results of inductive training in these skills indicates that "participants became more perceptually aware of the essential steps of a decision-making process and were able to verbalize this awareness in response to a written problem situation."[5] Research indicates that teachers must become aware of decision-making skills, study, learn, plan, act, and evaluate in order to become proficient in making "why" decisions with a greater degree of assurance.

It becomes clear that only the teacher who becomes capable of making decisions that lead to supportable answers to the question "Why?" will be able to provide a satisfying answer to "why" questions posed by students, administrators, fellow teachers, or the community. It is the thesis of this article that a serious effort to decide "why" results in the teacher's formulation of a basic rationale—a consciously derived position upon which classroom decisions are based. Rationale forces the teacher into direct confrontation with basic decisions about curricular objectives, implementation, and evaluation. The basic "why" question—(Why is this course being offered?) forces the formulation of objectives. Implementation leads to "therefore" decisions—("Therefore" these materials and activities are best suited to help students develop knowledge, skills, and attitudes.") Finally, an evaluation is necessary and the question for consideration becomes, "Is the course succeeding or failing to reach the stated objectives?"

Curricular Objectives. Whether the teacher is attempting to analyze and interpret the curricular objectives on which reformers have based innovative practices or attempting to identify and clarify his own curricular objectives, he is seeking an understanding of the philosophical framework and the assumptions on which curriculum is based. Inherent within the philosophy are certain value positions about what society "is" and thus, what the student "should be."[6] The vast number of potential objectives available for selection forces an effort to answer a major "why" question—Why is it valid to consider a particular course based on a particular philosophical framework beneficial to society and the students?

What student behaviors will the course promote? Will the course develop a student who is:

inquiring, analytical, hypothetical, and rational in his thinking; or

sensitive, intuitive, spontaneous, and creative in his responses; or knowledgeable, revolutionary, competitive, and confident in his problem-solving; or

deliberate, responsible, normative, and evolutionary in his approach to social order; or

some combination of these or other objectives which have not been considered?

Identifying desired student attributes, which are relevant to the needs of students and society, brings the teacher to decisions concerning the usefulness of the discipline(s)—(social science, mathematics, music, science, etc.) in terms of a specific contribution to the student. That contribution may be in the form of:

knowledge unique to that discipline; or

the methodological approach of the discipline; or

symbolic and empiric qualities of the discipline; or

ethical and moral meanings within the discipline;[7] or

some combination of these or other contributions.

"Whys" Lead to "Therefores." The decisions reached in answering the question "Why is this course being offered?" become the rationale for the course—the reasoned justification for the materials and activities through which content, processes, and attitudes are developed. The teacher's answer to that all-important "Why?" leads him directly into a series of "therefores" or implementations of his rationale.

As he clarifies which knowledge, skills, and attitudes are consistent with his rationale, the teacher realizes that these decisions eventually dictate that "therefore" the students will be:

studying certain topics rather than other topics; or

selecting their own topics for study; or

listening to a lecture; or

performing an experiment; or

reading a textbook; or

examining several types of sources; or

memorizing factual information; or

categorizing information according to a conceptual framework; or

writing a paper; or

discussing an issue; or

engaging in field work; or

creating an aesthetic work; or

participating in some combination of these or other alternatives.

It is the "therefores" in the form of classroom materials and activities that students experience most directly. It is "therefores" that students may misunderstand and question. It is the "therefores" that the teacher must be able to explain and justify to students, not only because they ask, but because the teacher has a responsibility to know.

Why Know "Why?" Knowing "why" enables a teacher to make logically consistent decisions in terms of a basic rationale. It also leads to curricular materials and activities—"therefores"—which are consistent with the rationale and thus, defensible to students. Students are going to ask "Why?" (whether vocally or not). They really want to know "Why?" They want to be engaged in experiences that "make sense" to them. They have a right to feel the security that comes from an open discussion of the rationale supporting a position—assuring them that it is not the first instant that the teacher has thought about "Why?" A reasonable answer, that the teacher is willing and able to share with students, increases student understanding and often enables them to feel the confidence necessary to proceed to the study of unfamiliar material or participation in a new activity.

Evaluation. Are the "whys" the best goals possible? Do the "therefores" represent the best possible material and activities to implement the "whys"? To what extent are the goals being accomplished? So run the questions of evaluation that have yielded millions of words written about such topics as:

domains—cognitive, affective, psychomotor;

implementation—content, process, or values orientation;

testing—norm vs. criterion referenced tests, or unmeasurable intangibles;

accountability—credibility to the public and/or funding agencies—

and on and on.

Not minimizing the importance of these issues, it does seem that one immensely important and very basic viewpoint, less often considered, is the students' perceptions of "what" they are doing in a course and "why." Obviously, the teacher has a legitimate right to arrive at certain educational decisions based on experience and expertise. At the same time, one important decision the teacher might easily make is that some time can profitably be devoted to student viewpoints and questions. A student's questions (both "Why?" and "Why not?") are an excellent mirror in which the teacher can see the image of a student's expectations[8] and perceptions of course goals, materials, and activities. Even though rationale leads to reasonable, defensible choices, these choices and the rationale itself represent only certain alternatives to the exclusion of many others which must remain viable and open to continual review. Students are often in a good position to be constructively critical of some aspect of the course, since the teacher is already intellectually and personally committed to the rationale—a *certain* point of view. A change or modification made in response to a substantiated student concern, or an explanation as to why the student's suggested change is unadvisable, is tantamount to saying to the student that he is important, his ideas are significant, and the course is a co-operative educational venture for all involved.

Picture this—a class of thirty active students mentally engaged and discussing course goals, or content, or activities. Asking "Why?" Receiving rationally decided answers; sensing the assurance that comes from participating in a thoughtfully conceived program; proposing alternatives; knowing that alternatives are carefully considered and often implemented. A phantom of the past? No. A vision of the future? No. *A current possibility*—thirty thinking, inquiring, creative beings working co-operatively with a teacher in evaluating decisions concerning their course and its "whys" and "therefores."

Notes

1. Richard J. Shavelson, "What is the Basic Teaching Skill?," *The Journal of Teacher Education* 24 (Summer 1973): 144.
2. Ibid., p. 144.
3. F. Douglas Bowles, "Decision Making in Instruction," *The Journal of Teacher Education* 24 (Spring 1973): 39.
4. John Hill and William R. Martin, "Training for Educational Decision Making," *The Journal of Teacher Education* 22 (Winter 1971): 443-45.
5. Ibid., p. 447.
6. Paul Trudinger, "Patterns of Diversity and Unity: Pedagogical and Curricular Reflections and Suggestions," *Journal of General Education* 25 (April 1973): 54-55.
7. Philip Phenix, *Realms of Meaning: A Philosophy of the Curriculum for General Education* (New York: McGraw-Hill Book Co., 1964).
8. John J. Painter and Kent L. Granzin, "Consistency Theory as an Explanation of Students' Course Evaluation Tendencies," *The Journal of Experimental Education* 41 (Fall 1972): 78.

Teaching: A Questionable Career

JAMES J. O'CONNOR

For many years American society has faced critical teacher shortages. But now it finds itself in the position of having a surplus of overtrained professionals. It is not, however, my purpose to explore what brought about this reversed trend. Anyone who reads the news of bond issue disasters, override tax defeats, or school district cutbacks is well aware of how and why the teacher surplus transpired. The situation, in fact, could trigger a panicky exodus by college students from teaching credential programs which would ease the surplus and deprive the profession of badly needed new blood. Assuming that prospective teaching candidates are panicky over possible career opportunities, I would like to pose some questions and ideas for those individuals to ponder.

When a candidate walks through my office door and asks what it takes to be a teacher, I hedge in giving a direct answer. Why? It is an honest question and deserves an honest answer. Yet the questioner seldom realizes the extent of the teacher surplus and, more importantly, how to avoid becoming part of it. My responsibility is to advise prospective social science teachers, hence the seriousness of such ignorance is even more acute. So before I attempt to answer the above query, I pose several questions.

1. What can you offer the teaching profession?
2. What subjects are you willing to teach?
3. Where are you willing to teach?
4. What can you do besides teach?
5. Is obtaining a credential just a security measure?

These are questions the advisee should ponder before seeking teacher certification, and as a guide I offer the following answers.

What can you offer the teaching profession? At first glance the question seems unfair. How does one answer it without appearing conceited? Conceit, however, is the least of the student's worries. The question is purely a philosophical one, and it asks why an individual would be a successful teacher, not how he is different or unique. The old bromide "We will always need good teachers" is philosophically sound but misleading. Administrators and department heads as well as instructors hold varying opinions on what constitutes a "good" teacher, so the question posed will not deal with that issue. Instead I believe that the individual credential candidate will find the answer if he can accept the following principles:

A teacher must love the company of students and the atmosphere generated

---

The somewhat homely advice to the prospective teacher takes on sharp relevance in view of the predicted teacher glut. JAMES J. O'CONNOR *is Assistant Professor of Social Studies Education at Oregon State University at Corvallis and a teacher of social science at the Junior High, Senior High, and Junior College levels. He did his doctoral work at the University of the Pacific.*

by them. Obvious? Perhaps, but many teachers envision their role as one of "setting the students straight."

A teacher must be accessible to students as both an advisor and listener. Sounds easy, yet one need only visit a school to observe the number of teachers who hide in the faculty lounge. More instruction in life's problems can be given outside of the classroom than within it, but how often do teachers desire to get away from their students?

The credential aspirant must want to guide, not accompany. He is not the students' peer and should never seek to be one of them. Such action on his part could only result in rejection by both students and colleagues.

The candidate must have an idea of why his subject is important and what he hopes to accomplish by giving instruction in his chosen area. How often do newly-credentialed instructors suggest that their courses are going to be interesting and relevant, and discover to their dismay, that what is interesting to them is boring and irrelevant to their secondary protégés? Many new history instructors are going to "really" teach what has not been taught. Washington, for example, was no saint; Thomas Jefferson was a racist; and Woodrow Wilson, Well! Such debunking techniques do not necessarily result in a relevant, interesting, or meaningful class. In fact, to be honest solely for shock effect may be the worst form of dishonesty. Seamy facts need not be hidden, but the assumption that their revelation will enhance relevancy or substantive meaning is questionable. The teacher should be more concerned with the development of critical thinking skills, which would provide his students with greater perceptual and conceptual understanding of the particular subject area. I would suggest that the "shockers" have little understanding of what or why they are teaching and very likely lack the skills and abilities they are supposed to impart to their students.

What subjects are you willing to teach? While history, modern problems, and government are the usual answers, little consideration is given to economics, anthropology, geography, psychology, speech, journalism, English including literature, and in some areas, religious studies. The candidate may not be qualified to teach many of these subjects, but the situation may arise where he is called upon to do so because of his supposedly broad general background and the likelihood that he has to his credit at least one college level survey course in the subject. If this occurs, then the beginning teacher may have three and perhaps even four preparations—a prodigious task for any teacher new or experienced.

No one who receives a secondary credential in the social sciences, however, can expect to be a pure historian or political theorist. He will have to be adaptive and willing to teach outside of his area and in courses for which he has had minimal training and virtually no experience. The credential aspirant should study all courses as if he might be required to teach them. If he cannot accept that premise, he should seek an alternative to teaching.

Where are you willing to teach? Perhaps another way of posing this question would be to say, where are you willing to go for a position? With the teacher surplus situation, desirable districts have lists of applicants, and unless one is adaptable to their program or has a unique talent, such as coaching winning teams, he will very likely be placed at the bottom of the list. An applicant should never state "I'll go anywhere just as long as it's a job." My experience shows that people who give this kind of answer usually are inconsistent. They receive a possible interview offer from Cayumas or Pisgah and suddenly are upset because the district does not have the cultural amenities they desired or it is too remote from larger cities for week-end flings. They will take any job but . . .

Then how should one answer the question? Initially the individual should sit down with a good Atlas and by order of preference list states in which he is willing to teach. Once this is done, the applicant should select certain communities within each state and note size, location to the nearest graduate school, geographic position in respect to nearby major cities, and travel connections to points of interest. The individual then should prepare a standard form letter. Since administrators receive vast amounts of dittoed or mimeographed material, each letter of inquiry should be typed separately. The applicant could, however, enclose a dittoed *vita* for the recipient's consideration. If a promising response is received, the individual should complete and return the application form which accompanied the reply and ask for some material on the community. Most cities and townships are willing to provide civic propaganda. Having some knowledge of a community often makes an offer easier to accept or reject.

What about applications to distant areas and the cost of traveling for an interview? If the applicant cannot afford this expense, the prospective employer must be told. On the other hand, an interview is advisable if the individual can stand both the financial cost and the possibility of a turndown.

What can you do besides teach? I find it disturbing when I overhear a credential holder complain that all he can do is teach. He feels that other job opportunities are closed to him because of his teacher training. The credential only certifies that the individual is legally qualified to teach. In no way does it limit choice of profession. After all, a student who possesses a teaching credential also has a college degree, so any job that requires only the latter is available to him. If the individual views receipt of a credential as job imprisonment, the teaching profession is better off without him. Indeed, one should *want* to teach, not *have* to teach.

Is obtaining a credential just a security measure? If one's answer is yes, my advice is not to get a credential. This may be a biased attitude but my rationale is quite simple. An individual who chooses a teaching career as a secondary or even tertiary goal will very likely be dissatisfied with the profession. In no time this dissatisfaction will be felt by both the students and faculty in the school where one is teaching. The attitude of credentialed security might be humorous considering the present surplus, but unfortunately, it is people with this attitude who create such a surplus. The proverbial statement "You can always teach" has done the profession in.

What does it take to become a teacher? This was the original question posed, and I will begin by giving the usual institutional answer. To be a teacher requires so many units of study, a certain grade point average, specific related activities as determined by professors, and fulfillment of state requirements. These are the obvious aspects of becoming a teacher, but what about the unexpected? A potential teacher expects stubborn children who refuse to study or matter-of-factly take their "F's," administrative clashes or misunderstandings, hall duty, chaperone duty, irate parents, and assorted classroom disasters. But I have often wondered if an aspiring teacher expects to encounter some of the following:

a. Jealous colleagues who deprecate a successful innovation.
b. Student's cruel ability to find a weakness and parlay it into a major disaster.
c. Malicious gossip based on half-truths or truth taken out of context.
d. Student competition with the teacher.
e. Stubborn resistance to change by colleagues who feel threatened by their own inability or inadequacies.
f. Evaluation forms for student failures that seem to invite blackmail.
g. Continual public address interruptions that break the atmosphere of a smoothly running class.
h. Admonitions not to discuss controversial issues that would call for an opinion.
i. Continual meetings for no other reason than adherence to a schedule.
j. Outdated texts and equipment.
k. State-approved and controlled syllabi that pre-empt any originality on the teacher's part.
l. Obligations to pass students who academically deserve to fail.
m. Demands to explain and defend every innovative act.
n. Expectancy to yield free periods without notice.
o. Administratively imposed methods or course changes.
p. Ambiguously worded faculty handbooks.
q. Requisitions slips for so much as a paper clip.
r. Open house where the teacher seldom sees the parents of "problem" students.
s. Rental materials that do not arrive on time and thereby ruin the day's preparation.

And so on *ad infinitum*. After a brief tenure, the instructor will come to realize that what appears to be obvious may really be unique. Thus what he had taken for granted becomes indefensible.

His position at the head of the classroom is challenged. Effective teaching is hard work and encompasses much more than the impartation of textual knowledge. Yet how often do we remember the teachers who did just that? Why? Because it was easy.

Lastly, as a note of encouragement, one should remember that all of the above will not likely happen in one day or even one year of teaching. On the other hand, an individual should never take solace in the bromide "teaching is a lot of little rewards." There is really only one reward and that is to teach well and know it.

Reprinted from The Educational Forum, Kappa Delta Pi, Volume 37, Number 2, January, 1973.

SEMESTER: WEEK THIRTEEN

REQUIRED READINGS

Church

Part IV: School and Community, Progressivism in Education, 1890-1940, Chapter 12: <u>American Education Between the Wars, 1918-1940</u> (58 pp.)

Dye

Goodenow, Ronald K. "The Progressive Educator, Race and Ethnicity in the Depression Years: An Overview" <u>History of Education Quarterly.</u> V.15, No.4, Winter, 1975. (30 pp.)

Violas, Paul. "Fear and the Constraints on Academic Freedom of Public School Teachers, 1930-1960" <u>Educational Theory</u>. V.21, No.1, Winter, 1971. (11 pp.)

American Federation of Teachers. "Bill of Rights of the American Federation of Teachers" 1976. (03 pp.)

National Education Association. "Bill of Teacher Rights" 1976. (04 pp.)

MEETINGS

Monday

Lecture: Akron, The Klan, The Depression

Tuesday

Lecture: Eight Year Study of the P.E.A.

Wednesday

Lecture: Teacher Organizations

Thursday and Friday

Small Groups:

CHURCH TEXTBOOK STUDY GUIDE: CHAPTER 12

AMERICAN EDUCATION BETWEEN THE WARS, 1918-1940

1. John B. Watson
2. behaviorism
3. hollow man
4. Sigmund Freud
5. the unconscious in behavior
6. the emotional in behavior
7. drives
8. irrationality
9. application of expert knowledge to social problems
10. the expert
11. The New Deal
12. Civilian Conservation Corps, CCC
13. National Youth Administration, NYA
14. nationalism
15. provincialism
16. transmission of traditional values
17. intelligence testing
18. individual testing
19. group testing
20. psychometricians
21. nature-nuture debate
22. heredity-environment debate
23. eugenics movement
24. Ku Klux Klan
25. Scopes trial
26. Robert and Helen Lynd
27. Ball State Teachers College, Muncie, Indiana
28. safe college
29. enhancement of community pride
30. organized athletics

31. organized extracurriculum
32. sustaining community pride
33. entrepreneurs
34. island community
35. protectionistic function of schooling

36. dress codes
37. management of student life
38. drinking
39. high school raternity and sorority
40. students' home life

41. work ethic
42. depressed economy and youth frustration
43. adolescent crime rate
44. youth unemployment
45. custodial function of schooling

46. general prevocational education
47. irreplaceable vitamin
48. physical manual labor
49. modernists
50. Progressive Education Association, PEA

51. radical pedagogy
52. social reconstruction
53. George S. Counts
54. excessive individualism
55. Isaac L. Kandel

56. eclectic
57. Kilpatrick's project method
58. social learning and social efficiency
59. Bruce Barton's The Man Nobody Knows (1924)
60. Dale Carnegie's How to Win Friends and Influence People (1936)

The Progressive Educator, Race and Ethnicity in the Depression Years: An Overview*

RONALD K. GOODENOW

FEW historians have analyzed the attitudes of major white progressive educators on race and ethnicity. Very little is known about what they did in the area of race relations and the schooling of minority and ethnic groups or about efforts sponsored by the Progressive Education Association to deal with racial tension and the "place" of blacks and white ethnics in American society. Likewise, the response and contribution of blacks and ethnics to progressive education has received little attention from scholars.

To fill some of these gaps this paper will briefly focus on the Depression years, a period of diverse and highly publicized progressive activity to (1) illustrate the place of race and ethnicity in the thinking and activities of prominent progressive educators; (2) outline the position of race and ethnicity in the programs of the PEA; (3) discuss the response of black educators in the South to the progressive education movement; and (4) point to a rich variety of sources which have been generally overlooked by historians. In so doing, regional differences will be considered and preliminary observations of a conceptual nature will be made.

Social Reconstruction: Intellectual Crosscurrents

The seminal social reconstructionist statement, *The Educational Frontier* (1934), edited by William Heard Kilpatrick, did little more than pass on a cruel black stereotype (1) and the major reconstructionist journal *The Social Frontier* (*Frontiers of Democracy*) failed to address racial or ethnic

---

Mr. Goodenow teaches at the State University of New York at Buffalo.

* The State University of New York Research Foundation funded some of the research for this paper, which is an outgrowth of the author's dissertation, "The Progressive Education Movement and Blacks in the 1930s: An Exploratory Study" (Ph.D., University of California at Berkeley, 1973).

discrimination until the late 1930s. Nevertheless, several prominent progressive educators associated with the social reformist wing of the progressive education movement were cognizant of these problems. If low on their agenda, they were on them, and enough documentary evidence exists to enable the historian to draw some conclusions on the "place" of race and ethnicity in progressive theory and ideology in the years of the Great Depression. This interest, moreover, provides insights into the manner in which liberal educators have reacted to a fundamental set of contradictions and conflicts in American life and culture, several of which surfaced as the result of international developments and a breakdown in a political economy dominated by capitalist modes of production and distribution. It further reflects on the nature of progressivism, illustrating its paradoxical and complex nature.

By 1935 a general consensus had formed among social reconstructionists on the dangers of racial conflict and forced "melting pot" assimilation processes. To combat anti-Semitism, racial discrimination and such "unhealthy" forms of ethnic expression as the German-American Bund they focused on the building of tolerance. In so doing, they endorsed cultural pluralism, the use of intercultural education, programs in human relations and other techniques to foster "communication," "understanding," and awareness of the "commonness" of all human beings. They also argued that a welfare state which practiced social planning could eliminate many of the cultural lags, such as racism and prejudice, which plagued a social order undergoing rapid change and technological development. The "glue" to hold this educational state together would be a set of commonly embraced democratic ideals and a faith in progress.

This consensus on race and ethnicity (phenomena which were often indistinguishable in discussion) grew in large part out of two basic positions. The first, as represented by John Dewey and George S. Counts in the 1920s and early 1930s, emphasized the extent to which racism and ethnic conflict were outgrowths of the social-structural and institutional nature of American life. The second, as reflected in the work of William Heard Kilpatrick and Harold Rugg, did not disregard the arguments of Dewey and Counts. It was, however, more inclined to emphasize the cultural and psychological components of racial prejudice and ensuing forms of discrimination, a position that indicates a conservative trend in reconstructionist thought and which Dewey and Counts, as well as most progressive literature and programs, increasingly supported.

John Dewey persistently referred to racial and ethnic matters with particular emphasis on problems related to intolerance. Among the white progressives who joined the "call" for the NAACP in 1909 (2) he, and his

Columbia University colleague Horace Kallen, were among the early advocates of cultural pluralism. (3) Dewey's pronouncements suffered from some inconsistency, however. He seemingly lent support to segregated schools when he praised an all-black neighborhood school in Indianapolis and the schools of Gary, Indiana, in *Schools of Tomorrow* (1915), a volume that he co-authored. The Gary public schools openly practiced discrimination as a matter of policy even as it was publicly attacked by the NAACP. (4) He also assumed what appears to be a rigidly assimilationist position in a report on Polish-Americans submitted to the War Department during World War I. Indeed, this volume has become a center of controversy among historians, some arguing that it shows Dewey's basic conservatism, others arguing the contrary. (5)

If there is dispute over where Dewey stood on race and ethnicity his position cannot be fairly judged on the basis of one episode. There is evidence that he did not isolate them from his general social theory and other social variables. Nor did he tie the best interests of racial and ethnic minorities to the well-being of a capitalist order. To the contrary; in a 1922 address to the Chinese Social and Political Science Association he noted the newcomer status of many immigrants and the ways in which they were often brought to America and, like blacks, stereotyped in order to serve the narrow interests of an economic system that needed cheap labor. Ethnic conflict, he held, was perpetuated by these self-serving interests. The way out of this dilemma he argued, was not easy. Although individuals could be educated to be less prejudiced, there would have to be fundamental change in "political and industrial organization" in order truly to remedy problems of mass ethnic and racial hatred. (6) A few years later he attacked South Africa for exploiting blacks in the name of profits, the only American to do so at an international conference on progressive education held in that country. (7)

The essentials of Dewey's position were repeated in a 1932 speech to the NAACP, where, reflecting his perspective as a politically active socialist in an election year, he reportedly declared that blacks faced discrimination primarily because they were part of a laboring underclass. The solution to their problems he suggested was to be found in

...a party which recognizes that we are living in a time of collective operation in which individuals must use all the agencies of law and administration to promote their common interest and build a cooperative society. (8)

This linking of racial exploitation and discrimination with the structural features of American life is also to be found in the work of George S. Counts. To bolster his arguments, moreover, Counts conducted empirical research in the 1920s which presented the ways in which urban educational politics were deeply influenced by elites who promoted conflict between ethnic and religious minorities for purposes of conservative social selection and control. In *School and Society in Chicago* he probed the nature of ethnic educational politics and in discussing working class opposition to the Gary Plan made some important observations on the functions of educational reform. This book, which shows a sensitivity to the relationship between pedagogical change and educational reform that was unique for its day also contained a contention by its author that the pluralistic nature of the American city be recognized and preserved. (9) Counts did not confuse voluntary pluralism with forced separation, however. Racial segregation, when the result of economic and social discrimination, he stated could not be condoned. In the early 1930s he declared that in modern America there could be no "separate but equal" treatment for blacks because they did not enjoy political and economic power, an observation seldom made by prominent white educators. (10)

If Dewey placed a great deal of faith in a socialist party in the early 1930s, Counts tended to see professional educators as enjoying a potential for inducing social reform. It was in this arena that he focused much of his attention throughout the decade. In his explosive address to the Progressive Education Association in 1932—later published as *Dare the School Build A New Social Order?*—he accused progressives of not considering carefully the nature of the "real" world and its conflicts. Portraying the members of his audience as well-meaning but often romantic advocates of pedagogical change, he attacked them for practicing discrimination in their own schools and not confronting racism and other social issues. (11)

The perspectives of Dewey and Counts reflected their unique political concerns, strains in progressive thought and, in the case of Counts, empirical inquiry on configurations of power and the social functions of education in a society where values were strongly influenced by industrial capitalism. Although they were not always explicit on this point, racism and the ways in which immigrants were Americanized were seen as problems in the sociology of knowledge. The economic system and the structure of American social and political life formed attitudes and habits that were psychologically unhealthy, dangerous to the building of social change and destructive of important democratic values that were deeply ingrained in the culture. The work of Counts shows a consistent interest in institutionalizing the processes of revolution in a democratic state responsive to popular will. (12) If Counts seemed more "radical" than Dewey in his emphasis on specific institutional causes of racial and ethnic conflict and discrimination, both men were concerned with the relationship between mind and social process and in the

1920s and early 1930s tended to stress the power of social and economic conditions to form and shape ideas and knowledge itself.

Counts wrote little on race and ethnicity after 1935. As he came to stress the positive power of democratic ideology and consensus in his work there is evidence to suggest that he believed that because of their controversial nature, problems related to them would "distract" educators and the public from broader social change processes. (13) Dewey, on the other hand, continued to speak out on racial intolerance and discrimination. On numerous occasions he lent his name to attacks on anti-Semitism and racism, and he used public forums to issue strong statements on the dangers posed to American values and institutions by prejudice. There is, however, a more defensive and non-political tone to his pronouncements.

There are two themes in Dewey's work which help explain this "new" stance on race and ethnicity. The first is a growing belief in the power of expertise and rational planning. In *The Public And Its Problems,* published in 1927, he provided an interesting insight into this faith. "The questions of most concern at present may be said," he declared

to be matters like sanitation, public health, healthful and adequate housing, transportation, planning of cities, regulation and distribution of immigrants, selection and management of personnel, right methods of instruction and preparation of competent teachers, scientific adjustment of taxation, efficient management of funds, and so on. These are technical matters, as much so as the construction of an efficient engine for the purpose of traction or locomotion. (14)

Dewey's socialism was pragmatic and based, to a great extent, on an integration of method and attitudes. As capitalism was fundamentally changed, new forms of social life and governance would, with the aid of education, alter belief and create a consciousness that change involved a delicate interplay between expertise and public consensus. Hence, while he recognized that the New Deal represented bourgeois interests aimed at the preservation of class privileges, he nevertheless argued that it must be seen not as a final solution to America's problems, but as a stopping off place, a period of transition. In *Liberalism and Social Action,* published in 1935, he wrote that New Deal social legislation had

... considerable importance in educating the public mind to a realization of the possibilities of organized social control. It has helped to develop some of the techniques that in any case will be needed in a socialized economy. But the cause of liberalism will be lost for a considerable period if it is not prepared to go further and socialize the forces of production, not at hand, so that the liberty of individuals will be supported by the very structure of economic organization. (15)

In the maelstrom of the 1930s with signs of American fascism, open persecution of the Jews in Germany and increased anti-Semitism in America, urban racial unrest in New York and elsewhere and the terrible realization that world war was on the horizon, educators and intellectuals alike groped for means to stem intolerance and foster American democracy. Democratic rhetoric permeated educational literature and the position papers of the National Education Association's Educational Policies Commission and the American Historical Association's Commission on the Social Studies, both of which were deeply influenced by the work of George Counts, Charles Beard and other progressive intellectuals.

If there was a defensiveness and ideological tone in much of the literature produced in this period, Dewey recognized that racial conflict and intolerance were more than temporary phenomena related to specific temporary social conditions. There was, he wrote, much that was contradictory in American culture, a position not readily apparent in the commentary of Counts and others on the nature of the nation's core values. Hence, Dewey observed in *Freedom and Culture,* published in 1939, that

The case of intolerance is used as an illustration of the intrinsic connection between the prospects of democracy and belief in the potentialities of human nature not for its own sake, important as it is on its own account. How much of our past intolerance was positive and how much of it a toleration equivalent to 'standing' something we do not like, 'putting up' with something because it involves too much trouble to try to change it? For a good deal of the present reaction against democracy is probably simply the disclosure of a weakness that was there before; one that was covered up or did not appear in its true light. Certainly racial prejudice against Negroes, Catholics, and Jews is no new thing in our life. (16)

What is important about this statement is that Dewey here leans towards a treatment of intolerance as a problem of attitudes, a general condition which may apply to race and religion; it does not necessarily grow out of caste and class relationships. As he dwelled on the subject in the late 1930s this matter of attitude was emphasized, particularly as he spoke to his educational publics. In what appears to be a reversal of his advice to the Chinese Social and Political Science Association in 1922, for example, he informed the Progressive Education Association in 1939 that

Intolerance, abuse, calling of names because of differences in race, color, wealth, or degree of culture are treason to the democratic way of life. For everything which bars freedom and fullness of communications sets up barriers which divide human beings into sets and cliques, into antagonistic sects and factions, and the democratic way of life is undermined. Merely legal guarantees of free belief, free expression, free assembly are of little avail if in daily life freedom of communications, of give and take of ideas, facts, experiences is couched by mutual suspicion, abuse, by fear and hatred. (17)

Here Dewey appears at glaring odds with his earlier analysis on the determining power of institutions in the realm of ideas. "Instead of thinking of our own dispositions and habits as accommodating to certain institutions," he observed, "we have to think of the latter as expressions, projections and extensions of habitually dominant personal attitudes." (18)

Dewey's theory of aesthetics provided a second theme that doubtlessly struck a vital chord in those progressive educators who were as concerned with racial conflict and intolerance in the daily life of the school as with the question of social change or reform. In *Art As Experience* (1934) he made a statement that was profound in its implications for the methods by which progressive pedagogy would stress culture. Claiming that knowledge of the integration of meanings inherent in works of art could help eliminate racial prejudice, he wrote that as one comes to know an artistic creation

... to some degree we become artists ourselves as we undertake this integration, and, by bringing it to pass, our own experience is re-oriented. Barriers are dissolved, limiting prejudices melt away, when we enter into the spirit of Negro or Polynesian art. This insensible melting is far more efficacious than the changes effected by reasoning, because it enters directly into attitude. (19)

Social planning, the attitudinal roots of intolerance and the curative power of the arts were major themes in the progressive approach to race in the 1930s. If articulated in the philosophy of John Dewey they were also expressed in the work of two of his most important disciples, William Heard Kilpatrick and Harold Rugg.

Kilpatrick and Rugg generally wrote of the psycho-social roots of prejudicial behavior. Reflecting the influence of the emerging field of social psychology they also, along with many of their contemporaries, incorporated into their writing research on race and culture conducted by such anthropologists as Margaret Mead, Ruth Benedict and Franz Boas. These influences were complemented by the work of President Hoover's Research Committee on Social Trends, and ideas on cultural lag as used by two sociologists, Howard Odum, of the University of North Carolina, and William Ogburn, of the University of Chicago.

The Southern-born Kilpatrick, a man of paternalistic manners and magnetic appeal, approached prejudice on a number of fronts. Concerned with preserving the "heart and mind" of the South he showed a persistent fear of such "irrational" forces as white populism and the Ku Klux Klan. (20) Blacks, he believed, should seek the counsel of Howard Odum and other middle and upper class members of the Commission on Interracial Cooperation, a progressive organization primarily interested in peaceful race relations to facilitate regional planning, industrial development, rational urbanization, modern social services and careful capital investment. (21) In line with this advice he urged blacks to approach legal action with the utmost caution. Clearly, he preferred that they obtain change through educational means. Taking a somewhat conservative, if not Sumnerian position, he warned that changes in customs and regional folkways must precede racial equality and justice. Behind this cautious approach was not only Southerner gentility, but a fear of communism. Direct political action on the part of blacks was not only likely to stir up violent white passions, he suggested, but it could also benefit "foreign" influenced radicals. (22)

Kilpatrick's interest in race was not confined to the South. He was an active member of the New York Urban League, serving as its President in the early 1940s. He was editor of *The Social Frontier-Frontiers of Democracy* and *Intercultural Education News,* and in those capacities presented his views on intolerance and intercultural education. Indeed, as editor of the former he not only published more materials on race and ethnic related matters than any previous editor, but also included much on national and regional planning. (23) Moreover, he became a prominent member of the Service Bureau for Intercultural Education, endorsing its interest in reducing racial and ethnic tensions and lending his prestigious name to its efforts at public acceptance.

Rugg, one of the leaders of the "child centered" movement in the 1920s and a foremost author of social studies textbooks in the 1930s, urged that the social studies curriculum and the study of art and creativity be used to eliminate fear and prejudice. In one of his early texts he passed on unflattering stereotypes of blacks and other minorities and opted for a combination of hard work—he emphasized the "usefulness" of immigrants to American industry—and tough Americanization as a way of creating a peaceful melting pot. (24) But by the late Depression he became an avowed pluralist who saw the school as playing a key role in the reconstruction of individual attitudes on race. (25) To eliminate stereotyping and its underlying fears he urged that teachers stress the commonness of all peoples as expressed through their art and contributions to American society. He would harness the creativity of the child and encourage him to recognize his own potential and the creativity of others so that hatred, and the belief that "strange" groups were threatening could be overcome.

Kilpatrick and Rugg did not discuss links between tolerance and social change in great detail. It is, however, evident that the relationship between the structural and institutional features in American life and intolerance are difficult to discern in their work. Their enthusiasm for social planning and corresponding forms of education also rendered insignificant social realities in the late Depression. Indeed, the tone of much progressive rhetoric in this period was not only ideological but extremely optimistic. Instead of focusing upon the contradictions and failings in American life educational leaders often turned to the future, arguing that the Depression must be seen in terms of opportunity. Rugg typically asserted in a 1939 *Frontiers of Democracy* piece that

> ... the Great Depression precipitated a deep social crisis and with it a breath taking era of creative effort. The breakdown of critical parts of the social system after 1929 had the positive effect of galvanizing much of our latent ability into dynamic action; a brigade of creative workers quickly emerged to study the problem and to design ways out. Already our years appear to mark the beginning of the most creative era in American history. (26)

Rugg here expressed some of the same sentiments as Dewey regarding planning and taking advantage of social crisis, a tact that he took on the positive attributes of war. (27) He also expanded the concept of creativity to include the artistry of social planning and engineering. Thus, to the progressive educator's belief in tolerance and planning must be added creativity at two levels. Although there was some variation in approach, it was through a synthesis of these interests that racial and ethnic conflict and tension was addressed in the 1930s and early 1940s.

The Functions of Tolerance: Intercultural Education

In a movement as diverse and complex as the one for progressive education there have doubtlessly been individuals and programs that have been unacknowledged in their search for racial justice and for equitable solutions to problems posed by the assimilation process. One need only mention the work of Mabel Carney at Teachers College, Columbia University, to eliminate discrimination against blacks in the 1930s. (28) Another example is Buell Gallagher, the white Kilpatrick student who, as President of Talladega College in Alabama, consistently crusaded for quality education, racial integration and social change in the South during the Depression years. (29) Indeed, the local historian could probably uncover numerous men and women who in a lonely and difficult manner tried to change the grave conditions faced by Americans of all colors and ethnic backgrounds in the Great Depression. For purposes of clarity and definition, however, it is necessary to briefly examine the Progressive Education Association, an organization which popularized and coordinated many national efforts at educational change in the 1930s. It likewise is of value to consider the positions of some individuals who were associated with it.

The PEA's interest in race and ethnicity grew out of an increasing concern for social issues in the late 1930s. Some of its leaders, particularly Executive Secretary Frederick Redefer, urged the organization to be socially responsible and "relevant" on the educational scene as other professional groups, namely the National Education Association and the American Federation of Teachers, promoted many of the principles and the techniques of progressive education. (30) It was also influenced by the work of such scholars of race and ethnicity as Charles Adamic, and a desire to attract funding. Hence, through its journal *Progressive Education,* beginning in 1935, it published considerably on human relations, intercultural education and the uses of materials on ethnicity in the classroom. (31) Indeed, a *Harvard Educational Review* study in the 1940s suggested that *Progressive Education* published more on intercultural education and related matters than any other educational journal in the United States. (32)

From 1936 until 1938 the PEA also sponsored a Commission on Intercultural Education, essentially lending its name and status to the Service Bureau for Education in Human Relations (later the Service Bureau for Intercultural Education), which was founded in 1933 by the Commission's director, Rachel Davis-DuBois. (33) Moreover, with the support of the General Education Board, its Commission on Human Relations, under the directorship of Alice Keliher, produced materials which occasionally included reference to racial and ethnic conflict as a problem in human relations. Slightly more than the Commission on Intercultural Education, the Commission on Human Relations was concerned with the uses of the behavioral and social sciences. It was funded in order to bring together specialists from disparate disciplines and from the outset it emphasized evaluation of its work. The Commission also explored group learning techniques and the uses of the media as means of resolving interpersonal conflict and misunderstanding. (33)

The Commission on Intercultural Education reflected the philosophy and energy of Davis-DuBois, a white Quaker active in NAACP affairs (34) who brought to her work moral indignation, verve, a social reconstructionist philosophy and commitment to a "cultural contributions" approach to intercultural education. A prolific writer and visible advocate of intercultural education, she was called upon by the New York City schools and other urban school systems undergoing racial conflict and anti-Semitic outbursts to develop curricular materials, assembly programs, and workshops for teachers that incorporated progressive pedagogy and an emphasis on the virtues of cultural pluralism. (35) By the late 1930s, however, she had developed personal disagreements with other educators and her approach came under criticism for being simplistic and unconcerned with careful evaluation. In 1938, therefore, when the PEA believed that her presence hindered its ability to raise funds, her association (and that of the Service Bureau) with it was terminated. The PEA continued to seek funds for intercultural education. It met with some success when the General Education Board agreed to support the publication of *When Peoples Meet,* an intercultural education handbook which examined racism in anthropological and international contexts, was edited by Alain Locke and Bernhard Stern and published in 1942. (36)

The Service Bureau continued its work after its relationship with the PEA was severed, attracting to its ranks William Kilpatrick, Stewart Cole, H. H. Giles and others who subsequently became the dominant personalities in the organization and forced the removal of Davis-DuBois in 1940. (37) If these individuals were critical of her on philosophical and methodological grounds, however, there is evidence to suggest that they did not succeed where she allegedly failed. (38)

Because intercultural education represented a new approach to racial and ethnic conflict and its advocates were generous in the use of self-serving rhetoric it became the subject of numerous studies in the early 1940s. The one sponsored by the General Education Board and released in 1940 as the *Report of the Committee for Evaluation of the Work of the Service Bureau for Intercultural Education* was critical of the Service Bureau's methods, social and educational philosophy, lack of careful evaluation and failure to include substantial ethnic participation. Although it did note the zealousness of Rachel Davis-DuBois and it recognized her pioneering efforts, its criticism of the Service Bureau's administrative sloppiness and asociological nature clearly contributed greatly to her demise in the organization she founded.

This study and others conducted by Theodore Brameld and the City of New York pointed to several weaknesses in early intercultural programs. In sum, they did not encourage relations between social and ethnic groups on an on-going basis, frequently ignored the political and social contexts of schooling and over-stressed a cultural contributions approach without duly defining the nature of community and the participation of ethnic groups themselves in policy formation. Programs had considerable difficulty as they attempted to define their philosophical positions and integrate the findings of modern social science research into their work. There may have been substantial tension between the need for practical day-to-day efforts and more broadly based theoretical considerations. (39)

In part, however, intercultural programs suffered from the progressive spirit of the times. Their endeavors were only partly successful because they were highly committed to an ideology of national unity, democracy, and tolerance that would resist authoritarianism at home and abroad and defend America's national interests. Attacking anti-Semitism and other forms of intolerance the interculturalists focused upon international and cross-cultural aspects of racism and noted the "commonness" of all men to the point where they blurred the differences between ethnic groups. Drawing on anthropological and biological research they often failed to consider the structural and institutional nature of racism in the United States. Indeed, by planing considerable stress upon the past cultural contributions of ethnics and others to American life, pluralism was portrayed as a static phenomenon. (40) Virtually no attempt was made to suggest that these groups could themselves shape the nature of American society. While some of the blame for this situation may be placed on the state of assimilation theory at that time, the belief in social engineering, rational planning, and consensus that was at the center of much progressive thought contributed to the questionable effectiveness of many intercultural efforts. The links between the best intentions of individuals concerned with the evils of conflict and the real world of the Depression era school and society were not clear.

There were numerous other efforts at intercultural education at this time, some of which attracted the support and endorsement of major progressives. Dewey and Kilpatrick joined a cross-section of American liberals to found the Council Against Intolerance in America. The school literature produced by this organization was more sensitive to the need to study community settings and integrate into its program findings from the social sciences on the psycho-social roots of discrimination and racist propaganda than was that produced by the Bureau. (41) Indeed, the United States witnessed a burgeoning of intercultural programs prior to World War II. (42) If one generalization may be made about them it is that like progressivism in education, they often tended to be eclectic and concerned with producing social harmony. In many cases they therefore downplayed social change and forms of actual race relations that might prove disruptive.

Southern Progressivism

The Southern region has been a major and unique area of progressive educational change. In the 1920s it witnessed the beginnings of a modernization thrust that included standardized state-wide syllabi featuring core curricula and activity-oriented courses of study. Accompanying these changes were reform of teacher education, centralization of state control over schooling, and the development of regional professional organizations. Such foundations as the General Education Board supplemented the public funding for these changes, which also featured considerable progressive rhetoric and the contributions of influential progressive educators and the Progressive Education Association. They were intended not only to modernize the South and bring it into line with the rest of the United States, but they were also a response to the South's chronically depressed economic condition and, later, the Great Depression. It was argued that such reforms would provide efficiency in the face of chronic financial difficulty, (43) maintain enrollments (which increased dramatically in the South during the Depression Years), (44) develop loyalty and "good citizenship," (45) and adjust students to some of the stark realities of the economic crisis by making the school pleasant and seemingly "relevant." (46) Much Southern educational literature made reference to the work of the major social reconstructionists and contained progressive rhetoric on the potentials of the technocratic expert society promoted by Northern progressives; it did not simply use *au courant* educational terminology. There was a Southern variation on these themes, however, in that many Southerners decided to build a New South that would maintain important regional characteristics, would be increasingly urbanized and economically modern and, to some extent, self-supporting. (47) Moreover, educational change often paralleled improvements in health care and other state services and, to a lesser degree, reflected the influence of New Deal politics and policies. (48)

One major feature of progressive change in the South was the publication of curriculum guides for use by teachers. Written after state departments of education consulted with a variety of experts, local educators and, in some cases, separate black study grounds, these curriculum guides stressed progressive pedagogy. Because of the influence of Doak Campbell and Hollis Caswell of the Peabody Institute for Teachers, two nationally recognized progressive curriculum specialists, these guides often differed little from state to state. (49) They provide an interesting measure of the "place" of blacks and race in Southern progressive thought and show how progressive rhetoric could be used to "tolerate" the maintenance of segregation.

The guides provided for the continuation of rigid "bi-racialism" or segregation and assumed that the black people would continue to occupy an inferior economic position. Given Southern society in the 1930s this is not surprising. But it is informative to note the extent to which progressive theory and rhetoric were used to rationalize it. The state of Virginia, for example, called for the development of educational goals that "should lead to the cooperation of individuals *within* (emphasis added) groups, and to the cooperation of groups with other groups ... the aims [of which] should grow out of existing social life." The Virginia curriculum guide also promoted social tolerance, an important component of progressive thought. (50) In Southern-depression context, however, this meant that there must be tolerance of constituted authority and provision for success within the individual's group as "an antidote for anti-social conduct." (51)

Deep South states were less subtle. Alabama's guides contained stereotypes on black humor and the desirability of black "self-control," (52) a Louisiana study prepared by Carleton Washburne stressed the need for black loyalty and constructive labor (53) and Georgia's guides emphasized that blacks be prepared, not for college, but for a life of menial jobs. (54) Indeed, the latter expressed the concern that there be social tolerance and an end to class differences while blacks and whites were to remain "two totally diverse races" who must "work out their social and economic destinies together, without fusion." (55) Despite considerable rhetoric on equality of opportunity it nevertheless made its appeal to white self-interest at a rather base level by using old racial stereotypes, claiming that there could be "no permanent prosperity for the state with half of the population idle, unskilled, shiftless, ignorant, criminal." (56) In sum, blacks were "a constant menace to the health of the community, a constant threat to its peace and security, and a constant cause of and excuse for the retarded progress of the other race." (57)

Southern curricular revisions enjoyed considerable support and publicity from outside the region. They were praised in *Progressive Education,* by J. W. Wrightstone, and by Paul Hanna and J. Paul Leonard in the Dewey Society's *Democracy and the Curriculum,* virtually always without comment on their social context. (58) The Progressive Education Association, moreover, considered the South such an important region that it attempted to establish a special program there. This move was blocked by the hesitancy of the General Education Board to fund a regional program run by "outsiders" and by the subsequent development of programs of experimentation and evaluation under the auspices of the Southern Association of Colleges and Secondary Schools and the Association of Colleges and Secondary Schools for Negroes. (59) Both organizations were deeply influenced by the PEA's Eight Year Study and were funded in part by the Board to replicate aspects of the Study.

Although rebuffed in its effort to establish a distinct Southern regional program in the mid-1930s the PEA, with 743 Southern members out of a national membership of 8,635, nevertheless lent support to the Southern Association and developed a workshop model that was used widely in the South. (60) It also sponsored a series of Southern conferences and carried in its journals considerable material on progressive education in the South as well as Southern forms of regional planning. (61) Extremely sensitive to its "radical" image in the South the PEA and its literature contained virtually no reference to race, even though Southern writers on regional planning, such as Howard Odum, the University of North Carolina sociologist who showed strong interest in progressive educational theory, did not skirt the issue and William Kilpatrick made considerable reference to it in his work. (62)

Some white liberals did find much that was lacking in Southern progressivism. They saw it as not properly grounded in sociological realities, as representing a headlong drive for urbanization or as under the control of the same powerfully conservative interests which dominated Southern social, economic and political life. (63) Still others, such as Mabel Carney, argued that Southern progressivism did not adequately address the pernicious aspects of segregation. (64) This latter position was to be found, as well, in the work of Buell Gallagher, who not only advocated a more open society and racial consciousness among blacks, but extended progressive thought into a direct analysis of the social and economic conditions which oppressed poor blacks and whites. (65) Indeed, he concluded that racial integration would aid all Southerners. Howard Odum, moreover, made a trenchant comment on the status of progressive education in the South. In his seminal 1936 work, *Southern Regions of the United States,* he spoke of gaps between reality and rhetoric and the self-serving nature of much educational change. Progressive educational reform had changed Southern culture but little, he suggested. It had probably "assumed the form and ideology of ambiguous plans, sectional schemes or outlets for [the] personal expression of leaders." (66)

Despite the reservations of white liberals, many blacks recognized that progressive education offered considerable potential for racial uplift and the elimination of the tradition-bound and authoritarian forms of schooling which plagued blacks in the South. Directed by W. A. Robinson, the principal of Atlanta's University's Demonstration School, the Association of Colleges and Secondary Schools for Negroes' Secondary School Study carried out a program of evaluation, experimentation, regional coordination and in-service training with the support of the General Education Board. (67) Its vast literature was replete with progressive pedagogy and theory, reflecting Robinson's belief that blacks could use progressive education's democratic rhetoric and philosophy to advantage. (68) Noting that educational rhetoric was basically a function of economic and political interests, Robinson argued that progressivism's wide appeal had established a new conventional wisdom that provided a convenient shield behind which liberal and conservative alike could work for their own ends. Hence, although conservatives could use it against blacks, progressive rhetoric and philosophy made it slightly more difficult for them openly to oppose democratic change. Indeed, Doxey Wilkerson and other blacks in Virginia had obtained important concessions in the state curriculum on these very grounds. (69)

Black interest in progressivism, therefore, ran high. It was part of a growing assertiveness which, in the 1930s, included attacks on segregation and a variety of intellectual approaches which stressed the power and uses of schooling. Hence, many black educational journals widely touted and discussed progressive methods and philosophy. (70) Such major scholars as Alain Locke and Charles S. Johnson supported the PEA. Most of the editors of the *Journal of Negro Education* joined the PEA. (71) Ambrose Caliver, Senior Specialists in the Education of Negroes, U. S. Office of Education, prominently supported the philosophy of social reconstruction as did the journals published by the National Association of Teachers in Colored Schools—American Teachers Association. (72) An examination of black publications and statements on progressive education suggests that interest in progressive methodology and philosphy was often linked to a need for democratic social change and black awareness, a break from the "learning by doing" and social accommodationism of Booker T. Washington's brand of early twentieth century progressivism. Progressive education was not only healthy for the individual child, but for the race. Whether through the Secondary School sStudy or through the use of progressive techniques in day to day schooling blacks saw much in progressive education that would enable the development of a black agenda in the schools, teacher professionalism and more scientific schooling.

As in the case of whites there were liberal black critics of progressive education in the South. Some warned of the dangers of accepting progressive education without duly considering the social implications and setting of educational change. Walter White, Doxey Wilkerson and Reid Jackson accepted and supported many progressive premises but called for progressives to bridge important gaps between rhetoric and the realities of day to day schooling and racism. (73) Jackson's research was concerned with the uses and impact of progressivism in the South. His work provided further evidence of gaps between theory and reality and that despite considerable effort at curriculum revision and improved teacher education there was much to be accomplished in the everyday world of the teacher. (74)

Much black criticisms of progressive education centered upon curriculum revision, one of the major features of progressivism in the South. Horace Mann Bond, the black historian, wrote in 1935 that

> The chain of social causation in the creation of attitudes does not begin with the makers of our current Southern courses of study; rather, it is linked

to the highly complex forces and past institutions whose dead spirits are revived in the unconscious prejudices and conscious "patriotism" of our contemporaries. (75)

Contending that blacks were aware that virtually all educational planning was in reality conducted for the ultimate benefit of whites, he nevertheless saw much revision as an effort to divert the public and educators away from poor pay and low educational standards. The crux of his argument, however, was that if progressivism was to be truly experimental, it would have to deal directly with society as it existed. This most progressives failed to do because they assumed an open society already existed. "It should be realized," he wrote,

...that the method of "activity" analysis in the construction of a curriculum presupposed an elastic, democratic social order in which there are no artificial barriers set against the social mobility of the individual. In such a society classes are assumed to be highly fluid, and there can be no such thing as caste. (76)

Bond thus posed a dilemma. If whites were serious about developing a progressive curriculum for all children, they would have to acknowledge the "real" nature of both segregation and social stratification. To do otherwise would deny the concept of equalitarian democracy and render their revisions wholly irrelevant. There could be no "separate" curriculum for blacks or whites, just as there could be no wholly separate or special class interests in a truly democratic society. (77)

Bond was not naive. He knew that as instruments of dominant social forces schools were not about to build a new social order. But like many progressives he believed that technology and modernization would eventually bring prosperity to the South, void many populist excesses and signal a more stable social order. Along with Counts, Carter Woodson, E. Franklin Frazier, and W. E. B. DuBois, he warned that the schools might fall into the control of a new middle class which in its drive for status and power could well turn its back on the needs of his race and the poor. Bond further held that in the face of modernization and technological development, democratic cultural pluralism could negate alienation. Suggesting that blacks could play a vital role in this society he told members of the PEA that blacks had, in the face of considerable oppression, developed a social life that should be seen as a model of associated living. He thus addressed a paradox inherent in much progressive thought, claiming that there could be diversity amidst increasing interdependence and standardization. (78) By recognizing that caste and class were related, moreover, Bond argued in his work that the careful study of racism and its structural causes might save a technological or "progressive" society from itself. This insight, as well as others, was missing from the writing of Southern white progressives, many of whom were intimately tied to the control of the educational system.

Conclusion

The progressive education movement as represented by the Progressive Education Association, major social reconstructionists, and progressive journals became cognizant of problems related to race and ethnicity in America during the Depression years. While it is apparent that the 1930s witnessed a growth of interest on the part of American intellectuals in racism, there was much in progressive social philosophy and pedagogy that provided for the amelioration of conflict and the development of strong well-integrated personalities. In its stress on tolerance there is little evidence of interest in actual race relations or careful study of the place of race and ethnicity in the American social fabric. Questions of racial integration and politics were skirted, in part out of a desire to avoid further conflict. In the South, progressivism represented an expression of expertise through educational reform and change, regional planning and progressive pedagogy. Although it was in line with much that was liberal in Southern intellectual life and politics, there is a good deal to suggest that its progressive rhetoric was used by whites to justify and tolerate the continuation of segregation and economic exploitation of blacks.

Revisionist and some other historians have argued that liberal or progressive educators held to assimilationist or melting pot theories, even into the 1930s. This assertion is not unwarranted, particularly with regard to cities like Gary, Indiana. (79) But progressivism is a complex and shifting phenomenon about which over-generalization is dangerous. Many progressives in the Depression years advocated a welfare state and technological Great Society that essentially eclipsed and rendered obsolete the local neighborhood or ethnic community. (80) At the same time, however, they also groped towards a concept of cultural pluralism. That said, it should not be assumed that if assimilationism has been used for conservative purposes of social control and consensus, then pluralism was advocated for opposite purposes. To the contrary, the progressive approach to race and ethnicity as well as to pluralism in the 1930s contained much that was conservative, even when seen as a product of its times. This conservatism is related to the progressive world view, the functions progressivism served in American education and the place of the educator in American society in the 1930s.

Despite the importance of empiricism in progressive philosophy much of the progressive interest in race and ethnicity was asociological and divorced from empirical research, existing social theory, and from the changing nature of the American city. A reflection of the personalities of those interested in race and ethnicity, they also grew out of the inspirational and ideological tone of progressive thought in the 1930s and increasing interest in the educative potential of the New Deal. Many of the movement's leaders were members of university faculties, school teachers, or administrators. Thus its approach to race and ethnicity must also be linked to the growing acceptance of progressive education as a respectable phenomenon that, as Lawrence Cremin has pointed out, was synonymous with educational "professionalism." (81) There is much, therefore, to C. Wright Mills' argument that progressivism in the 1930s was a "professional ideology" that reflected the marginal condition of the teacher in American life. (82) Indeed, as Willard Waller suggested early in the decade, teachers thus saw themselves as "passing on the culture" far more than dealing directly with questions of a political or socio-economic nature. (83) In spite of the best efforts of George Counts and others to overcome this perspective, progressivism may have served very specific interests within the school and the educational community insofar as it provided for institutional homeostasis and professional security in a time of social unrest. The recent work of David Swift, Merle Borrowman and Charles Burgess on the uses of the consummatory values of progressivism shows that it has, in part, been reactive to the dislocating impact of economic crisis on the individual child and a "need" to divert educational clienteles from hopelessness, joblessness and direct protest. (84) Horace Mann Bond clearly anticipated this analysis.

Progressive education, like American progressivism itself, has been a highly complex phenomenon which defies easy definition. Indeed, like much liberalism, it is beset by paradoxes and contradictions caused by the marginal roles that educators play in a changing American society and the ways in which educational and social ideologies grow out of these roles. As Walter Feinberg and others have pointed out, there are basic conflicts in progressive thought between individualism and community, child-centeredness and social reconstruction and desires for pluralism and national unity. (85) A need for individual freedom and expression is often posited over and against a fear that groups have neither the education nor experience to act on their own behalf. Indeed, in progressive thought there is both a fear of *praxis* (86) and a strong manipulative strain which during the Depression years may be seen in the interest of Rugg, Kilpatrick and other social reconstructionists in expertise, social planning and other "educated" responses by the modern state to social problems. (87)

Progressives saw the state in increasingly educational terms and hence problems of race and ethnicity were not defined as requiring group action. Their programs placed considerable burden on the individual child to develop new habits and attitudes as the state planned a society of abundance in which old dislocations and conflicts would be rendered irrelevant. Their stress on tolerance, understanding and communication, as well as their interest in pluralism must thus be understood as one of the ways in which they perceived the development of a liberal state that slowly and educationally reoriented American life. (88)

Because there was much paradox in progressive education, blacks recognized that it could be therefore used to advantage. In the rhetoric and ideology of progressivism there was an opportunity to test whites while creating a black school system featuring professional organizations, regional planning, testing and black consciousness. Aware that they were not about to obtain political freedom and cognizant of the way in which educational change was intimately related to Southern power structures, they nonetheless saw progressive education as a part of a slightly more liberal and humane progressivism that, while attempting to maintain law and order and the inferior economic status of blacks, held out some hope for a better future. Horace Mann Bond and others attempted to show whites that their rhetoric and ideals indeed would be meaningless unless they were willing to at some point eliminate caste barriers and the constraints of rigid social stratification. This strategy grew out of a historical quest for the change of social conditions through education. It was deeply influenced by developments in educational thought and practice as well as the Depression's impact on national life. Historians have yet to probe the impact of these trends on subsequent black strategy and, indeed, on the consciousness which led to the post-war Civil Rights movement.

In conclusion, progressivism served a variety of functions in the area of race and ethnicity. At its worst it upheld segregation and attempted to use tolerance and pluralism for self-serving and ideological purposes. In some cases humane and liberal educators were perhaps blind to the real social and economic consequences of what they were saying and doing. Continued repression in a society that was still dominated by capitalist modes of production was not their intention in the face of the promise of social reconstruction and the inroads of the New Deal upon an archaic state that served special interests. But if the latent functions of progressive reform in the 1930s meant that the fundamental nature of race and ethnic relations was not to be changed, major progressives openly addressed and publicized problems related to these relations and applied their educational and social philosophy to them. In some respects, interest in ameliorating racial and ethnic conflict accompanied a growing conservatism on the part of many progressive educators and so their position on these issues must be seen in terms of shifts in their ideology and the nature of progressive education itself.

Finally, this entire issue calls for considerably more research. Little is known about what members of oppressed and minority groups have actually had to say about many of the most cherished and humane beliefs held by liberal educators just as comparatively little is yet known about the positions of these educators on race and ethnicity. Likewise, it is important to study the functions of educational language and theory. Educational historians must look at the dynamics of acculturative and socializing forces in a changing capitalist society which often in the name of progress, creates unrest and tensions that well-meaning educators find difficult to face or understand.

Notes

1. William Kilpatrick, *et al.*, *The Educational Froniter* (New York, 1933), p. 8.
2. See Charles Flint Kellogg, NAACP: *A History of the National Association for the Advancement of Colored People*, 1, 1909–1920 (Baltimore, 1967): 20.
3. There is little literature on this topic. For an examination of Dewey's early views see J. Christopher Eisele, "John Dewey and the Immigrants," *History of Education Quarterly*, 15 (Spring 1975): 67–85.
4. See John and Eveyln Dewey, *Schools of Tomorrow* (New York, 1962). In January, 1971, *The Crisis* quoted William Wirt, the Superintendent of the Gary schools, as saying that "the colored children in the public schools of Gary, Indiana, have been segregated from the very beginning. It is a settled policy in this community to continue this segregation." *The Crisis,* 13 (January 1917): 121. See also Raymond A. Mohl, "Socialization and Americanization in the Gary Public Schools, 1906–1938," a paper presented to the American Historical Association (Chicago, 1974).
5. John Dewey, *Conditions Among the Poles of the United States* (Confidential Report) (1918). See also Walter Feinberg, "Progressive Education and Social Planning," *Teachers College Record,* 73 (May 1972): 485–505, and the following in the *History of Education Quarterly,* 15 (Spring 1975); Paul F. Bourke, "Philosophy and Social Criticism: John Dewey 1910–1920," 3–16; Charles L. Zerby, "John Dewey and the Polish Question: A Response to the Revisionist Historians," 17–30; Alan Lawson, "John Dewey and the Hope for Reform," 31–66; and Eisele.
6. John Dewey, "Racial Prejudice and Friction," *The Chinese Social and Political Science Review* (1922): 1–17.
7. John Dewey, "The Need for a Philosophy of Education," in E. G. Malherve (editor), *Educational Adaptations in a Changing Society: Report of the South African Education Conference Held in Capetown and Johannesburg in July, 1934, Under the Auspices of the New Educational Fellowship* (Capetown and Johannesburg, 1937), pp. 27–28. See also "South African Conference," Institute of International Education, *News Bulletin,* 10 (December 1934): 8–9.

8. "Dewey Urges Negroes to Join New Party," *The New York Times* (May 20, 1932), 2. See Edward J. Bordeau, "John Dewey's Ideas about the Great Depression," *The Journal of the History of Ideas*, 30 (January–March 1971): 67–84, for the extent to which Dewey committed himself to specific social and political goals in the 1930s. For a history of the NAACP in the 1930s see Raymond Wolters, *Negroes and the Great Depression: The Problem of Economic Recovery* (Westport, 1970). For older discussions which suggest that Dewey was unspecific and vague on matters political see Morton White, *Social Thought in America* (Boston, 1957), p. 201, and Seymour Itzkoff, *Cultural Pluralism in American Education* (Scranton, 1969), pp. 59–60.
9. George S. Counts, *School and Society in Chicago* (New York, 1928). See also George S. Counts, *The Selective Character of American Secondary Education* (Chicago, 1922), pp. 122–123; J. Crosley Chapman and George S. Counts, *Principles of Education* (Chicago, 1924), pp. 179–180; and George S. Counts, *The Social Composition of Boards of Education: A Study in the Social Control of Public Education* (Chicago, 1927).
10. George S. Counts, *The American Road to Culture: A Social Interpretation of Education in the United States* (New York, 1930), pp. 82–83, 116.
11. George S. Counts, "Dare We Be Progressive?" *Progressive Education*, 9 (April 1932): 258–259.
12. This question is discussed at length by Wayne J. Urban. See "The Dimensions of an Ideological Liberalism: George Counts and the Communists," (Unpublished manuscript, c.a. 1974). It is linked to Counts' view of race and ethnic relations in Ronald K. Goodenow and Wayne J. Urban, "George S. Counts (1889–1974): A Critical Appreciation" (unpublished manuscript, 1975). Copies of these papers are available from the authors.
13. George S. Counts, *The Prospects of American Democracy* (New York, 1938), p. 241.
14. John Dewey, *The Public and Its Problems* (Denver, 1927), pp. 124–125.
15. John Dewey, *Liberalism and Social Action* (New York, 1963), p. 48.
16. John Dewey, *Freedom and Culture* (New York, 1963), pp. 127–128.
17. John Dewey, "Creative Democracy—the Task Before Us," in *John Dewey and the Promise of America* (Progressive Education Association Booklet Number 14, Proceedings of the 1939 National John Dewey Conference of the Progressive Education Association) (Columbus, 1939), 15. Dewey's message to the meeting of 1,000 was read by Horace Kallen. *The New York Times* (October 21, 1939), 19, emphasized Dewey's discussion of tolerance. See also "Democracy Ailing, Dr. Dewey Asserts," *The New York Times* (October 25, 1938), 7.
18. Ibid., 13.
19. John Dewey, *Art As Experience* (New York, 1958), p. 334.
20. See William Heard Kilpatrick, *Our Educational Task As Illustrated in the Changing South* (Chapel Hill, 1930).
21. For discussions of the work of the Commission see Wilma Dykeman and James Stokely, *Seeds of Southern Change: The Life of Will Alexander* (Chicago, 1962); George B. Tindall, *The Emergence of the New South 1913–1945* (Baton Rouge, 1967), pp. 175–83; and Edward Flud Burrows, "The Commission on Interracial Cooperation: A Case Study in the History of the Interracial Movement in the South," Ph.D. dissertation (University of Wisconsin, 1955).
22. William Heard Kilpatrick, "Resort to Courts by Negroes to Improve Their

Schools a Conditional Alternative," *The Journal of Negro Education* 4 (July 1935): 412–418. For a further expression of his views on education see William Kilpatrick, foreword to Buell Gallager, *American Caste and the Negro College* (New York, 1938), pp. vii–xii. See also Ronald K. Goodenow, "Progressive Education in the South: The Depression Years," a paper presented to a conference of the History of Education Society and the Southern History of Education Society (November 14, 1974) for a detailed discussion of Southern progressive education.

23. See William Heard Kilpatrick, "Education and Intolerance," *The Social Frontier*, 5 (May 1939): 230–231; William Heard Kilpatrick, "The Problem of Minorities, an Editorial," *Frontiers of Democracy*, 6 (April 15, 1940); William Heard Kilpatrick, "Through the Looking Glass," *Intercultural Education News*, 2 (October 1940): 1; and the following in *Frontiers of Democracy*, 6 (April 15, 1940): Margaret Mead, "The Student of Race Problems Can Say...": 200–202; Henry Pratt Fairchild, "Who is American?": 203–205; Stewart G. Cole, "The Meaning of the Term: *Minorities*": 205; Eugene Horowitz, "The Social Roots of Prejudice": 206–208; Alain Locke, "With Science as His Shield the Educator Must Bridge Our 'Great Divides' ": 208–210; and Herbert L. Seamans, "Schools and Jews": 211–213; See also Ruth Benedict, "Differences vs. Superiorities," *Frontiers of Democracy*, 9 (December 15, 1942): 81–82; Edward G. Olsen, "Perspective in Race Relations," *The Social Frontier*, 1 (November 1934): 29; Theodore Brameld, "Karl Marx and the American Teacher," *The Social Frontier*, 2 (November 1935): 56; H. J. Boyden, "Which America?" *The Social Frontier*: 4 (May 1938), 268; and Broadus Mitchell, "Excluded Because of Color," letter to *Frontiers of Democracy*, 6 (March 1940): 191.

24. Harold Rugg, *America and Her Immigrants* (n.d. 1922) and Harold Rugg, *An Introduction to Problems of American Culture* (Boston), p. 561.

25. See "Education and National Unity," *Intercultural Education News* 2 (January 1941): 3.

26. Harold Rugg, "Creative America: Can She Begin Again?" *Frontiers of Democracy*, 6 (October 1939): 9. See also Gordon R. Clapp, "The Program of the Tennessee Valley Authority," *Frontiers of Democracy*, 6 (November 15, 1939): 48–55, 61; George F. Gant and S. E. Thorsten Lund, "Education and Regional Growth in the Tennessee Valley," 6 (November 15, 1939): 49–51; and George Soule, "The National Resources Planning Board," *Frontiers of Democracy*, 6 (March 15, 1940): 168-170.

27. See especially Harold Rugg, *The Teacher of Teachers: Frontiers of Theory and Practice in Teacher Education* (New York, 1952), p. 78.

28. See Walter G. Daniel, "Negro Welfare and Mabel Carney at Teachers College, Columbia University," *The Journal of Negro Education*, 11 (October 1942): 560–562; and "Trends and Events of National Importance in Negro Education," *The Journal of Negro Education*, 7 (January 1938): 92–93.

29. See Buell G. Gallagher, *American Caste and the Negro College*; plus footnote 65 below.

30. See "Report of the Executive Secretary," (1936), 2, Progressive Education Association Mss., University of Illinois.

31. There were too many articles published to provide a complete citation. For representative pieces see the March, 1935 issue.

32. Abraham Citron, Collins J. Reynolds and Sarah W. Taylor, "Ten Years of

Intercultural Education in Educational Magazines," *Harvard Educational Review*, 15 (March 1945): 129–133. For valuable insights into the development of intercultural education in the 1930s see Mordecai Grossman, "The Schools Fight Prejudice, An Appraisal of the Intercultural Education Movement," *Commentary*, 1 (March 1946): 34–42; "Brief Report of Specific Organizations and Their Programs," *Harvard Educational Review*, 15 (March 1945): 134–146; Feinberg, "Progressive Education and Social Planning"; and Theodore Brameld, *Minority Problems in the Public Schools: A Study of Administrative Policies and Practices in Seven School Systems* (New York, 1946). On the influence of urban unrest see Eve Thurston, "Ethiopia Unshackled: A Brief History of the Education of Negro Children in New York City," *Bulletin of the New York Public Library*, 69 (April 1965): 227–230. For a general overview of the relationship between the progressive education movement and intercultural education in the 1930s, see also Ronald K. Goodenow, "The Progressive Educator and Racial Tolerance: Intercultural Education, 1930–1941," a paper presented to Division F of the American Educational Research Association (April 1975). The author has benefited from the insights of Nicholas Montalto on intercultural education.

33. For an overview of its literature see Graham, *Progressive Education..., op. cit.*, 138–139. Its activities and philosophy are summed up in Alice V. Keliher, "The Commission on Human Relations: Its Work and Relation to the Defense of Democracy," *Progressive Education*, 17 (November 1940): 487–504.

34. Davis-DuBois was a "young militant" in the NAACP who supported black economic separatism in the early 1930s. See Wolters, *Negroes and the Great Depression . . .*, pp. 310–311, 313, 318. Her NAACP interests went unmentioned in Davis-DuBois' intercultural education publications. For information on the early work of Davis-DuBois see Rachel Davis-DuBois, *A School and Community Project in Developing Sympathetic Attitudes Toward Other Races and Nations* (New York, 1934); Rachel Davis-DuBois, "The New Frontier," *Opportunity*, 12 (February 1934): 40–41; and Rachel Davis-DuBois, "Practical Problems of International and Interracial Education," *The Clearing House*, 8 (April 1936): 486–490. For an extensive review of the work of the Service Bureau see the "Report of the Committee for Evaluation of the Work of the Service Bureau for Intercultural Education" prepared by a Committee appointed by the General Education Board. This report is on file at The Rockefeller Foundation Archives in New York City. Genivieve Chase served as Director of Research. Committee members included Otto Klineberg, Hugh Hartshorne, E. Franklin Frazier, Willian G. Carr, Harry Stack Sullivan and Leonard W. Doob.

35. See, for example, Rachel Davis-DuBois, "Intercultural Education at Benjamin Franklin H.S.," *High Points in the Work of the High Schools of New York City*, 19 (December 1937): 23–29; Benjamin Fine, "Schools to Open Intolerance Drive," *The New York Times* (January 16, 1939), Section II, 3; and "Courses in Intercultural Education Given by Service Bureau Staff," *Intercultural Education News*, 1 (September 20, 1939): 3. Local 5, the New York Teachers Union eventually purged from the American Federation of Teachers showed strong interest in race and ethnicity. It is evident that its membership included a substantial black representation. Its publications addressed racism and intolerance within the context of the historical job ceiling which faced blacks as well as specific depression conditions. It generally applauded the efforts of the PEA and

Service Bureau. See, for example, Celia Lewis, "Schools for Tolerance I," *The New York Teacher,* 4 (December 1938): 10–11; and Marion Milstein and Jenny L. Mayer, "Schools for Tolerance II," *The New York Teacher,* 4 (January 1939): 10–11.

36. See "Report of the Committee...."
37. For valuable research on the recollections of various progressives, including Kilpatrick, Stewart Cole, H. H. Giles and Helen and Frank Trager, who assumed power in the Service Bureau in the late 1930s, see the series of interviews conducted by Olive Hall of the Boston Univerity Human Relations Center c.a. 1958. The original manuscripts are on file at the Boston University Human Relations Center. The author wishes to acknowledge the generous assistance of Walter Feinberg of the University of Illinois in obtaining this material. One particularly helpful document in this collection is Stewart Cole, "The History of the Bureau of Intercultural Education," an unpublished manuscript made from tape recordings of an interview by Hall.
38. See Cole, "The History of the Bureau...," *op. cit.*
39. Brameld, *Minority Problems...*, *op. cit., passim.* Louis Yavner, *Administration of Human Relations Program in New York City Schools, Report to Hon. F. H. La Guardia, Mayor of the City of New York* (New York, 1945), pp. 99–102. The General Education Board Report noted that interculturalists were at times naive regarding the sociology of the school itself. See *Report of the Committee..., op. cit.*
40. This rather static view of pluralism may be related to the emphasis of existing pluralist theory and many interculturalists on description and stress upon "differences" and "contributions." It must also be seen within the context of the progressive educator's interest in building national consensus and unity around democratic ideology. For a valuable discussion of the ahistorical and asociological aspects of this approach see William M. Newman, *American Pluralism: A Study of Minority Groups and Social Theory* (New York, 1973), especially pp. 69–70. For an overview of arguments favoring "the Great Society" see Fred M. Newman and Donald W. Oliver, "Education and Community," *Harvard Educational Review,* 37 (Winter 1967): 61–106. Leonard J. Fein in *The Ecology of the Public Schools: An Inquiry into Community Control* (New York, 1971) takes up the question to the historical attitude of liberals on legitimacy.
41. Council Against Intolerance in America, *An American Answer to Intolerance* (Teachers Manual No. 1, Junior and Senior High Schools, Experimental Form) (New York, 1939).
42. See "Brief Report on Specific Organizations...,".
43. See, for example, Frank W. Cannaday, "Arkansas," in Jim B. Pearson and Edgar Fuller (editors), *Education in the State: Historical Development and Outlook* (Washington, 1969), p. 86, and Helen Heffernan, "The School Curriculum in American Education," in Edgar Fuller and Jim B. Pearson (editors), *Education in the States: National Development Since 1900* (Washington, 1969), p. 241. For an overview of the entire efficiency in education question see Raymond E. Callahan, *Education and the Cult of Efficiency: A Study of the Social Forces That Have Shaped the Administration of the Public Schools* (Chicago, p. 1962).
44. The South, in the period from 1930 to 1940, saw an increase in public

school enrollment of over 300,000, despite national trends to the contrary. See United States Office of Education, *Biennial Survey of Education in the United States*, 1939–1940, Vol. I (Washington, 1947), pp. 60, 113.

45. The General Education Board, which funded many curricular revision projects in the South, numerous PEA programs and the regional endeavors of the Southern Association of Colleges and Secondary Schools and the Association of Colleges and Secondary Schools for Negroes was motivated to a significant degree by these motives. See, for example, Robert Havinghurst and Flora Rhind, "The Program in General Education," General Education Board, *Annual Report* (New York, 1941), p. 34.

46. This function of progressive education is discussed in David Swift, *Ideology and Change in the Public Schools: The Latent Functions of Progressive Education* (Columbus, 1969) and in Charles Burgess and Merle L. Borrowman, *What Doctrines to Embrace: Studies in the History of American Education* (Glenview, 1969), pp. 113–141.

47. For insights on recent Southern history, New South ideology and Southern progressivism see George B. Tindall, *The Emergence of the New South* 1913–1945 (Baton Rouge, 1967); Thomas D. Clark, *The Emerging South* (New York, 1968); Paul M. Gaston, *The New South Creed: A Study in Southern Mythmaking* (New York, 1970); and Hugh G. Bailey, *Liberalism in the New South: Southern Social Reformers and the Progressive Movement* (Coral Gables, 1969).

48. Tindall writes that Georgia's program was part of an attempt by Governor E. D. Rivers to create a "little New Deal" in his state. See Tindall, pp. 617–618.

49. For their social philosophy and ideas on the extent to which children must be trained to understand the "realities" of depression see William H. Martin's comments in Virgil A. Clift, Archibald W. Anderson and Gordon Hullfish, *Negro Education in America: Its Adequacy, Problems, and Needs*, Sixteenth Yearbook of the John Dewey Society (New York, 1962), pp. 72–73. In their *Curriculum Development* (New York, 1935), they stress the need to keep students busy in the face of both increased opportunity for leisure and unemployment (406). Children must also be educated for the "planned social order" (29–30) in which urbanization (32) and the fostering of individualism within a cooperative context (36) were to be among the major goals of schooling. Both taught at the Peabody College for Teachers in Nashville. Caswell later went on to Teachers College, Columbia University.

50. *Procedures for Virginia State Curriculum Program*, Bulletin, State Board of Education, 14 (Richmond: November 1932), 24.

51. Ibid., 31.

52. Division of Instruction, State Department of Education, Montgomery, *Report of the Committee on Social and Economic Conditions in Alabama and Their Implications for Education*, Alabama Education Association, Bulletin No. 3 (Montgomery: May 15, 1937), 124–125.

53. See his "Summary of Recommendation in Regard to Negro Education," in *Louisiana Educational Survey*, Vol. 4 (Baton Rouge, 1942), pp. 239–240.

54. Georgia Program for the Improvement of Instruction in the Public Schools, *The Open Road: A Teacher's Guide for Child, Adult and Community Development in Negro Elementary Schools*, Bulletin No. 2A (Atlanta, 1938), pp. 32–34;

and Georgia Program for the Improvement of Instruction in the Public Schools, *Guide to Life-Related Teaching in the Negro High Schools of Georgia,* Bulletin No. 4 (Atlanta, October, 1938), pp. 27, 60–61.
55. *Georgia Program for the Improvement of Education,* State Department of Education, Bulletin No. 2 (Atlanta, May 1936), pp. 25–26.
56. Ibid.
57. Ibid., 26.
58. J. W. Wrightstone, *An Appraisal of Newer Elementary School Practices* (New York, 1938), pp. 27–31; and Paul Hanna and J. Paul Leonard, "Promising Efforts at Curriculum Improvement," Chapter 10, in Harold Rugg (editor), *Democracy and the Curriculum* (New York, 1939), pp. 475–512.
59. The PEA's position was developed in "Field Work in the South, Sponsored by the Progressive Education Association," a position paper submitted by Frederick J. Redefer to the GEB, March 15, 1939. See also two internal memorandam of Leo M. Favrot of the General Education Board of an interview of Frederick L. Redefer of the PEA, April 17, 1939 and Interview Re: "Redefer's Request for Aid on Field Work in the South," Leo Favrot to Frank C. Jenkins, Director, Southern Association of Colleges and Secondary Schools, March 27, 1939, GEB Mss. There is also considerable evidence in these and other materials that the PEA's image in the South was either self-serving or too "radical." For information on the extensive program of the Southern Association see Frank Jenkins, et al., *The Southern Association Study: A Report of the Work With the Thirty-Three Cooperating Secondary Schools* (The Commission on Curricular Problems and Research of the Southern Association of Colleges and Secondary Schools, 1941). This publication discusses cooperation with the PEA and contains a complete bibliography on its activities.
60. See "Comparative Membership Breakdown, PEA," PEA Mss., University of Illinois Archives.
61. See W. Carson Ryan and Ralph Tyler, *Summer Workshops in Secondary Education* (New York, 1939), George Redd, "Experimenting with the Workshop and Seminar in the Education of Teachers," *The Quarterly Review of Higher Education Among Negroes,* 9 (January 1941): 10–15; and George Redd, "An Analysis of Teacher Education Trends in Negro Colleges," *Educational Administration and Supervision,* 35 (November 1949): 461–474.
62. See especially Howard Odum, *Southern Regions of the United States* (Chapel Hill, 1936) and Howard Odum, *Race and Rumors of Race: Challenge to American Crisis* (Chapel Hill, 1943).
63. See, for example, B. J. O. Schrieke, *Alien Americans* (New York, 1936), pp. 175–176; and Leo Favrot, "How the Small Rural School Can More Adequately Serve Its Community," *The Journal of Negro Education* 3 (July 1936): 433–438.
64. See especially Mabel Carney, "The Pre-Service Preparation of Rural Teachers," *Teachers College Record,* 34 (1932–1933): 111–113; Mabel Carney, "Desirable Rural Adaptation in the Education of Negroes," *The Journal of Negro Education,* 5 (July 1936): 448–452; and *National Conference on the Fundamental Problems of Negroes* (Washington, 1934), pp. 62–66. For information on Carney's role in countering discrimination at Teachers College see Walter G. Daniel, "Negro Welfare and Mable Carney at Teachers College, Columbia University,"

The Journal of Negro Education, 11 (October 1942): 560–562; and "Trends and Events of National Importance in Negro Education," *The Journal of Negro Education,* 7 (January 1938): 92–93.

65. See Buell G. Gallagher, *American Caste and the Negro College, op. cit.;* Buell G. Gallagher, "Christians and Radical Social Change," *The World Tomorrow,* 15 (June 1932): 170–172; Buell G. Gallagher, "College Training for the Negro —To What End?" *Opportunity,* 15 (September 1937): 273–275, 282; Buell G. Gallagher, "What Would Constitute Progress?" *The Journal of Negro Education,* 8 (July 1939): 571–582; and Buell G. Gallagher, "The Dilemma of America in the Defense of Democracy," *The Journal of Negro Education,* 10 (July 1941): 442–452.
66. Odum, *Southern Regions,* p. 515.
67. See William H. Brown and William A. Robinson, *Serving Negro Schools: A Report of the Secondary Study, Its Purposes, Working Techniques and Findings* (Atlanta, 1946), pp. 58–72. See page 71 for a listing of workshop publications. For the General Education Board's role in the Study see Albert R. Mann, "The Program in Southern Education," General Education Board, *Annual Report,* 1943 (New York, 1944), The General Education Board Mss. in the Rockefeller Foundation Archives contain considerable materials on the study and the Board's motivation in funding it. Complex as these motives were, it came after continual prodding by several black educators and the refusal of the white Southern Association of Colleges and Secondary Schools to include blacks in its programs of regional planning and evaluation.
68. W. A. Robinson, "Progressive Education and the Negro," *Proceedings Association of Colleges and Secondary Schools for Negroes* (1937) (n.d.), 57–60. See also W. A. Robinson, "What Peculiar Organization and Direction Should Characterize the Education of Negroes?" *The Journal of Negro Education,* 5 (July 1936): 393–400; W. A. Robinson, "A New Era for Negro Schools," *Progressive Education,* 7 (December 1940): 541–565; and W. A. Robinson, "What is Progressive Education?" *The Virginia Teachers Bulletin,* 14 (February 1937): 23–26.
69. See D. A. Wilkerson, "Viewpoint of the Advisory Committee on Negro Schools, Virginia State Curriculum Revision Program," *The Virginia Teachers Bulletin,* 11 (January 1934): 7–9; Edna Colson, "The New Virginia Courses of Study," *The Virginia Teachers Bulletin,* 10 (January 1934): 21; Doxey Wilkerson, "A Guide for the Study of the Teneative Course of Study for Virginia Secondary Schools," *The Virginia Teachers Bulletin,* 2 (May 1935): 2–5; and Tinsley L. Spraggins, "A Democratic Program," *The National Educational Outlook Among Negroes,* 19 (October 193): 19.
70. See, especially, *The Bulletin* (late in the decade, *The National Educational Outlook Among Negroes*) published by the National Association of Teachers in Colored Schools, renamed the American Teachers Association in the late 1930s, and the many journals published by black state teachers groups in the South. These publications are on file at the Schomberg Collection of the New York Public Library.
71. Charles S. Johnson, the black Fisk University sociologist, served on several PEA advisory committees in the late 1930s and early 1940s, and Alain Locke, a PEA member, appeared on PEA panels in the North. Very few blacks participated in the affairs of the PEA at the national level. For a strong attack on the gen-

eral failure of the progressive education movement to include blacks see Robinson, "A New Era . . . ." There is some evidence that the officers of the PEA agonized slightly over segregation as early as 1935. In 1937, the Board of Directors passed a resolution by W. Carson Ryan that after March 1, 1937 *national* conferences would be held where "people of all races (could) ... attend without discrimination in any way whatsoever all sessions of the conference." This resolution, which said nothing with regard to housing, was apparently the result of difficulties surrounding an upcoming conference in St. Louis. See "Minutes of Board of Directors," April 7, 1935 and January 9–10, 1937. PEA Mss. Teachers College.

72. See Ambrose Caliver, "The Role of the Teacher in the Reorganization and Redirection of Negro Education," *The Journal of Negro Education,* 5 (July 1936): 508–516; and Ambrose Caliver, "The Negro Teacher and a Philosophy of Negro Education," *The Journal of Negro Education,* 2 (October 1933): 432–447. See also, "Report of the Committee on Resolutions of the American Teachers Association," *The National Educational Outlook Among Negroes,* 18 (September 1937): 24–25; and John W. Scott, "The New Deal in Education," *The Bulletin,* 12 (January 1934): back cover.
73. See, for example, Walter White, "The Progressive School and the Race Problem," *School and Home,* 15 (November 1932): 33–36; D. A. Wilkerson, "A Determination of the Peculiar Problems of Negroes in Contemporary American Society," *The Journal of Negro Education,* 3 (July 1936): 325–350; and Ried E. Jackson, "A Democratic Philosophy for Negro Teacher-Education Institutions," *The Quarterly Review of Higher Education Among Negroes,* 6 (April 1938): 108–122.
74. See especially Reid E. Jackson, "A Critical Analysis of Curricula for Educating Secondary-School Teachers in Negro Colleges of Alabama," Ph.D. dissertation (Ohio State University, 1937).
75. Horace Mann Bond, "The Curriculum and the Negro Child," *The Journal of Negro Education,* 4 (April 1935): 160.
76. Ibid., 168.
77. Horace Mann Bond, *The Education of the Negro in the American Social Order* (1934) (New York, 1966), p. 9.
78. Horace Mann Bond, "Democracy and the Problem of Minority Groups," *Progressive Education,* 18 (October 1941): 282. See also Horace Mann Bond, "Education in the South," *The Journal of Educational Sociology,* 12 (January, 1939): 264–274; Bond, *The Education of the Negro,* pp. 48–149. Horace Mann Bond, "The Extent and Character of Separate Schools in the United States," *The Journal of Negro Education,* 4 (July 1935): 327, and Horace Mann Bond, "The Liberal Arts College for Negroes: A Social Force," in *A Century of Municipal Higher Education* (A Collection of Addresses Delivered During the Centennial Observance of the University of Louisville, America's Oldest Municipal University) (Chicago, 1937), p. 363.
79. See Mohl.
80. For an excellent recent discussion see Walter Feinberg, *Reason and Rhetoric* (New York, 1975).
81. See Lawrence Cremin, *The Transformation of the School: Progressivism in American Education 1876–1957* (New York, 1961), and Patricia Graham, *Pro-*

gressive Education: From Arcady to Academe: A History of the Progressive Education Association 1914–1955 (New York, 1967).

82. C. Wright Mills, *Sociology and Pragmatism: The Higher Learning in America* (New York, 1964).
83. Willard Waller, *The Sociology of Teaching* (1932) (New York, 1967), especially pp. 1–19.
84. See Swift, and Burgess and Borrowman.
85. See especially Walter Feinberg, *Reason and Rhetoric: The Intellectual Foundations of Twentieth Century Liberal Educational Policy* (New York, 1975).
86. The author has benefited from Michael Simmons, Jr., "The Function of Praxis in the Philosophy of Education," unpublished manuscript (1974).
87. See Feinberg, *Reason and Rhetoric*.
88. For an excellent general discussion of the progressive view of politics see Rush Welter, *Popular Education and Democratic Social Thought in America* (New York, 1962).

Fear and the Constraints on Academic Freedom of Public School Teachers, 1930-1960

BY PAUL VIOLAS

Freedom and fear are rather strange bedfellows. A study of the history of the idea of academic freedom for public school teachers from 1930 to 1960, however, reveals an intimate relationship between the two. During this period over twelve hundred articles dealing with various aspects of the concept of public school teachers' academic freedom appeared in educational, legal, and popular journals. An analysis of these articles discloses the academic freedom dialogue reflected the fears emerging from successive crises in American society.

The thirty year period was trisected by three of the most traumatic events in American social history: the Great Depression, World War II, and the Cold War. During each era, the trauma which dominated it gave rise to a peculiar set of social fears. These fears had an important impact on the academic freedom dialogue because: first, the objectives of the school were ascribed in response to society's fears; and, second, the justification of academic freedom rested upon the teachers' function in implementing those objectives.

This relationship, however, was complex. The crescendo of fear did not necessarily mean a closure on teachers' freedom. On the contrary, it often provided the impetus for development of the rationale which enhanced certain aspects of academic freedom. All too often, this rationale supporting teachers' freedom was based on a sacrifice of the freedom of students. Because of the limitations of space, all of the dialogue cannot be examined here. This paper will analyze the dialogue surrounding one academic freedom issue during each of the three eras and illustrate the impact of the relationship of fear and freedom.

The portrait of the academic freedom dialogue during the 1930's was strongly colored by the fears arising from social issues stemming from the economic dislocations caused by the Great Depression. The feelings of fear and frustrations which one can sense in the literature of the era, however, was not directed toward the entire economic or social system. While the overwhelming majority of Americans had not lost faith in the system, it was obvious, nevertheless, that all was not right. Some evil had penetrated the Edenic American Garden. It was necessary, then, to dislodge the evil without

---

PAUL VIOLAS *is Assistant Professor of History of Education, Department of History and Philosophy of Education, University of Illinois at Urbana-Champaign.*

destroying the Garden. When the evil had been expelled, America would again become the New Israel. The national mood was for reform rather than revolution, and the support accorded to Franklin Roosevelt and his New Deal evidenced that most Americans favored a patchwork approach to reform — reform which amounted to little more than a minor reshuffling of the deck. Within this context there were two satanic enemies: the selfish businessmen who had stacked the deck and those who would overthrow the system — the revolutionaries who wanted a new game rather than a new deal to continue the old game.

The school, as often in the past, was viewed as a vehicle to alleviate social problems.[1] An important objective now assigned to the schools was the creation of safeguards against the dual threat to the Garden. This objective required that the schools produce a special kind of citizen — a citizen who possessed what was termed "critical intelligence." This kind of intelligence would lead the citizen to understand that both the selfish businessmen and the revolutionaries would contaminate Edenic America. Many writers were able to translate this objective into a persuasive rationale for increased teacher freedom. An analysis of the dialogue concerning the question of loyalty oaths provides a typical example of this process.

During the thirties, considerable effort was directed toward the passage of laws requiring loyalty oaths for teachers. By 1935, over twenty states had passed such laws.[2] The major thrust of these laws was to eliminate radical teachers. Most of the support for loyalty oaths stemmed from the belief that there existed a real danger to the Republic in the person of teachers who were imposing un-American and subversive doctrines on the nation's school children. The 1934 American Legion National Convention passed a resolution demanding that schools hire only teachers who were "citizens of unquestioned patriotism and advocates of American ideals."[3] William Kelty of the Y.M.C.A. contended, "There are forces at work in the schools, as elsewhere, that are insidiously undermining the confidence of children in their government. Teachers have been guilty of subversive indoctrination of their classes . . . the truly American forces are taking steps to eradicate the un-American ones. One of the most important moves in this campaign has been the loyalty pledge."[4] The president of the New York City Board of Education wrote to the Board of Examiners instructing them to go beyond the mere requirement

---

[1] For a history of the idea that the schools could solve America's social problems see: Henry J. Perkinsen, *The Imperfect Panacea* (New York: Random House, 1968).

[2] "Loyalty Oaths for Teachers," *School and Society*, vol. 42, No. 1078, August 24, 1935, pp. 267-269.

"Loyalty Oaths," *Social Frontier*, vol. 2, No. 1, October, 1935, p. 23.

[3] Quoted in "Educational Resolutions by the American Legion," *School and Society*, vol. 40, No. 1943, December 22, 1943, p. 839.

[4] "Is It 'Misguided Patriotism'?" *School and Society*, vol. 41, No. 1066, June 1, 1935, p. 735.

See also Glenn W. Moon, "Club Activity as Training for Democracy," *Social Education*, vol. 3, No. 1, January, 1939, pp. 103-107.

of the loyalty oath and "make personality and character your first consideration, and that under the head of character you consider loyalty and love of country."[5] These writers typified those who feared the radical as the greatest threat to the American system and believed the best weapon to expurgate the Garden was the loyalty oath.

This position, however, conflicted with the liberal reformers who were certain that selfish business interests posed the greater threat. They argued that loyalty oaths hindered the development of "critical intelligence" necessary to return America to its promise. One approach suggested that the oaths were neither needed nor effective. In 1936, the N.E.A. passed a resolution condemning loyalty oaths for teachers. This resolution attacked the basic premise of the oath supporters as it stated, "We hold that the loyalty of the teachers of America is beyond question."[6] In a somewhat different mood, H. L. Mencken had expressed the same disdain for the supposed threat of radical teachers as he commented on the proposed Maryland oath law: "The Halloway-American Legion Bill is foolish enough to be worthy of its sponsors. Its ostensible aim is to smoke out schoolmarms who poison their pupils with Marxian heresies . . . it is almost as rare for one of them to hatch sedition as it is for one of them to go up in a balloon."[7]

If the opponents of loyalty oaths believed there were too few un-American teachers to make oaths necessary, they even more strongly denied that such oaths would inhibit any few disloyal teachers that might exist. Abraham Lefkowitz pointed out that, "since these so-called dangerous 'reds' do not believe in bourgeois morality, they will be the first to take such silly oaths and then laugh at bourgeois stupidity and morality."[8] But, if these oaths could not solve American society's problems, their opponents believed they were detrimental to the development of that solution.

The opponents of loyalty oaths contended the depression had shown that a major responsibility of the schools was to develop students with "critical intelligence." They argued it could only be accomplished by professional teachers who were free from fear. Loyalty oaths would cause fear and inhibit this development. William H. Kilpatrick stated that the Constitution was held as a symbol of those supporting the status quo. The oaths, he believed, would be used to retard responsible social change and reduce reasonable social criticism.[9] Florence Curtis Hanson argued that the loyalty oath laws would produce fear among teachers. "Such legislation creates an atmosphere of fear

---

[5] Quoted in "Qualifications for Teachers in the New York City Schools," *School and Society*, vol. 40, No. 1033, October 13, 1934, p. 484.
[6] "Platform and Resolutions," *NEA Addresses and Proceedings*, vol. 74, 1936, p. 216.
[7] "Chasing the Reds," *Teachers College Record*, vol. 36, No. 8, May,, 1935, p. 721.
[8] "Academic Freedom and Progress," *The American Teacher*, vol. 19, No. 4, March-April, 1935, p. 11.
See also "Teachers' Loyalty Oath," *The American Teacher*, vol. 19, No. 5, May-June, 1935, p. 24.
[9] "Loyalty Oath—A Threat to Intelligent Teaching," *Social Frontier*, vol. 1, No. 9, June, 1935, pp. 10-15.

in which it is impossible to develop critical intelligence... Effective teaching can be carried on only under conditions of freedom from fear of official discipline for thinking thoughts that may be different from those approved by the guardians of status quo."[10] These writers believed the "guardians of the status quo" represented the same selfish business interests which had caused the depression. In a sense, this demand for the expulsion of the influence of the guardians of the status quo was not significantly different from the nature of the demand to eliminate the radical influence in the school. The presence of either would prevent the teacher from doing the right things to the student, i.e., equip him with "critical intelligence" that he might understand reality in a way to insure the continuation of the American system.

Perhaps the most interesting, and most visible, of such oaths was the "little red rider" which appeared as an amendment to a June, 1935 appropriations bill providing funds for the Washington, D.C. public schools. The amendment stated: "Hereafter no part of any appropriation for the public schools shall be available for the payment of the salary of any person teaching or advocating Communism."[11] The United States Controller-General interpreted this to mean that school employees could not discuss Communism either in or out of school. Before each payday, every teacher was required to sign a statement swearing that he had not violated this edict. The effect of this was the omission of any discussion or reading material dealing with Communism, or the history, geography and current events of the U.S.S.R., in Washington Public Schools.[13] Representative Thomas Blanton, author of the rider, went so far as to send a questionnaire to the teachers on June 11, 1936, asking if they believed in God, approved of the writings of George S. Counts or Charles H. Beard or were members of the N.E.A. and, if so, who had suggested such membership.[14] Reactions against such measures were swift and forceful. They came from both individuals and educational organizations. A concentrated effort against the law resulted in its repeal in May, 1937. The most effective arguments against the law focused on its debilitating effect on the development of effective, i.e., "critically intelligent," citizens.

It is interesting to note that the arguments both for and against loyalty oaths were not based on the need for individual freedom. The conservative who believed the radical posed the greatest threat to American Society wanted the school to produce students whose outlook corresponded to this world view.

---

[10]"Loyalists' Oaths," *Social Frontier*, vol. 2, No. 2, November, 1935, pp. 47-49.
See also Charles L. Bane, "Oaths for Teachers," *School and Society*, vol. 42, No. 1080, September 7, 1935, pp. 330-31.
Franklin W. Johnsen, "The Teacher's Oath," *School and Society*, vol. 43, No. 1121, June 20, 1936, pp. 832-35; and, "Teachers' Loyalty Oath," p. 25.
[11]Quoted in "The Little Red Rider," *School and Society*, vol. 43, No. 1111, April 11, 1936, p. 513.
[12]*Ibid.*, pp. 513-14.
[13]Caroline William, "Congress Legislates Character," *Social Frontier*, vol. 3, No. 22, January, 1937, pp. 107-110.
[14]Ellen Thomas, "Sequelae of the 'Red Rider'," *Progressive Education*, vol. 13, No. 8, December, 1936, pp. 606-608.

The liberals opposing the oaths based their rationale on the necessity of developing students whose world view saw the selfish business interest as the greatest threat. The rationale for increased teacher freedom was dominated by the desire to utilize this freedom to alleviate a social problem. A concern for the freedom of the individual teacher, apart from its social utility, did not constitute even a minor eddy in the main stream of the rhetoric.

The World War II Era saw a new threat and the development of a different complex of fears which then directed the academic freedom dialogue. This threat, represented by the Fascist dictators of Germany, Italy, and Japan, was both visible and foreign based. The Garden had been cleansed and now the crusade was sanctioned to protect democracy against totalitarianism. This crusade required a unified national effort. Groups and individuals who contributed toward that effort consequently were awarded increased esteem. Such groups included the American industrialists, women workers and veterans' organizations. Any tendency which seemed to weaken the drive for national unity, the war effort, or "democracy" was immediately suspect.

Within this context, the schools were assigned two somewhat conflicting roles: to extend and protect democracy and, to aid in the drive for national unity. Because these roles were somewhat contradictory, their impact on the function of the teacher was felt in contradictory ways. The need to protect democracy lent credence to the arguments for increased academic freedom, while the necessity for unity suggested restrictions.

The most interesting example of the effect of these fears on the academic dialogue concerned the development of the rationale for the exclusion of teachers from the profession because of their association with undesirable groups. In an important sense this rationale was similar to the dialogue of the depression era. The production of student attitudes conducive to effecting national unity became a primary objective of the schools. Educators now campaigned to purge teachers who might detract from that objective because of their associations with groups which displayed any tendency away from the norms of "Americanism." It is also interesting to note that this rationale developed during the war years by educators was not entirely dissimilar from the later rationale expounded by the professional patriots of the McCarthy Era.

The chairman of the N.E.A. Academic Freedom Committee, responding to the pressures of nationalism and fears of European war, declared, "the time has come when we should rethink and rewrite the statement of principles which was adopted in 1937."[15] The direction the rethinking and rewriting was going to take was accurately forecast when he continued:

> There is, we realize, always a danger that certain persons may hide under the cloak of academic freedom and disseminate propaganda in our public schools in

---

[15] William S. Taylor, "Academic Freedom," *NEA Addresses and Proceedings*, vol. 78, 1940, p. 879.

behalf of doctrines that will not bear public scrutiny. Occasionally one finds an individual who takes advantage of academic freedom in a subtle way in an effort to undermine the fundamentals of democratic government. The Committee must not and will not be a shield for Fifth Columnists in the United States of America![16]

The statement of principles drafted by William S. Taylor affected a significant closure on the concept of teacher's freedom in extra-school citizenship.[17] It cautioned teachers that intellectual integrity was indispensable to education and to qualify as teachers they must be certain that their associations would not prostitute their integrity. The Committee bluntly asserted: "Any suspicion, therefore, that the teacher is externally controlled or otherwise unduly influenced in reaching his opinions or in expressing them honestly must call into question his intellectual integrity and so work against the desired integrity in all whom he influences."[18] It is important that there was no discussion about how to determine whether a teacher was, in fact, "externally controlled." The statement simply said, "any suspicion." Not even a well-founded suspicion was required to "call into question his intellectual integrity." Significantly, the N.E.A. Committee on Academic Freedom did not find it necessary to even discuss the question of what kind of external control would in fact compromise one's "intellectual integrity."[19] Should, for example, a Baptist, or a Catholic, or a Republican, or a Communist have been disqualified as a teacher because each of them might in some way have been externally controlled? Or did this prohibition apply only to bad external control? If so, who would define 'bad'? The reflex expressed in 1941 by the N.E.A. Academic Freedom Committee was one which teachers would hear again at a later time. The 1941 N.E.A. National Convention adopted a resolution with reference to this question which was more precise than its Academic Freedom Committee. The resolution read: "The N.E.A. is opposed to the employment in any school, college or university, of any person who advocates or who is a member of any organization that advocates changing the form of government of the United States in any means not provided for under the federal constitution."[20] This resolution, while more precise than the Academic Freedom Committee's statement, nevertheless, made association, rather than acts, cause for summary condemnation and punishment.

The American Federation of Teachers under the direction of its President George S. Counts, took similar action in its 1941 Convention. After revoking the charters of three of its local unions, No. 5, No. 192, and No. 537, for Communist domination, the convention amended its constitution to exclude

---

[16]*Ibid.*, p. 879.
[17]"Principles of Academic Freedom," *NEA Journal*, vol. 30, No. 5, May, 1941, pp. 142-43.
[18]*Ibid.*, p. 142.
[19]It seems from the context in which the phrase "externally controlled" is used that it is meant to indicate control from outside one's own rational decision-making process as by some body of dogma or set of preconceptions which would short-circuit the process of inquiry. The context does not seem to indicate control from outside the country as by some foreign power. This lack of preciseness, however, which forces speculation from context, is part of the difficulty with the statement.
[20]Resolutions Committee, *NEA Addresses and Proceedings*, vol. 79, 1941, p. 906.

from membership an "applicant whose political actions are subject to totalitarian control such as Fascist, Nazi, or Communist."[21] The rationale offered by the A.F.T. paralleled that of the N.E.A. point for point and could be subjected to the same criticism as the rationale of the N.E.A. It is interesting during this time that such criticism was not voiced in the academic freedom dialogue.

What did appear was an attack on the Rapp-Coudert Committee. This committee was set up by the New York State Legislature in 1939 to examine state aid to education and investigate subversive activities in the schools. Oddly enough, the same 1941 American Federation of Teachers' Convention passed a resolution condemning the aims and methods of this committee. It charged that teachers should not be dismissed "until legitimate and specific charges for dismissal have been presented and substantiated in a fair public trial."[22]

Although a member of the 1941 N.E.A. Academic Freedom Committee, William H. Kilpatrick also challenged the activities of the Rapp-Coudert Committee.[23] He believed if it was indeed true that Communist teachers had rejected democratic standards of truth and honesty, then this rejection should be scored against their right to remain teachers. He argued, however, it was important to show that the individual teacher had actually subscribed to the alleged Communist tenets regarding truth and then show that this subscription had adversely affected his teaching. He said, "It is not hated ideas but wrong conduct which calls for penalty."[24] His arguments against guilt by association and his demands for proof of wrong actions represented, unfortunately, only a small minority view-point. Even Kilpatrick's lonely voice was raised only against legislative committees. Its impact was considerably diminished by the appendage of his name to the 1941 N.E.A. Academic Freedom Committee report.

Moreover, less than four months after his attack on the Rapp-Coudert Committee, Kilpatrick wrote an article defending the American Federation of Teachers' expulsion of the allegedly Communist dominated locals.[25] He argued that liberal democratic methods demanded free and open discussion as a means to apply intelligence to problematic situations in order to arrive at optimal solutions. The Communists, according to Kilpatrick, rejected open discussion and relied upon "obstructive and browbeating tactics so as seriously to hamper the legitimate deliberations."[26] When this happened, he believed

---

[21] "The Twenty-Fifth Annual Convention," *The American Teacher*, vol. 26, No. 1, October, 1941, p. 8.
[22] *Ibid.*, p. 23.
[23] "The Coudert Investigation," *Frontiers of Democracy*, vol. 7, No. 58, January 15, 1941, pp. 102-103.
[24] *Ibid.*, p. 103
[25] "Liberalism, Communist Tactics and Democratic Efficiency," *Frontiers of Democracy*, vol. 7, No. 60, March 15, 1941, pp. 167-68.
[26] *Ibid.*, p. 168.

"the bounds of toleration have been passed."[27] In effect Kilpatrick argued that the Communist locals should be denied entrance to the arena of open discussion because they had not abided by the ground rules and had sought to destroy the process to gain their own ends. This may have been a valid account of the activities of those locals. The difficulty, however, occurred as this analysis was generalized from this specific instance and Kilpatrick's argument used against all Communist teachers.

Such an argument was presented in 1942 by V. T. Thayer.[28] He believed it was time for liberals to rethink their traditional commitment to complete freedom of speech and of teaching. This commitment was based on the belief that in a completely free exchange of ideas man would use his reason to determine truth. Education was the agency, according to Thayer, charged with instructing future generations with this method, therefore, it must not attempt to inculcate dogmas or beliefs. Its commodity was method, not conclusions.

The teacher who was a Communist or a Fascist could not meet the qualifications Thayer set for membership in this agency. His first reason acknowledged its close allegiance with those who saw the teacher as an exemplar. He argued, "No conscientious teacher can ignore the fact that there is a relationship between his life outside school and his influence within the classroom."[29] Because his out-of-school behavior was to be an example for his students, it was obvious to Thayer that "conduct becoming a teacher cannot rightfully include membership in any group or party dedicated to a policy of undermining the essential structure of our government or our way of life."[30] Thayer apparently did not think it necessary to show the individual's compliance or involvement with the organization plans. Nor did he explain what he meant by "undermining our way of life."

Thayer's second reason for expelling Communists and Fascists from the teaching profession borrowed heavily from Kilpatrick's argument against the three Communist dominated A.F.T. locals. He contended that the Communist teachers violated the belief that the teacher should be free from dogma and restraint which would prohibit his arrival at undictated conclusions. The key assumption in Thayer's argument was the statement that "The Communist Party, and doubtless Fascist groups as well, secretly controls the activities of its members for purposes that can properly be termed subversive."[31] Armed with this assumption, which he considered a fact, Thayer believed that it was no longer necessary to demand proof of wrong action before the expulsion of a teacher from the profession. Proof of association with an undesirable group, i.e., membership in a Communist or Fascist Party, was accepted as sufficient cause for punishment.

---

[27] *Ibid.*, p. 168.
[28] "Should Communists and Fascists Teach in the Schools?" *Harvard Educational Review*, vol. 12, No. 1, January, 1942, pp. 7-19.
[29] *Ibid.*, p. 14.
[30] *Ibid.*, p. 16.
[31] *Ibid.*, p. 17.

Long before the red-baiting, Cold War Era, leading educators had developed the guilt by association arguments which they would again hear from men like Senator Joseph McCarthy and Congressman Richard Nixon. The rationale supporting this closure on academic freedom was based on what the teacher was supposed to do to the student — i.e., develop attitudes facilitating the intensification for national unity. It was necessary to expel those teachers whose associations indicated that they might be ineffective examples for the molding of effective citizens.

Several conditions obtaining in the Cold War Era produced a new fear. The increasing hostilities between the United States and the Soviet Union dashed the earlier hopes for world peace which had attended the end of World War II. A series of sensational espionage trials in the U.S., Canada, and Great Britain not only informed Americans that their international enemies had acquired the means to destroy American urban areas, but also that they had acquired this capacity through the conspiratorial efforts of faceless and silent traitors, some of whom were undoubtedly still lurking undetected. Thus, the awesome and constant fear of total annihilation was reinforced with the fear of internal conspiracy.

These fears were reflected in the definition of the role of the school. As in World War II, the school was to protect democracy against a totalitarian threat. The Communist threat, however, appeared more insidious in that it seemed to involve a significant internal conspiracy. The school had to do more than simply facilitate national unity. Its role now included the preparation of the sentinels of democracy. The teacher's function was to insulate the student from the evil effects of Communism and to outfit him for efficient service in the nation's struggle. One significant aspect of the academic freedom dialogue concerned the degree to which the teacher should be confined by this role.

An example of this was the demand that the teacher become an instrument of national policy and indoctrinate his students for patriotism and against Communism. The writers who supported this idea wanted education to be used as an instrument of social control and teachers to become agents for obtaining that control. The N.E.A. lent credence to this position when its Educational Policies Commission stated in a 1949 bulletin: "If the schools develop programs that contribute to the nation's needs in this time of crisis, and if they can convince the public that these contributions are useful, then education can command the support it will deserve as an instrument of national policy."[32] This statement suggests not only that education should attempt to become an instrument of national policy, but, that it will be less susceptible to attack and perhaps better financed if it does so.

When Massachusetts established the position of director of civic education in 1951, Henry W. Holmes, former Dean of Harvard's Graduate School of Education supported the creation by endorsing the statement subscribed to

---

[32]*American Education and International Tensions*, Washington, D. C. 1949, p. 35.

by the Massachusetts Association of School Superintendents. This statement called for the use of the school as an instrument of national policy. It listed several reasons for supporting the post. They included the following:

> *First,* the fight against Communism calls for all the weapons in the arsenal. If we neglect education, we are missing an opportunity so important that it may be impossible to make up, later, for what we fail to do now....
>
> *Third,* the Department of Education is the key place for a leader ... as we see it; *education for citizenship is a grass roots investment in national security; the schools are asking for help in meeting this great need; and the Massachusetts plan is to put an experienced leader in a key spot.*[33]

Similarly, William F. Russell, Dean of Teachers College, Columbia University asserted that the schools might be more secure if they could convince the public that they were aiding in the national defense. He said, "The basic reason for the attacks on the schools is that many people believe that the schools are not doing as much as they should for the national defense; or that what they are doing is hurting the national defense; or that doing something else might strengthen the national defense."[34] In a later article, Russell asserted that patriotic history could be one way of aiding national defense. He argued that an analysis of the post-war crisis "points to the supreme importance, in the better prosecution of the cold war, of bringing every American into close relationship with the glorious history of his country. When he knows it he will thrill to it. He will sense that he is a part of it. He will make the sacrifices."[35] This statement left little doubt about the kind of history and the kind of education the Dean of Teachers College supported.

Erling M. Hunt agreed that the social studies provided an effective avenue for developing right answers regarding the dangers of Communism.[36] Although he argued for a "full study of facts" and contended that "Americans are strong enough and smart enough to compare the theory and the realities of American democracy and Communism, and come out with the right answers," he still favored inoculation.[37] Hunt said, "So far as Communism is concerned, the schools are, I believe, basically responsible for inoculating young citizens against it. But the serum must be strong enough to be effective. I grant that there are risks in inoculation, but the risks of no inoculation are far greater."[38] Apparently Professor Hunt would support full and open study by American public school teachers and students only when there were guarantees that such study would lead to acceptable answers. This analysis is supported by his statement: "Perhaps we can safely admit that our democ-

---

[33]"Civil Education: Massachusetts Steps Ahead," *School and Society,* vol. 75, No. 1948, April 19, 1952, p. 242. Author's emphasis.

[34]"The Caravan Goes On," *Teachers College Record,* vol. 54, No. 1, October, 1952, p. 4.

[35]"Education and the Cold War," *Teachers College Record,* vol. 55, No. 3, December, 1953, p. 118.

[36]"Teaching the Contrasts Between American Democracy and Soviet Communism," *Teachers College Record,* vol. 55, No. 3, December, 1953, pp. 122-27.

[37]*Ibid.,* p. 123.

[38]*Ibid.,* p. 123.

racy has not yet achieved perfection . . . and yet have plenty of margin of attractiveness for our youth."[39] In a "full study of facts," it would seem that the admissability of a fact would be determined by its validity not by its effect on the conclusion the teacher wanted his students to reach.[40]

Although the belief that education should be an instrument of national security did not go unchallenged during the Cold War Era, its proponents were the most vociferous and occupied the most prestigious positions in the educational establishment.

Throughout this thirty year period the academic freedom dialogue was closely related to societal fears. Arguments for increased or decreased academic freedom rested on the function of the teacher. This function was determined by the purposes which society assigned to the schools. When one examines the history of American education and particularly its recent history, it becomes clear that most often those purposes have been in response to the fears and anxieties felt in American society. The idea of academic freedom for the public school teacher, then, has been shaped by what American society, in response to its fears, has decided that the teacher should do to the student to render him a more effective citizen.

---

[39] *Ibid.*, p. 125.
[40] Other writers who also argued that teachers should insure the acceptance by their students of those attitudes and beliefs most beneficial to the national security included: Louis William Norris, "The Teacher as Prophet," *School and Society*, vol. 71, No. 1831, January 21, 1950, pp. 36-39; and Philip H. Phenix, "Teacher Education and the Unity of Culture," *Teachers College Record*, vol. 60, No. 6, March, 1959, pp. 337-43.

Reprinted from <u>Educational Theory</u>, Volume 21, Number 1, Winter, 1971.

BILL OF RIGHTS OF THE AMERICAN FEDERATION OF TEACHERS

The teacher is entitled to a life of dignity equal to the high standard of service that is justly demanded of that profession. Therefore, we hold these truths to be self-evident:

(1)   Teachers have the right to think freely and to express themselves openly and without fear.

   This includes the right to hold views contrary to the majority.

(2)   They shall be entitled to the free exercise of their religion.

   No restraint shall be put upon them in the manner, time, or place of their worship.

(3)   They shall have the right to take part in social, civil, and political affairs.

   They shall have the right, outside of the classroom, to participate in political campaigns and to hold office.

   They may assemble peaceably and may petition any government agency, including their employers, for a redress of grievances.

   They shall have the same freedom in all things as other citizens.

(4)   The right of teachers to live in places of their own choosing, to be free of restraints in their mode of living, and the use of their leisure time shall not be abridged.

(5)   Teaching is a profession, the right to practice which is not subject to the surrender of other human rights.

   No man shall be deprived of professional status, or the right to practice it, or the practice thereof in any particular position, without due process of law.

(6)   The right of teachers to be secure in their jobs, free from political influence or public clamor, shall be established by law.

The right to teach, after qualification in the manner prescribed by law, is a property right, based upon the inalienable rights of life, liberty, and the pursuit of happiness.

(7)   In all cases affecting a teacher's employment or professional status, a full hearing by an impartial tribunal shall be afforded with the right to full judicial review.

No teacher shall be deprived of employment or professional status, but for specific causes established by law having a clear relation to the competence or qualification to teach provided by the weight of the evidence.

In all such cases the teacher shall enjoy the right to a speedy and public trial, to be informed of the nature and cause of the accusation, to be confronted with the accusing witnesses.

In supoena, witnesses and papers, and the assistance of counsel.

No teacher shall be called upon to answer any charge affecting his employment or professional status, but upon probable cause, supported by oath or affirmation.

(8)   It shall be the duty of the employer to provide culturally adequate salaries, security in illness, and adequate retirement income.

The teacher has the right to such a salary as will:

- a. afford a family standard of living comparable to that enjoyed by other professional people in the community,
- b. to make possible freely chosen professional study, and
- c. afford the opportunity for leisure and recreation common to our heritage.

(9)   No teacher shall be required under penalty of reduction of salary to pursue studies beyond those required to obtain professional status.

After serving a reasonable probationary period, a teacher shall be entitled to permanent tenure terminable only for just cause.

They shall be free as in other professions in the use of their own time.

They shall not be required to perform extracurricular work against their will or without added compensation.

(10)   To equip people for modern life requires the most advanced educational methods.

Therefore, the teacher is entitled to good classrooms, adequate teaching materials, teachable class size, and administrative protection and assistance in maintaining discipline.

(11)   These rights are based upon the proposition that the culture of a people can rise only as its teachers improve.

A teaching force accorded the highest possible professional dignity is the surest guarantee that blessings of liberty will be preserved.

Therefore, the possession of these rights impose the challenge to be worthy of their enjoyment.

(12)   Since teachers must be free in order to teach freedom, the right to be members of organizations of their own choosing must be guaranteed.

In all matters pertaining to their salaries and working conditions, they shall be entitled to bargain collectively through representatives of their own choosing.

They are entitled to have the school administered by superintendents, boards, or committees, which function in a democratic manner.

BILL OF TEACHER RIGHTS
NATIONAL EDUCATION ASSOCIATION

PREAMBLE

We, the teachers of the United States of America, aware that a free society is dependent upon the education afforded its citizens, affirm the right to freely pursue truth and knowledge.

As an individual, the teacher is entitled to such fundamental rights as dignity, privacy, and respect.

As a citizen, the teacher is entitled to such basic rights as freedom of religion, speech, assembly, association, and political action and equal protection of the law.

In order to develop and preserve respect for the worth and dignity of humankind, to provide a climate in which actions develop as a consequence of rational thought, and to insure intellectual freedom, we further affirm that teachers must be free to contribute fully to an educational environment which secures the freedom to teach and the freedom to learn.

Believing that **certain** rights of teachers derived from these fundamental freedoms must be universally recognized and respected, we proclaim this Bill of Teacher Rights.

ARTICLE ONE:
RIGHTS AS A PROFESSIONAL

As a member of the teaching profession, the individual teacher has the right:

Section 1. To be licensed under professional and ethical standards established, maintained, and enforced by the profession.

Section 2. To maintain and improve one's professional competence.

Section 3. To exercise professional judgment in presenting, interpreting, and criticizing information and ideas, including controversial issues.

Section 4. To influence effectively the formulation of policies and procedures which affect one's professional services, including curriculum, teaching materials, methods of instruction, and school-community relations.

Section 5. To exercise professional judgment in the use of teaching methods and materials appropriate to the needs, interests, capacities, and the linguistic and cultural background of each student.

Section 6. To safeguard information obtained in the course of professional service.

Section 7. To work in an atmosphere conducive to learning, including the use of reasonable means to preserve the learning environment and to protect the health and safety of students, oneself, and others.

Section 8. To express publicly views on matters affecting education.

Section 9. To attend and address a governing body and be afforded access to its minutes when official action may affect one's professional concerns.

A R T I C L E   T W O:
R I G H T S   A S   A N   E M P L O Y E E

As an employee, the individual teacher has the right:

Section 1. To seek and be fairly considered for any position commensurate with one's qualifications.

Section 2. To retain employment following entrance into the profession in the absence of a showing of just cause for dismissal or nonrenewal through fair and impartial proceedings.

Section 3. To be fully informed, in writing, of rules, regulations, terms, and conditions affecting one's employment.

Section 4. To have conditions of employment in which health, security, and property are adequately protected.

Section 5. To influence effectively the development and application of evaluation procedures.

Section 6. To have access to written evaluations, to have documents placed in one's personnel file to rebut derogatory information, and to have removed false or unfair material through a clearly defined process.

Section 7. To be free from arbitrary, capricious, or discriminatory actions affecting the terms and conditions of one's employment.

Section 8. To be advised promptly in writing of the specific reasons for any actions which might affect one's employment.

Section 9. To be afforded due process through the fair and impartial hearing of grievances, including binding arbitration as a means of resolving disputes.

Section 10. To be free from interference to form, join, or assist employee organizations, to negotiate collectively through representatives of one's own choosing, and to engage in other concerted activities for the purpose of professional negotiations or other mutual aid or protection.

Section 11. To withdraw services collectively when reasonable procedures to resolve impasse have been exhausted.

ARTICLE THREE:
RIGHTS AS AN ORGANIZATION

As an individual member of an employee organization, the teacher has the right:

Section 1. To acquire membership in employee organizations based upon reasonable standards equally applied.

Section 2. To have equal opportunity to participate freely in the affairs and governance of the organization.

Section 3. To have freedom of expression, both within and outside the organization.

Section 4. To vote for organization officers, either directly or through delegate bodies, in fair elections.

Section 5. To stand for and hold office subject only to fair qualifications uniformly applied.

Section 6. To be fairly represented by the organization in all matters.

Section 7. To be provided periodic reports of the affairs and conduct of business of the organization.

Section 8. To be provided detailed and accurate financial records, audited and reported at least annually.

Section 9. To be free from arbitrary disciplinary action or threat of such action by the organization.

Section 10. To be afforded due process by the organization in a disciplinary action.

SEMESTER: WEEK FOURTEEN

REQUIRED READINGS

Church

Part V: Redefining Commonality, 1940-1975, Chapter 13: <u>The Reaction Against Progressivism, 1941-1960</u> (30 pp.)

Dye

Goetz, William W. "The Schools and Their Critics: An Angry Comment From Within the System" <u>Phi Delta Kappan</u>. December, 1974. (04 pp.)

Gowin, D. Bob. "The Structure of Knowledge" <u>Educational Theory</u>. V.20, No.4, Fall, 1970. (10 pp.)

National Education Association. "Code of Ethics of the Education Profession" 1976. (03 pp.)

MEETINGS

Monday

Lecture: James Bryant Conant and the American High School

Tuesday

Lecture: Ethics for the Education Profession

Wednesday

Lecture: The Structure of the Disciplines Movement

Thursday and Friday

Small Groups: Initial Field Experience Essay is due.

CHURCH TEXTBOOK STUDY GUIDE: CHAPTER 13

THE REACTION AGAINST PROGRESSIVISM, 1941-1960

1. life adjustment movement
2. NEA Educational Policies Commission
3. U.S. Office of Education
4. USOE's Commission on Life Adjustment Education for Youth(1945)
5. Charles A. Prosser
6. marginal
7. criticism of American public education
8. back to the basics theme
9. Council on Basic Education. CBE
10. professional education establishment
11. teacher training
12. teacher certification
13. humanistic goals
14. Arthur Bestor
15. Mortimer Smith
16. efficiency goals
17. James Bryant Conant
18. Admiral Hyman Rickover
19. identification of the intellectual elite
20. goal of political and technological leadership
21. intellectual meritocracy
22. put efficiency back into education
23. intensified school guidance system
24. school curriculum revision
25. mastery of the disciplines
26. disciplinary methods
27. inquiry method
28. teacher proof curriculum
29. role of the federal government in the financing of American public education
30. National Science Foundation, NSF

31. <u>National Defense Education Act</u>, NDEA
32. cognitive psychology
33. Jerome Bruner
34. <u>The Process of Education</u>(1960)
35. baby boom of the 1950's and the 1960's
36. conformist
37. organization man
38. other-directed
39. intellectual merit becomes the central criterion of success
40. suburbanites
41. educational change
42. implementation

William W. Goetz

THE SCHOOLS AND THEIR CRITICS: AN ANGRY COMMENT FROM WITHIN THE SYSTEM

A classroom teacher calls for professional educators to take up the challenge to a "great debate" in public education. So far the "nasty critics" have won by default.

Four years ago Charles E. Silberman's *Crisis in the Classroom* appeared amidst rather extraordinary fanfare. *The New York Times* predicted the beginning of a "great debate" on public education in the United States. Since the publication of the Silberman report, I find that the "great debate" has consisted of reviews breathlessly endorsing the report's main arguments, a spate of articles in popular magazines lamenting the sad shape of American public education, and the National Education Association's embracing the report with baffling warmth. On the college and university level, teachers who have made careers of educating teachers are suddenly discovering that the contributions of public schools have been exaggerated. I would like to suggest that there has been no "great debate" since the appearance of *Crisis in the Classroom;* that, instead, there has been a relentless and patently uncritical attack on all public education.

At the inception of this assault I welcomed, as a social studies teacher, outside criticism from social scientists whom I had long admired. But the vehemence and unreasonableness of the criticism and the absence of an effective counterattack has prompted me to express an admittedly angry — but I hope critical — comment on the content and style of this criticism.

An appropriate starting point might be *Crisis in the Classroom*. First, I would suggest that it is, among other things, a remarkable synthesis of much that has occurred in American education since 1960. It could serve as a

WILLIAM W. GOETZ *is social studies coordinator of the New Providence (N.J.) Public Schools.*

history of American education for that period, providing an apt sequel to Lawrence Cremin's *The Transformation of the School*. There is, moreover, a critical balance in the report that has gone unnoticed. American schools have failed in many respects, but their successes and accomplishments are dutifully recorded; the English primary schools are seemingly superior to ours, but there are as yet no hard data to support this contention. Finally, there is a chapter on teacher education that is astonishingly incisive and accurate.

Yet, for such a serious study, *Crisis in the Classroom* is extraordinarily impressionistic and derivative. In addition to heavy reliance upon *The New York Times Magazine,* one finds introductions to college anthologies, a letter from a teacher to her former dean, and the author's own intellectual metamorphosis creeping into the data. The primary data seem to be many observations of the schools and what the schools reported, but nowhere is there any indication of how the data were sifted and organized. Many of the observations appear as an "item" to illustrate a generality, but there is no indication of how the generalities were produced.

I make the above observations with some uneasiness, considering the array of authorities amassed in the introduction, and of course I assume there was rigorous analysis that did not appear in the final draft. Yet it was reassuring to note that George R. LaNoue makes the same observation ("The Politics of Education," *Teachers College Record*, December, 1971) when dealing with school critics. He notes that such critics have not taken the failure of the schools "seriously in quantitative terms" and points out the dearth of conceptual models with which to evaluate efficiently the quality of schools. I do not intend to be pedantic about methods of quantification, a field in which I am obviously not an expert, but I think there is ample evidence to suggest that the critics have granted themselves inordinately wide latitude in producing generalizations about what is going on in schools. And what may be more significant, no one seems anxious to challenge this arrogance.

The Silberman report, unlike more radical works, does not advocate dismantling the system but would reform the present one, drawing largely on the experience of the English primary system. The most conspicuous recommendation is the use of the "open classroom" or "informal education" concept, which features greater freedom for children to set their own goals and select their own activities. As an experienced teacher, I have no quarrel with this recommendation. It may indeed be an idea whose time has come in American education. I applaud the attempts of districts and teachers who have initiated such programs. It could be the crowning achievement of the report to have popularized this concept for the American public.

Still, there is an idyllic tone that runs through the chapter on the open classroom (children kissing the bald pates of principals) that makes me just a little skeptical. Given many positive factors such as energetic, competent teachers and supervisors, well-organized curricula and activities — open classroom strategies require much more intensive and sophisticated preparation — and appropriate physical facilities, the concept may work very well for many students unable to relate to more traditional schooling. I have seen what I consider to be open classrooms in action, and I have been reasonably well impressed by the progress that is being made.

At the same time, I have observed experiments in "informal education" that have bombed out egregiously. At meetings and conventions I am beginning to pick up rumblings that all is not well in districts where open classroom techniques have been adopted. I am not anxious to see this concept fail; I realize the need for different situations in which more people can learn better. I do question whether open classrooms are the universal panacea for elementary and secondary education; I do wonder if infatuation with the concept will not distract many from less exotic instructional problems such as curriculum construction and the development of diverse types of teaching strategies and models; and I do object to its being used as a handy shibboleth to prove (before its merits have been verified) how "bad" and "oppressive" the present system is.

Another theme stressed by the Silberman report, and a recurring dirge of many other school critics, is the schools' obsession with rules and control. Silberman comments:

> These petty rules and regulations are necessary not simply because of the importance schoolmen attach to control — they like to exercise control, it would seem, over what comes out of the bladder as well as the mouth — but also because schools and school systems operate on the assumption of distrust.

A very cute statement and one I would like to examine more closely.

Of course schools and schoolmen are concerned over rules and regulations; of course there are many of us who still administer these rules with the finesse of a steam locomotive. But I have a feeling that schools are going to be social organizations for some time, demanding some types of social control. Hall passes and lavatory passes may seem petty and are easily caricatured (especially by those without any responsibility for the social control), but they represent an attempt to deal with hundreds of youngsters of different types and backgrounds interacting with each other and the institutional structure in rather limited space. Is it advisable to tell these students, "Rules reflect distrust. I trust you; therefore, no more rules"? Some students do find rules petty and a source of resentment. Other students find in them a source of security and direction and will admit quite candidly that they need them. I suspect that the rules bother critics of the schools far more than they do the rank and file of secondary students. What bothers students is when the rules are administered unfairly or inconsistently, changed constantly, or ignored by those responsible for their enforcement.

Another aspect of the school debate deserving attention is the constant if ambiguous theme that schools should concern themselves more with moral questions, with fundamental questions of right and wrong, with the quality of life, or with "values." The Silberman report supports this theme; it raises questions that have received scant attention.

One of the questions can be put quite simply: Whose "morality" and whose "quality of life" should be promoted? My impression is that those most anxious about values are individuals and interest groups with a rather definite conception of the values they want youngsters to learn. But how is pluralism protected if public education moves toward specifying moral and value goals? Weren't parochial schools criticized just a short time ago as a divisive influence in American society? If alternative schools are set up, say, under a voucher system, would each school have its own morality and lifestyle?

Edgar Z. Friedenberg has written an engaging and provocative analysis of high school students in *Coming of Age in America*. It is an exceptionally popular book, widely cited in the best journals, placed on the reading lists of foundations courses in schools of education. Despite the sociological framework established in the book, Friedenberg makes it quite clear that he brings "feelings" and "prior judgments" to his study.

These feelings revolve around the "vulgar-minded middle class" that mans the schools and the role it plays in producing students who are essentially anti-intellectual, devoid of self-knowledge, and lacking in concern for human dignity. Friedenberg would resolve this problem by establishing academic and residential schools manned by the upper classes. It is clear that Friedenberg has a certain set of values in mind when he speaks of "self-knowledge" and "human dignity." But few, it seems to me, have asked the questions: From whence has Friedenberg drawn his values? How valid and viable are these values?

Here I would like to engage in a little sociological prying myself, with the aid of David Riesman. (I am indebted to the Silberman report for calling this to my attention.) Riesman comments on the "aristocratic insouciance" that many school critics display when dealing with teachers and schools. Is "aristocratic insouciance" part of the explanation for the considerable interest in values displayed by academic critics? (You know, really *you* should be like *us*.) Does it help explain the personal, sometimes emotional, style of critics when dealing with schools? Does it explain why "values" can be presented with the arrogance and self-assurance of an absolutist ontology and encounter such weak resistance?

Thus far I have suggested that the sweeping indictment of the schools has escaped vigorous criticism. At this point, legitimate questions may be posed: Are not schools "bad"? Have they not "failed"? Is there not a school "crisis"? Is there nothing more to the criticism than the words of a few cantankerous writers?

My answer is yes, there is certainly more to be considered — much more, as a matter of fact — than the literary efforts of a few intellectuals. But, although it sounds terribly defensive and small (which could be the reason it is rarely stated), I do not want to minimize the role of critics and their followers in the debate. They have set the tone for debate; their rhetoric prevails; we fight on their conceptual battleground. It is the critics who have sensed the rhythm of the nation's intellectual life and who use it to their advantage. By design or otherwise, they set norms and expectations for others in academic circles. (Aristocratic insouciance again?) Many critics, I suspect, may be embarrassed by this acceptance based on faddishness. But it is a phenomenon which must be taken into consideration if the "debate" is to be analyzed fully.

Let us now deal with the badness and failures of the schools. Consider the statement of the late Columbia University historian, Richard Hofstadter, in *Anti-Intellectualism in American Life*, that there is a "general acceptance" of the fact that schools have been an "educational failure" and a "constant disappointment." Hofstadter came to this conclusion after reviewing the literature of criticism from the nation's colonial beginnings through the school reforms of the late nineteenth century to the school crisis following Sputnik.

But in accepting Hofstadter's statement, I would also like to accept his broad historical framework as a springboard for further analysis. Unlike many contemporary critics, who wrench the concepts of "the schools," "schoolmen," and "the system" out of any meaningful historical context, Hofstadter saw the failure as part of the total social and intellectual climate of the nation's history. Given the anti-intellectual tradition of American life, Hofstadter argued that schoolteachers from colonial times would be accorded low salaries and status and that the teaching profession consequently would acquire an image as a haven for the shiftless, the mediocre, and even the eccentric. Schools have failed historically to attract the exceptionally ambitious and the exceptionally competent, Hofstadter suggested, creating a self-perpetuating system of a less than first-class corps of professional educators.

This image continues to haunt development of the teaching profession, despite the progress made in recent years. Many outstanding young teachers leave the classroom for administrative positions, doctoral studies, or more "challenging" vocations. Classroom teaching is still not viewed as a prestigious *final* career-goal. (But a pleasant haven in times of economic distress? Yes.) Despite the tons of rhetoric, a system for identifying and rewarding an excellent classroom teacher has not yet been produced. The ideal of a self-correcting, self-improving profession does not come easily to teaching.

But where does one place "blame" for a phenomenon so deeply rooted in the history and culture of society? (As Hofstadter concluded: "The country could not or would not make the massive effort necessary to supply highly trained teachers for this attempt to educate everybody.") Perhaps it is enough to recognize the historical reality and its implications, to be thankful for recent improvements, and to work for additional progress.

Hofstadter was predictably critical of the turn-of-the-century school reforms associated with progressive education, which he treated under the label of "life adjustment." Even here, however, he has a message for those who would like to gain insight into a controversy overrun with rhetorical exuberance and moral fervor. Witness this statement:

> There is an element of moral overstrain and a curious lack of humor among American educationists which will always remain a mystery to those more worldly minds that are locked out of their mental universe. The more humdrum the task the educationists have to undertake, the nobler and more exalted their music grows. When they see a chance to introduce a new course in family living or home economics, they begin to tune the fiddles of their idealism. When they feel they are about to establish the school janitor's right to be treated with respect, they grow starry-eyed and increase their tempo. And when they are trying to assure that the location of the school toilets will be so clearly marked that the dullest child can find them, they grow dizzy with exaltation and launch into wild cadenzas about democracy and self-realization.

Lest one consider the above a historical aberration or collection of clever phrases, I point to the ponderous statements of state education committees, the philosophies of school districts, and even the introductions to courses of study within the schools. In this the silly season of educational criticism, it is well to recall that there have been many silly seasons of educational bombast about what the schools should and could do – a process which, I suggest, has snared the schools in their own rhetoric and made them vulnerable to attack from both the educational and political communities. The lesson should be clear: Institutions that claim they can do almost everything should not be surprised if they are accused of "failing" to do anything.

Despite his overall conclusion regarding the failure of American schools, Hofstadter was too astute a historian and too nuanced a thinker to neglect their obvious achievements or "successes." He commended the common school for forging "a vast and heterogeneous and mobile population" into a nation and for providing "at least the minimum civil competence" essential to the operations of republican institutions. Despite his academic bias, he agreed with Lawrence Cremin that the progressive or life adjustment program, while it did encourage much nonsense in the classroom, made positive contributions in many areas.

> Whatever may be said about the qualitative performance of the American high school, which varies widely from place to place, no one is to deny that the secondary education of youth was a signal accomplishment in the history of education, a remarkable token of our desire to make schooling an instrument of mass opportunity and social mobility.

How quickly we seem to have forgotten the educational "crisis" created by Sputnik – Admiral Rickover lamenting the level of high school math and science, Arthur Bestor talking of "educational wastelands," the Rockefeller Report calling for excellence in education, Silberman calling for masses of intellectuals, federal money to support university-based curriculum projects, honors courses and advanced placement fever in our high schools. But the frantic drive in this direction was abortive. Toward the end of the sixties a new wave of criticism appeared, proclaiming that the academic reforms had failed or were not meeting existing needs and that the schools had better look elsewhere to justify their existence.

It is understandable that social critics and schools under pressure of social disorganization would move away from preoccupation with academic programs primarily designed to prepare students for college. But it is another thing to write off the curriculum efforts as "failures," or to ignore their accomplishments, or to engage in polemics about the "inhumanity" of the entire endeavor. I suggest that the accomplishments and even the failures of these reform efforts deserve closer study. La Noue observes: "College Board scores show that the public schools in the sixties *did accomplish their post-Sputnik mandate* of producing students with higher mathematical, scientific, and technological skills." (The italics are mine, to suggest yet another "success" for American schools.) He then places the school debate in a broader context:

> ... the debate has been dominated by the educational romantics whose rhetoric fits the current intellectual mood of condemning all American institutions, the Presidency, the Congress, the judi-

ciary, state and local governments, the military, medicine, business, universities, etc., etc., as failures. Such an undiscriminating mood may be personally cathartic, and many of us indulge in it at times, but no rational public policy can be based on it. Both the achievements and problems of public education should be recognized.

After working closely with the curriculum reforms for close to a decade, I can report that these reforms have produced both achievements and problems. I recall the cry in the middle sixties for a "new" social studies to follow the "new" math and "new" science. I remember the frenzied articles in our professional literature castigating traditional social studies and heralding the university projects as the savior of the field. Then the interminable debates over semantics come to mind. (What does Bruner mean by "structure"? What's a "concept"?) Finally, new materials were made available. Some are outstanding, some mediocre, some miss the mark completely. Some teachers thrive on them, some use them moderately, some ignore them. Some students love them, some tolerate them, some despise them. Slowly, we all began to realize how really complicated the teaching process is — a process not to be simplified by catchy phrases, publishers' blurbs, or administrators looking for instant success.

Despite the difficulties that must still be worked out, there is a verve and urgency in teaching that was not present in the fifties. Many teachers are able to work with concepts such as "organic curriculum," "inquiry teaching," and even "modulating the cognitional activity." As I have already suggested, it has not been idyllic. There is still a long, hard road ahead to create learning environments where more of our young people can learn better. It would be tragic if the present debate were to distract us from the curriculum reforms started in the sixties. Bruce Joyce of Teachers College, Columbia, noted the challenge in his introduction to *Models of Teaching*, stating that, "despite the fearsome troubles besetting education, there presently exists a really delightful and vigorous array of approaches to schooling which can be used to transform the world of childhood if only we will employ them."

But perhaps the most biting criticism

> "Despite their nastiness, the school critics have the talent and wit to offer keen insights into the teaching process and the total school environment. And, for all their arrogance, they possess the energy and charisma to touch many of us within the system."

comes from those students who see the school as a "drag," "oppressive," and "boring." This phenomenon is exceedingly intricate and has no easy solution. There are indeed students who are bored for one reason or another with school and who are achieving very little academically. If there is one positive effect of the type of criticism I am counter-criticizing, it is the unique and dramatic way it has portrayed the plight of this type of student.

It should be remembered, however, that many of today's youth grew up very fast in an electronic age; to them, the pacing and atmosphere of most schools seem like a kindergarten existence. Still, there are many who are reasonably content and who make adequate and sometimes outstanding academic and social progress. There are still others who have induced a kind of boredom in themselves and others by constantly talking of "boredom." (Recently I heard a girl remark that she was bored with the talk of boredom.) Unfortunately, the critics, despite the incisiveness of some of their remarks, have given this boredom their blessing, though it is hardly representative of the complex reality of today's students.

How complex this reality is can be appreciated to some extent by examining the results of attempts to end boredom. I have observed some situations where students granted more freedom to study what interests them have grown even more bored with school. (What happens when a student given the privilege to study that which interests him or her decides that he or she is interested in nothing?) I have observed situations where overempathetic teachers caused bored students to become even more bored with the empathetic teacher. I have observed situations where rules have been modified to help students relax but, instead, the at-

mosphere has become more tense and the students more disgruntled. Of course I have also witnessed individual teachers working with groups of students (many of whom are "dropouts" in other classes), ignoring the rules, and working personal and pedagogical wonders. I have heard of students praising the accomplishments of free school or alternative school experiments. But my main point is that these situations are difficult to analyze; and to draw any meaningful generalizations is as yet a terribly hazardous task. I am convinced that the answer does not lie in peremptorily discarding in word or in fact the existing system of rules and curricula. There is still much to be learned about how the schools, students, and curricula interact.

In a *New Republic* article ("Our Public School Monopoly," September 15, 1973), S. Francis Overlan noted, after some study of public opinion samplings, that most citizens still view the public schools and their curricula as "fine." Obviously I do not find this surprising; but I do not feel like gloating. Could it be that while we are engaged in a tireless and unproductive debate, the taxpayers' revolt and an aloof national administration may do us all in? And this is happening when there seems to be evidence of real progress in the areas of curriculum and pedagogy, when schools are beginning to take education seriously and are developing belatedly a code of professionalism, when more progress can be made with additional study, research, and experimentation. But to accomplish what I think can be accomplished requires a prodigious expenditure of resources, energy, expertise, and commitment. We need help; we even need our critics on our side.

Despite their nastiness, the school critics have the talent and wit to offer keen insights into the teaching process and the total school environment. And, for all their arrogance, they possess the energy and charisma to touch many of us within the system. They could, indeed, touch more if they were to accept the schools, the staff, and the students as they are and not as they wish they would be. Let me make an offer: We will accept them with their nastiness if they will accept us with our inefficiencies. Perhaps then we would have the end of fruitless debate and the beginning of a real one. ☐

The Structure of Knowledge[1]

BY D. BOB GOWIN

ONE OF THE UNWELCOME HARVESTS OF AN INSUFFICIENTLY UNDERSTOOD EDUCATIONAL PRAGMATISM WAS A LACK OF CONCERN WITH *WHAT* IS TAUGHT. Yet there is certainly nothing inherent in philosophical pragmatism that prevents subject matter analysis. Dewey, for example, thought that educative experiences should lead out into an expanding world of subject matter, a progression into a logical ordering of facts, concepts and generalizations. Dewey thought the teacher should have a mastery and command of his subject, highly organized and structured, *so that* the teacher could pay careful attention to the interests and points of view of the pupils. This mastery would permit the teacher the flexibility to enter into the subject at any of a large number of points of pupil interest. The point of Dewey's pedagogical prescription of progressiveness is to grow *from* these initial interests *through* the educative episodes *into* a world of warranted knowledge claims. Unless the teacher knows his subject he will be unable to judge when pupils have arrived there. Somehow the doctrine got perverted. A teacher did not have to know any subject matter as long as he was competent enough in psychological and social processes to facilitate pupil activities of whatever sort. However good this concept of teaching as facilitating learning might be for a number of human concerns—socialization, emotional health, functional autonomy—if the concern with knowledge claims is missing, something central to education is lost. Dewey, I believe, presupposed that teachers would know their subject; that he did not have to worry about. He was concerned with what they did with it in teaching.[2]

D. BOB GOWIN *is a Professor of Educational Foundations and Chairman of the Division of History, Philosophy, and Sociology of Education in the Department of Education at Cornell University, Ithaca, New York. He served as President of the Philosophy of Education Society for 1969-70.*

---

[1] Presidential Address at the Twenty-sixth Annual Meeting of the Philosophy of Education Society; March 21, 1970; Sheraton-Biltmore Hotel; Atlanta, Georgia. Part of the work of this paper was done while the author was supported by a postdoctoral fellowship from the U.S. Office of Education.

[2] Representative statements from Dewey may be cited:

". . . the significance of a knowledge of subject matter, going far beyond the present knowledge of pupils, is to supply definite standards and to reveal to him (the instructor) the possibilities of the crude activities of the immature."

John Dewey, *Democracy and Education* (New York: The Macmillan Co., 1916), p. 214.

"When engaged in the direct act of teaching, the instructor needs to have subject matter at his fingers' ends; his attention should be upon the attitude and response of the pupil." *Ibid.*, p. 215.

(Footnote continued)

Recently, under a classic slogan system[3] featuring "the structure of knowledge," concern with the variable of "what is thought" has emerged dramatically. A benchmark book, *The Process of Education*,[4] was put together by Jerome Bruner from the papers and discussions of some thirty-five scientists, scholars and educators who met at Woods Hole in September, 1959. By 1962 more than one hundred national projects attempting curricular revision were underway.[5]

The pattern for these revisions is roughly as follows: A group of scholars is convened to sort through and select the significant concepts in their field. Writers, sometimes including teachers in these subjects, are hired to prepare these materials. Tryouts are held in selected schools and classes. Revisions are completed and the materials published in some form. Whatever emerges from this process is the new curriculum. Sometimes, as in math, several such working groups are convened, and alternative sets of materials are prepared. A basic assumption of this approach is this: When it comes to analyzing what is to be taught, no one is better qualified than the scholar in the discipline. It is the scholar who must tell us what is known, and as a consequence, what is to be taught. This assumption is plausible, but it is a half-truth. The scholar in a field is rarely the most likely candidate to provide us with knowledge about knowledge. He is willing to say what he knows, but not to talk *about* it. His very expertness in establishing specialized knowledge claims prevents him from developing a second-order knowledge which is about these first order claims.[6] This second-order knowledge has been called knowledge about knowledge by B. O. Smith.[7]

Neither the doctrine according to Saint John nor Saint Jerome is adequate and for the same reason. Both approaches to the process of education fail to supply teachers with a systematic method for the analysis of the knowledge claims in their special area. Dewey's concern with the method of inquiry re-

---

". . . simple scholarship is not enough. In fact, there are certain features of scholarship or mastered subject matter — taken by itself — which get in the way of effective teaching *unless* the instructor's habitual attitude is one of concern with its interplay in the pupil's own experience." *Idem.*

"The problem of teaching is to keep the experience of the student moving in the direction of what the expert already knows. Hence the need that the teacher know both subject matter and the characteristic needs and capacities of the student." *Ibid.*, p. 216.

3B. Paul Komisar and James E. McClellan, "The Logic of Slogans" in B. O. Smith and R. H. Ennis, editors, *Language and Concepts in Education* (Chicago: Rand McNally Co., 1961) Ch. 13.

4Jerome Bruner, *The Process of Education* (New York: Vintage Books, 1960). See especially Ch. 2 for the discussion of the importance of structure.

5William T. Lowe, *Structure and the Social Studies* (Ithaca: Cornell University Press, 1969).

6My discussion of this point is documented in a monograph now out of print. D. B. Gowin and Cynthia Richardson, *Five Fields and Teacher Education* (Ithaca: Project One Publications, 1965), Ch. 6.

7B. O. Smith (and others), *Teachers for the Real World* (Washington, D.C.: American Association of Colleges for Teacher Education, 1968), Ch. 9 and 10 especially.

sults in a formula *for* inquiry; it does not present a method for the recovery of meaning from the completed results of inquiry. Bruner, and the others who labored to deal with the structure of knowledge (Bruner wrote of the "fundamental ideas of a field"), expected the scholar to identify this structure; once identified, it was simply to be learned by teachers as such and taught in ways which assumed its correct centrality in the discipline. Teachers must of course learn much from the scholars in their special areas; the question is: How are teachers to comprehend knowledge claims for pedagogical purposes? The place of this analysis is the interface between the teacher and his subject matter.

The point of this paper is to present, largely without supporting argument, one method that teachers can use to unpack the knowledge claims in their special field. A good test of the method is its use; and its expression through a well-worked example would help to clarify the issues. Two recent publications contain my examples: "The Far Side of Paradigms,"[8] which is a paper in English education; and an opening essay in the December, 1969, issue of the *Review of Educational Research* on research methodology, with references to the variety of research fields in education.

Part II

Knowing is literally something man does. Knowledge claims are something man makes. The making and doing aspect of knowledge leads us to think of it in the category of the productive (rather than the theoretic as is usual). The first and simplest question we can ask of the structure of knowledge in any field is this: What are the typical products? And: What characteristic form do these products take? And: What performances are required in the acts of production?

Five additional topics are related to this one. It is a matter of preference which topic is to be considered next. Because most academic products consist of intellectual matters, we can ask: What key concepts and conceptual systems are produced by the field? Or, more loosely, we can ask: What are the generative ideas? The telling questions? The intellectual frameworks? The theories?

Concern with concepts, key questions, basic ideas, and the like, composes Topic Two. Topic Three concerns methods and techniques of work—the many ways of answering key questions. Studies of method, i.e., methodology, are also found in this topic. Topic Four moves us toward metaphysical questions. Inquiry is *about* something; knowledge is *of* something. The term often used to identify this topic is 'nature,' but I prefer the somewhat more neutral term, 'universe.' Questions arise concerning the background scene and the foreground phenomena of interest, the context of inquiry, and the portion of nature and experience illuminated by the knowledge claims of any work.

---

[8] D. B. Gowin, "The Far Side of Paradigms: Conditions for Knowledge Making in English Education," *The English Record* (October, 1969), pp. 7-22.

The fifth topic concerns the agent, the human doer, the audience, or stated in another way, the psycho-social setting of inquiry. Familiar questions arise about the roles of the individual researcher and the community of workers in establishing knowledge claims.

The sixth topic concerns values. What is knowledge good for? Is it good in itself? All the kinds of values, when identified, generate questions for this topic. Does the set of knowledge claims have value that is: commercial, moral, aesthetic, pedagogical, political, religious, social? Since values are created at every phase of disciplined inquiry, the value topic is both a separate topic and one which is found in the other topics as well.

These six topics constitute the framework for the claim that the structure of knowledge in any field may be characterized by its telling questions, key concepts and conceptual systems; by its reliable and relevant methods of work; by its central and common products; by its internal and external values; by its agent and audience; and by the phenomena the field deals with and the occasions which give rise to the quest for knowledge.

Part III

Products

I begin with products. Usually I ask students as teachers-to-be to decide what field of knowledge they know the most about (or are most interested in) and to select from that field two or three exemplary works. They may bring a reprint of a paper someone has judged to be a classic in the field. I ask the students to locate the knowledge claims in the work. Next comes a task of identification and classification of a whole variety of knowledge elements. These elements include facts, concepts, generalizations, explanations, theories, predictions, interpretations, value judgments, justifications, definitions, constructs, models, metaphors, and so on. Each of these knowledge elements is philosophically controversial; I have found in the process of analyzing specific works that philosophical distinctions seemingly necessary for the solution of a philosophical issue may actually be more misleading than illuminating because of the shift of intellectual context.[9]

In some fields, like history and literature, questions arise concerning literary style and form and the deliberate use of a given style to contribute to the meaning of the content. The analysis of the form-content interaction is often very fruitful. Another fruitful way to look at products of a field is to think of them as *productions*. The production of a dramatic play, a poetic reading, a surgical operation, and an experimental crop of vegetables are examples of performances expressing knowledge claims. In addition, the products of a field sometimes have a tangible or material mode. In history the term 'document' is often used to refer to the collection of things: diaries,

---

[9] D. B. Gowin, "Generalization and History," reprinted in R. Guttchen and B. Bandman, editors, *Philosophical Essays on Curriculum* (Philadelphia: J. B. Lippincott Co. 1969), pp. 265-78.

letters, coins, photographs, ledgers, tools, cavedrawings, artifacts and so on. Some works contain products which are new statements of the problematic; new questions, uncertainties, puzzles, and stimulating speculations can be said to be products of inquiry. They are knowledge claims only in the sense that the author asserts that he knows there is something he does not know.

Concepts

The next helpful question to ask is: What is the telling question in this work? The recovery of the basic question may require the student to make inferences from the work itself or to go beyond it to other material in his field of study. It is surprising how often telling questions are not explicit in a work.

It is seemingly impossible to ask truly telling questions about phenomena of interest without some set of fairly clear concepts. In Schwab's view the conceptual system initiates and guides the inquiry. A study may begin in virtual ignorance (Why undertake it unless there is something to be found out?), but "ignorance cannot originate an enquiry."[10] The conceptions which guide inquiry constitute for Schwab the substantive structure of a discipline.

Specific questions we can ask about the concepts in a study include the following:

What are the key concepts and how are they related to each other?

What are the undefined or primitive terms?

How does the conceptual framework organize the field for inquiry in the data that are selected? In the treatment of the data? In the interpretation of the data?

What is the relationship between the conceptual framework and the principle of verification? And the form of explanation?

What is the relationship between concepts and facts?

I now wish to give a very brief example of the sort of extension of meaning apparently required if we are to develop this method. I choose 'concept' and 'fact' as my examples. Other examples could have been chosen: 'theory,' 'assumption,' 'explanation.'

No single agreed-upon meaning for the terms 'concept' and 'fact' exists in philosophic discourse.[11] I have found the following definitions useful in the analysis of specific knowledge claims.

---

[10] J. J. Schwab, "The Structure of the Disciplines: Meanings and Significances," G. W. Ford and L. Pugno, editors, *The Structure of Knowledge and the Curriculum* (Chicago: Rand McNally & Co., 1964), p. 25.

[11] Hospers provides a brief introductory discussion of many of the philosophical problems of 'concept'. He asks, "What is a concept?" but as is usual in much philosophical analysis he does not provide an answer, or at least an answer that is extractable for use in

(Footnote continued)

'Facts' may be given three distinct but related meanings. Fact **One** is an event which occurs (either being made to occur by the researcher or merely happening). This event must leave a record in order to be chosen for study. Much time of actual inquiries is spent in inventing techniques and devices for making a record which will serve as an index to the phenomena of interest. The record is Fact Two. Fact Three is a factual statement, typically in verbal or mathematical form. Factual statements are based on records of events occurring in the phenomena of interest. Since concepts are related to facts in all three senses (the events, the record, and the statement), it is important for purposes of recovery of meanings to be clear about the different levels of fact. And the pedagogical significance is immense. Finding the key concepts, the conceptual system, and the way they relate to other aspects of inquiry is to get at one piece of the structure of knowledge. Concepts are not "at large," as platonic entities, but "at home" in the context of inquiry.[12]

How shall *concept* be defined? For all of its frequent use in educational writing, little has been done to clarify its conflicting meanings. In general there is a tension in meanings between the psychological (studies in concept formation) and the logical (concept as a class, as a construct, as a carrier of meaning). A child possesses the concept of "liquidity" when he correctly identifies milk, oil, honey and water as liquids; he sees what is common in events which are quite different. Thus, there are three elements tied together in the meaning of concept: the stability of response, the linguistic sign, and the commonality of different events. We stipulate the following definition of *concept*: A concept is a sign which points to a commonality in events and which permits the concept user to make relatively stable responses to those

---

other than philosophical contexts. John Hospers, *An Introduction to Philosophical Analysis* (Englewood Cliffs, N.J.: Prentice-Hall, 1967), pp. 101-13.

M. R. Cohen writes that "Concepts are signs (mainly audible or visible words and symbols) pointing to invariant relations or transformations in the natural world." Morris R. Cohen, *Preface to Logic* (New York: Meridian Books, 1958), p. 70.

'Fact' for Cohen and Nagel means four different things:
a. as certain discriminated elements in sense perception,
b. as propositions which interpret what is given in sense experience,
c. as propositions which truly assert an invariable sequence,
d. as denoting things existing in space or time together with the relations between them in virtue of which a proposition is true.

M. R. Cohen and E. Nagel, *Introduction to Logic and Scientific Method* (New York: Harcourt, Brace & Co., 1934), pp. 217-18.

The unresolved problem with these meanings is that 'fact' may be something "out there" or a statement about it. The definition I propose attempts to relate events to records to statements as posing three levels of meaning of 'fact.'

[12]The context is critically important. Schwab writes:

". . . most statements of most disciplines are like the single words of a sentence. They take their most telling meanings, not from their dictionary sense, not from their sense in isolation, but from their context, their place in the syntax. The meaning of $F = MA$ or of free fall, of electron or neutrino, is understood properly only in the context of the enquiry that produced them." Schwab, Ford and Pugno, *op. cit.*, p. 24.

This fact seriously brings into question efforts at interdisciplinary coherence and cross discipline borrowings.

varied events. The signs which are vehicles for the concept are largely linguistic and conventional. The commonality in events may range from simple similarities to regularities to law-like invariance.

I now return to the presentation of the remaining four topics.

Methods of Work

Problems and questions found in the pathway of inquiry are well known elements of knowledge claims. Perhaps among the most important questions is this: What sort of thing is to count as evidence? What principles or reasons are given to suggest the value of some data to count as evidence? This principle can apply to a variety of choices: subjects, observations, documents, instruments, index phenomena, record making, place of observation. Another way to ask this question is this: What reasons can be given to suggest that if the worker studies XYZ materials, he will then have an answer to his telling question?

A method is a procedural commitment, a collection of techniques or ways of doing things that may be generalized to a variety of situations. Method includes reasoned steps. Questions of method, then, suggest the connectedness between steps, sequences, phases, stages of inquiry. It is my contention that Dewey's quest for the supremacy of method obscures rather than illuminates the rich variety of methods and techniques of work. Inquiry is constantly inventive and continuous, as Dewey knew; but Schwab's distinction between stable and fluid inquiry, and the radically different syntax that each presents, seems to me to be the more accurate and helpful view. Schwab's description of the short-term and long-term syntax is required reading for anyone interested in the syntactical structure of knowledge.[13]

The Universe, the Scene and the Phenomena of Interest

Ontological questions are never finally settled, but they can be identified, and the role they play in giving structure to knowledge can be clarified. It may be true that distinctively different phenomena require different approaches. Schwab notes that the persistent and rewarding differences among the sciences encourage a conviction that there are real and genuine differences among phenomena. Differences in questions put and data sought are not merely the products of historical habits among the practitioners of the science, but also they reflect some actual stubbornnesses of the subject matters.[14]

What marks off these subject matters? This stuff?

I am persuaded by Dewey's assertion that a tertiary quality pervades a situation, and the shift in this pervasive quality is the mark of a shift in the phenomena of interest. In a developing situation such as a piece of

---

[13] *Ibid.*, pp. 31-44.
[14] J. J. Schwab, "The Concept of the Structure of a Discipline," *The Educational Record* (July, 1962), pp. 197-205.

inquiry, Dewey holds that the pervasive and underlying quality exerts a regulative influence on the direction of the development of that situation.[15]

Questions such as the following help to reveal the metaphysical foundations of knowledge claims:

Is the universe thought by the author to be ordered? Chaotic? Random? Only capable of becoming ordered?

What is the "reality" the author interacts with or describes?

How does the author convert the events within the phenomena of interest to a record which is publicly examinable?

The Agent and the Audience

The psycho-social setting of any work is significant. In general this category permits the examination of the frame of reference assumed or made explicit by the inquirer as a necessary condition for his communication to his intended or actual audience. This frame of reference may be revealed by finding answers to questions like the following:

What is the point of view of the inquirer?

Does the person of the inquirer make any special difference to the establishment of the knowledge claims? Is he, for example, in a privileged position for observation of events or in receipt of special information?

For whom is the work intended? Relevant?

Is any social bias detectable in the work?

Does the audience (e.g., the scholarly community) play any special role in giving warrant to knowledge claims?

Is the work culture-bound?

Can the work be considered propaganda? Doctrine? Persuasive, even in lieu of its truth value?

Values

Values are created at all phases of disciplined inquiry. As a consequence they constitute both a separate category and an aspect of each of the other categories. The following questions help to reveal the relation between the values of a work and its constituent knowledge claims.

---

[15] John Dewey, "Qualitative Thought," R. J. Bernstein, editor, *John Dewey: On Experience, Nature and Freedom* (New York: Library of Liberal Arts Press, 1960), pp. 176-98. Sociologists Harp and Richer recently reported: "The pervasive character of an ideology of equal opportunity and the continuing role assigned to education as an avenue of mobility in American society could not help but influence the direction and character of sociological research in this area (education).

John Harp and Stephen Richer, "Sociology of Education," *Review of Educational Research*, Vol. 39, No. 5 (1969), p. 673.

What reasons are given to justify the belief that:

a. the telling questions are important?
b. the selected materials will answer these questions?
c. the methods and techniques of work will not do violence to the relationship between a. and b.?
d. the conclusions and interpretations are fair?

What intrinsic values are thought to be contained within the work?

What instrumental values does the work have? That is, what is the work good for: As a stimulus to further research? As propaganda for a cause? As a commercial product?

I have waited until the end to define "structure of knowledge." 'Structure' simply means elements and their relation. Since everything under some description can be shown to have structure, this seemingly solid idea dissolves into an ocean of ubiquity. The next question becomes: What constitutes significant structure? I think no rule can be given to cover all cases. Anything at all which purports to present knowledge claims can be analyzed by using this method. The analysis will help to arrive at a judgment of significance, but the analysis alone cannot determine significance; other factors enter in because not all, or even most, of human experience is encompassed by knowledge claims.

The concept of teaching I favor[16] is one which stresses the active intervention of the teacher in the lives of the taught. The moral justification for this intervention is to be found in the human values of knowledge and truth. Unless the teacher intervenes with material which purports to be knowledge, and knowledge which has some acceptable test of truth applied to it, a necessary condition for the moral justification of teaching is missing. When the educative process is seen as simply facilitating the learning process, the moral justification for so acting lies elsewhere (social welfare, respect for persons, the innate goodness of man).

Teachers must try to get their content under intellectual control. A detailed, reflective scrutiny of the knowledge claims within representative works is a good place to begin. The method of analysis I commend to you has the virtue of forcing considerations beyond the work itself and beyond sole reliance upon the specialist in the discipline. Teachers in art history, physical education, physics, English literature, political science, have reported to me their successful use of this method. I have been surprised and pleased that this approach has been relatively successful in such diverse fields.

---

[16] The concept of teaching sketched in my essay, "Teaching, Learning and Thirdness" still seems to me to point in the right direction. D. B. Gowin, "Teaching, Learning and Thirdness," *Studies in Philosophy and Education,* Vol. I, (Autumn, 1961), pp. 87-113.

Instead of talking about a direct or even indirect relation between teaching and learning, we should talk more as if teaching were to change the meaning of experience of the pupil through a triadic transaction involving an active teacher, knowledge claims, and an active pupil.

(Footnote continued)

It is a curious fact that Peirce's definition of "thirdness" is what I now propose as a definition of 'concept.' Peirce is quoted by me as writing: "Thirdness is the triadic relation existing between a sign, its object, and the interpreting thought, itself a sign, considered as constituting the mode of being of a sign. A sign mediates between the interpretant sign and its object." Gowin, *op. cit.*, p. 105.

CODE OF ETHICS OF THE EDUCATION PROFESSION

ADOPTED BY THE 1975 N.E.A. REPRESENTATIVE ASSEMBLY

PREAMBLE

The educator, believing in the worth and dignity of each human being, recognizes the supreme importance of the pursuit of truth, devotion to excellence, and the nuture of democratic principles.

Essential to these goals is the protection of freedom to learn and to teach and the guarantee of equal educational opportunity for all.

The educator accepts the responsibility to adhere to the highest ethical standards.

The educator recognizes the magnitude of the responsibility inherent in the teaching process. The desire for the respect and confidence of one's colleagues, of students, of parents, and of the members of the community provides the incentive to attain and maintain the highest possible degree of ethical conduct.

The Code of Ethics of the Education Profession indicates the aspiration of all educators and provides standards by which to judge conduct.

The remedies specified by the N.E.A. and/or its affiliates for the violation of any provision of this Code shall be exclusive and no such provision shall be enforceable in any form than one specifically designated by the N.E.A. or its affiliates.

PRINCIPLE ONE: COMMITMENT TO THE STUDENT

The educator strives to help each student realize his or her potential as a worthy and effective member of society.

The educator, therefore, works to stimulate the spirit of inquiry, the acquisition of knowledge and understanding, and the thoughtfull formulation of worthy goals.

In fulfillment of the obligation to the student, the educator --

(1) Shall not unreasonably restrain the student from independent action in the pursuit of learning.

(2) Shall not unreasonably deny the student access to varying points of view.

(3) Shall not deliberately suppress or distort subject matter relevant to the student's progress.

(4) Shall make reasonable effort to protect the student from conditions harmful to learning or to health and safety.

(5) Shall not intentionally expose the student to embarrassment or disparagement.

(6) Shall not on the basis of race, color, creed, sex, national origin, marital status, political or religious beliefs, family, social or cultural background, or sexual orientation, unfairly:

    (a) Exclude any student from participation in any program;

    (b) Deny benefits to any student;

    (c) Grant any advantage to any student.

(7) Shall not use professional relationships with students for private advantage.

(8) Shall not disclose information about students obtained in the course of professional service, unless disclosure serves a compelling professional purpose or is required by law.

PRINCIPLE TWO:
COMMITMENT TO THE PROFESSION

The education profession is vested by the public with a trust and responsibility requiring the highest ideals of professional service.

In the belief that the quality of the services of the education profession directly influences the nation and its citizens, the educator shall exert every effort to raise professional standards, to promote a climate that encourages the exercise of professional judgment, to achieve conditions which attract persons worthy of the trust to careers in education, and to assist in preventing the practice of the profession by unqualified persons.

In fulfillment of the obligation to the profession, the educator --

(1) Shall not in an application for a professional position deliberately make a false statement or fail to disclose a material fact related to competency and qualifications.

(2) Shall not misrepresent his/her professional qualifications.

(3) Shall not assist entry into the profession of a person known to be unqualified in respect to character, education, or other relevant attribute.

(4) Shall not knowingly make a false statement concerning the qualifications of a candidate for a professional position.

(5) Shall not assist a noneducator in the unauthorized practice of teaching.

(6) Shall not disclose information about colleague obtained in the course of professional service unless disclosure serves a compelling purpose or is required by law.

(7) Shall not knowingly make false or malicious statements about a colleague.

(8) Shall not accept any gratuity, gift, or favor that might impair or appear to influence professional decisions or actions.

SEMESTER: WEEK FIFTEEN

REQUIRED READING

Church

Part V: Redefining Commonality, 1940-1975, Chapter 14: <u>Changing Definitions of Equality of Educational Opportunity, 1960-1975</u>(46 pp.)

Dye

Covert, James R. "Second Thoughts About the Professionalization of Teachers" <u>The Educational Forum</u>. V.39, No.2, January, 1975.(06 pp.)

Taggart, Robert J. "Accountability and the American Dream" <u>The Educational Forum</u>. V.37, No.1, November, 1974.(10 pp.)

Carper, James C. "In The Way He Should Go: An Overview of the Christian Day School Movement" <u>Review Journal of Philosophy and Social Science</u>. V.4, No.2, 1980. (14 pp.)

MEETINGS

Monday
Lecture: Private and Sectarian Education

Tuesday
Lecture: Contemporary Reform Criticism

Wednesday
Lecture: Federal Legislation in Education

Thursday and Friday
Small Groups: Course Evaluation will be administered.

CHURCH TEXTBOOK STUDY GUIDE: CHAPTER 14

CHANGING DEFINITIONS OF EQUALITY OF EDUCATIONAL OPPORTUNITY, 1960-1975

1. President John F. Kennedy
2. President Lyndon Baines Johnson
3. War on Poverty programs
4. Office of Economic Opportunity, OEO(1964)
5. cyclical nature of American poverty

6. urban violence
7. urban alienation
8. educational expansion
9. American slums as social dynamite
10. National Association for the Advancement of Colored People, NAACP

11. Plessy vs. Ferguson(1896)
12. separate, but equal doctrine
13. Sweatt vs. Painter(1950)
14. Brown vs. Board of Education of Topeka(1954)
15. segregation

16. integration
17. gerrymander
18. de jure
19. de facto
20. racial imbalance

21. metropolitanism
22. civil rights movement
23. nonviolent protest
24. Jim Crow laws
25. Reverend Martin Luther King, Jr.

26. gradualism
27. tactics of demand
28. tactics of demonstration
29. James Coleman
30. Equality of Educational Opportunity(1966), The Coleman Report

31. compensatory education
32. <u>Head Start</u>, OEO(1965)
33. <u>Operation Follow Through</u>, USOE(1968)
34. <u>Elementary and Secondary Education Act</u>, <u>ESEA(1965), Title One</u>
35. more relevant curriculum
36. black studies movement
37. minority hiring in professional education
38. integration movement
39. community control movement
40. performance contracting
41. Arthur Jensen
42. Christopher Jencks
43. <u>Inequality: A Reassessment of the Effect of Family and Schooling in America(1972)</u>, Inequality

Second Thoughts About the Professionalization of Teachers

JAMES R. COVERT

ONE of the most perplexing problems for teachers during the past century has been the upgrading of their occupation to a profession. While it is generally conceded that the various professional ranks engaged in "higher education" are professional, those lesser teachers hired in "lower education" must still fulfill a few more vital criteria before they are granted the esteem and prestige that professionals enjoy. Some skeptics point out however, that even when teachers fulfill all of these enumerated criteria, they will still not be thought of as professionals because that title is granted only to a few traditional occupations by society. Though this latter statement may have some validity, we must not revert to accepting the contemporary connotations and definitions assigned to professions. There must be some difference between a professional hockey player, a professional union organizer, and a professional surgeon. Unless we can agree on certain definite criteria to distinguish the accepted professions from those aspiring to professional status, all is lost. We might as well await the conferring of the honor by the society.

James R. Covert is an assistant professor in the Department of Educational Foundations at Memorial University of Newfoundland.

As society changes it becomes increasingly difficult to separate the traditional, established professions from their aspiring counterparts. Many of the distinguishing features which used to separate professions from crafts have become less distinct in the past decade. The notion of a professional private practice for doctors and lawyers and a public practice for teachers and social workers is no longer important with lawyers working in large partnerships and doctors joining to form clinics and even participating in socialized medicine. Such incompatible ideas as autonomous professionals working in bureaucracies, joining unions or associations, and even striking are no longer seen as incongruous. While the traditional professions have redefined what being professional means, aspiring occupations have made little headway in gaining professional standing, in spite of constant efforts in that direction. Social work has made its program more rigorous by introducing social science. Teachers have doubled their number of years of college training from two to four. Nurses have raised their requirements for admittance into the training program and have made acceptance into the occupation conditional on passing a rigorous standardized test. Following each of these exercises they have proclaimed themselves as more professional and sought public recognition as a full-fledged profession.

For those occupations that aspire to professional status and prestige, this can be a very frustrating experience. They often feel a "sense of calling" to their chosen "profession" and can demonstrate, in large measure, the fulfillment of the two basic criteria of the established professions. That is, they can provide empirical evidence: "(1) that social function is the primary reference point for guiding their activity or work and (2) they possess at this point in time, a specialized knowledge and means for verifying claims to knowledge that enable them to perform this function with an economy unique to that individual or group."[1]

While arguments continue to rage about the social function that is unique to education, the optimists can gain considerable support for the notion that socialization into the ongoing culture is their social function and pessimists can claim organized and essential baby sitting as their social function. The claim to a specific body of knowledge has also been a thorny problem for education. There may be an unexpected source of relief for this dilemma as we review the diverse nature of the bodies of knowledge possessed by the traditional professions. Medicine and law have always found it difficult to retain some definite and unique body of knowledge and are continually being forced to introduce interdisciplinary modes of information gathering and knowledge verification to educate their professionals. We are seeing, for instance, a new movement toward producing more general practitioners in medicine who must have an even wider-range of ability, drawn from a greater variety of disciplines.

The issues raised here are vital to the definition of a profession. Such things as changing social definitions, selection, education and entry requirements, a unique social function, and a specialized body of knowledge all play an important part in identifying those occupations designated as professions. I would like to explore certain aspects of the professional model that do not frequently appear in the literature and suggest that teachers review the very basic question of the desirability of becoming a profession.

Four Basic Questions

There is one issue that is becoming increasingly important to the established professions which hinges upon the very professional claim of a unique service performed by experts in their field. With the increasing number of malpractice suits brought against people in all professions, it might give teachers reason to pause and consider that which might readily be considered malpractice, should the profession firmly establish an area of competence. The list might be staggering as well as frightening. There has been no case tried, to my knowledge, where a teacher has been charged with malpractice as opposed to incompetence or improper supervision in a particular situation. In most cases the courts have been very careful to not attribute any special expertness or superior powers to a teacher. As a matter of fact, they have ruled that a teacher was no more responsible than any common man acting in a similar situation.[2]

This argument is not to be misconstrued as a reason for teachers not to pursue the professional promised land; it is rather to serve as a warning flag hoisted by the established professions. When teachers begin to strike for benefits other than wages, it seems likely they are claiming that there are certain benefits to be gained from instituting such practices as class size, special education classes, and increased per pupil expenditures. The school, being a part of a pragmatic pluralistic society, is likely to expect increased returns in the form of increments of learning. If a profession fails to deliver what it professes, or actually inflicts some harm on the client, then they may leave themselves open to charges of malpractice. If, as in other professions, educators were to define explicitly what constitutes standards of teaching performance and the duties to be performed by a competent teacher in this professional capacity, the possibility of inflicting "emotional damage" would become immense. For instance, is reprimanding a child in front of his peers not conducive to at least temporary emotional damage and perhaps a permanent emotional disability? Another case of malpractice might involve the "graduation" of an illiterate passed through the grades for compassionate reasons. A second point arises concerning the description of a competent teacher. Professions, through their rigorous selection and demanding educational programs, certify that all graduates are competent to perform the minimal professional service. This faith in the preparation of professionals is the result of a long history of tight controls exercised by the professionals themselves, building mutual trust within the profession and faith from the general public. It is not necessary for professionals to advertise because all are competent, nor is it likely that any professional will speak disparagingly of his colleagues because all are aware of the certification program and its safeguards against allowing incompetents to practice.[3]

Teacher education institutions, however, have not enjoyed this same degree of professional control nor public faith and trust. In most instances, teachers have been mass produced in response to crisis situations and professional control was not of major concern. With the advent of mass education nearly everyone has experienced some public education, and familiarity has not only bred contempt but an assumed understanding of what constitutes good teaching. This notion of a common understanding of education has been encouraged by public ownership of schools and a vast social institution that offers an open invitation to the public to visit and inspect their schools. Many argue that in a democratic society the schools should be shaped by the pressures of a pluralistic society, but the point remains that the openness of the public school system and its lay control does not lead to the development of a traditional profession.

Educational experts have provided only limited assistance in the solution of this problem. While there are extensive lists of criteria and competencies of good teachers, there is no consensus on this point.[4] Once again the problem of quality control rears its ugly head. Unless an adequate description of what constitutes a competent teacher can be agreed upon, the control mechanism of the traditional professional model will fail to function.

The third argument involves the superior-subordinate relationship of the traditional professions. In all established professions the client comes to the professional in ignorance of the special information which the professional possesses and professes. The client may bring certain information about the particular circumstances of his predicament, but he comes with complete faith that the professional will act beneficially on his behalf. This necessitates a superior-subordinate relationship, and, as a matter of fact, the professional must maintain this situation in order to retain his professional status. In a strictly professional situation the client is at the mercy of the professional, and their continued relationship depends upon the maintenance of these role relationships.

Most teachers would reject this drastic kind of superior-subordinate relationship. While many speak of maintaining a certain degree of social distance, they would flatly reject the notion that learning takes place primarily in school and mostly under the supervision of a teacher. Children come to school with vast amounts of varied knowledge which teachers may try to build on or try to "unlearn." Most teachers assume that education is an ongoing process which takes place both inside and outside of school and continues throughout our lifetime. There can be no monopoly on knowledge, which raises the question of how teaching may best be executed.

There is a vocal group of educators that suggests teachers should be guides and reference persons assisting students in pursuing their own interests rather than acting in the traditional superior-subordinate mode.[5] While there is no overwhelming majority that would support this position, it is sizeable enough to pose a reasonable doubt about the superior-subordinate relationship that the professional must establish and encourage.

The final point has been hinted at in the previous section and is the most damaging of all arguments put forward. In order for a profession to maintain its superior-subordinate relationship, it is essential for the occupation to remain shrouded in secrecy. It should be obvious that education is the antithesis of this position. The very nature of education is a sharing of information. Withholding information for the purpose of exercising power should be a foreign concept to education.

The traditional profession is built on a rigorous selection system and a stringent socializing program which insures that those people who are chosen do not allow their professional knowledge to become public knowledge. If wills and deeds were written in language that lay people could understand, the need for the lawyer would be greatly diminished. If the clergy performed their services in anyone's home and did not invoke some special knowledge of a spiritual being, their clients would soon lose the faith that perpetuates their position. The more the professions are exposed to public scrutiny, the less professional they become and their previous advantage is eroded away. Professions are built on knowledge not common to all people, and the more the mystery is removed from the profession, the more each person feels competent in performing the professional function.

It can be seen that this latter position is diametrically opposed to the purpose of education. It is the function of a teacher to explain to the student and assist him in understanding and knowing, not only all that the teacher knows, but more. The best teachers will be those that encourage and facilitate their students learning more than they ever knew themselves. This cannot be accomplished by withholding information and maintaining the advantage of mysterious knowledge. The teacher must be giving of knowledge, and the occupation must be built on the idea of shared information.[6]

As can be seen from this discussion, there are some real difficulties when the aspiring public occupations seek to adopt the model of the traditional professions. However, most teacher education institutions seek to adopt the traditional professional model and have overlooked the difficulties outlined here primarily because of the desirable status and prestige that accrue to professionals. Even the more recently initiated programs of teacher education retain the professional title in certain parts of their program or as a title for their entire program, constructed on the unexamined traditional professional model.

From the evidence presented in this article it might seem to be a more profitable venture for teachers to explore the changing models of the traditional professions to examine how the theoretical model has been altered in practice. It would appear that the traditional professions are becoming more like the public professions. If we could curb our aspirations toward an outmoded model, we might find that they are trying to emulate us. At least we should become less paranoid about the prestige and status accorded to our occupation and get on with the business of establishing an optimal learning climate for all students.

Notes

1. Frank H. Blackington and Robert S. Patterson, *Schools, Society and the Professional Educator* (New York: Holt, Rinehart and Winston, 1968), p. 21.

2. By common man it is meant that teachers are required to exercise only that degree of care in the management and supervision of pupils that might reasonably be expected of any prudent person in the same or similar circumstances. Johnson devotes one paragraph to explaining incompetence, but a chapter to exploring tort liability. See George M. Johnson, *Education Law* (East Lansing, Mich.: Michigan State University Press, 1969), p. 41.

3. Howard Becker in his construction of the ideal professional model makes these points in greater detail. See Howard S. Becker, "The Nature of a Profession," *Education for the Professions*, Sixty-first Yearbook of the National Society for the Study of Education, Part II (Chicago: Chicago Press, 1962), p. 30.

4. For explication of this point refer to Harry S. Broudy "Criteria for the Professional Preparation of Teachers," *Journal of Teacher Education* 16 (December 1965): 408-15.

5. Such authors as John Holt, William Glasser, Carl Rogers, and George Dennison are exemplars of this position.

6. It might be argued that there are mysteries of knowing that are kept secret until a certain level of learning has been attained. That is, only the initiated can properly understand sophisticated concepts. This presupposes a certain sequential way of knowing which ignores some of the more esoteric modes such as insight, intuition, and revelation. Furthermore, it forces us into a sequential, lock-step arrangement of teaching which may be seriously questioned.

Reprinted from The Educational Forum, Kappa Delta Pi, Volume 39, Number 2, January, 1975.

Accountability and the American Dream

ROBERT J. TAGGART

IN the words of Leon Lessinger,[1] accountability's leading proponent, our schools have "failed" to educate our children because not every child has competency in the basic skills. As the price of success, therefore, we must systematically and objectively provide the means to make "every kid a winner" by requiring intransigent professional educators to become responsive to the public's needs through external auditing of objectives stated so clearly that failure can be distinguished from success easily. Like so many previous reforms, success is virtually assured by advocates if only the formula is followed. And like so many earlier reforms, there is little thought as to the consequences of the reform beyond the attainment of the reform itself. Will success in the basic skills of reading and writing fulfill the American dream for those who have, up to now, been bypassed?

Accountability is dangerous to public education. At the time we should be asking ourselves what education can effectively provide, a group of reformers is insisting that more efficient education can provide everything. If education is streamlined, if the professional educators can be made responsive to public demands, if we can objectify, systematize, and analyze our procedures, then multitudinous rewards will apparently follow. Yet modeling our schools after the aerospace industry ("where 'zero defect' of

---

Robert J. Taggart is an assistant professor in the College of Education at the University of Delaware.

Reprinted from The Educational Forum, Kappa Delta Pi, Volume 37, Number 1, November, 1974.

components is the rigorously sought-after goal")[2] suggests a simplistic view of the educational process and a terrifying expectation of what education is expected to achieve in our society.[3] One might shrug off the pretensions of yet another wave of reformers and wait for their eventual demise. Unfortunately, these reformers base their assumptions about the nature and possibilities of education on expectations which the public has adopted from the past rather than on the concrete reality they so much prize; expectations rooted in the rhetoric of nineteenth century reformers which have been expanded in the twentieth century and are now accepted by the public.

Americans have assumed a high correlation between educational attainments and social and economic success for several decades.[4] In the minds of parents, success in the outside world has become so dependent upon school success that schools are thought of as the prime instruments of social mobility. Accountability proponents promise educational success in the guise of skill training as if the three Rs will automatically provide life success.[5]

There is great danger in this position for public education, however. If parents are convinced that such skills lead to automatic social and economic rewards, what happens to their support of public education—no matter how misplaced—when the successful acquisition of basic skills for everyone is discovered to be unattainable? Will the public see this as willful professional negligence? Further, when those who have attained the skill competency turn out not always to be "winners" in society, how will that be viewed? The accountability coalition of businessmen and "experts" as proposed by Lessinger will not be hurt, for they will reappear in another form.[6] It is the educators and the schools themselves that will face the wrath of a public self-righteously assured that the professionals have failed them again because of unresponsiveness to the public demands. Educators will find they are expected to deliver the impossible, yet be blamed for not attaining it.

After decades of growing public support and educators' promises, we have tended to confuse extended school attendance and social success. The earliest advocates of public education did not make this mistake. Republicans of 170 years ago believed *access* to learning would increase social and economic opportunity. Schooling was seen as an instrument of limited capabilities for individual use. Thomas Jefferson did not promise that schools would guarantee social or economic success for all individuals; they certainly could not guarantee equality. That would be a patent absurdity to a Republican from Virginia. He insisted, in his unsuccessful plans for Virginia, that all citizens should become literate, which he believed possible in three years of universal education. The opportunities in America were so great this minimal skill training would enable every willing individual to better himself as much as he wished—although not likely through further public schooling. Additional formal education was reserved for those who could benefit from it in order to fit themselves for social and political leadership. Basic education was a limited tool necessary to free the masses from ignorance.[7] It could not in itself make individuals wealthy, powerful, or wise. Only individuals themselves could achieve that.

During the nineteenth century the coalition of reformers who publicized and designed mass education insisted that common schooling should be much more than a tool of individual advancement. Republican optimism was diminished because the Whig reformers believed the cultural homogeneity that allowed individual improvement in a comparatively stable society was gone. Jefferson had believed in change, but like most of his fellow Republicans, change was "progress" because an independent class of intelligent people who believed in common Republican principles could be depended upon to guide that change. By the 1830s reformers feared the inherent instability of democracy which had the temerity to insist that all human beings were created equal. It was no longer enough to free people from ignorance; they now had to be consciously indoctrinated in social, economic, moral, and political duties.[8] The alternative was a deposition of authority and the destruction of civilization itself. Social disintegration was inevitable in a democracy unless the individual could be literally "re-formed."

The pressure on schools to mold obedient adults increased after the Civil War.[9] Professional and business classes feared the changes they could not control, even though much of the transition from rural-agricultural to urban-industrial life was due to them.[10] When the "native" middle class looked about they saw an undisciplined, proletarian mob, unassimilated immigrants of strange mores and a crass, philistine materialism of the upper classes which threatened the whole social order. Horace Mann had wanted to make better human beings for a slowly evolving society; postbellum reformers insisted on new people for a new industrial society. The stakes were the same—social order—but the cost was higher to the democratic viability of the public schools than ever before. When compulsory education laws became enforced after 1880, the school monopoly tightened. Reformers still insisted on high individual student performance, but by insisting on a universal common system they were, in effect, placing the burden for social mobility on the shoulders of the public schools. In extending its control, the public school enslaved itself.

By the late nineteenth century, education was defined as the total shaping of an American, and unless schools delivered on their promise to fulfill this broad definition for all Americans, they were believed to be failing in the popular mind. Monopoly institutions are disadvantaged in that there is no competition to blame for failures. The public school protected itself against the negative results inevitable with an undifferentiated population by maintaining that the individual was responsible for his own success. The social philosophy of most educators after the Civil War supported the inviolable position of the public schools. City superintendents and board members tended to accept the social-Darwinian ideal of the survival of the fittest, while ignoring the laissez-faire implications of that ideal for a democracy, much as did Carnegie and Rockefeller.[11] The school people were able to maintain their monopoly without commensurate responsibility for individual academic success. In any case, most reformers of the era believed in reform through individual improvement, but the ideology served the monopoly position of the public schools particularly well. It freed school people to demand more public support for education without apparent responsibility for public accountability, except as the school bureaucracy defined it. And they defined pupil success in gross, mechanistic terms, not individually. Accountability was always present in terms of system goals as established and maintained through a bureaucratic hierarchy, but not in terms of client goals.

Schools were expected to graduate productive, obedient citizens, and since school people believed they knew how exactly to define such a citizen and had the faith in themselves to attain their goal, the schools simply had to ensure a standardized, efficient production line in order to be consistent with these goals. Schools relied on truant officers to keep students in the institutions, therefore, and counted success in terms of attendance and graduation figures; that is, in terms of completing a prescribed course on time. The attention of late nineteenth century school people to attendance figures is amazing to the twentieth century person. School people would report figures upwards of 97 percent, while admitting, privately, that the figures were purposely misleading. For instance, students were often counted as no longer on the official rolls if they failed to attend for three consecutive days.[12] Those who fell behind were held back a year, and by the early 1900s if a student fell behind more than two years he was labeled a retardate and sometimes placed in a special class for the slow. This system seemed efficient as long as the school system was not in itself considered responsible for individual success and as long as high schools were viewed as leadership preparation and not mass education. There was no "dropout problem" in the American city of the 1880s and 1890s beyond the eighth grade, because elementary education was believed sufficient to provide useful, obedient Americans. There was also no "dropout problem" because the admission of a problem would have meant the institution had responsibility for student academic success.

The Progressives attacked the educators' assumption that school success could be measured in terms of producing graduates on time who had taken a certified course of study. Schools were supposed to revolve around the individual children's needs and the full development of each child in the present for the future. While it was not true, as the Lynds noted in *Middletown* in 1929,[13] that progressivism changed the structure or methodology of education in the average American public school, the rhetoric of education placed a significant burden on schools for personal student success in school and in life. Perhaps the Progressive rhetoric was inevitable in the democratic heritage of educational opportunity,[14] but no longer could school people ask for public support and pretend not to have responsibility for individuals.

Furthermore, Progressives insisted that secondary education was no longer primarily a preparation for college, but a necessity for all in an urbanized, industrial society. This aggravated the differences in pupil achievement, and made school people and the public more aware of deficiencies in the schools. The Cardinal Principles of 1918 summarized the Progressive stand on the new-found usefulness of secondary education.[15] The Principles stressed that all students should receive the same education and participate in common activities in a comprehensive high school. Since schools could not make students equal through secondary education and still justify several distinct courses of study, as outlined in the openly elitist Committee of Ten proposal of 1893, the educators tried to deny that any particular curriculum was superior to any other for citizenship.

By 1947, a Presidential Advisory Commission stated that even secondary education was insufficient; America owed it to her youth and to herself to attain a goal of 50 percent of the college-age youth in college.[16] The decade of the 1960s also demonstrated the grasping of Americans for more education as the answer for their dreams, as the nation committed a three-fold increase in public funds for higher education. However, the late 1950s and the 1960s saw a backlash of the tough-minded against the popular belief in education as instrumental for personal advancement. Following the lead of the Bestors and Rickovers, many citizens now demanded quality. This was, after all, the original goal of secondary education in this country. But people who clamored for better quality usually failed to recognize that such quality implied clear differentiation according to intellectual abilities. Tracking and the American dream of uninterrupted social mobility simply do not mix.

The pressure upon education for guaranteeing the American dream has increased almost to the breaking point with minority group pressure. Blacks long ago realized that they were not receiving their fair share of society's spoils. With the Brown decision of 1954 destroying the rationale for de jure segregation, blacks began believing they had the power as well as the right to expect the schools to serve as the prime method of mobility. Now that inequality in the form of separate but equal was no longer legal in education, blacks and other minorities began demanding the same as their suburban neighbors. That is, not merely success in school, but success in life. But urban parents are mistaken if they think that the apparent success of suburban children in life is due necessarily to the physically superior suburban school. Suburbia believes that schools are only supplemental to the importance of the family in educating their youth, and that they can maintain school quality through local control.

Urban parents know suburbia controls their own schools and assume that this control is the reason for the superior suburban schools rather than the nonschool factors delineated by the Coleman and Jencks reports. Therefore, since urban populations neither believe that their schools are as good as suburban schools nor that they control the schools, urban parents have often turned to community control, decentralization, and other forms of lay accountability. Perhaps, it is reasoned, the public can force urban educators to guarantee the same results as their suburban neighbors receive. Yet all the community pressure that can be mustered on the public school system will not achieve the same academic or social results from the Cleveland city schools as from Shaker Heights.[17] If most children in suburbia are "winners," the evidence of the Coleman report and other research would suggest it is due to nonschool conditions.

In and of itself, accountability in the form of lay control can only provide a public veto over professional actions in the present system of public education. It cannot ensure equal school or life success.[18] However, as long as disgruntled urban parents believe that schools can guarantee life success and equate poor student performance with poor teaching and school performance, there will be friction between lay people and educational professionals.

The most striking aspect of the accountability phenomenon is its negativism toward professional educators. Whether accountability is minority-inspired community control or the specific relationship of a performance contract, educators are presumed guilty of ineptitude or even criminal negligence whenever children do poorly in school. This negativism of the public is the price for professional success in a system of local control. While most of the public has accepted the attainment of mobility through education, public acceptance has always depended upon the assumption that the schools were "theirs," and the development of an education profession has always been antithetical to the popular notion of local or lay control.[19] The hostility between lay people and professionals occurred as soon as the reformers and other proponents of public education insisted upon a universal, tax supported system. They succeeded only at the cost of their original aim of an effectively centralized system.[20] The public agreed to support universal education only if they could maintain both lay control and local control. Since universal-schooling advocates could not have their way directly, they worked from within the local district system in the towns and cities where they could most easily perfect an efficient system through standardization and consolidation.

An education profession came into being, but not because of federal or state fiat or because of public clamor for such a profession. A group of politically-astute, ambitious men met together in state and national educational organizations even before the Civil War. Neither the public nor the teachers themselves played a large part in these meetings or in designing the business-hierarchical model upon which city school systems were patterned. Lay boards, being largely business people, tended to approve of the model, but the public itself was recognized only through the board. While the motives of professional educators and lay boards may have been the highest, that is, the design of educational institutions which were educationally efficient, these superintendents, principals, professors, and other "experts" controlled the actual operations of the schools. The public was not asked what they wanted so much as told what they needed.

Sometimes there were setbacks. As Michael Katz has amply illustrated in his *Irony of Early School Reform,* the public did not always passively accept tax supported education, especially at the secondary level. In Beverly, Massachusetts, in 1856, the public actually destroyed the high school.[21] But the new professional class did not give up easily. The "great victory" at Kalamazoo in 1874, which extended common schooling through the secondary level, was a victory of the professional class over a large segment of the public, and not necessarily over reactionary religious elements or wealthy conservatives, as historian Cubberley would have put it in 1920. Neither the public school ladder system, now accepted as characteristically American, nor the education profession itself, was public-initiated. Neither was viewed as legitimate by the taxpayers, except to the extent that they controlled them.

Much of the public's mistrust of educators stems from a clash of expectations as to what and how the school system should deliver. Parents expect the system to respond to each of their children's needs, and have accepted schooling as a personal tool by which to gain social mobility. Professional educators have for over a century promised mobility through schooling, but only if students accepted a model of accountability based on a hierarchical system of responsibility which rewards individuals for conforming to accepted norms of behavior and levels of achievement. Whether it was the graded system of William Torrey Harris at St. Louis or the N.E.A. Committees of Ten (1893) and Fifteen (1895), educators imposed standardization upon the "chaotic" elementary and secondary schools which was defined by the professionals for the public. Even progressivism did not return the schools to public control. For all the talk of democratic, community schooling, Progressives desired to impose their own, albeit wider set of goals upon the schools than was already the case. The schools were now not only to attempt to give intellectual, moral, and citizenship training, but—in the words of the Cardinal Principles of 1918—confront the "main objectives" of health, home-membership, vocation, and avocation.

By the early twentieth century, professional educators had popularized to the public the notion that there was practically nothing that education could not achieve if just given the financial resources, manpower, and moral support of the public. The last two decades have demonstrated the futility of this position. The attack of educational conservatives after 1945 demanding at least proficiency in the "basics" received substantial public support. Educators had claimed so much for themselves, much of the public could no longer believe them. Even though the public was partially led by self-interested pressure groups, lay people had a right to demand that educators clarify the school's role in society in more specific terms than "life adjustment," so popular in the 1940s and early 1950s. Yet the reaction of the later Progressives to this challenge was reflected in a 1951 pamphlet entitled *Danger! They're After Our Schools*.[22]

Ostensibly, the Progressives believed that "they" were, by definition, a reactionary coalition of pressure groups. As professional educators, the Progressives never seemed to question that they, themselves, best represented the public.

The tension between the public, which believes that it controls public education and also believes in schools as personally instrumental for the public's purposes, and the professional educators, who believe that only they know best, has produced two conceptions of accountability. Professionals have insisted it is to be internal or system oriented, while the public has always conceived the schools as externally accountable to their own legitimate power. The current popular definition of accountability as a guarantee of specific results is inherent to the power conflict between the public and professional. Accountability thus defined becomes a weapon of the public (or those speaking for the public) against the professional. By making educational results more specific, failures would be more evident. Since failures could be easily known, presumably the public could rectify the weakness by applying pressure to the professional educators who have promised so much yet delivered so little. Furthermore, lay people could reassert control over what results should be attained in a public school and perhaps over the curricula itself, and so force the system to guarantee competency rather than differentiate the superior from the inferior student in a selective process for society.

Yet what can accountability accomplish as compared to what society expects from the schools? Educators are attacked because they promise mobility through schooling and fail to deliver, but why should education-for-results achieve mobility? Lessinger might insist that he promises only to free the teacher from inefficiency by giving her new tools to manage learning.[23] But this begs the real question. What goals are implicit in the engineering of results which can be externally audited in relation to costs? Even Lessinger admits that "We can apply an educational engineering system only to those basic skills we can measure reliably."[24] One must assume from a model of guaranteed results, then, that a child can be kept up to grade standards for twelve grades, that it will necessarily make a difference for him in real life, and that education-for-results can achieve that goal. The latter is in deep question, as the cancelled performance contract at Gary's Banneker School suggests.[25]

It is the long-term difference that is most important for the child. Can success in the basics for several consecutive years assure success in life? In other words, can success in reading by itself assure economic and social success? If not, then why bother with specified, guaranteed results for narrow objectives which will not make any difference to the student in the long run?

Accountability proponents tend to consider educational success as a linear production of skills; as if society did not exist apart from the schools. The fact that teachers have always been expected to teach ethical, social, and political attitudes as well as academic knowledge and basic skills is an admission that schools exist in a pluralistic society consisting of conflicting cultural values and expectations. To expect that educational success can be sufficiently defined in narrow terms so that the results can be "audited" is to deny the reality of schools in society.

This is not to say that teachers should not be given the tools to produce learning skills in a more effective manner in place of inefficient memorization of sterile information. Teachers might then be able to diagnose learning problems more effectively. However, when outside contractors assume that they have better techniques, they also assume that educators are incompetent. Given the Banneker example, teachers find that they are forced to defend the minimal professional integrity still allowed them and perhaps sabotage such an obvious attempt to ignore their present skills.[26] Accountability proponents are unfortunately more interested in "remodeling" teachers in their own image than in considering teachers as autonomous and worthy professionals capable of self-improvement.

If education-for-results using performance contracts and outside audits gains favor, there is little gain likely for either the public or the student. In fact, the present interlocking directorate of educationists, against whom so much complaint has raged, will simply be supplemented or replaced by an even less accountable coalition of outsiders from business and government. Clearly specified contracts might increase short-term reading levels, as Head Start quickly increased IQ scores five to ten points, but neither the public nor teachers would have more control over educational procedures or goals.[27] And there would be no guarantee either of long-term academic effects or of the life success which should be the major reason for improving educational performance.

What is most dangerous about education defined as guaranteed results is that failure is considered either impossible or a breach of faith. Yet even if we assumed that all students worked up to their ability in a competency-based model, would this ensure that all students were at grade-level? If this result is not attained for everyone, then is that school a failure? If so, then there is no successful school anywhere that accepts a differentiated clientele.

Certainly no student should be cheated of opportunities to learn as efficiently as possible. If more accountable, more objectively-based schools can achieve a faster, more complete achievement in reading and arithmetic with less pain, then surely the public must approve. However, the public must not be misled into believing that a performance contract or other methods of "guaranteed results" can, by themselves, significantly affect the social, economic, and political realities of public education. Accountable standards of local achievement may streamline certain school operations. The public, unfortunately, will continue to find that the American Dream is as elusive for their children as ever if they believe holding schools "accountable for specified results" will make "every kid a winner" where it counts—in the real world outside the public school.

Notes

1. Leon Lessinger, *Every Kid a Winner: Accountability in Education* (New York: Simon and Schuster, 1970).
2. Ibid., p. 5.
3. Robert J. Nash and Russell M. Agne, "The Ethos of Accountability—A Critique," *Teachers College Record*, February 1972, pp. 357-70.
4. Henry J. Perkinson, *The Imperfect Panacea: American Faith in Education, 1865-1965* (New York: Random House, 1968).
5. For example, Kenneth Clark, "Just Teach Them to Read," *New York Times Magazine*, March 18, 1973, pp. 14ff.
6. Lessinger, *Every Kid*, pp. 91-92, 125-29. The coalition present at Texarkana is listed in the Appendix, pp. 156-58.
7. Thomas Jefferson, "From a Letter to George Wythe," August 13, 1786, in *The Papers of Thomas Jefferson*, ed. Julian P. Boyd, vol. 10 (Princeton, N.J.: Princeton University Press, 1950), pp. 243-45.
8. Henry Barnard, "Sixth Annual Report of the Superintendent of Common Schools to the General Assembly of Connecticut for 1851," *American Journal of Education* 5 (1865):293-310.
9. "Compulsory Education," in *Report of the Board of Public Charities of the State of Pennsylvania* (1871), pp. 5-30 is typical of demands for knowledge and morality training in the face of urbanization.
10. Robert H. Wiebe, *The Search for Order, 1877-1920* (New York: Hill and Wang, 1967), Chapters 1-5.
11. Selection from "A Statement of the Theory of Education in the United States of America as Approved by Many Leading Educators—1874," cited in David B. Tyack, *Turning Points in American Education History* (New York: Blaisdell, 1967), p. 324.
12. Michael Katz, *The Irony of Early School Reform* (Cambridge: Harvard University Press, 1968), p. 87.
13. Robert S. Lynd and Helen Merrell Lynd, *Middletown, A Study in Modern American Culture* (New York: Harcourt, Brace and World, 1929).
14. Richard Hofstadter, *Anti-Intellectualism in American Life* (New York: Knopf, 1963), Chapters 12, 13, and 14.
15. Commission on the Reorganization of Secondary Education, *Cardinal Principles of Secondary Education*, U.S. Bureau of Education Bulletin no. 35 (Washington: Government Printing Office, 1918), pp. 7-11.
16. U. S. President's Commission, *Higher Education for American Democracy*, vol. 1 (New York: Harper and Bros., 1948), p. 37.
17. Witness the sad decline of the New York public schools in reading norms, even after decentralization into thirty-one districts. Gene Maeroff, "Reading Scores Decline in the City Schools Again," *New York Times*, March 18, 1973, p. 1.
18. Harry S. Broudy, *The Real World of the Public Schools* (New York: Harcourt, Brace, Jovanovich 1972), pp. 146-47.
19. Myron Lieberman, *The Future of Public Education* (Chicago: University of Chicago Press, 1960), Chapter 3.
20. The lack of executive authority for early state superintendents of education is evident in the career of Horace Mann. See Jonathan Messerli, *Horace Mann, A Biography* (New York: Alfred A. Knopf, 1971).
21. Katz, *Irony*, p. 85.

22. Progressive Education Association, *Danger! They're After Our Schools* (Urbana, Ill.: PEA, 1951).
23. Lessinger, *Every Kid,* pp. 133-34.
24. Ibid., p. 131.
25. James A. Mecklenburger, "Epilogue: The Performance Contract in Gary," *Phi Delta Kappan,* April 1973, pp. 562-63.
26. Ibid., p. 562.
27. Ivor Kraft, "Head Start to What," *The Nation,* September 5, 1966, pp. 179-82.

IN THE WAY HE SHOULD GO : AN OVERVIEW OF THE CHRISTIAN DAY SCHOOL MOVEMENT

James C. Carper

The American social order has recently emerged from a period of unprecedented upheaval, agonizing self-appraisal, and change. From the early 1960s until the mid-1970s American institutions and the values, traditions, and purposes undergirding them were subjected to poignant criticism and often scorn. Although it is too early to assess accurately the total impact of these years of profound disenchantment, it is apparent that they witnessed a collapse of consensus concerning the basic nature and function of our institutions, an erosion of American civil religion. As the sense of national cohesiveness evanesced, alternative modes of thinking, believing, and acting appeared. Some were new while others were merely old options revivified.[1] These phenomena, exemplified by, among other things, the apotheosis of self, a decline of belief in all forms of obligation, the rejection of the past, and confusion about the meaning of progress, morality, authority, justice, responsibility, and civility, suggest a "watershed" in American history. As the noted American historian Henry Steele Commager has observed, "Perhaps the 60s and the 70s are a great divide–the divide of disillusionment."[2]

This disillusionment and collapse of consensus was reflected clearly in Americans' dissatisfaction with public education. While schooling has been the object of much acrimonious discussion since its inception, never before has the criticism been so mordant.

The lay public and commentators of all socio-political persuasions scrutinized the schools and found them wanting. Charges leveled at public education were legion and, indicative of the fragmented nature of the society, often contradictory. Schooling was simultaneously characterized as racist, permissive, authoritarian, trendy, irrelevant, too conservative, too liberal, an instrument for maintaining the status quo, too involved in social change, and generally unresponsive.[3]

Solutions to the school crisis were many and varied. Some observers proposed reforms of the curriculum, while others advocated changes in school governance patterns, teacher education, and methods of school finance. Several commentators eschewed reform altogether and argued for the abolition of schools.

Of all the proposed remedies, one of the most heralded was the free school movement which emanated originally from the socio-political left. Dedicated to a more "humane" and "liberating" education and opposed to standardization and regimentation, several hundred of these institutions were established outside the public school system in the late 1960s and early 1970s. Variations of the free school concept were eventually incorporated within the public system. While much has been written about the successes and failures of the free school and related alternative education schemes, one has received little scholarly attention.[4]

The alternative is the Christian day school. Since the mid-1960s evangelical Protestants have been establishing interdenominational Christian Schools at a phenomenal rate.[5] Not only do these schools constitute the fastest growing segment of formal education in America today, but they also represent the first widespread secession from the public school pattern since the establishment of Catholic schools in the nineteenth century.

Protestant-sponsored weekday education is not a contemporary phenomenon. Since the nineteenth century most denominations have experimented with parochial schooling. The vast majority of Protestants, however, have shown scant interest in such an educational arrangement. Only certain Lutheran bodies, the

Seventh Day Adventists, and the Christian Reformed Church have sponsored a significant number of weekday schools.[6]

Most Protestants have supported public schooling since its inception in the mid-nineteenth century. Early public education enjoyed their approval because it reflected the Protestant values of the society and was viewed as an integral part of the Protestant crusade to establish a Christian America. According to church historian Robert T. Handy, elementary schools did not need to be under the control of particular denominations because "their role was to prepare young Americans for participation in the broadly Christian civilization toward which all evangelicals were working."[7] While the public school via Bible reading, prayers, and the ubiquitous McGuffey readers emphasized nondenominational evangelical Protestantism, the American civil faith for the better part of nineteeth century, the Sunday School stressed the particular teachings of the various denominations. To most evangelical Protestants this "parallel institutions" educational strategy was quite satisfactory. As William B Kennedy, an authority on Protestant education, has argued:

> By 1860 there had emerged a general consensus in American Protestantism that the combination of public and Sunday school teaching would largely take care of the needed religious teaching of the young. In that pattern the public school was primary; the Sunday school was adjunct to it, providing specific religious teaching it could not include.[8]

Much has changed in America since the establishment of this dualistic educational strategy. No longer does evangelical Protestantism influence the society and the schools as it did in the nineteenth century. The past six decades have witnessed its rapid decline as the moving force behind cultural and behavioral patterns and its eventual demise in the 1960s. Despite this radical alteration of the American scene, most Protestants have clung to the myth of the "parallel institutions" educational arrangement. The rapid expansion of Christian day schools during the past fifteen years suggests, however, that a growing number of evangelicals are not only wrestling with the impact of the collapse of Protestantism as a social foundation but also questioning their long standing commitment to public schooling and the dualistic strategy of education.

Just what is a Christian day school? The term has been used recently to describe those schools, many of which are interdenominational, founded in the past decade and a half by evangelical Protestants. In numerous ways these institutions are quite diverse. Facilities, for example, range from poorly equipped church basements to modern multibuilding campuses. Enrollments vary from less than fifty to over two thousand. The atmosphere in these schools runs the gamut from exacting discipline and dress codes to moderate regulation of student life. Curricular offerings range from the most rudimentary to the most comprehensive available anywhere. Some mix healthy doses of pre-1960 "Americanism" with religious belief while others shun this unfortunate practice. Some Christian day schools are attended by whites only, sometimes, regretably, because of segregative intent, while many are integrated. A militant rejection of any state regulation characterizes some schools while others cooperate to varying degrees with state education agencies.[9]

Although these institutions are diverse in many respects, they all profess the centrality of Jesus Christ and the Bible in their educational endeavors. Regardless of the subject matter, a conservative Christian perspective is employed. For example, history is generally viewed as the record of God's involvement in human affairs and science is perceived as the outworking of His laws. Moral education, an important aspect of the instructional program, is also biblically based. Students are instructed to search the Scriptures as the final authority for value judgments. Summing up the difference between the ethos of the Christian school and that of the public school, Paul A. Kienel, Executive Director of the newly formed Association of Christian Schools International, has observed:

> ... Christian schools are Christian institutions where Jesus Christ and the Bible are central in the school curriculum and in the lives of the teachers and administrators. This distinction removes us from direct competition with public schools. Although we often compare ourselves academically, we are educational institutions operating on separate philosophical tracks. Ours is Christ-centered education, presented in the

Christian context. Theirs is man-centered education presented within the context of the supremacy of man as opposed to the supremacy of God. Their position is known as secular humanism.[10]

How rapidly are Christian day schools multiplying? "There's a grass-roots explosion taking place among church-related schools in the United States," according to Thomas W. Klewin, an observer of the Christian day school movement. "It's happening, strangely, not among the traditional parochial-school systems, but in the interdenominational, multicongregational Christian schools of the evangelical Protestants."[11] Some have estimated that such schools are being established at the rate of almost two a day.[12] While there is no doubt that these schools have burgeoned recently, particularly since 1967, it is difficult to assess their number and student population precisely. The very character of the Christian day school movement prohibits an accurate accounting. Many schools are of such a separatist persuasion that they refuse to report enrollment and related figures to state and federal education agencies. For similar reasons some schools do not join one of the approximately fifty state and regional associations of Christian schools which are currently the primary sources of data. Also, the rapid growth of these schools is so unorganized that accurate figures are difficult to obtain.

Illustrative of these problems is the variation in estimates of the number of Christian day schools and their enrollment. Calculations of the number of these schools founded since the early 1960s range from 4,000 to as many as 10,000. Enrollment figures for these schools range from 250,000 to over 1,200,000. Based on the best available data, an estimate of between 5,000 and 6,000 recently established schools with a student population of approximately 950,000 seems reasonable.[13]

Perhaps the most concrete evidence of the "boom" in Christian day schools can be seen in the figures of several associations. For example, the Western Association of Christian Schools, which merged recently with two other groups to form the Association of Christian Schools International, claimed 102 schoools with an enrollment of 14,659 in 1967. By 1972 the figures were 246 and 34,949 respectively, and in 1978, 763 and 93,576. The American

Association of Christian Schools was founded in 1972 with eighty schools enrolling 16,000 students. In 1978 the association boasted better than 800 schools with a student population in excess of 100,000.[14] Despite the fact that a few schools probably hold dual memberships and some were founded long before they affiliated, these figures indicate the phenomenal growth of a movement which shows no sign of abating.

Why are these schools proliferating? Why are many Protestants forsaking their traditional commitment to public schooling and the "parallel institutions" educational strategy? There are a number of reasons involved. Some are symbolic of evangelical Protestants' growing alienation from the American social order. To many of them the public school exemplifies the trends they deplore in society, such as the decline of authority, lapse of standards, rejection of the Judeo-Christian value system, loosening of custom and constraint, scientism, sexual permissiveness, government social engineering, and hedonism. Thus when they establish schools which stress the Bible, moral absolutes, basic subject matter mastery, academic standards, discipline, and hard work, they are not only protesting the secular nature of public education, unsatisfactory academic and behavioral standards, and unrest in the schools but also expressing disillusionment with the society that sustains the educational enterprise.

While many evangelicals have pointed to discipline problems, declining educational standards, federal meddling, the drug culture, race-related problems, and unresponsive educators as reasons for abandoning the public schools, secularism has disturbed them the most.[15] Although the United States Supreme Court decisions in 1962 and 1963 outlawing mandatory prayer and devotional Bible reading in tax supported schools merely marked the culmination of better than a half-century long process of "de-Protestantization" of public education, many evangelical Protestants translated the removal of these symbols as yanking God out of the schools.[16] Rather than making the schools neutral on matters related to religion, many believed that, despite the intent of the majority of the Court, these decisions were a victory for secular humanism— Such a belief sensitized them to what was being taught in the schools. So while these decisions did not cause directly the rapid growth of Christian day schools, they certainly provoked many

Protestants to scrutinize the public schools as never before. The result of such scrutiny was often disillusionment with the secular character of the schools and, in many cases, consequent founding of Christian educational institutions. As Richard N. Ostling, a staff writer for the religion section of *Time*, has observed, "there is little doubt that the rulings produced anxiety about the climate in public schools that is boosting Protestant schools many years later."[17]

Evidence of this anxiety can be seen in the curriculum controversies of the past decade in, among other places, West Virginia, New Jersey, California, Virginia, Minnesota, and Texas where evangelical Protestants have complained about the secular humanistic slant of the schools. Examples of what is perceived as bias abound. For instance, many have protested the well-known elementary social studies curriculum *Man : A Course of Study*. In this course they see moral absolutes undermined in favor of situation ethics. Likewise, science textbooks which proclaim evolution as dogma offend those who believe creationism should be considered as well. Many evangelicals also see evidence of secular humanism in values clarification programs which assume there are no absolutes. Behavioral sciences texts which imply that man is an animal, rather than a being created in the image of God, belittle the belief in an omniscient creator, and equate the Bible with myth also trouble them.[18] Floyd Robertson of the National Association of Evangelicals summed up the thinking of many of his fellow believers concerning the charactor of public education when he wrote : "It has become quite obvious to many that this religion of secularism has indeed pervaded our public school system and created an anti-Christian attitude in all too many cases."[19] Although a majority of evangelical Protestants still enroll their children in the public system and continue to wrestle with its secular character, an increasing number are opting for Christian day schools. Like nineteenth century Catholics who established parochial schools to preserve their religion and culture, a significant number of evangelicals are founding schools to counter the secular influence of society and its institutions on their children.

Awakening and profession as well as alienation and protest are involved in the growth of these schools. The movement is more than just a "counter-cultural" phenomenon. A recrudescent evangelical consciousness, one manifestation of the spiritual ferment of the past fifteen years, has prompted many to promote Christian education beyond the home and the marginally effective efforts of the Sunday School.[20] Realizing that all education is value oriented and Christian nurture is a full-time endeavor, they have founded schools that profess the biblical beliefs of the church and home. As one parent affirmed on a Christian school application form, "We believe that our children are gifts of the Lord. We are responsible as parents to train them according to His Word not only at home and in church, but in school as well."[21] By enthusiastically establishing schools to complement the home and church, a significant number of evangelical Protestants believe they have fashioned an "educational configuration" in which all components are engaged in their conception of the scriptural command to "train up a child in the way he should go ... ... "[22]

Zeal for Christian day schools is not universal. Some have argued that such schools represent an abdication of Christian social responsibility rather than a Christian witness as their proponents proclaim. They believe that Christians have a moral obligation to support public education rather than private schools. To them the public school is a mission field to be cultivated, not abandoned. William H. Willimon of Duke Divinity School enunciated this position in an article which raised the perennially controverted question of how to be in the world but not of it:

> In too many communities, parents who are talented, educated, committed Christians have withdrawn their children (along with their time, talent, and prayers) from the public schools without a thought for their responsibility as their brother's keeper. Without children in the public schools, they have little interest in the needs of public education ...... Certainly there is much wrong in today's public schools—mostly the same things that are wrong with our society as a whole. Christian parents have good reason to feel alarmed over many recent developments in public education. But who will improve it? What kind of society will we have if all Christians abandon the public schools?[23]

Others have charged that many so-called Christian schools were established to maintain racial segregation. A recent study by David Nevin and Robert E. Bills suggests, regretably, that racism was an important factor in the founding of many schools in the South which purport to be "Christian." This is by no means true of all Christian schools in the region since many of them enroll minority students.[24] In other areas of the country busing has played a role in the creation of some schools Often it was the "straw that broke the camel's back." But it is unclear as to whether the reaction to busing was because of racism, or resentment of federal coercion, or fear of unrest, or a combination of all three.[25]

Although racism has, unfortunately, been a factor in the founding and maintenance of some of these schools, the vast majority of Christian schools eschew racial exclusion. Most Christian school associations and spokesmen for the movement condemn racially motivated schooling. In the words of D. Bruce Lockerbie, a respected Christian educator, "The Racist Stronghold claiming also to be a 'Christian school' is, by definition, an imposter, a fraud. Its reason for being is indefensible by standards of Scripture, the Constitution, ... or common decency."[26] Besides professing nondiscrimination, it appears that and increasing number of Christian schools, in fact, are enrolling minority students.

Questions have also been raised by proponents as well as opponents of Christian day schools relative to the quality and nature of the education provided by these schools. Several observers have lamented the poor academic quality of some schools. Critics have rightly deplored the "super-patriotism" which characterizes a number of Christian schools. Commentators have also suggested that perhaps these schools shelter students and therefore fail to prepare them for life in the "real world."[27]

In 1967 Henry A. Buchanan and Bob W. Brown co-authored an article in *Christianity Today* entitled, "Will Protestant Church Schools Become a third Force?". They answered their query in the affirmative.[28] While Christian day schools have yet to attain the stature of either the Roman Catholic school system or the public educational enterprise, they are becoming increasingly visible on the educational landscape and offer many opportunities for research. Whether or not they will become a "third force" depends not only on the resolution of some of the aforementioned problems but also on answers to a number of questions. For example, how will these schools relate to state and federal regulatory agencies whose actions have at times bordered on harassment? Four state court cases already have been argued on this touchy question where free exercise of religion collides with state interests.[29] Will evangelical Protestants be able to afford to support both public schools and parochial schools? How will graduates of Christian schools fare in society? To what extent will they "systematize" their schools? To what extent will the public school establishment attempt to accommodate disgruntled evangelicals? Will proponents of Christian schools accept the discredited assumption that schooling is a panacea for all problems? What direction will the apparent evangelical "awakening" take in the next decade?

The future of the Christian day school will be determined by answers to these and related questions. Regardless of its future as a possible "third force," it now stands as a viable alternative to the public school system, as evidence of evangelical Protestant reconsideration of educational strategy, a symbol of profession as well as protest, an attempt on the part of a significant number of parents to regain authority over those with whom they share the task of raising their children, and an indication of the crisis in American civil religion and one of the main vehicles of its transmission, the public school.

REFERENCES

[1] Daniel E. Griffiths, "The Collapse of Consensus," *New York University Education Quarterly* 7 (Fall 1975) : 2–3. See also Robert N. Bellah, *The Broken Covenant : American Civil Religion in Time of Trial* (New York : Seabury Press, 1975); Christopher Lasch, *The Culture of Narcissism : American Life in An Age of Diminishing Expectations* (New York : Norton, 1978); William L. O'Neill, *Coming Apart : An Informal History of America in the 1960's* (New York : Quadrangle Books, 1971).

[2] "In Quest of Leadership," *Time*, 15 July 1974, p. 23.

[3] For example, see Carl Bereiter, *Must We Educate?* (Englewood Cliffs, N. J. : Prentice-Hall, 1973) ; Harry S. Broudy, *The Real World of the Public Schools* (New York : Harcourt Brace Jovanovich, 1972);

R. Freeman Butts, "Assaults on a Great Idea," *The Nation*, 30 April 1973 pp. 553-60; Ronald and Beatrice Gross, eds., *Radical School Reform* (New York: Simon & Schuster, 1969); Allan C. Ornstein, "Critics and Criticism of Education," *Educational Forum* 42 (November 1977): 21-30; Peter Witonski, *What Went Wrong With American Education and How to Make It Right* (New Rochelle, N. Y.: Arlington House 1973).

[4]Lawrence A. Cremin, 'The Free School Movement: A Perspective," *Notes on Education* 2 (October 1973): 1-11; Mario Fantini, ed., *Alternative Education* (Garden City, N J.: Anchor Books, 1976); Allen Graubard, "The Free School Movement," *Harvard Educational Review* 42 August 1972): 351-73; David Thornton Moore, "Social Order in an Alternative School, "*Teachers College Record* 79 (February 1978): : 437-60.

[5]Evangelical Protestantism is composed of several ideological subgroups. Richard Quebedeaux has identified four. Ranging from the most conservative to the least conservative on theological and social issues, they are "Separatist Fundamentalism," "Open Fundamentalism," "Establishment Evangelicalism," and "The New Evangelicalism." Although no research has been done on the matter, one would speculate that enthusiasm for Christian schools is greater in the "fundamentalist wing" than in the "evangelical wing." Richard Quebedeaux, *The Young Evangelicals* (New York: Harper & Row, 1974).

[6]Francis X. Curran, *The Churches and the Schools: American Protestantism and Popular Elementary Education* (Chicago: Loyola University Press, 1954); Otto F. Krauhaar, *American Nonpublic Schools: Patterns of Diversity* (Baltimore: The Johns Hopkins University Press, 1972); Edwin H. Rian, *Christianity and American Education* (San Antonio, Tex.: Naylor, 1949).

[7]Robert T. Handy, *A Christian America: Protestant Hopes and Historical Realities* (New York: Oxford University Press, 1971), p. 102. See also James C. Carper, "A Common Faith for the Common School? Religion and Education in Kansas, 1861-1900," *Mid-America* 60 (October 1978): 147-61; Timothy L. Smith, "Protestant Schooling and American Nationality," *Journal of American History* 53 (March 1967): 679-95; David Tyack, "The Kingdom of God and the Common School," *Harvard Educational Review* 36 (Fall 1966): 447-69.

[8]William B. Kennedy, *The Shaping of Protestant Education* (New

York : Association Press, 1966), p. 27. See also Robert W. Lynn, *Protestant Strategies in Education* (New York : Association Press, 1964).

[9]B. Drummond Ayres, "Private Schools Provoking Church-State Conflict," *New York Times*, 8 April 1978, sec. A, pp. A1, A23; William J. Lanouette, "The Fourth R Is Religion," *National Observer*, 15 January 1977, pp. 1, 18; Roy W. Lowrie, Jr., "Christian School Growing Pains," *Eternity*, January 1971, pp. 19–21; Richard Ostling, "Why Protestant Schools Are Booming," *Christian Herald*, July-August 1977, pp. 44–47; Ken Ringle, "D. C. Suburban School Systems Are Swept By Changes—'Christian Schools'," *Washington Post*, 31 December 1973, sec. B, p. B1; Elmer Towns, "Have the Public Schools Had It ?," *Christian Life*, September 1974, pp. 18–19, 50–51.

[10]Paul A. Kienel, "The Forces Behind The Christian School Movement," *Christian School Comment* 8 (n. d.) : 1.

[11]Thomas W. Klewin, "Make Way for the Christian School," *Liberty*, September-October 1975, p. 18.

[12]Lanouette, "The Fourth R Is Religion," p. 1.

[13]Ayres, "Private Schools Provoking Church-State Conflict," p A23; Lanouette, "The Fourth R is Religion," p. 1; Dave Raney, "Public School vs. Christian School," *Moody Monthly*, September 1978, p. 42; Towns, "Have the Public Schools Had It ?," pp. 18–19.

[14]Gerald B. Carlson, American Association of Christian Schools, personal letter; Paul A. Kienel, Western Association of Christian Schools, personal letter, See also Paul A. Kienel, "Status of American Christian Schools," National Institute of Christian School Administration, Winona Lake, Ind., 25–30 July 1976.

[15]John P. Blanchard, Jr., "Can We Live With Public Education ?," *Moody Monthly*, October 1971, pp. 33, 88–89; Klewin, "Make Way for the Christian School," pp. 18–19; Lanouette, "The Fourth R Is Religion," p. 1; Raney, "Public School vs. Christian School," pp. 44–45.

[16]Engle v. Vitale, 370 U. S. 421 (1962); Abington School District v. Schempp, 374 U. S. 203 (1963); Murray v. Curlett, 374 U. S. 203 (1963).

[17]Ostling, "Why Protestant Schools Are Booming," p. 45.

[18] James C. Hefley, *Textbooks on Trial* (Wheaton, Ill.: Victor Books, 1976); George Hillocks, Jr., "Books and Bombs: Ideological Conflict and the Schools — a Case Study of the Kanawha County Book Protest," *School Review* 86 (August 1978): 632–54; Dorothy Nelkin, *Science Textbook Controversies and the Politics of Equal Time* (Cambridge: MIT Press, 1977); Ostling, "Why Protestant Schools Are Booming," p. 45; Gerald J. Stiles and Louis R. Rittweger, "The Dichotomy Between Pluralistic Rhetoric and Bias Practices," paper presented at the annual meeting of the American Educational Studies Association, Philadelphia, Penn., 3 November 1977.

[19] Floyd Robertson, "The Declining Support for Public Schools," *Christian Teacher*, November-December 1976, p. 19.

[20] Adjustments in institutional arrangements are linked frequently to religious awakenings. For an interesting, albeit highly speculative, discussion of different aspects of the current ferment and possible outcomes, see William G. McLoughlin, *Revivals, Awakenings, and Reform* (Chicago: University of Chicago Press, 1978).

[21] Paul A. Kienel, "Ten Reasons Why You Should Send Your Child to A Christian School," *Christian School Comemnt* 7 (n. d.): 1.

[22] Proverbs 22:6.

[23] William H. Willimon, "Should Churches Buy Into the Education Business?," *Christianity Today*, 5 May 1978, p. 22. See also Ethel L. Herr, "Who's Salting the Schools?," *Eternity*, February 1976, pp. 16, 18, 58–59.

[24] David Nevin and Robert E. Bills, *The Schools That Fear Built* (Washington, D. C.: Acropolis Books, 1976).

[25] Russell Chandler, "Popularity of Religious Schools Rising," *Los Angeles Times*, 18 June 1978, p. 14; Towns, "Have Public Schools Had It?," pp. 19, 50.

[26] D. Bruce Lockerbie, "The Way We Should Go," *Christian Teacher*, September-October 1976, p. 7. See also "Creed and Color in the School Crisis," *Christianity Today*, 27 March 1970, pp. 32–33; Lowrie, "Christian School Growing Pains," p. 20; Ostling, "Why Protestant Schools Are Booming," pp. 45–46.

[27] Herr, "Who's Salting the Schools ?," pp. 16, 18, 58–59; Lockerbie, "The Way We Should Go," pp. 6–7, 29; Lowrie, "Christian School Growing Pains," pp. 19–21; Willimon, "Should Churches Buy Into the Education Business ?," pp. 20–22.

[28] Henry A. Buchanan and Bob W. Brown, "Will Protestant Church Schools Become a Third Force ?," *Christianity Today*, 12 May 1967, pp. 3–5.

[29] "Christian Schools : Learning in the Courtroom," *Christianity Today*, 22 September 1978, pp. 36–37; Russell Kirk, "Locking Up Christian Parents," *National Review*, 17 September 1976, p. 1008 For a discussion of the issues involved in the Internal Revenue Service's recent attempts to regulate private schools, see current issues of *Inform*, published by the Center for Independent Education, and *Outlook*, published by the Council for American Private Education.

SPONSORSHIP OF THE PERIODICALS IN THIS TEXT

The Educational Forum
> Kappa Delta Pi, An Honor Society in Education

Educational Theory
> Philosophy of Education Society

History of Education Quarterly
> History of Education Society

The Journal of Teacher Education
> American Association of Colleges of Teacher Education

Ohio History
> Ohio Historical Society

Review Journal of Philosophy and Social Science
> College of Education, Arizona State University

The Phi Delta Kappan
> Phi Delta Kappa, Professional Fraternity in Education

Washington University Magazine
> Washington University Alumni Association

BIBLIOGRAPHY OF PROFESSIONAL PERIODICALS

The professional periodicals in the following bibliography are available at the Bierce Library, The University of Akron, and contain articles appropriate to the introductory, foundational study of American education.

Note that the citations contain current and old titles and the extent of the holdings of that particular journal in the Bierce Library.

American School Board Journal
    January, 1922 - Present

American Secondary Education
    December, 1970 - Present

American Vocational Education
    January, 1966 - Present

Black Scholar
    November, 1969 - Present

Catholic Educational Review
    January, 1936 - November, 1969

Changing Education
    Winter, 1967 - Spring, 1970

Christian Education
    October, 1919 - October, 1941

College Student Journal
    (was College Student Survey)
    September, 1971 - Present

Community and Junior College Journal
    (was Junior College Journal)
    August-September, 1972 - Present

Education
    September, 1916 - 1964
    1964 - Present (on microfilm)

Education and Urban Society
    November, 1968 - Present

Educational Forum
    (was Kadelphian Review)
    November, 1936 - Present

Educational Leadership
    October, 1943 - 1966
    1966 - Present(on microfilm)

Educational Record
    January, 1920 - Present

Educational Review
    (now School and Society)
    January, 1891 - October, 1928

Educational Theory
    May, 1951 - Present

Harvard Educational Review
    February, 1962 - Present

History of Education Journal
    (now History of Education Quarterly)
    Autumn, 1949 - November, 1959

History of Education Quarterly
    (was History of Education Journal)
    March, 1961 - Present

Indian Education
    October, 1960 - May, 1966

Jewish Education
    October, 1965 - Present

Journal of Education
    October, 1918 - Present

Journal of Experimental Education
    September, 1932 - Present

Journal of General Education
    October, 1946 - Present

Journal of Higher Education
    June, 1930 - Present

402

Journal of Negro Education
    1965 - Present

Journal of Nursery Education
    (now Young Children)
    January, 1957 - September, 1964

Journal of Outdoor Education
    Fall, 1971 - Present

Journal of Special Education
    Fall, 1966 - Present

Journal of Teacher Education
    January-March, 1950 - Present

Journal of Value Inquiry
    Spring, 1967 - Present

Junior College Journal
    (now Community and Junior College Journal)
    October, 1930 - June-July, 1972

Liberal Education
    March, 1959 - Present

N.E.A. Journal
    (now Today's Education)
    April, 1913 - May, 1968

National Association of Secondary School Principals Bulletin
    January, 1945 - Present

National Elementary Principal
    October, 1955 - Present

Negro Educational Review
    January, 1969 - Present

Ohio Department of Education Newsletter
    Five years kept, plus current year

Ohio Educational Monthly
    January, 1882 - June, 1926

Ohio Parent - Teacher
    November, 1930 - Present

403

Ohio School Boards Journal
    February, 1957 - Present

Ohio Schools
    January, 1926 - Present

Ohio Teacher
    June, 1905 - December, 1932

P.T.A. Magazine
    February, 1961 - 1968
    1968 - Present (on microfilm)

Peabody Journal of Education
    July, 1923 - Present

Phi Delta Kappan
    September, 1949 - Present

Quarterly Review of Higher Education Among Negroes
    1933 - 1960 (on microfilm)

Record
    (was Teachers College Record)
    1967 - Present

Religious Education
    January, 1941 - Present

School and Community
    1963 - Present

School and Society
    1929 - Present

School Review
    1907 - Present

Social Education
    January, 1937 - Present

Studies in Philosophy and Education
    January, 1961 - Present

Teachers College Record
    (now Record)
    January, 1922 - May, 1967

Today's Education
    (was N.E.A. Journal)
    September, 1968 - Present

Urban Education
    Summer, 1964 - Present

Women's Education
    Five years kept, plus current year

Young Children
    (was Journal of Nursery Education)
    October, 1964 - Present